P9-EMH-301

DATE DUE

OCT 1 5 2003	
OCT 2 9 2003	
DEC 0 5 2003	
NOV 2 3 2004 MAY 0 2 2005	
MAY 0 7 2005 APR 1 2 2007 APR 1 2 2010	
AUG 1 4 2010 SEP 2 3 2015	
NOV 0 2 2015	
MAR 0 8 2018	

ARMED

New Perspectives on Gun Control

Gary Kleck & Don B. Kates

 Prometheus Books

59 John Glenn Drive
Amherst, New York 14228-2197

Published 2001 by Prometheus Books

Inquiries should be addressed to
Prometheus Books
59 John Glenn Drive
Amherst, New York 14228–2197
VOICE: 716–691–0133, ext. 207
FAX: 716–564–2711
WWW.PROMETHEUSBOOKS.COM

04 03 02   5 4 3 2

Library of Congress Cataloging-in-Publication Data

Kleck, Gary, 1951–
    Armed : new perspectives on gun control / Gary Kleck and Don B. Kates
        p. cm.
    Includes bibliographical references and index.
    ISBN 1–57392–883–6 (cloth : alk. paper)
    1. Gun control—United States. 2. Firearms ownership—United States. I. Kates, Don B., 1941– II. Title.

HV7436 .K538 2001
363.3'3'0973—dc21

                                                                00–069932

Printed in Canada on acid-free paper

Gary Kleck dedicates this book to Diane, Matt, and Tessa.

Don Kates dedicates the book to E. Spector and P. Kates, in memorium; to C. B. Kates in perpetuity.

Contents

1. Introduction
by Don B. Kates

2. Guns and Public Health: Epidemic of Violence, or Pandemic of Propaganda?
by Don B. Kates

3. "Poisoning the Well" for Gun Control
by Don B. Kates

4. Absolutist Politics in a Moderate Package: Prohibitionist Intentions of the Gun Control Movement
by Gary Kleck

5. Modes of News Media Distortion of Gun Issues
by Gary Kleck   **173**

6. The Frequency of Defensive Gun Use: Evidence and Disinformation
by Gary Kleck   **213**

7. The Nature and Effectiveness of Owning, Carrying, and Using Guns for Self-Protection
by Gary Kleck   **285**

8. The Second Amendment: A Right to Personal Self-Protection
by Don B. Kates 343

Subject Index 357

Name Index 361

Introduction

by Don B. Kates

T his book seeks to redress a remarkable dissonance that exists in the American gun control debate. On many issues the conventional wisdom is substantially, or even diametrically, inconsistent with criminological, legal, and other scholarship. Contrast conventional wisdom, as revealed in the editorials and columns of our leading newspapers and magazines, to the following summary statements from the social scientific literature: Repudiating his own prior support for banning handguns, Professor Hans Toch of the School of Criminology, State University of New York (Albany), concludes that the best available current evidence shows that:

> when used for protection firearms can seriously inhibit aggression and can provide a psychological buffer against the fear of crime. Furthermore, the fact that national patterns show little violent crime where guns are most dense implies that guns do not elicit aggression in any meaningful way. Quite the contrary, these findings suggest that high saturations of guns in places, or something correlated with that condition, inhibit illegal aggression.[1]

An article analyzing violent crime patterns in Canada and the United States by Professor Brandon Centerwall of the School of Public Health, University of Washington, states the following:

> If you are surprised by my findings, so am I. I did not begin this research with any intent to "exonerate" handguns, but there it is—a negative finding, to be sure, but a negative finding is nevertheless a positive contribution. It directs us where not to aim public health resources.[2]

From an article on urban youth violence by Dean Joseph Sheley of the School of Social Science, California State University at Sacramento, and his colleagues, we learn that:

> [The problem of urban youth violence] will not yield to simplistic, unicausal solutions. In this connection, it is useful to point out that everything that leads to gun-related violence is already against the law. What is needed are not new and more stringent gun laws but rather a concerted effort to rebuild the social structure of inner cities.[3]

Substantially similar views are expressed by Dean Alfred Blumstein of the Heinz School of Public Policy and Management at Carnegie-Mellon University.[4] (At a symposium presentation of that paper he added jocularly that banning guns or handguns to the general public is "like trying to stop sexually transmitted disease by forbidding sex.")

Our goal is to acquaint readers who do not regularly peruse scholarly journals with the findings therein that are so little reported in the major popular news sources. If we seem derisive about the conventional wisdom, it may be because both my coauthor and I began working in this area under its influence. Laboring under that same misleading influence, lay readers are unlikely even to know of the vast gap that exists between the conventional wisdom and modern scholarly findings. So let me begin with some glaring examples of how thoroughly modern scholarship has discredited the popular media's conventional wisdom about firearms regulation.

Gun Accidents versus Self-Defense

How often is a small child killed in a handgun accident? From the national publicity such deaths often receive, lay readers are likely to assume them to be as frequent as they are tragic. In fact, gun accidents kill only ten to twenty children under age five each year. Tragic as each such death is, they are only about as numerous as the equally tragic deaths of children that age who are poisoned by ingesting iron supplements that look like candy and are often prescribed for mothers after birth. Indeed, handgun accidents kill only about half as many children under age five annually as does the ingestion of common household poisons (roach spray, lighter fluid, ammonia, iron supplements, ant poison, and so forth).[5] In fact, gun accidents rarely involve preadolescents of any age. (See figures in chapter 2.)

Typical of the wild exaggeration that regularly appears is *USA Today*'s claim that fourteen *thousand* fatal gun accidents occur each year; the actual number is fourteen *hundred*.[6] In comparison, as many as 2.5 million victims use guns to defend against crime each year. (See discussion and evidence presented in chapter 6.) If the public is unaware of this, it is because the media do not mention the 2.5 million figure and report only a tiny proportion of such defense incidents. Nevertheless, the total number of defense uses is so large that the tiny proportion reported still constitute a goodly number. Yet consumers of the popular media are unlikely to realize how common such incidents are because even when reported locally, defensive gun uses somehow never manage to make the national news, unlike the far, far fewer instances of children being killed in gun accidents.

The one exception is that a defensive gun use that seems to have gone wrong can become nationwide news; for example, when a Louisiana man mistakenly killed a Japanese student who menaced him in a Halloween prank, and when a Texan who had received a concealed handgun carry license under Texas's new right to carry law killed a man who attacked him in a traffic dispute. (In fact, both shooters were cleared, the Texan because he fired in reasonable fear of death or great bodily harm from his larger and younger attacker.[7]) Those who get their information from the popular media are unlikely to realize that erroneous killings (which the Texas case was not) by civilians total only about thirty per year; even less likely is the average person to know how favorably this compares to the police who erroneously kill five to eleven times more innocent people each year.[8]

The nonreporting of successful victim self-defense incidents lends spurious credence to another argument that dates back to early in this century. Conventional wisdom holds that guns are not useful for self-defense. Defensive gun ownership is a "dangerous self-delusion," and groups like Handgun Control, Inc., advise victims who are attacked by a rapist, robber or other felon that "the best defense against injury is to put up no defense—give them what they want or run."[9]

This conventional wisdom persists only because the definitive contrary facts receive little or no attention in the popular media. Criminological data and studies have definitively established that, compared to victims who resisted with a gun, *victims who submitted were injured about twice as often*; also, of course, nonresisters were much more likely to be raped or robbed.[10]

Nevertheless, until quite recently the sparsity of statistical information made it possible to still argue that guns are rarely used for self-defense. But a series of seminal studies by my coauthor Gary Kleck have now demonstrated beyond peradventure that handguns are actually used by victims to repel crime far more often than they are by criminals in committing crimes—as much as three times more. I shall not review the evidence here since Kleck does so in chapters 6 and 7. I raise the point only because Kleck's studies either go unreported in the nation's press or are derided. This media dubiety contrasts strikingly with a remarkable accolade accorded the Gary Kleck and Marc Gertz study on defensive gun use by the doyen of American criminologists, University of Pennsylvania Professor Marvin Wolfgang, who wrote:

> I am as strong a gun control advocate as can be found among the criminologists in this country. If I [had the power] . . . I would eliminate ALL guns from the civilian population and maybe even from the police. I hate guns—ugly, nasty instruments designed to kill people. . . .
>
> Nonetheless the methodological soundness of the current Kleck and Gertz study is clear. I cannot further debate it. . . .
>
> The Kleck and Gertz study impresses me for the caution the authors exercise and the elaborate nuances they examine methodologically. I do not like their conclusions that having a gun can be useful, but I cannot fault their methodology. They have tried earnestly to meet all objections in advance and have done exceedingly well.[11]

I can only speculate as to why the popular media omits any mention of this tribute even as they continue to ignore Kleck's work or treat it as doubtful. What can be said is that here again the popular media is suppressing scholarly research that contradicts conventional wisdom.

It is interesting to consider how the popular media treated two studies coming to opposite conclusions about the effects of laws passed by thirty states to allow all qualified applicants to carry concealed handguns for self-defense. Though these laws had been enacted in many more urbanized states for five or more years when it was done, the first study was limited to just five selected cities in Florida, Oregon, and Mississippi.[12] In none of these cities had a murder been committed by a permit-holder. Yet this small, city-level study concluded that widespread carrying of concealed guns had not reduced crime and perhaps even increased gun homicides in three of the five cities whose data were examined. These conclusions are a spurious artifact of the use of city-level data and of the cities selected. Had the study looked at state-level data—even for just the three states selected—it would have found that overall homicide declined. (It may be coincidental that the study's conclusions here dovetail with the hypothesis its authors advance elsewhere that self-defense is not a personal right but rather a social evil that ought to be eliminated to the extent possible.[13]) Yet the media gave this study extensive publicity. The *New York Times* actually reported it twice. Though the authors themselves qualified their results, neither their caveats nor criticisms by other scholars have received attention in popular media reports of the study.[14]

Contrast the *New York Times*'s total silence regarding a later study that differed from the earlier one both in its conclusions and in the extensiveness of its data. Done by University of Chicago economists, its findings were based on data from all 3,054 American counties. Perhaps more important to the *Times*, however, was that the data showed that liberal allowance of concealed handgun carry by thirty-one states had coincided with a reduction of thousands of murders, rapes, and other violent crimes in those states.[15] The authors tentatively concluded that adoption of such policies by the other nineteen states would save many more lives and prevent thousands more violent crimes. Other popular media did not follow the *New York Times* in completely blacking out the University of Chicago study. But insofar as it was reported, the results were denigrated by falsely reporting that the study had been sponsored by the gun industry.[16] (In turn, these falsehoods led to editorials denouncing the study as a fraud.[17])

Similar contrasts are endless. For instance, to their credit, the *New York Daily News* and several other New York City papers have noted that the New York City police, having unfettered discretion under New York law, issue concealed handgun carry licenses only to especially influential people, including Donald Trump; numerous Rockefellers and DuPonts; and a raft of politicians, millionaires, and/or celebrities. Perhaps because its own publisher was one of these licensees, the *New York Times* never found this story "fit to print." It is ironic (to say the very least) that in lieu of such information, the *Times* gives readers editorials asserting that "the urban handgun offers no benefits," inter alia, because "most civilians, *whatever their income level* are likely to lack the training and alertness" required to "use a gun to stop an armed criminal."[18]

Returning to the issue of accidental death, a child under age fifteen is 351 percent more likely to drown at home in an unattended swimming pool or bathtub than to be killed in a handgun accident.[19] Editorialists often assert that no one really needs a handgun. It would be more accurate to say that no one, except the disabled, needs a bathtub (as opposed to a shower) and that in most areas even Olympic swimmers do not need home swimming pools. Does it follow that home swimming pools and bathtubs should be subject to a licensing system under which they are forbidden to all except the disabled and anyone else who can satisfy the authorities that they have a pressing need that cannot otherwise be met? In raising this rhetorical question I am aware that handguns and swimming pools are different things and may require different policy responses. A vital difference, for instance, is that swimming pools do not prevent millions of violent crimes annually.

The Character of Gun Owners

The popular media's depiction of the character of the 50 percent of the American populace who own a firearm provides another example of how far conventional wisdom differs from sociological fact. News columnists, cartoonists and the media in general contemptuously dismiss such people as deluded, uneducated, intellectually and socially backward, and morally obtuse. To their credit American news media do not normally air stereotypical condemnations of entire groups. But to this there is one exception. *As a class*, gun owners are routinely reviled by the popular media as "gun lunatics who silence the sounds of civilization," "gun nuts," "gun fetishists," "traitors, enemies of their own *patriae*," "terrorists," "anti-citizens," sexually warped "bulletbrains," Klansmen, thugs, and vigilantes who represent "the worst instincts in the human character."[20]

Contrast the facts sociological and psychological research reveal about the character of gun owners as a class (as summarized by Professor Kleck and in studies sponsored by the National Institute of Justice):

> Middle- and-upper income people are significantly more likely to own [firearms] than lower-income people. . . .
>
> Gun owners are not, as a group, psychologically abnormal, nor [do attitude surveys show them to be] . . . more racist, sexist, or violence-prone than nonowners . . . Gun ownership is higher among middle-aged people than in other age groups, presumably reflecting higher income levels and the sheer accumulation of property over time. Married people are more likely to own guns than unmarried persons.
>
> Probably fewer than 2 percent of handguns and well under 1 percent of all guns will ever be involved in even a single violent crime. Thus, *the problem of criminal gun violence is concentrated within a very small subset of gun owners.*[21]

* * *

> It is clear that only a very small fraction of privately owned firearms are ever involved in crime or [unlawful] violence, the vast bulk of them being owned and used more or less exclusively for sport and recreational purposes, or for self-protection.[22]

Studies find gun owners do differ from nonowners in some ways. Gun owners are more likely to approve "defensive" force, i.e., force used to defend victims; in contrast, those with "violent attitudes" (who condone violence against social deviants or dissenters) are no more likely to own guns than not.[23] A study of citizens who rescued crime victims or arrested violent criminals found these Good Samaritans were two-and-half times more likely to be gun owners than nonowners.[24]

In sum, the conventional wisdom about gun owners perpetuated by their enemies (among which the popular media must be counted) is a bigoted stereotype that would be recognized and denounced as such if directed against gays, Jews, African Americans, or virtually any group other than gun owners. This bigotry is particularly hard to dispel because the generally good-hearted, progressive liberal people who perpetuate it are wholly incapable of understanding that any opinion they fervently embrace could be bigotry.

The Myth That Ordinary People Murder

This brings me to a related character issue, the conventional wisdom that most murders are perpetrated by ordinary people, and only because they had firearms available in a moment of ungovernable anger. The endlessly repeated argument for banning firearms is that "most [murderers] would be considered *law-abiding citizens* prior to their pulling the trigger"—"most shootings are not committed by felons or mentally ill people, but are acts of passion that are committed using a handgun that is owned for home protection."[25]

The point of these falsehoods is to evade the problem of gun bans being unenforceable. The embarrassing fact that criminals are not going to obey gun bans can be evaded by misrepresenting murder as something committed by "law-abiding citizens." But "the use of life-threatening violence in this country is, in fact, largely restricted to a criminal class and embedded in a general pattern of criminal behavior."[26] This is documented by homicide studies so numerous and consistent that their findings "have now become criminological axioms" about the "basic characteristics of homicide. . . ."[27] Local and national studies dating back to the 1890s show that in almost every case murderers are aberrants exhibiting life histories of violence and crime, psychopathology, substance abuse, and other dangerous behaviors.[28] Looking only to prior crime records, roughly 90 percent of *adult* murderers had *adult* records, with an average adult criminal career of six or more years, including four major *adult* felony arrests.

I emphasize adult murderers' records to distinguish the minimum 10 percent of murderers who are minors. By definition, they cannot have adult records, and state law has long made juvenile crime records unavailable. But several recent criminological studies at Harvard University have gained access to some of those records. They show the average minor who murders has compiled (in less than twenty-one years of life) at least five to ten prior arrests. Between them, the "relatively small number of very scary kids" who were identified as murderers in Boston in the years 1990 to 1994 had previously been charged with: three murders; 160 armed violent crimes; 151 unarmed violent crimes; 71 firearms offenses, 8 involving other weapons; and hundreds of property offenses and drug offenses. The great majority of these murderers were gang members, though their murders were not necessarily "gang-related" (e.g., gang member beats girlfriend to death believing she has been unfaithful to him).[29]

In short, available evidence as to juveniles who murder shows them to be as aberrant as adult murderers. By the same token, if the juvenile records of adult murderers were reviewed, criminal careers—juvenile and adult together —would show much more than their average of four major adult felonies discussed above. Thus the fact that most murders occur among acquaintances does not mean they arise out of neighborhood or family disputes among previously law-abiding people. The typical "acquaintance homicide" involves murders between members of the same or rival gangs, or between drug dealers and their customers, or the murder of a woman by a brutal man who has savaged her on numerous prior occasions. And the oft-mentioned (by antigun advocates) fact that many murders occur in homes fails to belie this since criminals have homes too. National data on acquaintance gun murders in homes show "the most common victim-offender relationship" was "where both parties knew one another because of prior illegal [drug] transactions."[30] Local homicide studies show that: 80 percent of homicides in Washington, D.C., are "drug-related"; 84 percent of 1990 homicide victims in Philadelphia had crime records or showed ante-mortem use of illegal substances; 71 percent of Los Angeles child and teenage drive-by shooting victims are documented members of violent street gangs; 71 percent of shooting victims in 1992 in Charlotte, North Carolina, had criminal records; likewise, trauma centers find recurrent gun and knife wounds to be virtually a disease common to "unemployed, uninsured law breakers"; substance abusers, those with subpar intelligence, and those with major mental disorders are each several times more likely to commit a violent crime than are ordinary citizens.[31]

In sum, the possession of firearms by the responsible, law-abiding citizenry is not a cause of murder. On the contrary, murders are committed by "a relatively small number of very scary" aberrants. It is desirable to prohibit guns to such aberrants as our laws already do.[32] But it is unreasonable to think any law can disarm such people. As a National Institute of Justice-funded evaluation of the literature on the criminology of firearms put it:

> [t]here is no good reason to suppose that people intent on arming themselves for criminal purposes would not be able to do so even if the general availability of firearms to the larger population were seriously restricted. Here it may be appropriate to recall the First Law of Economics, a law whose operation has been sharply in evidence in the case of Prohibition, marijuana and other drugs, prostitution, pornography, and a host of other banned articles and substances, namely, that demand creates its own supply. There is no evidence anywhere to show that reducing the availability of firearms *in general* likewise reduces their availability to persons with criminal intent or that persons with criminal intent would not be able to arm themselves under any set of general restrictions on firearms.[33]

Likewise an English gun control analyst has commented that no matter how restrictive and severe its laws, in any society there will always be enough guns available to arm those who are willing to obtain and use them illegally.[34] Thus, "conventional wisdom" is as wrong in thinking that gun laws (of any kind) can substantially reduce crime as it is in thinking that widespread gun ownership leads the law-abiding to murder.

The Threat of Long Gun Substitution

Indicative of the truly lamentable intellectual quality of the argument for banning handguns is that for more than thirty years it has rested on the (correct) premise "*guns* are much more deadly than other methods of assault"—from which it jumps to the conclusion that "reducing the availability of [only] *hand*guns" (my italics) will reduce murder—even though those so concluding concede that such a reduction "will not reduce the number of violent confrontations. . . ."[35] The error lies in assuming that without *hand*guns attackers would substitute knives (weapons that kill only about 2.4 percent of those they wound, where handguns kill 10 to 15 percent). Never examined is the possibility that at least some assailants might turn to rifles, weapons that are about fifteen times more deadly than knives, and, therefore, 5 to 11.4 times more deadly than handguns;[36] or shotguns, which are so much deadlier yet that for medical purposes the wounds they cause ought not to be "compared with other bullet wounds. . . . [A]t close range they are as deadly as a cannon."[37]

Criminological studies demonstrate "that anywhere from 54 percent to about 80 percent of homicides occur in circumstances that would easily permit the use of a long gun."[38] Professor Kleck modeled what would happen if differing shares of prospective attackers, who otherwise would have used handguns, instead substituted long guns of differing lethalities. He showed that a net increase in homicide deaths as a result of long gun substitution was likely, and that the only way eliminating handguns would not increase homicide would be if there were some combination of unrealistically low level of substitution of long guns, or substitution of unusually low lethality long guns (e.g., long guns being substituted that were only twice as deadly as handguns rather than four or five times as deadly) in combination with less than half of attackers substituting a long gun. How likely is it that if criminal attackers were deprived of handguns they would substitute long guns? Of the two thousand incarcerated felons who were queried in a National Institute of Justice survey, 82 percent said, "If a criminal wants a handgun but can't get one he can always saw off a long gun"; 87 percent of inmates who often used handguns in crime felt that sawing a long gun off to make it concealable for carrying would be "easy"—with which 89 percent of those who had often used shotguns criminally agreed.[39] Based on these responses, Professor Alan Lizotte, of the School of Criminal Justice at SUNY-Albany, estimated that the murder rate would triple if a handgun ban were actually effective enough to make felons substitute long guns at the rates indicated.[40] Another National Institute of Justice-sponsored analysis facetiously suggests:

> If someone intends to open fire on the authors of this study, our *strong* preference is that they open fire with a handgun, and the junkier the handgun, the better. The possibility that even a fraction of the predators who now walk the streets armed with handguns would, in the face of a handgun ban, prowl with sawed-off shotguns instead, causes one to tremble.[41]

The Second Amendment
Constitutional Right to Arms

Conventional wisdom calls the Second Amendment to the Constitution a mere "collective right" that guarantees nothing to individuals. A typical assertion in the popular media is that of Leonard Larsen (Scripps-Howard News Service): "only gun nut simpletons, NRA propagandists, and tinhorn members of Congress striving for careers at the public trough defend against gun controls on constitutional grounds."[42]

Unlike journalists, however, "almost all the qualified historians and constitutional-law scholars who have studied the subject [concur] . . . that the Second Amendment establishes an *individual* right to bear arms, which is not dependent upon joining something like the National Guard. [Representing] the overwhelming weight of authority,"[43] this view so dominates the scholarly literature that it is acknowledged as "the standard model" of the amendment even by opponents.[44] Of law review articles in the 1990s, forty-two endorsed the standard model view, while only six dissented.[45] Significantly, this "overwhelming weight of authority" is *nonpartisan*: though the six dissents are authored by vehement opponents of gun ownership (mostly lawyers for antigun groups), the standard model is endorsed by law professors, many of whom have never owned a gun, and were surprised and dismayed at the conclusion the evidence forced upon them, including all the major figures in constitutional law who address the issue. Reviewing Leonard Levy's book *Origins of the Bill of Rights*, Professor Lucas A. Powe (himself an ardent liberal Democrat with scant affection for guns) notes that "all serious constitutional law scholarship over the past decade has shown the 'collective right' position to be historically bogus."[46]

Nonetheless, as I have urged in debate with the NRA,[47] the amendment does not forbid gun *control*, as opposed to wholesale prohibition. Registration, licensing and other regulations are permissible if, but only if, they do not unreasonably hinder the freedom of law-abiding, responsible adults to choose to acquire firearms. (For example, a one-day waiting period to check a gun buyer for criminal record is permissible; New York's eight-month waiting period is not.)

A 1939 U.S. Supreme Court case allowed a challenge to gun laws under the amendment by individuals who had no connection to a state militia, but held that it protects possession of only military type and quality weapons. If so, the amendment covers high-quality handguns and other firearms but not poor-quality or gangster-type weapons (Saturday night specials), switchblade knives, blackjacks, and so on. Three 1990s cases implicitly reject claims that the right to arms applies only to state militias. The amendment's wording "bear arms" was analogized to the carrying of arms by ordinary people; and the Court emphasized that its wording "right of the people" is used consistently throughout the Constitution to denote rights of individuals.[48]

Notes

1. From an article coauthored with his colleague Professor Alan J. Lizotte, "Research and Policy: The Case of Gun Control," in *Psychology and Social Policy*, ed. Peter Sutfeld and Philip Tetlock (New York: Hemisphere, 1992).

2. Brandon Centerwall, "Homicide and the Prevalence of Handguns: Canada and the United States, 1976 to 1980," *American Journal of Epidemiology* 134 (1991): 1245-65.

3. Joseph F. Sheley and James D. Wright, "Gun-Related Violence in and Around Inner-City Schools," *American Journal of Diseases of Children* 146 (1992): 682.

4. Alfred Blumstein, "Youth Violence, Guns and the Illicit-Drug Industry," *Journal of Criminal Law and Criminology* 86 (1995): 10-36.

5. Compare National Safety Council, *Injury Facts* (Itasca, Ill.: NSC, 1999), pp. 16-17, 32, 101 (seventeen child deaths from accidents with all firearms combined in 1996, an estimated nine from handgun accidents) to the following figures for accidental poisonings of children in 1991: twenty-four died from ingesting a variety of household poisons (ammonia, kerosene, pesticides); eleven dead from ingesting iron supplements; ten from antidepressants, "Iron Pills Lead List in Killing the Young," *New York Times*, 9 June 1992.

6. Compare NSC, *Injury Facts*, above, and the figures given in chapter 2 below, to *USA Today* editorial, "Stop the Madness; Pass Sane Gun-Control Laws," 17 October 1991, p. 10A.

7. See *Odessa* (TX) *American*, 21 March 1996, p. 3B, and Lori Shawn, "Violence Shoots Holes in USA's Tourist Image," *USA Today*, 9 September 1993, p. 2A.

8. John R. Lott and David B. Mustard, "Crime, Deterrence, and Right-to-Carry Concealed Handguns," *Journal of Legal Studies* 26 (1997): 3n. 8 (police erroneously kill eleven times more often than do civilians, based on 1993 figures); Don B. Kates, "The Value of Civilian Arms Possession as Deterrent to Crime or Defense Against Crime," *American Journal of Criminal Law* 18 (winter, 1991): 130 (5.5 times more erroneous police shootings, based on 1970s figures).

9. Father Robert Drinan, S.J., coined the term "dangerous self-delusion" in his "Gun Control: The Good Outweighs the Evil," *Civil Liberties Review* 3 (summer, 1976): 4. The Handgun Control, Inc., language quoted is from a book by its then chairperson, Nelson Shields, *Guns Don't Die, People Do* (New York: Arbor House, 1981): 124-25. To the same effect see, e.g., Matthew Yeager et al., *How Well Does the Handgun Protect You and Your Family?* (Washington, D.C.: Handgun Control Staff of the U.S. Conference of Mayors, 1976); Franklin E. Zimring and Gordon Hawkins, *The Citizen's Guide to Gun Control* (1987): 32, and public health articles cited in chapter 2.

10. See discussion in chapter 7 and Lawrence Southwick, "Self-Defense with Guns: The Consequences," forthcoming in the *Journal of Criminal Justice*, 2000.

11. Marvin E. Wolfgang, "A Tribute to a View I Have Long Opposed," *Journal of Criminal Law and Criminology* 86 (1995): 188.

12. David McDowall, Colin Loftin, and Brian Wiersema, "Easing Concealed Firearms Laws: Effects on Homicide in Three States," *Journal of Criminal Law and Criminology* 86 (1995): 193-206.

13. David McDowall and Colin Loftin, "Collective Security and the Demand for Legal Handguns," *American Journal of Sociology* 88 (1983): 1146.

14. *New York Times*, 2 November 1995, p. A-16; 15 March 1995, p. A-23; see the critique by Daniel D. Polsby, "Firearms Costs, Firearms Benefits and the Limits of Knowledge," *Journal of Criminal Law and Criminology* 86 (fall, 1995): 207-20 and the authors' response and additional discussion between them on pp. 221-30.

15. The earliest version of this study was Lott and Mustard, "Crime, Deterrance, Right-to-Carry"; a later version with greatly extended findings to the same effect is John R. Lott, *More Guns, Less Crime*, 2d ed. (Chicago: University of Chicago Press, 2000).

16. Typically, the Associated Press, and the newspapers that ran its story, simply accepted the false claims of antigun lobbying groups—though they would never have published a progun lobby group press release without checking its accuracy. Checking would have been easy in this case. As any reporter could have discovered by calling the University of Chicago, Professor Lott holds a position the Olin Foundation had endowed decades ago. Lott is just a successor to earlier holders of the same endowment. The Olin Foundation had no part in Lott's selection nor in the funding for his study. For an account by a *Chicago Tribune* columnist who did check, see Stephen Chapman, "Taking Aim: A Gun Study and a Conspiracy Theory," *Chicago Tribune*, 15 August 1996, p. 31.

As any reporter could have discovered by calling the Olin Foundation, it is entirely independent of the Olin corporation. The foundation was established in John Olin's will decades ago, and the corporation has no control over the Foundation or connection to it. See the Foundation chairman's letter to the editor: William

Simon, "An Insult to Our Foundation," *Wall Street Journal*, 6 September 1996, p. A15.

17. See, e.g., *Chicago Sun-Times* editorial, 11 August 1996, p. 35. When Lott published a brief popular article on his results in the *Wall Street Journal* ("More Guns, Less Violent Crime," 28 August 1996, p. A13), then-Rep. (now Senator) Charles Schumer (D-N.Y.) wrote a letter to the editor repeating the falsehood: "Gun Control Thesis Is a Shot in the Dark," *Wall Street Journal*, 4 September 1996. Perhaps aware of the falsity, Mr. Schumer carefully attributed this disinformation to the Associated Press's false report of the matter. Nevertheless the *Wall Street Journal* later printed both its own retraction and a letter to the editor by former Treasury Secretary William Simon, the chairman of the Olin Foundation. See last note.

18. Don B. Kates, "Handgun Prohibition and the Original Meaning of the Second Amendment," *Michigan Law Review* 82 (1983): 208, notes 16, 17. Emphasis added.

19. National Safety Council, *Injury Facts—1999 Edition*, 32; (138 children age 0 to 14 died in firearms accidents in 1996, an estimated 78 with handguns); *Accident Facts—1997 Edition*, 131 (470 drowned at home); National Safety Council, *Accidents Facts—1988 Edition* (Itasca, Ill.: NSC, 1988), p. 91 (three-fourths of home drownings are in swimming pools or bathtubs, implying approximately 352 such deaths of persons age 0 to 14 in 1996).

20. These are direct quotations from: Braucher, "Gun Lunatics Silence [the] Sounds of Civilization," *Miami Herald*, 19 July 1982; Lewis Grizzard, "Bulletbrains and the Guns That Don't Kill," *Atlanta Constitution*, 19 January 1981; *Washington Post* editorial, "Guns and the Civilizing Process," 26 September 1972; and a series of columns by Garry Wills, including, "The Terrorists Who Pack an NRA Card," *Albany, N.Y. Times Union*, 22 April 1996; "NRA Is Complicit in the Deaths of Two Children," *Detroit Free Press*, 6 September 1994; "Or Worldwide Gun Control," *Philadelphia Inquirer*, 17 May 1981; "Handguns That Kill," *Washington Star*, 18 January 1981; and "John Lennon's War," *Chicago Sun-Times*, 12 December 1980. See also the following cartoons: *San Jose Mercury-News*, 3 March 1989 ("I.Q.-47"); Morin (*Miami Herald*) cartoon showing gun store with sign "drug dealers, gangs, welcome" appearing in the *Arizona Republic*, 21 March 1989; Herblock cartoon, *Washington Post*, 21 March 1989 ("these guys who want to spray the streets with bullets"); *Los Angeles Herald Examiner*, 31 January 1989 (showing "Crips, Bloods and NRA" as "Three Citizen Groups Opposed to Outlawing Assault Rifles"); Interlandi cartoon, *Los Angeles Times*, 16 December 1980.

21. Gary Kleck, *Point Blank: Guns and Violence in America* (New York: Aldine, 1991), pp. 22, 47–48. Emphasis added.

22. James D. Wright and Peter Rossi, *Armed and Considered Dangerous: A Survey of Felons and Their Firearms* (New York: Aldine, 1986), p. 4.

23. Alan J. Lizotte and Jo Dixon, "Gun Ownership and the Southern Subculture of Violence," *American Journal of Sociology* 93 (fall 1987): 383.

24. Kates, "Civilian Arms," p. 125.

25. Quoting public health writers who hold leading positions in disparate antigun lobbying groups, respectively: Daniel W. Webster et al., "Reducing Firearms Injuries," *Issues in Science and Technology* (spring, 1991): 73 (emphasis added); and Katherine Kaufer Christoffel, "Toward Reducing Pediatric Injuries from Firearms: Charting a Legislative and Regulatory Course," *Pediatrics* 88 (1991): 300.

A host of such assertions by academic antigun advocates are quoted in Don B. Kates and Daniel D. Polsby, "Long Term Non-Relationship of Widespread and Increasing Firearm Availability to Homicide," *Homicide Studies* 4 (May 2000): 192.

26. Delbert S. Elliott, "Life Threatening Violence Is Primarily a Crime Problem: A Focus on Prevention," *Colorado Law Review* 69 (1998): 1085; see statistics cited on pp. 1085–97.

27. David M. Kennedy and Anthony Braga, "Homicide in Minneapolis: Research for Problem Solving," *Homicide Studies* 2 (1998): 267.

28. Unless otherwise referenced, all assertions in this paragraph are based on Kates and Polsby, "Long Term Non-Relationship"; Kennedy and Braga, "Homicide"; and Elliott, "Life Threatening."

29. See generally the following studies coauthored by David M. Kennedy, Anthony Braga, and their colleagues: "Youth Violence in Boston: Gun Markets, Serious Youth Offenders and a Use Reduction Strategy," *Law and Contemporary Problems* 59 (1997): 159–60; "Homicide in Minneapolis," pp. 263–90; and "Youth Homicide in Boston: An Assessment of the Supplementary Homicide Report Data," *Homicide Studies* 3 (1999): 277. Professor Kennedy tells me that he has comparable data on Baltimore and other cities that is being readied for publication.

30. U.S. Justice Department data analyzed by Gary Kleck, *Targeting Guns: Firearms and Their Control*, p. 236.

31. Daniel Polsby and Don B. Kates, "American Homicide Exceptianalism," *University of Colorado Law Review* 69 (1998): 969–1007.

32. Federal and state law generally bar gun ownership by felons, drug addicts, minors, and persons who have been formally committed to mental institutions. See statutes cited in James B. Jacobs and Kimberly A. Potter, "Keeping Guns Out of the 'Wrong' Hands: The Brady Law and the Limits of Regulation," *Journal of Criminal Law and Criminology* 86 (fall 1995): 93–95.

33. James D. Wright, Peter Rossi and Kathleen Daly, *Under the Gun: Weapons, Crime and Violence in the United States* (New York: Aldine, 1983), pp. 137–38. Italics in original.

34. Colin Greenwood and Joseph Magaddino, "Comparative Cross-Cultural

Statistics," in *Restricting Handguns*, ed. Don B. Kates (New York: North Point, 1979).

35. Quoting, respectively, Katherine Kaufer Christoffel and Tom Christoffel, "Handguns: Risks Versus Benefits," *Pediatrics* 77 (1986): 782-83 and Susan Baker, "Without Guns, Do People Kill People?" *American Journal of Public Health* 75 (1985): 587.

36. Gary Kleck, "Handgun-Only Gun Control: A Policy Disaster in the Making," in *Firearms and Violence: Issues of Regulation*, ed. Don B. Kates (Cambridge: Ballinger, 1984), pp. 186–94; Martin L. Fackler, "Physics of Missile Injuries," in *Evaluation and Management of Trauma*, ed. N. McSwain Jr. and M. Kerstein (Norwalk, Co.: Appleton-Century-Crofts, 1987).

37. M. Taylor, "Gunshot Wounds of the Abdomen," *Annals of Surgery* 177 (1973): 174–75.

38. Kleck, "Handgun-Only Control," 189.

39. Wright and Rossi, *Armed and Dangerous*, p. 221, table 11.3.

40. Alan J. Lizotte, "The Costs of Using Gun Control to Reduce Homicide," *Bulletin of the N.Y. Academy of Medicine* 62 (1986): 539.

41. Wright, Rossi, and Daly, *Under the Gun*, pp. 322-23. Italics in original.

42. Syndicated Larsen column in the March 27, 1989, *Evansville Courier*. Compare Knight-Ridder columnist, Don Shoemaker, endorsing stringent laws to "disarm the American people and keep them disarmed," and dismissing constitutional objection to such laws as "idiocy" which all "thinking people" reject. *Evansville Press*, Dec. 7, 1990; see also: Molly Ivins, "Ban the Things. Ban Them All," *Washington Post*, 16 March 1993; John O. Craig, "There Is No Constitutional Right to Bear Arms," *Pittsburgh Post*, 8 May 1993; *Los Angeles Times* editorial, "Taming the Monster: The Guns Among Us," 10 December 1993; Herbert Mitgang, "What Right to Arms?" *New York Times*, 5 May 1995, p. A15; *CBS Evening News with Dan Rather*, 2 August 1999.

43. Comments by constitutional law professor Daniel Polsby in the *Atlantic Monthly*, June 1994, p. 13. Italics in original.

44. The description "standard model" originated in a review of the scholarly literature by University of Tennessee constitutional law professor Glenn H. Reynolds, "A Critical Guide to the Second Amendment," *Tennessee Law Review* 62 (1995): 461. Vigorous opponents of the standard model who nevertheless accept it as such include Garry Wills, "To Keep and Bear Arms," *New York Review of Books*, 21 September 1995, and Andrew D. Herz, "Gun Crazy: Constitutional False Consciousness and Dereliction of Dialogic Responsibilities," *Boston University Law Review* 75 (1995): 57.

45. These endnotes name some publications on each side. For more compre-

hensive lists see David B. Kopel, "The Second Amendment in the Nineteenth Century," *Brigham Young Law Review* (1998): 1362-65; Randy E. Barnett and Don B. Kates, "Under Fire: The New Consensus on the Second Amendment," *Emory University Law Journal* 45 (1996): 1143-46.

46. Laurence H. Tribe, *American Constitutional Law*, vol. 1 (New York: Foundation Press, 2000): 901–92; Leonard W. Levy, *Origins of the Bill of Rights* (New Haven, Conn.: Yale University Press, 1999), chap. 6; William Van Alstyne, "The Second Amendment and the Personal Right to Arms," *Duke Law Journal* 43 (1994): 1236-55; Akhil Amar, "The Bill of Rights and the Fourteenth Amendment," *Yale Law Journal* 101 (1992): 1205-11, 1261-62; Sanford Levinson, "The Embarrassing Second Amendment," *Yale Law Journal* 99 (1989): 637-59.

47. Compare Don B. Kates, "The Second Amendment: A Dialogue," *Law and Contemporary Problems* 49 (1986): 143, to Stephen Halbrook, "What the Framers Intended: A Linguistic Interpretation of the Second Amendment," *Law and Contemporary Problems* 49 (1986): 153.

48. *United States* v. *Miller*, 307 U.S. 174 (1939), *United States* v. *Verdugo-Urquidez*, 110 S.Ct. 1056 (1990), *Planned Parenthood* v. *Casey*, 505 U.S. 833, 848 (1992), *Muscarello* v. *United States*, 118 S.Ct. 1911, 1915, 1921 (1998).

Guns and Public Health

Epidemic of Violence, or Pandemic of Propaganda?*

by Don B. Kates

[Knowledge is neither good nor evil, but takes its character from how it is used.] In like manner, weapons defend the lives of those who wish to live peacefully, and they also, on many occasions kill [murder] men, not because of any wickedness inherent in them but because those who wield them do so in an evil way.

—Boccaccio, *The Decameron*,
translated by Mark Musa and Peter Bondaella
(New York: Mentor-New American Library, 1982), p. 686.

---

*In 1995 four colleagues and I published a severe critique of the articles on firearms that routinely appear in medical and public health journals. My coauthors were a University of North Carolina biostatistician, Henry E. Schaffer, Ph.D.; a Columbia Medical School professor, John K. Lattimer, M.D.; and two Harvard Medical School professors, Edwin H. Cassem, M.D., and George B. Murray, M.D. Our article appeared in *Tennessee Law Review*, v. 62 (1995): 513–96.

Our criticisms were validated when (at our request) the law review invited those whose works were principally criticized to reply. *None deemed it prudent to do so.*

There are two reasons why I have updated and adapted much of that article for this book. First, it gives an introductory summary of the state of criminological learning, of research and findings discussed in the later chapters of this book. Second, it contrasts to criminological learning the result-oriented medico-public health literature that underlies standard antigun arguments. (In addition to updating parts, I have severely reduced the size of the notes and reduced or eliminated discussions of subjects that are addressed elsewhere in this book. Please note that I bear the responsibility for all changes from the original article.)

The Public Health Agenda

In 1979 the American public health community adopted the "objective to reduce the number of handguns in private ownership," the initial target being a 25 percent reduction by the year 2000.[1] Based on studies and leadership from the Centers for Disease Control and Prevention (CDC), the objective has broadened so that it now includes banning and confiscation of all handguns, and restrictive licensing of owners of other firearms, with the goal of eventually eliminating firearms from American life, excepting (perhaps) only a small elite of extremely wealthy collectors, hunters or target shooters as in Europe.[2]

In this connection, some clarification is needed of the term "gun control." That term could mean no more than noncontroversial measures to prohibit gun misuse or gun possession by high-risk groups. In the literature we are analyzing, however, "guns are not an inanimate object, but in fact are a social ill" and to "control" them means, initially, measures to prevent their acquisition, and, eventually, a wholesale confiscation so as to make guns unavailable to ordinary people (see note 2). This goal parallels the goals of political lobbying groups such as Handgun Control, Inc., and the National Coalition to Ban Handguns (renamed the Coalition to Stop Gun Violence [CSGV], reflecting its present advocacy of banning many long guns as well as handguns). In fact, the antigun public health agenda goes beyond that of those groups. Officially at least, Handgun Control seeks only to ban gun ownership for self-defense, but would allow licensed sportsmen to have both handguns and long guns for purely sporting purposes; and the CSGV would allow people to have long guns, and limited access to handguns, for sporting purposes.[3]

Perhaps surprisingly, neither medical and health writers nor the journals that publish them are embarrassed by their agenda's close relationship to that of political lobbying organizations. On the contrary, exhortations "to speak out for gun control" are seen as part of an admirable tradition of political advocacy by doctors and other health professionals in support of political measures designed to improve public health.[4] In that spirit, writers in such journals strongly avow the need for active, political advocacy, for concerted action with antigun groups, and for openly supporting their political initiatives.[4] (We use the phrase "antigun health advocacy literature" as a shorthand for medical and public health publications having this focus or agenda.[5])

Health advocates see no problem reconciling such an openly political agenda with the demands of scholarship. After all, guns are hateful things for which no decent purpose is imaginable, certainly not self-defense.[6] Society's need to radically reduce gun availability is an unarguable truth to which there can be no *legitimate* opposition. Arrayed against the beneficent alliance of health advocates and antigun political advocates are only sinister "powerful lobbies that impede constructive exploration of the full range of social options"[7] by nefarious machinations, including racist propaganda cunningly designed to exploit white Americans' irrational fears of crime.[8]

The outward forms of scholarship must be observed, but the academic ideal of scholarly detachment is inapplicable. This is a struggle between modern enlightenment and (at best) morally obtuse and intellectually benighted atavism. There is no time for arid, academic discussion; the need for gun control is too urgent to require, or allow, equivocation, doubt, debate, or dissent.[9] The following comments typify the both the comments and the tenor of the articles discussing firearms issues that will be found in such journals:

> The continued advocacy of long overdue gun control is a constructive long term approach to [reducing violence]. . . . We reason that the time has come for government and citizens to begin a reasoned dialogue on the "why not" of gun ownership. If the conduct of youth [sic] and the need for harmony of humans with Nature is valuable to health and civilization, the world's most powerful country may not find justification for an armed citizenry.[10]

Moreover, there is no point to discussion, detached reflection, or dissent in a struggle between the forces of light and darkness. Evidence or perspectives that might induce skepticism or produce delay are per se invalid, being espoused by the Neanderthal racist gun lovers.

The anomalies found in the antigun health advocacy literature against gun ownership arise from that literature's existence in a vacuum of lockstep orthodoxy almost hermetically sealed against any admission that contrary data or scholarship might exist. Such data and scholarship routinely go unacknowledged; at best, they are evaded by misleadingly associating them with the sinister forces of the gun lobby. With rare exception, reference citations in the antigun health advocacy literature are to other writings in that same literature. If the universe of sources thus circumscribed does not yield appropriately antigun data, editorials are cited as if they were data and without noting that they are mere expressions of editorial opinion. Sometimes publications by partisan antigun groups are cited for purported factual data—often without any warning to readers of the group's partisan affiliation.[11] (This is all the more striking because of its inconsistency with the way in which claims from gun lobby sources are mentioned in the health advocacy literature against firearms. When such claims are mentioned, their origin is noted both in the text and in the margin. Far from concealing or ignoring the potential for bias as health sages do with antigun lobby claims, progun bias is deemed to render progun claims specious per se.[12]) Sometimes health advocates cite partisan antigun groups for claims the advocates know are dubious and subject to contradiction by nonpartisan, scholarly sources—which, of course, the advocates do not cite.[13]

To use Znaniecki's frame of reference, the antigun health advocacy literature is a "sagecraft" literature in which partisan academic "sages" prostitute scholarship, systematically inventing, misinterpreting, selecting, or otherwise manipulating data to validate preordained political conclusions.[14] Consciousness that one represents the forces of light against those of darkness overwhelms not only the canons of scholarship but also the ordinary demands of personal honesty and integrity: given the urgent needs of political advocacy, all too often academic health "sages" feel no compunction about asserting falsehoods, fabricating statistics and falsifying references to counterfeit support for them. (See examples given below of "gun-aversive dyslexia" and "overt mendacity.")

The speciousness and atavistic, insidious malignancy of all opposition to gun control being presumed, there is no need for health advocacy periodicals to waste space on such views or time in evaluating inconsistent evidence. Typical is the statement by the president of the American College of Epidemiology who declares gun ownership the "primary cause" of murder—and *then* calls for research on the subject.[15] (Whether guns "cause" violence, rather than being only an instrument, is among the cardinal, and most mooted, issues in the gun control debate. For what it is worth, two decades of research and analysis have led most criminologists to discard the idea of guns as a *cause* of crime—something that results in crime by previously law-abiding, responsible adults—in favor of noting their role in *facilitating* crime by criminals, and in worsening or bettering those crimes.)

In sum, health leaders see violence as a public health crisis and the firearm as something akin to an infectious disease: "Guns are a virus that must be eradicated" is a typical declamation.[16] These views receive wide exposure because, unlike criminology and other social scientific journals, medical and health periodicals announce the appearance of their articles on firearms to the press with releases describing the antigun conclusions. This follows the avowed intention of the health advocate sages to promote the idea that firearms ownership is an evil and its elimination a desirable and efficacious means of reducing violence.

The Verdict of Criminological Scholarship

From the 1960s on, health advocate sages have churned out a vast and ever-increasing amount of antigun advocacy literature. But the view thus promulgated is strikingly different from the view concurrently emerging from criminological research and scholarship. Consider the leading researcher's description of the effect his (and others') research had on his own attitudes. (From an unpublished presentation to the National Academy of Sciences by Florida State University criminologist Gary Kleck):

> Up until about 1976 or so, there was little reliable scholarly information on the link between violence and weaponry. Consequently, everyone, scholars included, was free to believe whatever they liked about guns and gun control. There was no scientific evidence to interfere with the free play of personal bias. It was easy to be a "true believer" in the advisability of gun control and the uniformly detrimental effects of gun availability (or the opposite positions) because there was so little relevant information to shake one's faith. When I began my research on guns in 1976, like most academics, I was a believer in the "antigun" thesis, i.e., the idea that gun availability has a net positive effect on the frequency and/or seriousness of violent acts. It seemed then like self-evident common sense which hardly needed to be empirically tested. However, as a modest body of reliable evidence (and an enormous body of not-so-reliable evidence) accumulated, many of the most able specialists in this area shifted from the "antigun" position to a more skeptical stance, in which it was negatively argued that the best available evidence does not convincingly or consistently support the antigun position. This is not the same as saying we know the antigun position to be wrong, but rather that there is no strong case for it being correct. The most prominent

representatives of the skeptic position would be James Wright and Peter Rossi, authors of the best scholarly review of the literature. [See note 44.]

[Subsequent research] . . . has caused me to move beyond even the skeptic position. I now believe that the best currently available evidence, imperfect though it is (and must always be), indicates that general gun availability has no measurable net positive effect on rates of homicide, suicide, robbery, assault, rape, or burglary in the United States. This is not the same as saying gun availability has no effects on violence—it has many effects on the likelihood of attack, injury, death, and crime completion—but these effects work in both violence-increasing and violence-decreasing directions, with the effects largely canceling out. For example, when aggressors have guns, they are (1) *less* likely to physically attack their victims, (2) *less* likely to injure the victim given an attack, but (3) *more* likely to kill the victim, given an injury. Further, when *victims* have guns, it is less likely that aggressors will attack or injure them and less likely they will lose property in a robbery. At the aggregate level, in both the best available time series and cross-sectional studies, the overall net effect of gun availability on total rates of violence is not significantly different from zero. The positive associations often found between aggregate levels of violence and gun ownership appear to be primarily due to violence increasing gun ownership, rather than the reverse. Gun availability does affect the rates of *gun* violence (e.g., the gun homicide rate, gun suicide rate, gun robbery rate) and the fraction of violent acts which involve guns (e.g., the percent of homicides, suicides or robberies committed with guns); it just does not affect total rates of violence (total homicide rate, total suicide rate, total robbery rate, etc.) [Citations omitted; emphasis in original.]

Scholars engaged in serious criminological research into "gun control" have found themselves forced—often very reluctantly[17]—to four largely negative propositions: 1) there is no persuasive evidence that owning guns *causes* ordinary responsible, law-abiding adults to murder or engage in any other criminal behavior—though guns can *facilitate* crime by those who were independently inclined toward it; 2) the value of firearms in defending victims has been greatly underestimated; 3) gun controls are innately very difficult to enforce (see note 17).

Difficulty of enforcement crucially undercuts the violence-reductive potential of gun laws. Unfortunately, there is an almost perfect *inverse* correlation between those who are affected by gun laws (particularly bans) and those whom it is desired to affect. Those easiest to disarm are the responsible and law abiding whose guns represent no meaningful social problem. But the irresponsible and/or criminal owners whose gun possession creates or exacerbates so many social ills are also the ones most difficult to disarm. A leading English analyst's pessimistic view has been summarized as follows: "in any society the number of guns always suffices to arm the few who want to obtain and use them illegally."[18]

So the final conclusion criminological research and analysis forces on scholars is (4) while controls carefully targeted only at the criminal and/or irresponsible have a place in crime-reduction strategy, the capacity of any type of gun law to reduce dangerous behavior can never be more than marginal. Contrast the health perspective that "guns are not an inanimate object, but in fact are a social ill" with the conclusion from a Wisconsin State Legislative Reference Bureau summary:

> It is difficult to make rational decisions in an atmosphere where absolute moral values are assigned to an inanimate object. A gun, while powerful and often destructive, is no more than a tool controlled by the person who uses it. . . . Gun control legislation focuses on regulating access to firearms, but the availability of guns is only one of many factors contributing to crime. Any measures that attempt to restrict access to firearms without reference to drugs, poverty with its attendant lack of educational and employment opportunities, clogged courts and overcrowded prisons are bound to have only marginal effects on firearm crime.[19]

Fear and Loathing as Social Science

In stark contrast to this nuanced, sophisticated assessment, the spirit animating the health advocacy literature on firearms is illuminated by the frank admission of one outspoken advocate of its political agenda, Professor Deborah Prothrow-Stith of the Harvard School of Public Health:

> My own view on gun control is simple. I hate guns and I cannot imagine why anyone would want to own one. If I had my way, guns for sport would be registered, and all other guns [i.e., those designed for self-defense] would be banned. [See note 6.]

Our review of the antigun health advocacy literature suggests that such unconstrained, unabashed emotive bias helps account for many of its anomalies and for its remarkable difference in tone and conclusion from the criminological scholarship on firearms issues.

Antigun health advocates seem blind or unconcerned about the danger that their emotions may preclude rational evaluation of gun ownership. Psychiatrist Emmanuel Tanay, M.D., who admits that he loathes guns to the point of being unable to look upon or touch them with equanimity, asserts that gun ownership betokens sexual immaturity or neuroticism. Dr. Tanay deems it evidence of this: that gun owners actually "handle . . . with obvious pleasure" these horrid objects which so repulse him; that collectors "look after" their collections, "clean, pamper, and polish" their guns: "The owner's overvaluation of his gun's worth is an indication of its libidinal value to him."[20]

As further evidence, Dr. Tanay invokes Freud's view of the sexual significance of firearms in the interpretation of dreams. This is particularly ironic because Freud's comments were not directed at gun ownership or owners. Insofar as Freud addressed the matter at all, he seems to have deemed *fear and loathing of guns* a sign of sexual immaturity and neuroticism.[21] We are emphatically not endorsing Freud's view as applicable to Dr. Tanay or explanatory of his views. Our concern is with the effect fear and loathing of guns has on the intellect, not the libido. On Dr. Tanay at least the effect is that he can't recognize how gun collectors' tastes might differ from his own, and he cannot comprehend passages from Freud; in fact, he is unable to read them without imposing a meaning almost opposite to what they actually say.

Dr. Tanay is by no means the only antigun health advocate to exhibit such an emotion-based reading disability (or "gun-aversive dyslexia" as we shall hereinafter call it). Dr. Kellermann, one of the most prolific and influential health advocate sages, cites as *supporting* his view "that limiting access to firearms could prevent many suicides" an article expressly concluding the opposite.[22] An article in the *Journal of the American Medical Association* alleged, "Research examining the effectiveness of gun control in specific locales suggests that it can reduce violence"—but cited only articles supporting the opposite conclusion.[23] Another *Journal of the American Medical Association* article attributed increased homicide to increased cocaine use and gun availability among New York City minority teenagers. It did cite evidence to show increased cocaine use; but its citations for the supposedly increased firearms availability indicated the reverse.[24]

We do not suggest these gun-aversive dyslexic errors have any great importance in and of themselves. Their importance lies in what they, and innumerable other errors we document, collectively say about the effect of having advocacy deemed (even hailed as) a norm while scholarship receives only lip service. Error becomes endemic when the corrective effects of dissent and criticism are excluded. Lest our comments seem strident and extreme, recall that this is peer-reviewed literature. Each of these articles was peer-reviewed, as were almost all the other articles we cite. How did errors of easily establishable fact (e.g., that a source is cited for something opposite to what it says) slip past three reviewers? The short answer is that intellectual sloppiness prevails when political motivations reign and sagecraft displaces scholarship.

Worse yet, peer review, and the general process of criticism, actually exacerbates error, given the atmosphere of intellectual lockstep which prevails among health advocates. For instance, it wasn't enough for the *JAMA* reviewer of Dean Prothrow-Stith's book (see note 2) that it unreservedly avowed her hatred for guns. He reproached not her emotionalism (which he fervently endorses) but the failure to devote more space to teaching health advocates how to mobilize support for laws to rid our society of these evil objects.[25] An atmosphere in which criticism in general, and peer review in particular, comes from solely one perspective not only allows error, but promotes it—intentional error as well as inadvertent, serious error as well as minor. Locutional sloppiness and hyperbole reign in a health advocacy literature where advocacy has displaced scholarship and the only allowable peer review or criticism is that which arraigns authors for underemphasizing the baleful effect guns have on society.

A Nosology of Health Sage Error

The abysmal quality of the antigun health advocacy literature implicates six conceptually discrete factors: intellectual and locutional sloppiness; intellectual confusion; ignorance of criminological or other fact; omission of material fact, or statement of part of a fact in a way calculated to suppress the whole; overt misrepresentation of facts; and gun-aversive dyslexia, i.e., a fear and loathing of guns so profound that health advocate sages encountering adverse facts may be honestly unable to comprehend them.

Though these six aspects are conceptually discrete, they often run together in the health advocacy literature, so that it is not always easy to clearly distinguish them from each other and to disentangle their mutually exacerbating effects. Consider Judith Dolins and Katherine Christoffel's exhortation for health advocates to "educate" the public to believe there is no constitutional impediment to banning and confiscating guns because

> the Second Amendment does not guarantee the right to personal ownership of firearms. Legal decisions, including those of the Supreme Court, have repeatedly ruled in favor of this interpretation, and *none of the existing tens of thousands of [gun control] laws . . . has ever been ruled unconstitutional.*[26]

Particularly since neither author is a lawyer, it is impossible to disentangle how much of this results from overt deception and how much represents gun-aversive dyslexia, confusion, ignorance and/or locutional sloppiness. The authors may simply be unaware of the Supreme Court authority or that all but eight state constitutions guarantee the right to arms independent of the Second Amendment and these guarantees have been held to invalidate gun laws.[27] Likewise, when in another article Christoffel asserted, "Well-informed legal scholars agree that [gun bans] are indeed constitutional" (under the Second Amendment), she may not have known that the verdict of modern constitutional scholarship is overwhelmingly contrary.[28]

A related passage from Dolins and Christoffel illustrates the difficulty of distinguishing how much a particular health advocacy assertion owes to deception from what may be gun-aversive dyslexia. In the first of two consecutive sentences, they seek to discredit the individual right view of the Second Amendment by ascribing it to the sinister forces of "the gun lobby." In fact, one the most striking things about the scholarly consensus for that view is that it includes substantial numbers of scholars who have no liking for either guns or the gun lobby. The next sentence invokes the same specter to discredit two uncongenial sets of criminological data discussed by social scientists whom Dolins and Christoffel cite, but willfully mischaracterize as follows:

> *Gun supporters* contend that widespread gun ownership has helped to curb the increasing rates of violence and crime although most *epidemiologists* interpret the evidence as unconvincing.[29]

We have added emphasis to highlight the labels falsely bestowed on *both* sides in this dispute: On the one hand, the "epidemiologists" whose support Dolins and Christoffel invoke are not "epidemiologists" (i.e., health professionals) at all. They are criminologists, i.e., social scientists, just as are the social scientists whose findings they reject. This is important, because as we emphasize below, no health advocate sage has had the moral courage to even attempt to come to grips with either of the data sets involved here. Dolins's and Christoffel's reference quoted above is the only mention of one of these data sets in the entire health advocacy literature; the other set is almost never mentioned.

It is no less an overt misrepresentation to label the three scholars who published those two datasets "gun supporters." All three are liberal Democrats, two of them holders of endowed chairs in sociology who don't own firearms and don't urge that others do so. But labeling them "gun supporters" has the advantage not only of demeaningly misrepresenting their position, but also of suppressing two embarrassing, but material, facts. *First*, each of these "gun supporter" social scientists began his research as a believer in the health advocacy indictment of guns, but was reluctantly forced to conclude that it is simply wrong.[30]

Second, the contention that widespread gun ownership deters violent crime is not personal to Professors Wright and Rossi, but rather something they report from a survey of what might be called more percipient witnesses. The work Dolins and Christoffel cite is a report of the results of the survey Wright and Rossi conducted for the National Institute of Justice among two thousand inmates in state prisons across the United States. All Wright and Rossi do is report what the felons said: that 34 percent of them personally had been "scared off, shot at, wounded or captured by an armed victim"; that 69 percent said they knew at least one other criminal who had also. Answering two other questions: that 34 percent said that when thinking about committing a crime they either "often" or "regularly" worried that they "Might get shot at by the victim"; and that 57 percent agreed with the statement "Most criminals are more worried about meeting an armed victim than they are about running into the police."[31]

Dolins and Christoffel do not, because they cannot, deny this is what the felons said. Though Dolins and Christoffel find the felons' answers highly uncongenial, to label Wright and Rossi "gun supporters" for honestly reporting them is misleading and tendentious. To fully comprehend the deceptiveness of the entire passage we have quoted from Dolins and Christoffel, it must be understood that Dollins and Christoffel are linking together a book by Wright and Rossi and an article by Gary Kleck, though the two publications have nothing to do with each other, and neither do the respective authors. But linking them allows Dollins and Christoffel to falsely claim that other social scientists have analyzed and rejected the findings of each publication. One critique Dolins and Christoffel cite does reject Kleck's views—but makes no mention of Wright-Rossi. The other critique Dolins and Christoffel cite does not deem either Kleck or Wright and Rossi "unconvincing"; it describes Kleck's results respectfully and without any demurral, and seeks to put the Wright and Rossi data in perspective by noting that other surveys of criminals suggest dogs deter burglary more than do guns.[32] (In contrast, the critique Dolins and Christoffel do cite gives a far more negative appraisal of a study they rely on to assert the foolishness of defensive gun ownership. Of course that negative appraisal is yet another thing Dolins and Christoffel don't bother to mention.)

Our examples from Dolins and Christoffel, and others discussed below, may explain, if not justify, the antigun health advocacy literature's refusal to try to deal with uncongenial data and views. Yes, scholarship normally requires that opposing data and views be expressly cited and refuted. But what point is there in antigun health advocate sages doing that when their gun aversion precludes them from accurately perceiving the meaning of data or perspectives about guns which are inconsistent with their own views?

The Valor of Ignorance

An interview with Dr. Robert Tanz of Children's Memorial Hospital in Chicago is as illuminating in its way as Professor Prothrow-Stith's admission of the "hatred" of guns that underlies her antigun advocacy. Dr. Tanz affirms that he and his Children's Hospital colleague, Dr. Katherine Christoffel, "plan to do to handguns what their profession has done to cigarettes . . . turn gun ownership from a personal-choice issue to a repulsive, antisocial health hazard." Because the validity of this goal is severely undercut by Professor Kleck's research on the defensive value of firearms, the interviewer asked Dr. Tanz about that research.* This brings us back to Dr. Tanz, who has no place in this debate—no basis for forming an opinion, much less for commenting on it—for he "acknowledges that he has never read a single word Kleck has written," nor does he claim even to have read Kleck's critics. Yet Dr. Tanz unhesitatingly informed the interviewer that Kleck's figures are wildly exaggerated and that the actual number of cases in which guns are used defensively is "only about 80,000" annually.[34]

Dr. Tanz is apparently no less ignorant of the now established fact that the very data-source he embraces against Kleck confirms a different Kleck finding which would equally appall Dr. Tanz, if only he knew of it. These data show that, far from defensive gun use endangering them, gun-armed victims who resist robbery or rape are injured far less often than those who submit!† Gun-armed victims are also, of course, much less likely to be robbed or raped than those who take Handgun Control's advice to never resist: "the best defense against injury is to put up no defense—*give them what they want* or run."[35]

It bears emphasizing that Kleck and others who have discussed these facts add various caveats, the most important of which is that a gun is not a magic wand that renders resistance successful and risk-free regardless of the circumstances. Rather, a handgun is precisely analogous to a fire extinguisher. Each are tools that provide an option for action—an option that may be exercised or not, depending on what the circumstances dictate.

Issues, Data, and References "Missing in Action"

Prof. Kleck's research findings on the utility of defensive gun ownership first appeared in February 1988, based on the early data that were then available. That research and Kleck's later elaborations of it are appraised by one of Kleck's sometime critics as "the definitive study in this area" (personal communication from Professor Alan J. Lizotte). Health advocates are aware of the importance of the issue of defensive gun use. (Indeed, in the interview previously quoted, Dr. Tanz said: "If somebody were to turn

---

*I have here deleted a lengthy discussion of Kleck's work because a more up-to-date discussion appears in chapters 6 and 7 below.

†See Kleck, chapter 7 below.

around and prove that guns save more lives than they kill, then I think we [gun control advocates] would have to turn around."[36] What then accounts for their never citing and refuting the "definitive study" from 1988 until 1991 when a contrary article by Professor Cook became available for counter-citation?* On the very rare occasions on which they even cite Kleck's work, it is always negatively and almost always with the statement that it has been discredited.[37]

We are not, incidentally, suggesting that health advocate sages join their allies in the antigun lobby in counseling victim submission to rapists and other felons. While antigun health advocates freely counsel that victims never keep a firearm to defend self, home, or family,[38] what victims *should* do if attacked is yet another issue missing in action from the health advocacy literature.

Even now when the health sages have Cook's work to counteract Kleck, health sages who discuss defensive gun use virtually never cite Kleck's "definitive study in this area. . . ." Writing in 1993, James Mercy, CDC criminologist, and Mark Rosenberg, former head of CDC's Intertinal Injury section, admitted the great importance of the question "How frequently are guns used to successfully ward off potentially violent attacks?"—but did not cite Kleck, whose studies directly address that question.[39] Equally unfortunate is the following from a 1993 article by Stephen Teret, lawyer and professor of public health at Johns Hopkins, and Gwen Wintemute, doctor at the U.C. Davis Medical Center, which also fails to cite Wright and Rossi, Kleck, or the other studies discussed above: gun lobby or manufacturer "advertisements often portray a handgun as a necessary protection of oneself and one's family. However, data do not support this claim."[40]

Doubtless Mercy and Rosenberg and Teret and Wintemute would seek to excuse their suppression of the existence of Kleck's (and the other) contrary scholarship on the ground that they subscribe to Cook's views. The first difficulty with this is that only portions of Kleck's work have even been challenged; the rest have not, nor have the Wright and Rossi findings cited in note 31. The second difficulty is that the fact of Cook's disagreement with Kleck on a particular issue does not repeal the normal standards of scholarly discourse; quite the reverse. The normal standards of scholarly discourse demand that health sages do what Cook did: cite Kleck and explain

---

*For a discussion of Professor Cook's work, see chapters 6 and 7 below.

why they think he is wrong. Or, if they do not have the space to address the issue at length, cite both Kleck and Cook, declare their agreement with Cook, and let their readers decide for themselves. But the health advocacy political agenda requires that the existence of contrary scholarship or views be suppressed or misrepresented to readers as deriving solely from the dark forces of the gun lobby.

This leads to a more general point about the persona non grata status in the health advocacy literature of the entire corpus of Kleck's work, not just his research on defensive gun use. Over the past fifteen years Kleck has been the most important and prolific social scientific researcher in the area. In 1993 the American Society of Criminology bestowed its highest award on his book titled *Point Blank*, declaring it to be the single most important contribution to criminology over the preceding several years. American and foreign reviewers hail the book as *the* prerequisite to scholarly research or discussion of the issues; even those who disagree with Kleck's views call it the essential reference work, the "indispensable" text "for any serious scholar working in the area."[41]

So what does it say about the integrity, competence, and reliability of antigun health articles that we can find none of them citing *Point Blank* and virtually no citation of the rest of the vast corpus of Kleck's scholarly research? Insofar as Kleck is cited, health advocate sages deem they have refuted him without exposing any actual flaws, by just stating that Kleck questions the efficacy of gun control.[42] The antigun editors who print them presumably accept such refutations as condemning Kleck's work per se and without need for further discussion, much less for allowing Kleck or any scholar who agrees with him to argue its merits.

Returning to the example of Dr. Tanz with which we began, we see at least a limited defense for his disinclination to read anything adverse to his emotional bias against firearms. Perhaps his apparent failure to read any of Kleck's work is occasioned by the assumption that Kleck would simply shirk the evidence Dr. Tanz prefers to credit. Reasonable though such an assumption is to one whose ideas of scholarship are conditioned by the health advocacy literature, it is inaccurate as to the criminological literature in general and Kleck in particular. Dr. Tanz meticulously analyzes every major article in the health advocacy literature that preceded the publication of Kleck's verbal word; *Point Blank's* reference section cites at least twenty-five medical or health publications.

Unnatural Selection

Another "exception" to Kleck's persona non grata status in the health advocacy literature is particularly striking because it is the proverbial "exception that proves the rule." Despite Dolins and Christoffel's characterization of Kleck as a Neanderthal "gun supporter," he is actually a liberal Democrat, a member of the ACLU and Amnesty International, but not of any progun group. In fact, Kleck has angered the gun lobby by recommending gun controls it opposes. Long before the Brady Bill he supported a much more sweeping background check than provided in it.[43] Of all Kleck has written about firearms, this recommendation of a control is one of only two positive citations his work has received in the health advocacy literature.

It is noteworthy that this positive citation of Kleck in the health literature appears in the entire chapter devoted to firearms issues of a book. Given the available space, it is at once ironic and typical that the chapter's authors found no room for the more major points in Kleck's work as a whole—or even for the major points in the Kleck article they cited. To see why Kleck's major findings are avoided we need only quote from the abstract to the cited article:

> All of the following assumptions [of antigun advocacy] were found to be substantially at variance with the evidence: (1) Guns are five times deadlier than the weapons most likely to be substituted [if a gun ban made guns unavailable to criminals]; (2) The sight of a gun can elicit aggression . . . ; (3) If guns are made more expensive, more difficult to obtain, or legally risky to own, people will do without them; (4) Guns are useless for self-defense . . . and have no deterrent effect on criminals; (5) Homicides are largely "crimes of passion" committed by otherwise law-abiding citizens not distinguishable from other people. Therefore, control must be directed at all gun owners rather than select criminal subgroups. [See note 43.]

Since most of these insupportable assumptions are present in the health advocacy chapter on firearms, the failure to mention Kleck's (or any other) counter-showing is, once again, striking, yet all too typical of what passes for scholarship in the sagecraft literature of antigun health advocacy.

Despite its enormous bulk, the health advocacy literature has no comprehensive summary like *Point Blank*. Since citing *Point Blank* is inconceivable, health sages (including even Dr. Christoffel!) sometimes find themselves forced to cite a much earlier work by Wright, Rossi, and Kathleen Daly (professor of sociology at the University of Michigan) for some point that cannot otherwise be documented. It is truly wondrous how the need to cite this work transforms those discreditable "gun supporters" into credible, reliable scholars.[44] In yet another example of gun-aversive dyslexia, Dr. John Sloan and his colleagues even cite Wright, Rossi, and Daly as *supporting* their (the doctors') belief that "restricting access to handguns could substantially reduce our annual rate of homicide."[45] Now Wright, Rossi, and Daly had indeed evaluated that belief, but their actual appraisal was:

> It is commonly hypothesized that much criminal violence, especially homicide, occurs simply because the means of lethal violence (firearms) are readily at hand, and, thus, that much homicide would not occur were firearms generally less available. *There is no persuasive evidence that supports this view.*[46]

Two years later an NRA employee criticizing a new Sloan et al. article noted Wright and Rossi's highly adverse view of the doctors' prior article. Sloan et al. responded that "Wright's [and Rossi's] long held views on the subject of gun control are also well-known, and their criticism was predictable."[47] Yet, of course, if those "long held" views were "well-known" to them two years before, their apparent attribution of the opposite view to Wright and Rossi would cross the line from mere gun-aversive dyslexia to affirmative misrepresentation.

The quotation from Wright, Rossi, and Daly in the preceding paragraph is the centerpiece from their abstract to their *Executive Summary* of their massive NIJ-funded literature evaluation. Neither that quote nor their general conclusions which the quote expresses are ever mentioned in the health advocacy literature on firearms. Readers who get their information from the health sages will never know of these general conclusions or of their disagreement with the health advocacy position on firearms. Nor, with minimal exceptions, do health advocate sages inform readers of specific findings in Wright, Rossi, and Daly that are adverse to the health advocacy position.

In this connection we note Teret and Wintemute's brief mention, in a 1993 article, of prior reviews of scholarship and literature on the criminology of firearms. Wright, Rossi, and Daly and *Point Blank* are far and away the most important such reviews. But Teret and Wintemute choose not to share that (or any knowledge of either review) with their readers. Instead they cite an obscure, generally antigun, 1978 review only ninety pages long that has gone virtually uncited since the 600 page Wright, Rossi, and Daly review appeared in 1981. Instead of the 500 page *Point Blank* (1991) they mention a nine-page review done for the American Medical Association in 1989, again with generally antigun conclusions.

Health advocates are understandably uncomfortable with the criminological scholarship represented by Wright, Rossi, Kleck, Bordua, etc.—almost allergic to it, in fact. Yet ought they not to have some better response than just concealing this enormous body of contrary scholarship from their readers? It is trite, but apparently necessary, to say that if the health advocates have some meaningful answer to the criminologists' conclusions, health advocates ought to forthrightly describe those conclusions and tell their readers what is wrong with them.

"Sagecraft" and Scholarship

Though he has not read Kleck, Dr. Tanz has read—and highly recommends—a study the *New England Journal of Medicine* published extolling strict Canadian gun control. The study was a simplistic comparison of homicide rates in Vancouver to those in Seattle.[48] Being largely or completely ignorant of the vast body of competent contradicting research, health advocacy journals routinely cite this simplistic study for the shibboleth of the health advocacy faith:

> Lack of availability of guns can decrease the propensity of people to commit violent acts both toward others and themselves, [resulting in] an absolute reduction in the rate of penetrating trauma.[49]

But Dr. Tanz at least does know that opposite conclusions were reached in one of the few skeptical articles a medical or health journal has published, psychiatrist and University of Washington School of Public Health Professor Brandon Centerwall's exhaustive comparison of broad Canadian and U.S. homicide data.[50] That is, however, yet another uncongenial study Dr. Tanz never bothered to read before closing his mind.[51]

Presumably Dr. Tanz is unaware that the rosy conclusions he prefers about Canadian gun control have also been discredited in other studies as well.[51] But the fact that Dr. Tanz chooses to rely on conclusions he likes based on data from just two cities in the United States and Canada, while having no interest in the contrary conclusions dictated by much broader data comparisons, speaks for itself. Being intellectually indefensible, such a choice can only be explained, not justified; and the only explanation is that it is "result-oriented," i.e., it is dictated by Dr. Tanz's emotional bias in favor of reaching antigun results despite the contrary results dictated by the best available evidence. Regrettably, the health advocacy literature against firearms is consistently result-oriented. Again, the relevant paradigm is sociologist Florian Znaniecki's concept of "sagecraft" (see the discussion in note 14 and accompanying text). The health advocacy literature is a sagecraft literature in which academic "sages" prostitute scholarship, systematically inventing, misinterpreting, selecting, or otherwise manipulating data to validate preordained conclusions.

Dr. Tanz's preference for two-city data that supports his view over two-nation data which refute it is typical. And, that same intellectually indefensible, politically motivated choice was made first by the authors of the two-city comparison (who are among the most prominent of the health advocate sages); second by the *New England Journal of Medicine* which published that inferior data article; and third by the antigun health advocacy community ever since. Professor Centerwall has kindly consented to allow us to quote the following from a letter he wrote us: One of the authors of the two-city comparison, Dr. John Sloan,

> and I were both affiliated with the University of Washington [School of Public Health, where Centerwall still teaches] at the time that [Sloan] was working on his study comparing Seattle and Vancouver and I on my study comparing the United States and Canada. We were aware of each other's work. Shortly before he began writing his paper, I gave him a copy of my [mss.—title omitted], so *he was familiar with it in detail before he prepared his own work.*

We have added emphasis to the foregoing to spotlight the issue of sagecraft. Under normal standards of scholarly integrity, Dr. Sloan would have responded either by dropping publication efforts for his inferior-data study or by citing the Centerwall research therein and then explaining why its results were meaningful and valid despite their contradiction by the vastly larger, more meaningful Centerwall data set. But the sagecraft ethics prevailing among health advocates on gun issues allowed Dr. Sloan et al. to solve their problem more simply, if not more elegantly. They simply published their article and neglected to inform their readers that a far larger and more geographically diverse data set yielding contrary results existed.

Professor Centerwall's very different attitude toward scholarship is indicated by the fact that his article expressly called the two-city comparison to his readers' attention and then explained why its defective methodology and inferior data set invalidated its results.[53] We now resume quotation of Professor Centerwall's letter from the point at which we broke it off:

> By coincidence [Sloan] and I independently submitted our respective manuscripts to the *New England Journal of Medicine* which published that inferior data at the same time. Therefore, the editors had both manuscripts before them on the table, at least metaphorically, and perhaps literally. Thus both [Sloan] *and* the editors of the *New England Journal* knew that there was another study which flatly contradicted Sloan's findings and conclusions, yet Sloan chose not to acknowledge the existence of that study in his paper and the editors of the *New England Journal* did not require him to make reference to it. I might add that it is common for the *New England Journal* to publish two articles on the same subject back-to-back in the same issue when it seems opportune to do so. They have even published back-to-back articles which have flatly contradicted each other. Therefore, accepting one article in no way precluded accepting the other. [Italics in original.]

Predictably, the *New England Journal* rejected the Centerwall study; did publish the Sloan piece; and did not even require that Sloan et al. mention Professor Centerwall's uncongenial findings. The Centerwall article was belatedly published in the *American Journal of Epidemiology*, albeit under the unprecedented condition that an antigun author be invited to formally comment in response. Of course, none of the literally hundreds of antigun articles and editorials published by health advocacy periodicals over the past thirty years has required or received an invited commentary by either a progun or a neutral analyst. Indeed, only one progun commentary has even appeared in that period of time in contrast to all the antigun articles addressing gun issues in these supposedly scholarly periodicals.[54]

Remarkably, the antigun commentator on the Centerwall article ended up lauding its conclusions and urging careful attention to them by medical and health professionals interested in the firearms area.[55] Of course, this advice fell on deaf ears: the Centerwall article is almost never cited by health advocacy writers; nor is there ever any citation of the other two-nation studies reaching the same negative conclusion as to strict Canadian gun control; in contrast, Sloan et al.'s meager two-city comparison is among the most frequently cited studies in the health advocacy literature on firearms.[56]

Note that Prof. Centerwall is yet another non-gun owner, non-"gun supporter," whose research forced him to conclusions he did not desire. His comments on that should have particular interest for any health advocates who can rise above gun-aversive dyslexia:

> If you are surprised by my findings, so am I. I did not begin this research with any intent to "exonerate" handguns, but there it is—a negative finding, to be sure, but a negative finding is nevertheless a positive contribution. *It directs us where not to aim public health resources.*[57]

Other research has led Centerwall to link high violence rates to the effects of a generation or more children watching television. Predictably, health advocate sages who concur with Centerwall on that have no difficulty citing his work to that effect—even in the same works in which they ignore the uncongenial findings of his far broader handgun homicide study in favor of citing the congenial findings of the Sloan et al. two-city study.[58] The June 10, 1992, issue of the *Journal of the American Medical Association*, which was devoted to the issue of violence, included a piece from Centerwall on television as a cause of violence. Many of the other articles addressed firearms violence. Naturally, none cited Centerwall's piece on that subject or offered, or even mentioned, any view other than the health advocacy shibboleth that more-guns-mean-more-murder and strict-gun-control-means-less-murder. The remainder of this article will contrast the health advocacy literature's promotion of this shibboleth to the overwhelmingly adverse results of the criminological evidence.

International Disinformation

In a book published twenty years ago antigun activist Robert Sherrill derisively commented that no debate over gun policy would be complete without a plethora of brief, often inaccurate and invariably contradictory, references to foreign gun laws and crime rates.[59] The information necessary to avoid many such errors is available in Professor David Kopel's analysis of foreign gun laws, policies, and crime, which received the American Society of Criminology's Comparative Criminology Award in 1992.[60] Predictably, though foreign gun laws are frequently (and often erroneously) mentioned in the health advocacy literature,[61] we have been unable to find even a single reference to Professor Kopel's book in that literature.

Sloan's Vancouver-Seattle Comparison

The quality of health advocacy literature mentions of foreign gun laws and their supposedly miraculous reductive effect on crime ranges from ignorant and simplistic to half-truths to deliberate misinformation. Lest our assessment seem harsh, consider a *Canadian* criminologist's comment: all too often, asserts Professor Gary Mauser of Simon Fraser University, gun control "studies are an abuse of scholarship, inventing, selecting, or misinterpreting data in order to validate a priori conclusions." He then cites as "a particularly egregious example—'Handgun Regulations, Crime, Assaults and Homicide,' by John Sloan and his associates, which appeared in Volume 319 of the *New England Journal of Medicine* in 1988."[62]

Note that—entirely independent of the contradictory result from Centerwall's far superior data base (or Sloan's failure to mention it)—Sloan's two-city comparison is methodologically worthless, patently invalid, and insufficient to justify its conclusions. As Professor Kleck commented on National Public Radio's *All Things Considered* on December 16, 1989:

> There were only two cities studied, one Canadian, one U.S. There are literally thousands of differences across cities that could account for violence rates, and these authors just arbitrarily seized on gun levels and gun control levels as being what caused the difference. It's the sort of research that never should have seen the light of day.

Indicative of the methodological sophistication of health advocacy sages is that, with a straight face, they actually call the Sloan et al. study "elegant."[63] Of course, neither Sloan et al. nor any other health advocacy sage has even acknowledged criticism from scholars like Mauser and Kleck. Consistent with the health advocacy themes noted earlier, criticism of the article is attributed to the NRA and portrayed as part of its sinister attempts to stifle legitimate scholarly research.[64]

Israel and Switzerland:
Murder and the Availability of Guns

As Professor Kopel's prize-winning international study shows, there is no consistent correlation between gun laws or gun ownership rates and high murder or suicide or crime rates across a broad spectrum of nations and cultures. No health advocacy sage has cited Kopel or any of the other works cited in notes 50 and 52. No doubt health advocates sincerely do believe the coincidence of severe antigun laws and low violence rates in some foreign nations is a matter of cause and effect. The gun laws, crime and history of foreign lands are arcane matters, not likely to be within health advocates' ken. Moreover, the health advocates' ignorance of the criminological literature, and their allergy to neutral analysis or works that might contain uncongenial facts, precludes their discovering a fact that undercuts their simple-minded faith in foreign gun laws: such laws can't have caused the low European homicide rates because those rates long *preceded* the laws.[65]

The health advocate sages are, however, at least dimly aware of international data which contradicts their shibboleth that gun availability causes high homicide and suicide rates. The shibboleth is contradicted when it turns out that "low violence rates appear in Switzerland and Israel which encourage (even require) gun possession by their entire citizenry."[66] Health advocate sages evade those uncongenial facts by describing Israel and Switzerland as nations "that have strict handgun laws [and] report negligible deaths by handguns."[67]

The sages' statements to that effect are classic examples of deception by half-truth. Yes, Switzerland and Israel do have "negligible deaths by handguns." Yes, Israel has a license requirement to *buy and own* a gun (any gun, not just a handgun). But providing only that half of the story allows health sages to falsely imply handgun *unavailability*, so as to counterfeit support for their shibboleth—whose idée fixe is gun unavailability, not the existence of a particular regulatory scheme. Gun licensing does not, as they imply, equate to the gun scarcity their shibboleth deems the indispensable prerequisite to low homicide rates. Outside of the licensing system, Israel and Switzerland routinely *loan* guns to millions of civilians; for those desiring to *own* guns, licensure is available on demand to every law-abiding, responsible adult; and Swiss law allows, while Israeli law and policy actively promote, widespread *carrying* of handguns to maximize the likelihood that armed civilians will be present in every crowd spot and public place. As an Israeli criminologist notes, Israeli murder "rates are . . . much *lower* than in the United States . . . despite the *greater availability* of guns to law-abiding [Israeli] civilians."[68] (Credit being due, we take the opportunity to applaud a rare occasion of health advocacy candor on such matters. Lee, Kellermann et al. accurately state that "Israel and Switzerland [have] rates of homicide [that] are low despite rates of home firearm ownership that are at least as high as those noted in the United States."[69])

The reason relatively few Israelis *own* guns is because any law-abiding, responsible, trained Israeli who needs a submachine gun, or a handgun, just draws it out of the local police armory, unlike the United States where fully automatic weapons have been illegal or severely controlled since the 1930s and the importation and sale of even semiautomatic Uzis is now prohibited.[70] Unlike the United States where carrying a concealed handgun was, until recently, almost universally illegal, in Israel if you legally possess a firearm (by loan or licensure) you

> are allowed to carry it on your person (concealed or unconcealed). The police even recommend you carry it because then the gun is protected from thieves or children. The result is that *in any big crowd of citizens, there are some people with their personal handguns on them (usually concealed).* [See note 68.]

Swiss law is closely similar.[71] American massacres in which dozens of unarmed victims are mowed down before police can arrive astound Israelis[72] who note

> what occurred at a Jerusalem [crowd spot] some weeks before the California MacDonalds massacre: three terrorists who attempted to machine-gun the throng managed to kill only one victim before being shot down by handgun-carrying Israelis. Presented to the press the next day, the surviving terrorist complained that his group had not realized that Israeli

civilians were armed. The terrorists had planned to machine-gun a succession of crowd spots, thinking that they would be able to escape before the police or army could arrive to deal with them.[73]

Fraudulent Suppression of the Steep Decline in Fatal Gun Accidents

The health advocate shibboleth posits a simple, simplistic, patterned relationship between guns and social harms: more guns equals more homicide, suicide, and fatal gun accidents, stricter gun control equals many fewer tragedies. But this shibboleth is *diametrically* contradicted by the decline in accidental gun fatalities since the late 1960s. An unparalleled increase in handgun ownership coincided not just with no increase in fatal firearms accidents, but with a steep decline.*

In sum, over the thirty-year period from 1968 through the end of 1997, a 373 percent increase in the stock of civilian handguns, and a 262 percent increase in the civilian stock of guns overall, coincided with a 68.9 percent decrease in the number of fatal gun accidents—even as population substantially increased!†

Later in this article we note the correlation of this steady twenty-year decline with the steady displacement over that period of the long gun by the much safer handgun as the weapon kept loaded for defense in American homes and businesses. But for now we focus not on the cause of the decline but on health advocacy's uninterest in that cause or in the decline itself. For now we treat the cause as unknown (though not unknowable) so as to explore what the health advocates' uninterest reveals about their claim of studying gun issues out of a single-minded concern to preserve human life.

Were health advocates rationally concerned to preserve human life, a two-thirds decline in fatal gun accidents should have been of great interest to them. Even in the absence of such concern, any honest scholarly proponent of the health advocacy shibboleth would be deeply interested in a phenomenon that diametrically contradicts that shibboleth. The interest should have been particularly intense and urgent for scholars motivated not by

---

*The original text here presented a twenty-year comparison. Because a thirty-year comparison is now possible it has been substituted, per table 1 and the following text.

†The twenty-year comparison in the original text yielded similar figures. From here on these original figures are used.

Table 1: Thirty-Year Comparison of Gun Ownership Increase to Decrease in Accidental Firearm DEATHS:[74]

1968

	Total Gun Stock		Guns per 1,000 pop.	
Handguns	All Guns		Handguns	All Guns
25,431,479	97,087,751		128.8	491.7

Total gun accident deaths: 2896

1997

	Total Gun Stock		Guns per 1,000 pop.	
Handguns	All Guns		Handguns	All Guns
94,890,222	254,512,056		372.8	942.6

Total gun accident deaths: 900

academic curiosity alone, but also by concern to preserve human life. After all, there must be some explanation for a two-thirds reduction in accidental gun deaths, and particularly for it coinciding with a 173 percent increase in handguns. If that mysterious explanation could be determined, it might suggest strategies to reduce gun suicide or gun murders as well. (This potential should especially have attracted health advocates; for, as we shall see, they have a penchant for combining statistics of gun fatality by suicide, homicide, and accident into one homogenous group, as if the three were related or homogenous phenomena.)

Of course, on investigation it might turn out that no ready explanation can be found for the decline in gun accidents. Or, if an explanation is determinable, it might not be helpful in curbing gun murders and/or suicides. But the possibility that investigation *could* be fruitless does not explain, much less justify, the health advocates' total lack of interest in pursuing such an investigation—the fact that the decline itself has gone virtually unmentioned and that there has been no focus at all on its implications in the health advocacy literature against guns.[75]

This total disinterest has an interesting implication of its own. Without denying that health advocates do care about reducing gun death, their uninterest in the twenty-year decline in accidental death implies that their concern is severely compromised by their hatred of guns. Though avowing a deep and single-minded concern to save lives, they seem interested only in ways of doing so which involve reducing access to guns. At least we can think of no other reason for their total lack of interest in finding out how and why accidental gun death could decline by two-thirds over a period when the handgun stock was increasing by 173 percent.

Health advocacy's negativity about firearm safety training confirms our reasoning. The NRA's commitment to reducing accidents is expressed in decades of support for safety training, both in the home and for hunters. Most recently, the NRA has devoted significant resources to the "Eddie Eagle" program on firearms safety education for children, which is praised by the National Safety Council and even the vehemently antigun, anti-NRA *Washington Post*.[76] But the only "safety training" antigun advocates unreservedly approve is teaching that guns are evil and no one should have them.[77] Some admit the "Eddie Eagle" program promotes safety, yet reject it because it was originated by the NRA.[78] Health advocates worry that gun safety training may convey the wrong message: it may lead young people to consider guns and gun ownership a legitimate aspect of American life; it may even promote among children a desire to own guns when they grow up.[79]

No doubt health advocates genuinely desire that gun death be reduced. But that desire is constantly compromised by a hatred of guns which precludes serious consideration of any option other than reducing gun ownership as a way of reducing firearms fatalities. Consider the typical, and typically disingenuous, ratiocination given by Dolins and Christoffel for ignoring the potential of safety training: "Data showing that this strategy is effective are scanty, however."[80] Notice how opposite the lesson Dolins and Christoffel draw is to the lesson they would draw if their concern for saving lives were not alloyed by their desire to ban guns. An unalloyed concern to save lives would cause them to see a lack of data on the life-saving potential of safety training as an urgent basis to recommend study of that potential. But Dolins and Christoffel see the lack of data only as an excuse to dismiss that potential, focusing only on proposals to reduce gun ownership instead.

Of course, Dolins and Christoffel never tell their readers that some unknown factor has caused a two-thirds decline in accidental fatalities to coincide with a 173 percent enormous increase in handguns. For all Dolins and Christoffel know, this radical reduction in deaths is attributable to safety training. But they are not interested in having that explored or in their readers considering any program for saving lives except those involving reduced gun availability. Dolins and Christoffel ostentatiously lament accidental gun deaths among children—while, again, not informing their readers of the steady decline in such deaths (discussed below). Again, Dolins and Christoffel don't know whether that steady decline is attributable to increased safety training. And they are not interested in finding out. Their interest is in milking the highly emotive issue of dying children for all it is worth as an argument for reducing handgun availability to ordinary citizens.[81]

Again, we do not doubt that health advocates are sincerely concerned with reducing gun accident fatalities, and especially with saving children's lives. Why, then, is firearms safety training discussed so negatively in the health advocacy literature, to the extent that it is discussed at all? Again, the only hypothesis that seems to fit the facts is that the authors' overriding agenda of reducing gun ownership compromises their deep concern with saving lives (and especially children's lives).

We return to the issue of accidental death in a few pages. But now we want to consider homicide and suicide, these being the other elements of the shibboleth health advocates postulate: i.e., that more gun availability results in more homicide, suicide, and gun accidents, while strict gun control will result in fewer such tragedies.

No Observable Pattern in International Homicide and Suicide

As discussed below, the shibboleth is also refuted by a decline in domestic American homicide correlating to the vast increase in gun ownership during the 1970s and 1980s. To mask this embarrassing downward trend in murder, the health sages began in the mid-1980s "massaging" the statistics by combining homicide and suicide in one joint figure. This produced an "Intentional Homicide" rate which, once again, they claimed to have been caused by widespread gun ownership.[82]

But this combined homicide-suicide approach embarrasses the health advocacy shibboleth in another way which requires avoidance through yet another statistical manipulation. Antigun advocates like to compare American homicide rates to those of low-violence European nations as "proof" that strict European gun laws reduce homicide. Of course, when we remember that low European violence rates long *preceded* strict gun laws, what the comparison proves is that countries that differ in culture and institutional and socioeconomic arrangements are likely to have different violence rates. By the same token, though the U.S. suicide rate actually exceeds its homicide rate, European suicide rates are still much higher. These much higher suicide rates further confirm that the decisive factors in the social harms associated with guns are culture and other issues more fundamental than the mere availability of some particular kind of weaponry. So antigun advocates offer international homicide rate comparisons but never international suicide rate comparisons—even though they also emphasize *American* suicide rates which they attribute to widespread gun ownership. Thus, for instance, when the CDC discusses homicide alone, international comparisons are made, but whenever the CDC combines homicides and suicides, data is given only for the United States.[83]

The example of health sage Susan Baker is especially apt. She originated the idea of combining suicide and homicide in discussing *American* statistics, thereby both inflating the gun death total and concealing the fact that American homicide was declining as handgun ownership increased. If deception is not the object, why when she uses cross-national comparison to support the antigun shibboleth does she abandon her own supposedly preferable combined suicide-homicide creation and revert to the homicide-only approach? In arguing that restrictive gun laws reduce homicide she points out that Denmark's murder rate is about 7 deaths per 100,000 population lower than the United States.[84] If she had compared suicide rates, however, she would have had to admit the Danish rate is much higher. By the same token, had she compared the two nations' combined homicide-suicide rates according to her own supposedly preferable method, she would have had to admit the Danish combined rate was almost 50 percent higher than the American.

Curious about what would happen if Professor Baker's combined homicide-suicide rate were used in making international comparisons, we constructed a table 2.

How well do the results in table 2* comport with the health advocacy shibboleth that more access to guns means more homicide and suicide while strict gun laws reduce each? Of the nations for which figures were available, the United States ranks below the median when suicide and homicide rates are combined; the U.S. combined rate is less than half the combined rate in gun-banning Russia; such firearm-intensive countries as Australia and New Zealand rank very low on the table; and the lowest rate is for Israel, a country that actually encourages and requires almost universal gun possession.

In short, Professor Baker's combined suicide-homicide approach does not serve the health advocates' political agenda if applied in comparing the United States to gun-banning countries that health advocates cite as models for American policy. So it is only when they discuss U.S. figures that Professor Baker and the other health sages combine murder and suicide figures. Reviewing the entire health advocacy literature on guns and suicide, we have been unable to find even one reference to the much greater suicide rates in gun-banning European countries (or the much lower suicide rate in Israel).

The antigun literature never discusses the shibboleth in connection with the suicide rates of gun-banning foreign countries. The one exception is Sloan et al., who followed their Vancouver- Seattle homicide comparison with an (unintentionally) hilarious comparison of suicide rates in the two cities.[85] Unfazed by the fact that the Canadian city had the *higher* suicide rate, Sloan et al. emphasize that it had a lower suicide rate for one subgroup, adolescents and young men. This, they solemnly intone, is due to the United States's having lax gun laws and more gun availability. And what is the cause of Canada's having higher suicide rates overall? Sloan et al. do not venture to speculate on that.

That brings us to an issue health advocacy articles stressed during the 1980s: suicide among young males, a poignant phenomenon that, supposedly, was increasing in response to the ever-increasing numbers of firearms in the United States.[86] Naturally, the health advocate articles drawing this connection never mentioned that suicide among teenage and young adults has been increasing dramatically throughout the entire industrialized

---

*The table in the original text has been replaced with one covering later years. The information provided is generally from the latest available *U.N. Demographic Yearbook*. The years that it covers for each individual nation vary because the *U.N. Demographic Yearbooks* do not provide data that is consistent either by year or by the various nations they cover. Rather, they provide the latest data reported by whichever nations have reported the data to them.

Table 2: International Intentional Homicide Table

(In order of highest combine rate; nations higher than the United States in either suicide or murder rates are in bold face.)

	Suicide	Murder	Combined	Year
ESTONIA	**39.9**	**22.1**	**62.1**	1995
RUSSIA	**26.6**	**15.3**	**41.9**	1992
LATVIA	**26**	**9.2**	**35.2**	1990
LITHUANIA	**26**	**7.5**	**33.5**	1990
FINLAND	**27.3**	3.3	**30.6**	1994-95
UKRAINE	**20.6**	**8.0**	**28.6**	1990
DENMARK	22	5.0	**27**	1991
AUSTRIA	**22.3**	1.5	**23.8**	1991
SWITZERLAND	**20.8**	1.1	**21.9**	1994-95
FRANCE	**20.2**	1.1	**21.3**	1990
BELGIUM	**19.3**	1.4	**20.7**	1987
UNITED STATES	11.5	7.3	18.8	1995-96
SWEDEN	**17.2**	1.3	18.5	1990
GERMANY	**15.8**	1.8	17.6	1995
LUXEMBOURG	**15.1**	2.1	17.2	1991
NEW ZEALAND	**13.9**	1.9	15.8	1989
CANADA	**12.9**	2.0	14.9	1995
ISRAEL	7.3	1.2	8.5	1989

world.[87] By the same token, readers of health advocacy articles blaming American suicide increases on guns would never learn that while suicide among American males aged fifteen to twenty-four increased 7.4 percent in the period 1980 to 1990, the increase in suicide among English males of this age was over ten times greater (78 percent), "car exhaust poisoning [being] the method of suicide used most often."[88]

Despite recent increases in youth suicide, the population subgroup most likely to shoot themselves are elderly men.[89] We take leave to doubt that any health advocate (or anyone else) is wise enough to decide for a seventy-six-year-old man in failing health whether he should live or die. But such philosophical considerations are never mentioned by health sages asserting the more-guns-mean-more-suicide shibboleth. Modesty about their own wisdom is not likely to find favor with sages who are confident enough of it to be willing to promote their policy prescription for American society by cloaking sagecraft in pseudoscholarly literature.

Setting aside the philosophical issue, it is pragmatically arguable that, if guns are unavailable, people who are seriously enough interested in killing themselves to use a gun will find some other way.[90] On the other hand, some suicide may occur impulsively because of the immediate availability of a deadly mechanism to a person who might not have completed the act had time for reflection been required. The intellectual desert inhabited by health advocates is epitomized by their failure (inability) to cite the strongest empirical showing for gun control as a means of reducing suicide. They do not know of this study because it was done by Gary Kleck, whose work they compulsively avoid.[91] Suicide is a serious issue. It deserves serious, scholarly discussion, rather than being used as a political football by unscrupulous propagandists grasping at any opportunity to make a case for their preordained agenda.

Finally, consider the implications of table 2 for the health advocacy shibboleth that strict gun laws equals low homicide. The observable pattern that would exist if such were true simply does not exist. Denmark, whose strict antigun laws Professor Baker praises, has almost four times more homicide than Switzerland and more than four times more homicide than Israel. Switzerland's very gun-restrictive neighbor, Germany, has about 25 percent more homicide than Switzerland (and 50 percent more than Israel). Germany's very gun-restrictive neighbor, Belgium, has more than 20 percent more homicide than Germany, and their mutual neighbor, Luxembourg, where gun ownership is completely illegal, has more than 100 percent more. England, with its much-ballyhooed antigun policies, has the lowest homicide rate of all. But Scotland, with exactly the same laws, has almost three times as much homicide as England and much more than Israel or Switzerland.

These statistics are not intended to, nor do they, prove that strict gun laws "cause" homicide. What they do reinforce are the conclusions set out above in the section titled "The Verdict of Criminological Scholarship": gun ownership by responsible adults is not the cause of the social problems associated with guns; what causes those problems is gun possession by irresponsible people. Disarming criminals and irresponsible people is a highly desirable goal, but it is not reasonable to anticipate any more success than the law has in preventing or deterring them from violent acts. In every society the number of guns suffices to arm those who desire to misuse them.

Gun Availability, Social Harms, and Fraudulent Nondisclosure

Having dealt with the international statistics, we move now to domestic American statistics. Here, again, to sustain the health advocacy shibboleth, sages routinely suppress facts and truncate, select, or even falsify statistics and data. They must doctor the statistics because a full and accurate rendition would not show the easily observable, consistent, and coherent pattern of more guns equals more murder, suicide, and/or accident. (At this point we need to offer a caveat as to the health advocacy literature's suppression of data and/or relationships. When we say something is never mentioned or discussed in that literature, we are not denying that *independently knowledgeable* readers might be able to ferret parts of it out. For instance, we can find tucked away in a table the fact that young inner city black males have a homicide rate almost 1,000 percent greater than their counterparts in rural areas.[92] But a correlative fact will not be found, much less discussed, because it casts doubt on the shibboleth. The correlative fact is that rural blacks have this far lower murder rate *despite* having a rate of gun ownership and/or availability comparable to whites, i.e., a rate far, far exceeding that of urban blacks.[93] A fortiori, there is no discussion of how these correlated facts can be squared with the more-guns-equals-more-murder shibboleth.)

Suppression of Declining Accidental Gun Fatalities

We use terms like "suppression" and "nondisclosure" advisedly to describe a pattern of fact omission which renders the statements made deceptive or likely to mislead. Suppression thus differs in method, though not in effect, from affirmative misrepresentation (overt mendacity), which we separately catalog in antigun health advocacy writings. We earlier detailed suppression by health advocates of the fact that the two-thirds decline in fatal gun accidents over the twenty-year period from 1967 to 1986 coincided with a 173 percent increase in the handgun stock. This correlation goes so remarkably unremarked upon because it triply embarrasses the health advocate sages' political agenda. *First*, to acknowledge it would undercut their use of the danger of gun accident as a reason for opposing gun ownership. *Second*, such acknowledgement might lead to readers to well-justified skepticism about the shibboleth that increasing gun availability increases the rates of murder, suicide, and fatal accidents.*

Third, admitting the remarkable decline in fatal gun accidents might prompt inquiry about linkage to a correlative phenomenon that occurred during the same years: the handgun's replacement of the long gun as the weapon kept loaded for defense in American homes and stores. Handgun prohibition advocates themselves argue that banning handguns would reverse that trend, causing a return to long guns for home and office defense—weapons the advocates (in their abysmal ignorance of firearms) erroneously think are "safer" than handguns.[94] In fact, the necessary effect of such a reversal would be to increase accidental fatalities. If kept loaded and ready for rapid defensive deployment, long guns are both more likely to be accidentally discharged and much deadlier when discharged, than are handguns.[95] Moreover, a long gun is much more difficult to secure from children.

The comparative dangers are made clear by comparison of the available figures breaking down gun type involvement in fatal gun accidents: though 90 percent or more of the firearms kept loaded at any one time are handguns, handguns are involved in less than 14 percent of the accidental gun fatalities.[96] It is estimated that if the 85.2 percent of loaded handguns in American homes in the year 1980 had been long guns instead, the number of fatal gun accidents would have more than quadrupled, from 1,244 to about 5,346, *i.e., about 4,100 lives per year would be lost in accidental shootings in the home.*[97]

Table 3 provides all available comparative data on involvement of handguns, rifles, and shotguns in accidental death.

---

*As set out in table 1, the twenty-year figures in the original text are confirmed and extended by newly available figures for the thiry-year period from 1968 to 1997.

Table 3: National Safety Council Gun Accident Statistics[98]

	Total	H-gun*	Shotgun	Rifle	Unspecified	% H-gun**
1991	1,441	255	163	94	929	50%
1990	1,416	241	160	73	942	51%
1989	1,489	231	175	86	997	47%
1988	1,501	202	185	93	1,021	42%
1987	1,440	206	178	105	951	42%
1986	1,452	183	190	108	971	37%
1985	1,649	190	215	113	1,131	37%
1984	1,668	225	214	118	1,111	40%
1983	1,695	209	260	132	1,094	35%
1982	1,756	219	232	127	1,178	38%
1981	1,871	224	273	140	1,234	35%
1980	1,955	288	283	129	1,255	41%
1979	2,004	311	254	145	1,294	44%
1979-91:	21,337	2,984	2,782	1,463	14,108	41%

NOTES: *H-gun means handgun. **Percentages given in table 3 are rounded off.

Suppression of Decline in Accidental Child Gun Death

To help promote their gun control agenda, health advocate sages have long harped on the emotionally charged issue of child death by gun accident.[99] Naturally, sages cannot acknowledge the steep decline in such tragedies. Acknowledging that would, in and of itself, undercut their political agenda. Worse, it could hoist health sages on their own emotional petard: What if someone were inspired to ask whether their proposal to ban handguns might reverse the decline and cause many hundreds more children to die in gun accidents involving long guns? Finally, by suppressing any mention of the decline, health advocate sages leave themselves free to continue fabricating statistics to exaggerate the number of child deaths—statistics which, but for their tragic subject matter, would be comic in their wild inconsistency.[100]

Using these exaggerated figures allows health advocate sages to capitalize on the emotionalism of childhood fatalities, thereby evading legitimate questions about their nostrum of banning and confiscating handguns, or all guns, as a means of reducing such tragedies. We offer the following questions which, of course, are never discussed in the health advocacy literature on children and guns: 1) if so sweeping a measure as confiscating 230 million firearms is justified because some 273 children under age fifteen die in firearm accidents annually, is the less intrusive measure of banning child bicycles justified by the death of three times as many children in bicycle accidents annually?[101] If confiscating 80 (or more) million handguns is justified because approximately fifteen children under age five die in handgun accidents annually, is a ban on cigarette lighters justified by the fact that four times as many such children die from playing with them annually?

Consider these facts: more than 400 percent more children under age fifteen die in drownings than in gun accidents; and twenty times as many children under age five drown in bathtubs and home swimming pools as are killed in handgun accidents. Few people *need* a bathtub (as opposed to a shower stall) or a swimming pool. If the tragedy of accidental childhood gun fatalities justifies confiscating 80 million or more handguns, or all 230 million or more firearms, do the much greater numbers of tragic childhood drownings justify a licensing system under which only the disabled and others who show they "truly need" a bath or swimming pool will be allowed to have them?

Note: We do not pose these as rhetorical questions having only one clear "right" answer. Reasonable people may well differ vehemently over how they ought to be answered. That is precisely why *scholars* discussing the role of firearms and other potentially harmful media in society ought to disclose the facts and raise the questions. Regrettably, the possibility that honestly informing people might lead to differing conclusions is also the reason such facts and questions are never raised by health sages who capitalize on the issue of accidental childhood deaths to argue for banning handguns or all guns.

Suppression of Gun-homicide Comparison Data

[Editor's Note: Based on figures available when it was written, this section shows how the shibboleth is belied by the fact that massive long-term increases in the American gunstock have been accompanied by *declining* homicide rates. Later figures are available in the 2000 article by Don B. Kates and Daniel D. Polsby, cited at note 74. The following summarizes those figures: Implicit in the shibboleth is that major increases in availability of guns (or handguns) will be accompanied by regular, indeed, roughly corresponding, increases in the rates of homicide over that same period. But there has been no such coincidence in these data. That must at a minimum be regarded as an anomaly in, if not an outright refutation of, the hypothesis that gun availability is a main, if not the primary, cause of high American homicide rates.

Post–World War II American homicide rates peaked in 1979 and actually decreased over the fifteen years from 1980 to 1994. In this period the number of handguns in civilian hands increased from 51.7 million to 84.7 million, or by about 64 percent, while gun ownership overall increased about 40.5 percent, from 167.7 million to 235.6 million weapons. In this time period there was no increase at all (much less a corresponding increase) in homicide rates. In fact, the rate declined from 10.2 per 100,000 population in 1980 to 9.0 per 100,000 in 1994.

This was no anomaly. If one pushes out the study period to twenty-five years (i.e., the period from 1973 to 1997), the lack of correlation between homicide rates and firearms availability appears even more stark. Over that period homicides decreased by 27.7 percent (from 9.4 to 6.8 in 100,000 of population), despite an approximate 160 percent increase in the number of handguns owned by civilians (from 36.9 million to 94.9), and a 103 percent increase in civilian gun ownership (from 128 million to 254.5 million weapons) overall. The consistent, characteristic pattern of the entire postwar period has been that murder rates and firearms acquisition patterns have been uncorrelated, with only the relatively brief period from the mid-1960s to the late 1970s as the exception.

The increases in firearms over this period, moreover, have far outstripped population increases. In 1973 there were 610.3 guns (175.9 handguns) per 1,000 population; by 1994 the figures were 905 guns and 325.2 handguns per 1,000 population, respectively.

Of course within the 1973 to 1997 period homicide rates fluctuated considerably, rising in some years, falling in others. In themselves, these fluctuations provide further evidence that homicide rates are independent of gun availability levels. Gun, particularly handgun, availability levels exhibit no comparable fluctuation. While homicide rates rose and fell, handgun ownership only rose. Each year from 1973 through 1997 the existing stock increased by between 1.7 and 3.7 million new handguns. These increases were accompanied by a long-term decline in murder, not the increase that would have occurred, and that has insistently been predicted by believers in the shibboleth.] Once again, these are facts that readers whose information comes from health advocacy literature will never learn.

Shibboleth Diverts Attention from Actual Causes

Likewise never discussed (at least in connection with breakdowns of rates of firearms ownership by race) in the health advocacy literature is that the white homicide rate has steadily fallen since 1980.[102] The apparent increase in American homicide from the mid-1980s on is due entirely to that steady fall in white homicide being offset by a vast increase in homicide in drug and crime-ridden, poverty-stricken inner cities. Inner-city and minority youth homicide is a regular theme in the antigun health literature.[103] Of course, health sages never note that the whites whose murder rate is declining are far more likely to own guns per capita than African Americans in general, and that black gun ownership is *lowest* in the inner cities.[104] Mentioning that would at once disconfirm their shibboleth that gun availability causes homicide and support the leading English criminological analyst's pessimistic view that "in any society the number of guns always suffices to arm the few who want to obtain and use them illegally."[105] (In that connection remember the fact that young black inner-city males have a homicide rate about 900 percent greater than their counterparts in rural areas, even though *these low homicide rural blacks have far, far greater gun ownership than do urban blacks*. See notes 92 and 93.)

In sum, increased firearm availability to honest, responsible people (of any race) does not cause increased violence; neither is lower availability to such people associated with lower violence. Taken together or separately, data on firearm availability for the nation as a whole, and for discrete geographic or demographic subpopulations, discredit the shibboleth that "the possession of guns" is "the primary cause" of murder. The actual cause is hopelessness, poverty, and a lack of substantial employment opportunities—

(The post–World War II period is the earliest for which there are reliable data on American gun ownership. During the fifteen years from 1946 to 1960, the handgun stock increased by 43 percent and the total gunstock by 55.5 percent—yet the homicide rate decreased by 25 percent.)

other than competing in the murderous drug trade. Studies suggest black rates of homicide and other violence are no greater than those of similarly situated whites.[106] In that connection, consider the following remarks:

> Fixating on guns seems to be, for many people, a fetish which allows them to ignore the more intransigent causes of American violence, including its dying cities, inequality, deteriorating family structure, and the all-pervasive economic and social consequences of a history of slavery and racism.[107]
>
> Moreover, an overemphasis on [gun control] diverts attention from the kinds of conditions that are responsible for much of our crime, such as persisting poverty for the black underclass and some whites and Hispanics; the impact of post-industrial transition on economic opportunity for working-class youths; and the shortage of prison facilities that makes it difficult to keep high risk, repeat offenders off the streets.[108]

A Critique of Overt Mendacity

A 1989 article in the *Journal of the American Medical Association* approvingly quoted a Center for Disease Control official's assertion that his work for the CDC involved "systematically building a case that owning firearms causes death." The CDC official later claimed *JAMA* had misquoted him and offered the only repudiation of the antigun political agenda we have found in a health advocacy publication, characterizing it as "anathema to any unbiased scientific inquiry because it assumes the conclusion at the outset and then attempts to find evidence to support it."[109]

Unfortunately, that is precisely what CDC is doing. Indeed, this was subsequently avowed by the prior official's successor.[110] Even more unfortunately, CDC and some other health advocate sages build their case not only by suppressing facts, but by overt fraud, fabricating statistics and falsifying references to support them. The following are but a few of many examples documented in a paper by two of the authors of this article (cited in note 97):

One of these frauds is an exception to our generalization a few pages ago that the health advocacy literature never compares gun ownership and murder rates through the 1970s and 1980s. Some health sages claimed murder rates increased overall during that period—and then linked this falsehood to the same period's steady increase in gun ownership so as to lend spurious support to their more-guns-equals-more-murder shibboleth. Thus, a 1989 Report to the United States Congress by the CDC stated, "Since the early 1970s the year-to-year fluctuations in firearm availability has [*sic*] paralleled the numbers of homicides."[111] We leave it to the readers of this article to judge how a 69 percent *increase* in handgun ownership over the fifteen-year period from 1974 to 1988 could honestly be described as having "paralleled" a 14.2 percent *decrease* in homicide during that same period.[112]

Understandably, the CDC report offered no supporting reference for its claim of parallelism. But the inventive Dr. Diane Schetky, and two equally inventive CDC writers, George Smith and Henry Falk, in a separate article, actually do provide purportedly supporting citations for her claim that "handguns account for only 20 percent of the nation's firearms yet account for 90 percent of all firearms [*mis*]use, both criminal and accidental."[113] The problem is that the claim is false in every part and the citations are fabrications.

The purpose of Schetky's claim is to exaggerate the comparative risks of handguns vis-à-vis long guns so as to fortify the cause of handgun prohibition and avoid admitting the major problem we have already addressed: that, because handguns are innately far safer than long guns, if a handgun ban caused defensive gun owners to keep loaded long guns instead (as handgun ban advocates and experts concur would be the case), thousands more might die in fatal gun accidents annually (see discussion in text accompanying notes 74 and 97).

The only citation given by either Schetky or Smith and Falk to support their claim that handguns are but 20 percent of all guns, yet are involved in 90 percent of gun accidents and crime, is the FBI's *Uniform Crime Reports*. Understandably, no page citations are given because the citations are falsified. As anyone familiar with the *Uniform Crime Reports* knows, they provide: (a) no data on gun ownership—and thus, (b) no comparative data on handgun versus long gun ownership; (c) no data on accidents—and thus (d) no data on gun accidents—and thus (e) no comparative data on the incidence of handgun accidents versus long gun accidents. Schetky and Smith and Falk could have found firearms breakdowns on fatal gun accidents in the National Safety Council's *Accidents Facts* volumes. But those data would not have suited the purpose since they do not support the point Schetky and Smith and Falk set forth (see table 3).

Neither do the UCRs give any data on the number of persons injured in gun crimes or the number of such injuries in handgun crimes versus long gun crimes. The UCRs do give such data for gun murders but even those data do not support Schetky's claim that 90 percent are by handgun.[114] Every one of the other purported statistics given by Schetky and Smith and Falk in their above mentioned articles is not only wrong but wrong in only one particular direction, i.e., each false statistic supports their point, whereas an accurate rendition of the statistic would not have done so. It is, of course, elementary that innocent mistakes tend to be random, and even to balance each other, rather than all erring in favor of the position for which they are presented.

Next to be considered is the remarkable Dr. Sloan. Giving him the benefit of the doubt, we put down other mischaracterizations by him to gun-aversive dyslexia. But it strains even that generous category unduly to so classify an inability to accurately read and describe his own articles. The gravamen of the Sloan et al. two-city comparison discussed earlier (see notes 44ff.) was that a new, highly restrictive Canadian antigun law caused Vancouver to have less homicide than Seattle (where any responsible adult can buy a handgun). But an NRA representative noted in a critical letter to the *New England Journal of Medicine* that the authors had made no effort to determine how Canadian homicide had changed since adopting the law. In fact, the homicide rate had not fallen as Sloan et al.'s claims would have required, but rather *risen* slightly, with handgun use unchanged at about one-eighth of homicides. Sloan et al. tried to extricate themselves from this embarrassment by asserting that the "intent of our article was not to evaluate the effect of the 1978 Canadian gun law."[115] The mendacity of that is made clear by juxtaposing it to the article's actual conclusion: "Canadian-style gun control . . . is associated with lower rates of homicide."[116] Not surprisingly, that is exactly how other health advocates understood the article's intent: as "demonstrat[ing] the beneficial effect of [Canada's] tighter regulation" by "evaluati[ng] firearm mortality in Seattle and Vancouver, similar communities with vastly different regulatory strategies."[117]

It would be misleading to suggest that, heavily politicized though it is, the antigun health advocacy literature commonly exhibits overt falsehoods (as opposed to misleading by half-truth and suppression of material facts). Overt mendacity is not infrequent, however. Numerous examples will be documented in the next section and in the balance of this chaper.

The Myth That Murderers Are Ordinary Gun Owners

The case for reducing firearm availability to ordinary people rests on two interrelated myths endorsed explicitly and implicitly in the health advocacy literature on firearms. Those myths are: (1) that "most [murderers] would be considered law-abiding citizens prior to their pulling the trigger"; and (2) that "most shootings are not committed by felons or mentally ill people, but are acts of passion that are committed using a handgun that is owned for home protection."[118] From those myths other follow, e.g., that firearms availability to ordinary citizens is the "primary cause" of murder; that murder would radically decrease if ordinary citizens were deprived of those guns; and that it is unnecessary to worry much about the enforceability of gun bans because, even if *criminals* will not disarm, the law-abiding will—and they are the ones committing most murders.[119]

It simply isn't true that previously law-abiding citizens commit most murders or many murders or virtually any murders; and so disarming them could not eliminate most or many or virtually any murders. Homicide studies show that murderers are not ordinary citizens, but extreme aberrants of whom it is unrealistic to assume they will have any more compunction about flouting gun laws than about murder. The great majority of murderers have life histories of violence, felony records, substance abuse, and car and other dangerous accidents.*

The antigun health advocacy literature avoids the problems the aberrance of murderers raise for their view by just stating facts that are false. A truly startling example (because it contradicts his own writings!) is that of the CDC's Dr. Mark Rosenberg, who avows his desire to create a public perception of firearms as "dirty, deadly—and banned," (see note 2). To mislead readers into blaming firearms for crime rather than criminals, Dr. Rosenberg actually goes so far as to claim that

> most of the perpetrators of violence [*sic*—can he really mean not just murderers, but robbers and rapists as well?] are not criminals by trade or profession. Indeed, in the area of domestic violence, most of the perpetrators are never accused of any crime. The victims and perpetrators are *ourselves—ordinary citizens*, students, professionals, and *even public health workers*.[120]

---

*Because this point was discussed earlier in some detail in chapter 1, the discussion has been truncated here.

The falsity of this is apparent from other statements *in the same article* and in other articles by Dr. Rosenberg: "Violence is foreign to the lives of most public health professionals,"[121] and in others ("Most family homicides involve spouses and occur after a series of prior assaultive incidents"[122]).

"Gun Ownership as a Risk Factor for Homicide in the Home"

This is the title of a 1993 *New England Journal of Medicine* article whose authors include several of Sloan's coauthors on the Vancouver-Seattle two-city comparison discussed above.[123] Since space limitations constrain us to a brief summary of the vast majority of health advocacy articles, we have selected this article for a detailed critique. One reason is that this article (hereinafter called *NEJM-1993*) was widely publicized in the media and has been voluminously cited in the health advocacy literature. Moreover, this article continues a long series of prior widely publicized health advocacy studies. Regrettably, it and the prior studies would be more appropriately cited in a statistics textbook as a cautionary example of multiple statistical errors. Before addressing these, however, it is necessary to set out some basics of statistical analysis.

Statistical analyses are used to reach conclusions in the face of certain types of uncertainty. Uncertainty results from such factors as inherent variation in the subjects being studied, the effects of many other influences, both known and unknown, and limited resources which restrict the amount of data that can be collected and studied. Statistical analyses may result in erroneous conclusions for a variety of reasons, some acceptable, others not. We shall ignore, in this discussion, errors in recording data, and of calculation, because, though unacceptable, they have become less common with the use of computers and statistical analysis programs. But many other types of errors can occur and are of grave concern when the conclusions will be used to make decisions on how to act. In the medical area such decisions may affect the choice of medical treatment, or may affect policy decisions in the public sector. In either case, use of flawed conclusions may lead to literally fatal consequences.

When What You See Isn't Necessarily What You Get

We can safely assume that the statistical analysis program on the computer does the calculations of the statistical analysis correctly. This isn't always true. Moreover, data entry errors are sufficiently common to require careful checking by the analyst to catch them. But at least neither calculation errors nor any data entry errors that slip through will be consistently biased in favor of any particular agenda the analyst may have.

More serious concerns involve errors of the analyst which can be related to a conscious or unconscious agenda. The analyst is responsible for choosing the correct type of analysis, for making sure that the assumptions required for the use of a type of statistical analysis are met, and that the results are described correctly. When there are errors in any of these areas, the conclusions reached can be partially or completely wrong even in the absence of any other errors. The presence of these errors in a study does not guarantee that the conclusions are invalid. But the conclusions then are unsubstantiated, and the scientific impartiality of the analyst is called into question. Errors are of particular concern when they are made in such a way as to facilitate conclusions which confirm the previous stands of the analyst.

It is seldom possible to conduct a scientific study in which only the effects to be tested are operating. The statistical field of "experimental design" is concerned with methods which allow the detection of the effects to be studied even when other effects are operating.[124] Failure to separate the effects to be studied from extraneous effects leads to a confusion between them and the unintentional "confounding"[125] of extraneous effects with the effects to be studied. The resulting conclusions are not based on tests of the effects being studied; rather, they reflect some unknown combination of those effects and extraneous effects confounded with them. Thus, the hypotheses supposedly being studied are not in fact being studied— and what you see is not what you get.

Purpose and Design of *NEJM-1993*

The hypothesis *NEJM-1993* was supposedly studying is "whether keeping a firearm in the home confers protection against crime or, instead, increases the risk of violent crime in the home."[126] Very simplistically described, the study compares a sample of households in which homicide occurred to a supposedly similar sample in which they did not. It finds that the homicide households were more likely to have contained guns. From this it concludes that guns are more of a danger than a protection.

The study used data from three urban counties: Shelby County, Tennessee, containing Memphis; King County, Washington, containing Seattle; and Cuyahoga County, Ohio, containing Cleveland. The data consisted in all cases of homicide in the home during the chosen time periods. To compare with these homicide cases, a control was selected for each homicide victim. These control subjects were matched to the homicide victim with respect to sex, race, age-range, and neighborhood of residence. Various kinds of information were then obtained: by reading police or other official reports as to the homicide cases; by interviewing another occupant of the homicide case households (a case-proxy); and by interviewing either the control subject or another occupant of his or her household (a control-proxy).

Study Design Exaggerates Risks of Defensive Gun Ownership

The data presented in *NEJM-1993* do not show that even *one* homicide victim was killed with a gun ordinarily kept in that household, whether for defensive purposes or for any other reason. Indeed the indirect evidence presented indicates that the home gun homicide victims were killed using guns *not* kept in the victim's home.*

We do not, incidentally, deny the relevance of the murder household having a gun, even though that gun was not the murder weapon. But the nature of that relevance compromises *NEJM-1993*'s conclusions about the supposed risk of home gun ownership rather than validating them. What if it turns out that people who are at higher risk of being murdered are more likely to own guns than those at lesser risk?† If these higher-risk people own

---

*Subsequently available evidence has verified our speculation on this point. It is now clear that virtually all the homicides were committed by intruders who brought their own guns to the victim's household. Thus, Kellermann's claim that owning guns increased the owners' risk of murder is simply wrong. Moreover, it was highly misleading since when he made that point he had to have been aware that the victims were not killed with their own guns—and that his conclusion would have been unsupportable had he revealed what his own data showed on the point rather than suppressing it.[127]

†That is not only intuitively plausible, it is supported by the finding (especially in high density urban areas) that most victims of homicide and other severe violence tend to have criminal records and/or involvement in the illicit drug trade or with violent criminal gangs. See discussion of "acquaintance homicide" in chapter 1.

guns more often, *NEJM-1993*'s conclusion that murder victims owned guns at a higher rate than the control group of nonvictims does not at all follow. Rather, *NEJM-1993* has confused cause and effect: far from owning guns, having put the victims at risk, it was the victims' high-risk life-styles that caused them to own guns at higher rates than the members of the supposedly comparable control group. We take up this point in the next section.

Moreover an unstated, unsubstantiated tacit assumption is made by *NEJM-1993*'s consistent use of the word "victim" and by the abstract's introductory statement that the article's subject is "violent crime in the home." This assumption is that the deceased was the victim of the crime. In fact, the deceased may actually have been the attacker. In those cases, the homicide should be considered a benefit rather than a risk. The cases in which the "offender" is listed as "police officer" seem likely to fall under this misleading classification, as does even the categorization of police as "offender."*

Inadequate Consideration of High-Risk Career Criminality

NEJM-1993's authors were not unaware of the problem that their homicide cases might contain a disproportionate number of high-risk people. To attempt to avoid the problem, *NEJM-1993* tried to compare the homicide cases to the controls to see if there were differences in a variety of risk factors including drinking and drug problems, histories of domestic violence, whether the home was owned or rented, and particularly emphasizing gun ownership. *NEJM-1993* then reports differences in presence of these risk factors as being associated with an increase in the risk of homicide.

In this connection, note that gun ownership, the supposed risk factor *NEJM-1993* emphasizes, was far from the most strongly associated with being murdered. Drinking and drug problems, a history of family violence, living alone, and living in a rented home were all greater individual risk factors for being murdered than gun ownership, based on the *NEJM-1993* results. Even so, it is clear that yet other risk factors were not accounted for, e.g., number of criminal associates or frequency of high-risk or criminal activity. These and others which are ignored in this study will have their effects lumped in with the effects supposedly being studied and inadvertent statistical "confounding" can result. An "association" due to these ignored

†Health advocacy literature, and antigun literature in general, have a long, discreditable history of miscounting defensive homicides as murders in the home.[128]

confounding factors would be more accurately described as a "spurious association." Proper statistical design requires an effort to identify all the risk factors and to take the relevant ones into account by properly collecting the data and choosing the appropriate statistical analysis. *NEJM-1993* simply did not do this adequately, and therefore their strongly worded conclusions about the factors which they did include are not warranted.

For instance, though some account was taken of whether any member of either the homicide victim household or the control group had been arrested, no account seems to have been taken of the seriousness of the crime for which the arrest was made; of any conviction of crime; of whether the specific murder victim had been arrested or convicted and of the seriousness of the crime; and of how many arrests and convictions the murder victim (or others in that household) had had in comparison to the number of arrests in the control household, or other high-risk activity or gang affiliations of any member of the household.

These issues are particularly important because criminological studies indicate that the overall population may be divided into: (a) the overwhelming majority, who are law-abiding; (b) a minority of people who are criminals because they infrequently commit a crime, often a relatively trivial one; and (c) "career criminals" who, though relatively small in numbers, commit the majority of crimes, especially the more serious ones.[129] It may plausibly be postulated that a group containing more career criminals will have both a higher rate of gun ownership and a greater likelihood of being murdered than a supposedly similar control group of people who commit relatively less frequent and serious crimes. If so, that is a confounding factor which would produce a spurious association between owning a gun and being murdered.

This leads us to a more fundamental problem with the entire *NEJM-1993* study design. Let us suppose that the data problems with comparability of the murdered group to the control group had all been solved. Still, the cases are high-risk households unrepresentative of the general population. The controls, having been drawn from atypically high-violence geographical areas are unrepresentative, as well, of the general population. Therefore there is no formal research basis for applying any conclusions from this study about the effects of gun ownership to the general population.[130] Nonetheless, *NEJM-1993* reaches unqualified conclusions and presents them as applying to the general population.

False Minimization of Sampling Bias

Whenever only a portion of a phenomenon is studied, the conclusions reached may be in error if the portion selected for study is not representative of all of the cases. One way to avoid this error (which is called a "bias") is to scrupulously include all of the cases in the study. The authors of *NEJM-1993* are aware of this, and claim, "To minimize selection bias, we included *all cases* of homicide in the home. . . . High response rates among case proxies (94.6 percent) and matching controls (80.6 percent) minimized nonresponse bias."

Unfortunately, a rather different picture emerges from close examination of the numbers (instead of relying on the percentages given by the authors). There were actually 444 cases of homicide in the home reported in the counties studied, during the time period selected. Nineteen of the 444 cases were dropped from consideration because the authors deemed murder-suicides and multiple homicides as a single event each and included only one homicide per event. Five additional homicides were dropped for reasons relating to reporting or death certificate change. The remaining cases account for the 94.6 percent of the total cases the authors state were left in the study. An additional 7 percent were dropped because of failure to interview the proxy, and 1 percent more due to failure to find a control.

This left 388 matched pairs, i.e., only 87.4 percent of the cases. This lower percentage is not mentioned by the authors (though they do give the individual drop percentages), thereby downplaying the cumulative effect and the possible biases which could result. Nor is this the end point in the process of diminishing the number of cases included in the analyses. The authors were unable to obtain complete data on all of the matched pairs, but the form of statistical analysis used requires complete data. So 72 of the 388 matched pairs had to be excluded in the final multivariate analysis.[131]

The end result is that only 316 matched pairs were used in the final analyses, representing only 71.2 percent of the 444 homicide cases. It is very difficult to accept *NEJM-1993*'s claim of having examined "all cases" as a fair description of an analysis that was actually based on 71.2 percent of the cases. We hasten to add that this does not prove that there was any selection or response bias in this study. It just shows that there was ample room for such biases to act. It also shows that the authors avoided coming to grips with this issue and presented the data in a manner which would mislead the readers into thinking that there could be little or no such bias.

Further analysis of the 28.8 percent of the cases which were dropped might be able to shed some light on whether, and to what extent, *NEJM-1993* is compromised by the existence of such biases. But the senior author refuses to make these data available to others for reanalysis.[132]*

Control Group Selection Did Not Assure Comparability

The validity of *NEJM-1993*'s conclusions depends on the control group matching the homicide cases in every way (except, of course, for the occurrence of a homicide). The importance of proper control selection cannot be overemphasized, whether medical or policy implications are at stake. Use of an inappropriate control can lead to erroneous conclusions and then to harmful practices:

> It is thus, for want of an adequately controlled test, that various forms of treatment have in the past, become unjustifiably, even sometimes harmfully, established in everyday medical practice.[134]

The need for the controls to differ only with respect to the factor being studied is called an "obviousity" because it is so glaringly obvious.[135] In *NEJM-1993*, however, the controls collected do not match the cases in some important ways. The incomplete matching which was done had another untoward effect. It produced a control group which was not representative of the counties being studied, and therefore further decreased the inference which can be legitimately drawn from the data of this study.

The study did match the control group to the case group using several categorizations (sex, race, age range, and neighborhood of residence). But

---

*A peculiarity of Dr. Kellermann's work (including the Vancouver-Seattle article discussed above and many others) on guns is that the authors refuse to reveal the underlying data to scholars desiring to examine it. As George Mason University Law School Professor Daniel Polsby comments, this so far departs from the routine scholarly practice as to makes it "seriously debateable whether [this work] should be credited at all."[133]

this matching method selects controls which are not necessarily matched with the case group on other important factors. The control selection involved random selection of households that were at least a "one-block avoidance zone" away from the case homicide. The matching criteria did not include any lifestyle or related indicators. A number of lifestyle indicators (referred to as "behavioral factors") were studied but the large differences between the cases and the control for these invariably shows more substance abuse and other problems in the cases than in the controls, and this shows that matching was not done for these lifestyle indicators. Other lifestyle indicators such as single-parent versus two-parent homes were not included in the study or are not shown in the article.

If the population selected from is composed of subpopulations which differ in homicide rates, the matching control must come from the same subpopulation as the case it is supposed to match. This could happen with the matching method *NEJM-1993* used, but only if the subpopulations were settled in distinct and different large geographic areas. Because of the avoidance method used, these areas would have to be larger than one-block in size. How much larger is hard to tell, since the paper doesn't say how far outside the zone it was necessary to travel to find a matching control who would agree to cooperate.

In any event, risk subpopulations are not distributed in such a coarse-grain manner. Criminal residences and crime areas which define the homicide-risk subgroup factors (drug use and dealing, violent criminal events, violently abusive family relationships, etc.) are often fine-grained in their distribution. There are differences in areas within a city, but there is population heterogeneity within these areas.[136] Choosing a control living one or more blocks away will not assure matching with respect to the subpopulation.

Of particular interest here is the small violent high-risk subpopulation (violent predators) that may be disproportionately represented in the homicide cases. The chances are good that the "controls" with which they will be matched will come from the much larger nonviolent (or less violent) subpopulation(s). This will produce a "spurious association" since the matching is not as exact as it should be.

The control group may or may not differ from the homicide cases in another characteristic which is central to *NEJM-1993*. The conclusion that gun ownership is a risk factor for homicide derives from the finding that there was a gun in 45.4 percent of the homicide case households, but in only

35.8 percent of the control households. Whether that finding is accurate, however, depends on the truthfulness of control group interviewees in admitting the presence of a gun(s) in the home.[137] How much confidence can be reposed in the truth of persons asked about gun ownership by a surveyor?

NEJM-1993's authors themselves state that "underreporting of gun ownership by control respondents could bias our estimate of risk upward." So they realized that this is a critical point, but they conclude that there is no underreporting. Predictably, they do not mention the fact that false denial of gun ownership by survey respondents has long been deemed a major problem with calculating the true size of American gun ownership; neither, of course, do they cite Professor Kleck's exhaustive discussion of this issue.[138]

NEJM-1993's authors justify their dismissal of underreporting as a problem, noting that "a pilot study [conducted by four of the *NEJM-1993* authors plus one other person] of homes listed as the addresses of owners of newly registered handguns confirmed that respondents' answers to questions about gun ownership were *generally* valid."[139] It is reasonable to ask what "generally" means. In the study referred to, 97.1 percent of the families (34 of 35) listed as being the location of a registered handgun admitted to having guns in the home, either at the time or recently. Superficially this appears to be an impressive record of openness. It becomes less impressive when the numbers are placed in full perspective. Seventy-five homes were chosen from new handgun registration records. Due to false addresses and other difficulties, only 55 could be found, and of these only 35 consented to the interview. These are the 35 families mentioned previously. These families are unrepresentative in an even more significant respect. They are people who, by definition, have chosen to let others, i.e., the government, know that they own guns, and who have undergone some governmental approval process. To learn that this sample is willing to admit the same facts to survey interviewers can tell us nothing about gun owners in general, let alone about the lower-income gun owners in *NEJM-1993*.

In comparison with this sample of *registered* owners, it is likely that owners of unregistered guns would be even more reluctant to admit to ownership. Among other things, it may involve admission to a criminal offense.[140] The control group could be further biased if criminals and owners of illicit guns are more likely to refuse to be interviewed for a study such as this, let alone to admit to ownership. With these many discrepancies possible between measures of gun ownership in the homicide case and control homes, it appears that the authors are quoting their own previous work in a way which overstates its strength.

To reiterate, *NEJM-1993*'s conclusions depend entirely on there having been no substantial underestimation of the control group's gun ownership. It would take only 35 of the 388 controls falsely denying gun possession to make the control ownership percentage exactly equal to that of the homicide case households. If indeed the controls actually had equal gun ownership to that of the homicide case households (45.4 percent), then a false denial rate of only 20.1 percent among the gun-owning controls would produce the 35 false denials and thereby equalize ownership. Such a 20.1 percent false denial rate is smaller than either of the "refused consent for interview" category of the pilot study, or the "inaccurate registration data" category. Therefore the results of the pilot study are consistent with a false denial rate sufficiently high to bring the control group gun ownership rate up to a level equal to, or even higher than, the homicide case household rate, although the authors cite the pilot study to the reverse effect. Neglect of the false denial rate can produce a bias large enough, by itself, to account for the entire association between gun ownership and homicide claimed in this study.

Inappropriate Method of Statistical Analysis

NEJM-1993's authors chose to use the Case Control Method (CCM), a method accepted in medical research as an investigatory tool with a strength in its ability to generate hypotheses, rather than as a final test of hypotheses.[141] A relevant weakness of the CCM is that it has a susceptibility to bias.[142] In the social sciences it is seldom possible to do the properly blinded, randomized, and otherwise controlled studies which would be used to confirm a hypothesis. This makes it even more important to be sensitive to the possible existence of biases, and to attempt to minimize them. *NEJM-1993* makes claims about the association found between gun ownership and homicide, and presents those claims as conclusions rather than as tentative hypotheses. According to the conclusion of the abstract, ". . . guns kept in the home are associated with an increase in the risk of homicide. . . ." and "Our study confirms this association. . . ." The authors' occasional qualification of their results ("People who keep guns in their homes *appear* to be at greater risk of homicide in the home than people who do not"; emphasis added) indicate that they understand the tentative nature of the results of Case Control Method studies. Regrettably, this understanding does not appear to have tempered the presentation of their conclusions.

CONCLUSION

We believe we have documented an emotional antigun agenda in the treatment of firearms issues in the medical and public health literature. While the antigun editorials and articles discussed had the superficial form of academic discourse, the basic tenets of science and scholarship have too often been lacking. We call them "antigun health advocacy literature" because they are so biased and contain so many errors of fact, logic, and procedure that we can not regard them as having a legitimate claim to be treated as contributions to a scholarly or scientific literature.

This advocacy literature generally ignores the large amount of criminological and sociological research dealing with firearms and violent crime. Criminological and sociological analysis provides important, even crucial, information as to the role of firearms in violence and the utility and viability of potential gun control strategies. But virtually all of this information is ignored or affirmatively suppressed in the health advocacy literature. That literature also shows consistent patterns of making misleading international comparisons, mistaking the differences between handguns and long guns, and exaggerating the number of children injured or killed—which builds up the emotional content. Other distortions include presenting gun ownership in such a manner as to ignore or minimize the benefits, and measuring defensive benefits purely in terms of attackers killed, rather than considering attacks deterred or attackers repelled. The criminological and sociological research literature demonstrates the existence of high-risk groups for firearms misuse, and of the "career" criminals who commit many of the serious crimes in our society. Yet the antigun health advocacy literature consistently overlooks these data and attributes equal propensity to commit violent crime to all people.

The health advocacy literature exists in a vacuum of lock-step orthodoxy almost hermetically sealed from the existence of contrary data or scholarship. Such data and scholarship routinely goes unmentioned and the adverse emotional reaction of the gate-keepers of the health journals assures the elimination of contrary views from their pages, and even from their citation in the invariably antigun articles these journals carry. In the rare instances in which works with contrary views are cited at all, they tend to be dismissed with ad hominem comments, but without the presentation of evidence or analysis refuting them. The antigun health advocacy literature can be described with the derogatory term "sagecraft," implying that academics have gone beyond the pale. Superficialities of scientific methodology and presentation are used to counterfeit scholarship supporting an antigun agenda while the basics of sound research are ignored. This shameful performance implies the willing collaboration of the researchers, the journals, and the CDC as a federal governmental funding agency. While many medical and public health journals have participated in this, the *New England Journal of Medicine* has been one of the most noticeable. It has an editorial policy which is strongly and explicitly antigun, and not only has published poorly executed antigun articles, but has excluded articles which disagree with this editorial policy.[143] These actions forfeit its claim to be a research journal rather than just a political advocacy publication.

This indictment of the antigun health advocacy literature is extremely troubling in an era in which research and data are often sought as a basis for debate over guns and formulation of public policy. When emotionally based antigun pseudoscientific advocacy is presented in the guise of research, ill-founded policy decisions may ensue. This may waste public resources and directly harm many people. The medical and public health journals need to eschew their emotionally based advocacy role in favor of presenting scientific research results.

Finally, some remark must be made on the idea of violence as an epidemic and a public health emergency. For that purpose we are delighted to adopt some recent comments by a preeminent *neutral* scholar in criminology, Professor James D. Wright (of Wright, Rossi, and Daly):

> And there is a sense in which violence is a public health problem. So let me illustrate the limitations of this line of reasoning with a public-health analogy.
>
> After research disclosed that mosquitos were the vector for transmission of yellow fever, the disease was not controlled by sending men in white coats to the swamps to remove the mouth parts from all the insects they could find. The only sensible, efficient way to stop the biting was to attack the environment where the mosquitos bred.

Guns are the mouth parts of the violence epidemic. The contemporary urban environment breeds violence no less than swamps breed mosquitos. Attempting to control the problem of violence by trying to disarm the perpetrators is as hopeless as trying to contain yellow fever through mandible control.

NOTES

1. Quoting from CDC bulletin, "Firearm Mortality Among Children and Youth," *Advance Data #178 NCHS* (November 3, 1989). (Significantly, the authors, CDC firearms specialists Lois Fingerhut and Joel Kleinman, add, "The data presented in this report underscore these concerns." They could, without substantial exaggeration, have added that CDC publications on firearms can be reviewed, as they will be herein, without ever finding analysis of data leading to any other conclusion.) See also Public Health Service (hereinafter PHS), *Healthy People: The Surgeon General's Report on Health Promotion and Disease Prevention* (Washington, D.C.: PHS, 1979), pp. 9-21, and PHS, *Healthy People: The Surgeon General's Report on Health Promotion and Disease Prevention: Background Papers* (Washington, D.C.: PHS, 1986), pp. 18, 64-67, 465.

2. "Guns are a virus that must be eradicated. . . . They are causing an epidemic of death by gunshot, which should be treated like any epidemic—you get rid of the virus. . . . Get rid of the guns, get rid of the bullets, and you get rid of the deaths." Health activist Katherine Christoffel, M.D., profiled/quoted by Janice Somerville, "Gun Control as Immunization," *American Medical News* (January 3, 1994): 9 (also quoting approving comments by an AMA official and the CDC's Mark Rosenberg). See also Deane Calhoun, "From Controversy to Prevention: Building Effective Firearm Policies," *Injury Prevention Network Newsletter* (winter, 1989-90): 17 (praising National Coalition to Ban Handgun's change of name to indicate broader prohibition reflecting its "belief that guns are not just an inanimate object, but in fact are a social ill"); Deborah Prothrow-Stith, *Deadly Consequences* (New York: Harpers, 1991), p. 198; *Surgeon General's Workshop on Violence and Public Health: Report* (Rockville, Md.: PHS, 1985), p. 53 (need to ban private possession of handguns); Karl P. Adler and J. A. Barondess et al. "Firearms Violence and Public Health: Limiting the Availability of Guns," *Journal of the American Medical Association* 271 (1994): 1281; William Rasberry, "Sick People with Guns," *Washington Post*, 19 October 1994, p. A23 (quoting Dr. Mark Rosenberg on his, and the CDC's, agenda to create a public perception of firearms as "dirty, deadly—and banned"); Harold Henderson, "Policy: Guns 'n' Poses," *Chicago*

Reader, 16 December 1994 (quoting Chicago Drs. Robert Tanz and Katherine Kaufer Christoffel on the need to change public attitudes toward guns as public attitudes toward smoking have been changed); Jonathan Fielding and Neal Halfon, "Where Is the Health in Health System Reform," *Journal of the American Medical Association* 272 (1994): 1292, 1294 (prohibitory taxation as a way of deterring purchasing of cigarettes and firearms); Editorial, "Brady Bill Has Medicine's Support," *American Medical News* (May 20, 1991): 25 (firearms "are one of the main causes of intentional and unintentional injury. . . . [T]he real cure for the epidemic [of violence by guns] is to eliminate its cause"); American Academy of Pediatrics, "Policy Statement," *American Academy of Pediatrics (AAP)* News 20-3 (January 1992) (necessity to ban private possession of handguns); Judith Cohen Dolins and Katherine Kaufer Christoffel, "Reducing Violent Injuries: Priorities for Pediatrician Advocacy," *Pediatrics* 94 (1994): 638, 645 (defining gun control as a process of progressively removing weapons from home environments); Daniel W. Webster and Modena E. H. Wilson, "Gun Violence Among Youth and the Pediatrician's Role in Primary Prevention," *Pediatrics* 94 (1994): 617, 621 ("gun manufacturers are polluting our communities").

3. See Gary Kleck's piece in this volume, "Absolutist Politics in a Moderate Package," and sources cited and quoted in note 2 above.

4. Quoting Webster and Wilson, "Gun Violence Among Youth and the Pediatrician's Role in Primary Prevention," p. 622. See sources cited in notes 1 and 2 above; also William DeJong, review of *Media Advocacy and Public Health: Power for Prevention*, by L. Wallack et al., *Health Education Quarterly* 21 (1994): 543. Dr. DeJong, who teaches in the Harvard University School of Public Health, advises that "to advance the cause of public health, we need to move to a new paradigm, one in which health educators focus on galvanizing political action and change." In the same spirit he praises "work by a gun control advocate [which] shows us how researchers can choose projects that will bring attention to public policy," i.e., the need to prohibit firearms ownership. Compare Peter Edelman and David Satcher, "Violence Prevention as a Public Health Policy," *Health Affairs* 12 (1994): 123, 124. Edelman and Satcher emphasize the urgent need to reduce violence and decrying unwillingness to pursue "any potentially effective interventions" out of concern with finicky principles like scholarly neutrality. See also Stephen Teret, "So What," *Epidemiology* 4 (1993): 93, and Steven S. Coughlin, "A Ban on Policy Recommendations in Epidemiology Research Papers? Surely You Jest!" *Epidemiology* 5 (1994): 258; Kenneth Tardiff et al., "Homicide in New York City: Cocaine Use and Firearms," *Journal of the American Medical Association* 272 (1994): 43, 46; Jeffrey B. Kahn, "Firearm Violence in California: Information and Ideas for Creating Change," *Western Journal of Medicine* 161 (1994): 565; M. Denise Dowd

et al., "Pediatric Firearm Injuries, Kansas City, 1992: A Population-Based Study," *Pediatrics* 94 (1994): 867, 872; Lester Adelson, "The Gun and the Sanctity of Human Life; Or the Bullet as Pathogen," *Archives of Surgery* 127 (1992): 659, 663–64; Leland Ropp et al., "Death in the City: An American Childhood Tragedy," *Journal of the American Medical Association* 267 (1992): 2905, 2909–10; Katherine Kaufer Christoffel, "Toward Reducing Pediatric Injuries from Firearms: Charting a Legislative and Regulatory Course," *Pediatrics* 88 (1991): 294; and Katherine Kaufer Christoffel and Tom Christoffel, "Handguns: Risks Versus Benefits," *Pediatrics* 47 (1986): 781, 782.

5. Thus, as used in this article, that phrase does not include the minuscule number of articles on firearms topics in medical or health publications that treat the issues neutrally, e.g., Robert L. Ohsfeldt and Michael A. Morrisey, *Firearms, Firearms Injury and Gun Control: A Critical Survey of the Literature*, Advances in Health Economics and Health Services Research 13 (1992): 65, or even take a stance affirmatively supporting freedom of private choice regarding firearms ownership, e.g., Edgar A. Suter, "Guns in the Medical Literature: A Failure of Peer Review," *Journal of the Medical Association of Georgia* 83 (1994): 133.

6. See, e.g., Prothrow-Stith, *Deadly Consequences*, p. 198 (quoted in the text on p. 33). Inexplicably, the author, who is at the Harvard School of Public Health, indicates she would allow limited gun ownership for sport, however much she disapproves of it, but not for self-defense.

As a University of Chicago health advocate put it, "The only legitimate use of a handgun that I can understand is for target shooting." Testimony of Professor Robert Replogle, M.D., "Handgun Crime Control Hearings," 1975–76 Senate Judiciary Committee (Subcommittee re Juvenile Delinquency), *Oversight of the 1968 Gun Control Act*, v. II), p. 1974. See also Adler, Barondess et al., "Firearms Violence and Public Health; James A. Mercy and Mark Rosenberg et al., "Public Health Policy for Preventing Violence," Health Affairs 12 (1993): 7, 28 ; Andrew L. Dannenberg, Susan P. Baker et al., "Intentional and Unintentional Injuries in Women: An Overview," *Annual Epidemiology* 4 (1994): 133, 137; Susan B. Sorenson and Audrey F. Saftlas, "Violence and Women's Health: The Role of Epidemiology," *Annual Epidemiology* 4 (1994): 140, 145; Mark L. Rosenberg, James A. Mercy, and Vernon N. Houk, "Guns and Adolescent Suicides," *Journal of the American Medical Association* 266 (1991): 3030; Daniel W. Webster et al., "Parents' Beliefs About Preventing Gun Injuries to Children," *Pediatrics* 89 (1992): 908, 914; Daniel W. Webster et al., "Firearm Injury Prevention Counseling: A Study of Pediatricians' Beliefs and Practices," *Pediatrics* 89 (1992): 902, 907.

7. J. Michael McGinnis et al., "Actual Causes of Death in the United States," *Journal of the American Medical Association* 270 (1993): 2207, 2211,

Diane Schetky, "Children and Handguns: A Public Health Concern," *American Journal of Diseases of Children* 139 (1985): 229, 230.

Dr. Kassirer, the current editor of the *New England Journal of Medicine*, severely criticizes NRA lobbying as ultra vires to the NRA's historical mission as a group devoted to sports and citizen military preparedness. Jerome P. Kassirer, review Under Fire: The NRA and the Battle for Gun Control by Osha Gray Davidson, *New England Journal of Medicine* 373 (1994): 330. This is ironic, given his own lobbying for gun prohibitions and that of his predecessors.

8. Arlene Eisen, "Guns: In Whose Hands? A Portrait of Gun Owners and Their Culture," *Injury Prevention Network Newsletter* (winter, 1989-90): 9 (subsection entitled *"Fear and Racism Among Gun Owners"* and characterizing—but without providing any example or supporting citation—"the veiled racism of NRA literature promoting self-defense"; also p. 10: "The gun lobby grows fat . . . on a generalized fear and hostility toward African American people, especially on the association between African American men and crime in the white public's mind").

9. Compare the *Journal of the American Medical Association's* disparate treatment of two opposing article submissions: its April 27, 1994, issue carried an article by nineteen medical professionals, seven of them teachers at medical schools, including Columbia and Cornell, urging the banning and confiscation of all handguns, federal restrictive licensing for gun ownership and a host of other gun control laws. In response, *JAMA* promptly received an article submission arguing the other side from thirty-nine authors, twenty-three of them teachers at medical schools, including Harvard and Pennsylvania, and two of them being law professors. *JAMA* just as promptly rejected it. [Note: Subsequent to our article's publication, *JAMA* did publish an article by Professor Kleck. With only minuscule exceptions (see note 5), that remains the only article in any health advocacy periodical that is skeptical of banning firearms or even neutral on the subject.]

10. William C. Shoemaker et al; "Urban Violence in Los Angeles in the Aftermath of the Riots: A Perspective From Health Care Professionals, with Implications for Social Reconstruction," *Journal of the American Medical Association* 270 (1993): 2833, 2836.

11. See, e.g., Schetky, "Children and Handguns" (of eleven footnotes, one is to a book by Handgun Control, Inc. chairman Nelson Shields—whose affiliation is *not* identified—three are to other Handgun Control, Inc. publications, and one is to a publication by yet another antigun lobbying group). This lack of validation by independent references is particularly troublesome as to this author who, as we shall see, regurgitates false information from lobbying organizations and attributes it to a neutral source by fabricating references. See also: National Committee for Injury Prevention and Control, *Injury Prevention: Meeting the Challenge*, a supple-

mental edition of the *American Journal of Preventive Medicine* (1989) [hereinafter cited as National Committee], chap. 17, note 6 (describing—without identifying him as such—the spokesman for the National Coalition to Ban Handguns as "one researcher [who] has calculated that $500 million a year is spent on hospital care for handgun injuries," citing an article by the Field Director of the National Coalition to Ban Handguns); American Academy of Pediatrics Policy Statement, Firearms Injuries Affecting the Pediatric Population in *American Academy of Pediatrics (AAP) News* (January 1992): 22 (twice citing publications of antigun foundation without noting that it is the nonprofit research affiliate of Handgun Control, Inc. in whose offices it is situated), Christoffel, "Toward Reducing Pediatric Injuries from Firearms," *Pediatrics* 88 (1991): 305.

12. "Coming from an official spokesman for the National Rifle Association, Blackman's invective is no surprise. We understand [his] need to attack this paper; it is what he is paid to do." Sloan, Rivara, and Kellermann, "Correspondence," *New England Journal of Medicine* 323 (1990): 136.

13. For instance. the American Medical Association Council on Scientific Affairs article, "Assault Weapons as a Public Health Hazard in the United States," *Journal of the American Medical Association* 267 (1992): 3067, asserts that "assault weapons are meant to be spray fired from the hip," citing a Handgun Control, Inc. publication as authority. The immediately preceding reference cited a neutral publication for explanation of gun nomenclature, *Assault Rifle Fact Sheet 1: Definitions and Background* (Washington, D.C., 1989), a publication of the Institute for Research on Small Arms in International Security, then headed by the late Edward Ezell, curator of the Smithsonian's U.S. Armed Forces Collection, a preeminent expert. The *Fact Sheet* directly contradicted the AMA Council's claim about spray firing assault weapons from the hip. So, of course the AMA Council simply failed to mention the *Fact Sheet's* contrary statements: that such weapons are designed for aimed fire, *not* "spray fire"; and that anyone who shoots a semiautomatic gun rapidly without aiming will rarely hit the target.

14. See William Tonso, "Social Science and Sagecraft in the Debate Over Gun Control," *Law and Policy Quarterly* 5 (1983): 325 applying to the firearms regulation debate the concepts set out by Florian Znaniecki, *The Social Role of the Man of Knowledge* (New York: Harpers, 1968), pp. 72–74.

15. Quoted in Marsha Goldsmith, "Epidemiologists Aim at New Target: Health Risk of Handgun Proliferation," *Journal of the American Medical Association* 261 (1989): 675. It bears emphasis that the CDC and the Public Health Service were calling for reduction in handgun ownership as a means of reducing violence *before* any research had been done. It is little wonder that subsequent CDC publications on this subject uniformly support that preordained position. See notes 1 and 2.

16. Dr. Christoffel quoted in Somerville, "Gun Control as Immunization." The health advocacy literature regularly describes firearms as disease "vectors," "toxins" and/or causes of an epidemic. See, e.g., Christopher Durso, "Guns 'n' Doctors," *The New Physician* (December 1994); Paul Cotton, "Gun-Associated Violence Increasingly Viewed as Public Health Challenge," *Journal of the American Medical Association* 267 (1992): 1171–74; A. Colburn, "Gunshots as an Epidemic: Some Doctors Call Firearms a 'Toxin' in the Environment," *Washington Post* "Health," 1 November 1988.

17. See, e.g., Hans Toch and Alan J. Lizotte, "Research and Policy: The Case of Gun Control," in *Psychology and Social Policy*, ed. Peter Sutfeld and Philip Tetlock (New York: Hemisphere, 1992); James D. Wright, "Second Thoughts About Gun Control," *Public Interest* 91 (1988): 23; Ted Robert Gurr, ed., *Violence in America* (New York: Sage, 1989): 17-18; Chris Eskridge, "Zero-Order Inverse Correlations Between Crimes of Violence and Hunting Licenses in the United States," *Sociology and Social Research* 71 (1986): 55.

18. Don B. Kates, "Firearms and Violence: Old Premises and Current Evidence," in Gurr, *Violence in America*, p. 201, citing the views of Colin Greenwood, retired chief superintendent of the West Yorkshire constabulary, author of the seminal study of English gun control.

19. State of Wisconsin Legislative Reference Bureau, *The Gun Control Debate—An Update*, Informational Bulletin 94-3 (October 1994): 30.

20. Quoted in Don B. Kates and Nicole Varzos, "Aspects of the Priapic Theory of Gun Ownership," in William Tonso, ed., *The Gun Culture and Its Enemies* (Bellevue, Wash.: Merril, 1989), pp. 93, 95.

21. Sigmund Freud and D. Oppenheim, *Dreams in Folklore* (New York: Praeger, 1958), p. 33; see also *The Major Writings of Sigmund Freud* (Chicago: Great Books ed., 1952); p. 507.

22. Arthur Kellermann et al., "Suicide in the Home in Relation to Gun Ownership," *New England Journal of Medicine* 327 (1992): 467, citing Charles L. Rich et al., "Guns and Suicide: Possible Effects of Some Specific Legislation," *American Journal of Psychiatry* 147 (1990): 342, which found, based on empirical investigation, that in the absence of guns, suicidal individuals turn to other methods (e.g., leaping from great heights) so that any reduction in gun suicides is almost perfectly offset by an increase in suicide by other means.

23. Carol W. Runyan and Jonathon B. Gerken, "Epidemiology and Prevention of Adolescent Injuries," *Journal of the American Medical Association* 262 (1989): 2273, 2275, citing two articles by Colin Loftin and David McDowall which actually said (respectively) "the gun law did *not* significantly alter the numbers or types of serious crimes in Detroit" and "our current working hypothesis and by far the simplest interpretation of the data is that the FL gun law did *not* have a mea-

surable deterrent effect on violent crime." Emphasis added to both quotes which are (respectively) from "'One with a Gun Gets You Two': Mandatory Sentencing and Firearms Violence in Detroit," *Annals of the American Academy of Political and Social Science* 455 (1981): 150 and "The Deterrent Effects of the Florida Felony Firearm Law," *Journal of Criminal Law and Criminology* 75 (1984): 250, 258.

24. Tardiff, "Homicide in New York City," pp. 43, 45, blames increased homicide among minority teenagers on increased availability of firearms to them, but cites Centers for Disease Control, "Weapon-Carrying Among High School Students-U.S. 1990," *Morbidity and Mortality Weekly Report* 40 (1991): 681, which indicated a *decline* in gun carrying, not an increase. (Of the other two citations the article gives to the same point, citation 42 contained no information about firearm availability while citation 43 had no trend data.)

25. Abraham B. Bergman, review of *Deadly Consequences*, by Deborah Prothrow-Stith, *Journal of the American Medical Association* 267 (1992): 3089.

26. Dolins and Christoffel, "Reducing Violent Injuries," p. 647 Emphasis added.

27. For U.S. Supreme Court cases see chap. 1 of this volume and David B. Kopel, "The Supreme Court's Thirty-Four *Other* Gun Cases: What the Supreme Court Has Said About the Second Amendment," *St. Louis University Public Law Review* 18 (1999): 99. For state provisions and cases see Robert Dowlut and Janet Knoop, "State Constitutions and the Right to Keep and Bear Arms," *Oklahoma City University Law Review* 7 (1982): 177.

28. Quoting Christoffel, "Toward Reducing Pediatric Injuries from Firearms," p. 295; compare the discussion of the scholarly literature in chap. 1 above.

29. Dolins and Christoffel, "Reducing Violent Injuries," p. 649, citing as the "gun supporters" Kleck (see his discussion in chapters 6 and 7 below) and James D. Wright and Peter Rossi, *Armed and Considered Dangerous: A Survey of Felons and Their Firearms* (New York: Aldine, 1986) and (as the "epidemiologists") various pieces including the State of Wisconsin Legislative Reference Bureau, *The Gun Control Debate—An Update*, Informational Bulletin.

30. Compare Kleck's Address to the National Academy of Sciences quoted in the text above to Wright, *Second Thoughts*, above.

31. Wright and Rossi, *Armed and Considered Dangerous*, 145, 146, 150, 154, table 7.1.

32. Wisconsin Informational Bulletin, *The Gun Control Debate—An Update*, pp. 5–6.

33. Ibid., p. 6, discounting the conclusions in Arthur L. Kellermann and Donald T. Reay, "Protection or Peril?: An Analysis of Firearm-Related Deaths in the Home," *New England Journal of Medicine* 314 (1986): 1557–60, which Dolins and Christoffel extol in *Pediatrics* v. 94 p. 645.

34. All quotations from Dr. Tanz are from the interview "Guns 'n' Poses," in *Chicago Reader*, 16 December 1994, pp. 8, 22, 24, 33 respectively.

35. Quoting, with emphasis added, from then-Handgun Control, Inc. Chairman Nelson "Pete" Shields, *Guns Don't Die, People Do* (New York: Arbor, 1981), 124–25. Submission or running away or screaming is also the advice offered by Matthew Yeager et al., *How Well Does the Handgun Protect You and Your Family?*(Washington, D.C.: Handgun Control Staff of the U.S. Conference of Mayors, 1976).

36. See note 34.

37. See, e.g., Jerome P. Kassirer, "Editor's Reply," *New England Journal of Medicine* 326 (1992): 1161.

38. See, e.g., Patti J. Patterson and Leigh R. Smith, "Firearms in the Home and Child Safety," *American Journal of Diseases of Children* 141 (1987): 221, 223, Douglas S. Weil and David Hemenway, "Loaded Guns in the Home, Analysis of a National Random Survey of Gun Owners," *Journal of the American Medical Association* 267 (1992): 3033, 3037, and the following other articles cited above: Webster and Modena, *Pediatrics*, vol. 94, p. 621; Somerville; Webster, et al., "Parents' Beliefs," and "Pediatricians' Beliefs," both in *Pediatrics* vol. 89.

39. Mercy and Rosenberg, "Public Health Policy for Preventing Violence," p. 19.

40. Stephen Teret and Gwen Wintemute, "Policies to Prevent Firearm Injuries," *Health Affairs*, 12 (1993): 96, 105.

41. See, e.g., reviews by Lawrence W. Sherman, *The Criminologist* 18 (1993): 15 and by H. Laurence Ross, *American Journal of Sociology* 98 (1992): 661. [Note: In 1997 *Point Blank* was updated and largely replaced by Professor Kleck's *Targeting Guns*.]

42. See, for example Dolins and Christoffel discussed on p. 40, John H. Sloan et al., "Correspondence," *New England Journal of Medicine* 323 (1990): 136, and Arthur L. Kellermann, "Obstacles to Firearm and Violence Research," *Health Affairs* 12 (1993): 142, 150–51.

43. The Brady Bill is limited to a background check on *handgun* purchases from *dealers*. Long before Brady was proposed Kleck was supporting a background check as prerequisite to *all* firearms purchasing, including long guns as well as handguns and transactions between private persons as well as sales through dealers. Gary Kleck and David J. Bordua, "The Factual Foundation for Certain Key Assumptions of Gun Control," *Law and Policy Q Vatesly* 5 (1983): 271, 294, Gary Kleck, "Policy Lessons from Recent Gun Control Research," *Law and Contemporary Problems* 49 (1986): 35, 58–60; *Point Blank*, pp. 58–60.

44. See note 29 above and accompanying text. The work in question is James D. Wright, Peter Rossi, and Kathleen Daly, *Under the Gun: Weapons, Crime and Violence in the United States* (New York: Aldine: 1983).

45. John Sloan et al., "Handgun Regulations, Crime, Assaults, and Homicide:

A Tale of Two Cities," *New England Journal of Medicine* 319 (1988): 1256, purportedly citing Wright, Rossi, and Daly, but without supplying any specific page citation.

46. From the abstract to the Wright, Rossi, and Daly *Executive Summary*, p. 2. Emphasis added.

47. Sloan, Rivara, and Kellermann, "Correspondence," p. 136.

48. Sloan et al., "Handgun Regulations, Crime, Assaults, and Homicide."

49. See, e.g., Charles Mock et al., "Comparison of the Costs of Acute Treatment for Gunshot and Stab Wounds: Further Evidence of the Need for Firearms Control," *Journal of Trauma* 36 (1994): 516, 521; Editorial, *American Journal of Emergency Medicine* 11 (1994): 183, 184.

50. Brandon Centerwall, "Homicide and the Prevalence of Handguns: Canada and the United States, 1976 to 1980," *American Journal of Epidemiology* 134 (1991): 1245-65.

51. Three years after its publication, he told the interviewer "he's heard it was coming but didn't know it was out." "Guns 'n' Poses," *Chicago Reader*, 16 December, 1994, p. 24.

52. See, e.g., Robert Mundt, "Gun Control and Rates of Firearms Violence in Canada and the United States," *Canadian Journal of Criminology* 32 (1990): 137–53, and Gary Mauser and Richard Holmes, "Evaluating the 1977 Canadian Firearms Control Legislation: An Econometric Approach," *Evaluation Research* 16 (1993): 603.

53. Centerwall, "Homicide and the Prevalence of Handguns," pp. 1245–46. As discussed on pp. 53ff., even independent of its irreconcilability with Centerwall's much better data, the Sloan et al. article is methodologically worthless.

54. Richard Drooz, "Handguns and Hokum: A Methodological Problem," *Journal of the American Medical Association* 238 (1977): 43.

55. Harold B. Houser, "Invited Commentary: Common Wisdom and Plain Truth," *American Journal of Epidemiology* 134 (1991): 1261. The gravamen of the title and commentary is that, while "common sense" supports "recommending the reduction of access to handguns as the primary intervention strategy for reducing homicide," the "plain truth" of Centerwall's empirical finding refutes "common wisdom."

56. We have found no citation of the Mundt or Mauser and Holmes articles. Centerwall's article was cited dismissively by one of the authors of the Sloan article. Arthur Kellermann, "Preventing Firearm Injuries: A Review of Epidemiologic Literature," *American Journal of Preventive Medicine* 9 (1993): 12. Citations to the Sloan article are virtually endless and invariably favorable. See, e.g., Stefan Z. Wiktor et al., "Firearms in New Mexico," *Western Journal of Medicine* 161 (1994): 137, 139; Peter M. Marzuk et al., "The Effect of Access to Lethal Methods of Injury on Suicide Rates," *Archives of General Psychiatry* 49 (1992): 451, 458;

Charles M. Callahan and Frederick P. Rivara, "Urban High School Youth and Handguns: A School-Based Survey," *Journal of the American Medical Association* 267 (1992): 3038, 3042; Daniel W. Webster et al., "Reducing Firearms Injuries," *Issues in Science and Technology* (spring, 1991); Roberta K. Lee et al., "Incidence Rates of Firearm Injuries in Galveston, Texas, 1979-1981," *American Journal of Epidemiology* 134 (1991): 511, 520; Lois A. Fingerhut and Joel C. Kleinman, "International and Interstate Comparisons of Homicides Among Young Males," *Journal of the American Medical Association*, 263 (1990): 3292, 3295; Garen J. Wintemute, "Closing the Gap Between Research and Policy: Firearms," *Injury Prevention Network Newsletter* (winter, 1989-90): 21; James A. Mercy et al., "Firearm Injuries: A Call for Science," *New England Journal of Medicine* 319 (1988): 1283–84; and the following previously cited articles: Mock, "Comparison of the Costs of Acute Treatment for Gunshot and Stab Wounds"; Dolins and Christoffel, "Reducing Violent Injuries," p. 651; at 1777; Mercy and Rosenberg, "Public Health Policy for Preventing Violence," p. 28; Teret and Wintemute at 107; National Committee, *Injury Prevention*, p. 267.

57. Centerwall, "Homicide and the Prevalence of Handguns." Emphasis added.

58. See, e.g., Mercy and Rosenberg, "Public Health Policy for Preventing Violence," 28 (footnote 52, citing Sloan but not Centerwall) and 29 (citing B. Centerwall, "Exposure to Television As a Cause of Violence," in G. Comstock, ed., *Public Communications and Behavior* [Orlando: Academic Press, 1989].)

59. R. Sherrill, *The Saturday Night Special* (New York: Penguin, 1975), p. 176.

60. David B. Kopel, *The Samuraii, the Mountie, and the Cowboy: Should America Adopt the Gun Control of Other Democracies?* (Amherst, N.Y.: Prometheus Books, 1992), chap. 8.

61. See, e.g., Susan Baker, "Without Guns Do People Kill People?" *American Journal of Public Health* 75 (1985): 587 and the following previously cited works: Marzuk et al., "The Effect of Access to Lethal Methods of Injury on Suidide Rates"; Lee et al., Mercy, "Firearm Injuries"; Fingerhut and Kleinman, "International and Interstate Comparisons of Homicides Among Young Males," p. 3295; Callahan and Rivara, "Urban High School Youth and Handguns," p. 3042; Webster, Chaulk, Teret, and Wintemute, "Reducing Firearms Injuries," *Issues in Science and Technology* (spring, 1991): 76; Paul Cotton, "Gun Associated Violence Increasingly Viewed as Public Health Challenge," *JAMA* 267 (1992): 1171–74; Dolins and Christoffel, "Reducing Violent Injuries," p. 651; Mercy and Rosenberg, "Public Health Policy for Preventing Violence," p. 28.

62. Gary Mauser, "Gun Control in the United States," *Criminal Law Forum* 3 (1992): 147, n. 2. Emphasis added.

63. See, e.g., Wintemute, "Closing the Gap Between Research and Policy,"

p. 21, and D. A. Brent and J. A. Perper, "Reply," *Journal of the American Medical Association* 267 (1992): 3026–27.

64. See Arthur L. Kellermann, "Obstacles to Firearm and Violence Research," *Health Affairs* 12 (1993): 142, 150–51. Amusingly, Dr. Kellermann makes these comments without bothering to inform his readers that he himself is one of the authors of the article he portrays being so nefariously attacked by the dark forces of the NRA.

65. "But these countries' low crime rates seem to have preceded the gun laws that supposedly caused them. Violence was low (and falling) in Western Europe from at least the mid-19th Century, but antigun policies only came in after World War I aimed not at crime but at the political unrest of that tumultuous era . . . ; and if antigun laws explain low Japanese homicide why does Taiwan (where gun possession is a capital offense) have a higher murder rate than the U.S.; and why is South Africa's rate twice that of the U.S., despite some of the world's strictest antigun laws?" Kates, "Firearms and Violence: Old Premises and Current Evidence," p. 200 (footnotes omitted). See also Kopel, *The Samuraii, the Mountie, and the Cowboy*; Eric H. Monkkonen, "Diverging Homicide Rates: England and the United States, 1850-1875," in Gurr, *Violence in America*, pp. 80–81, and Colin Greenwood, *Firearms Control: Armed Crime and Firearms Control in England and Wales* (London: Routledge, Kegan, Paul, 1972), chaps. 1, 2.

66. Kates, "Firearms and Violence: Old Premises and Current Evidence," p. 200.

67. Schetky, "Children and Handguns," p. 230; see also the virtually identical statement in Fingerhut and Kleinman, "Correspondence," *Journal of the American Medical Association* 264 (1990): 2210.

68. Abraham Tennenbaum, "Israel Has a Successful Gun Control Policy," in Charles P. Cozic, *Gun Control: Current Controversies* (San Diego: Greenhaven, 1992): 250. Emphasis added.

69. Roberta Lee, Arthur Kellermann et al., "The Epidemiologic Basis for the Prevention of Firearm Injuries," *Annual Review of Public Health* 12 (1991): 17, 28.

70. Compare Swiss and Israeli laws and practices cited in Glenn H. Reynolds and Don B. Kates, "The Second Amendment and States' Rights: A Thought Experiment," *William and Mary Law Review* 36 (1995): 1737, and Don B. Kates, "Handgun Prohibition and the Original Meaning of the Second Amendment," *Michigan Law Review* 82 (1983): 203, 249, n. 193, to Title 18 U.S.C. § 922(o) and (v) and 26 U.S.C. § 5845.

71. For discussion of gun availability and carrying under Swiss law see David Kopel, "Peril or Protection? The Risks and Benefits of Handgun Prohibition," *St. Louis University Public Law Review* 12 (1993): 285, 299.

72. See Judge Tennenbaum's guest editorial, "Handguns Could Help," *Baltimore Sun*, 26 October 1991.

73. Don B. Kates, "Firearms and Violence: Old Premises and Current Evidence," in *Violence in America*, ed. T. Gurr (1989), p. 209. Such events are not uncommon in Israel, e.g., the following from an April 7, 1994, A.P. release which appeared in the *Marin Independent Journal* (p. A3): "JERUSALEM—A Palestinian opened fire with a submachine gun at a bus stop near the port of Ashdod today, killing one Israeli and wounding four before being shot to death by bystanders, officials said. . . . National police spokesman Eric Bar-Chen said today's attacker, who was armed with an Uzi submachine gun, was shot and killed by a civilian and a soldier who were at the bus stop and hitchhiking post used by soldiers. Ashdod is 15 miles south of Tel Aviv and 15 miles north of the Gaza Strip. . . . Bar-Chen identified the gunman as a Palestinian from the Shati refugee camp in the Gaza Strip. Six ammunition clips and a knife were found on his body, he added."

74. For the accidental firearms death figures see the table in National Safety Council [NSC], *Injury Facts 1999* (Itasca, Ill.: NSC, 1999), pp. 42–43. For the calculation of firearms stock see the discussion on pages 190–91 and notes 7 and 10-12 in Don B. Kates and Daniel D. Polsby, "Long Term Non-Relationship of Firearm Availability to Homicide," *Homicide Studies* 4 (2000): 185-201.

75. We can find *no* health advocacy publication that mentions—much less discusses—the correlation between a radically rising handgunstock and radically declining accidental firearms deaths. Nor does *any* health advocacy publication suggest that the decline in accidental firearms death rate requires or deserves exploration or study, or has any importance at all. Indeed, almost without exception health advocates inveigh against widespread gun ownership and discuss gun accidents without revealing to their readers the steep decline in accidental firearms fatalities over the 20 year period 1967-86. See, e.g., Dowd et al; "Pediatric Firearm Injuries, Kansas City, 1992," p. 867; Webster et al., "Parent's Beliefs About Preventing Gun Injuries to Children," pp. 902, 903, 906-7 (emphasizing child death nationally but giving no trend data); CDC, Firearm-Related Deaths—Louisiana and Texas, 1970-1990, *Morbidity and Mortality Weekly Report* 41 (1992): 213, 214-15 (giving neither local nor national trend data for accidental killings); Lee, Kellermann et al., "The Epidemiologic Basis for the Prevention of Firearm Injuries," pp. 26–27; National Committee, *Injury Prevention*, pp. 263–64, 266; AMA Council on Scientific Affairs, *Public Health Reports* (1989): 113 (emphasizing accidental gun deaths among children without giving either trend in general or for children); Patterson and Smith, "Firearms in the Home and Child Safety," p. 221.

A rare exception—which nevertheless proves the rule—is Garen J. Wintemute, "Firearms as a Cause of Death in the United States, 1920-1982," *Journal of Trauma* 27 (1987): 532, 533, 534, 536. He does admit accidental firearms fatalities have steadily declined throughout the twentieth century. But he treats the matter in a single sentence that assigns no importance to it and draws no implications from it. Citing no evidence at all, he denigrates safety education in general and attributes the decline to a trend of identifying suicides as such rather than as gun accidents.

76. *Washington Post*, 7 January 1992, p. B5 ("A must for any parent who keeps a gun in the home"). In 1993 NRA lobbyist Marion Hammer (soon to be NRA president) received a National Safety Council Outstanding Community Service Award for originating the Eddie Eagle program. *American Rifleman*, March 1994, p. 34; *Florida Times-Union*, November 1994, p. B2.

77. See, e.g., Deane Calhoun and Dr. Christoffel (both quoted in footnote 2) and citations given in notes 78–81.

78. Cheryl Jackson, "Gun-Safety Backers Shun NRA material," *Cleveland Plain Dealer*, 27 March 1992.

Amusingly, at its 1995 annual meeting the California Medical Association endorsed what the CMA's resolution described as "the California Department of Justice's [*sic*] safety instruction to children: 'If you [find a gun in some area], Stop. Don't touch. Leave the area. Tell an adult.' " Our [*sic*] emphasizes the deception employed by the resolution's proponents. The safety instruction is the NRA's, not that of the California Department of Justice (which has adopted it from the NRA's Eddie Eagle pamphlet, however). The resolution originally described the quoted admonition as deriving from the NRA. But when the resolution was pre-presented in that form to a county medical association the proponents were advised that if they wanted their resolution to pass they should delete any reference to the NRA. Reworded in that fashion, the resolution was unanimously adopted by the California Medical Association.

79. Compare National Committee, *Injury Prevention*, p. 266; American Academy of Pediatrics Committee on Adolescence, Policy Statement: "Firearms and Adolescents," *American Academy of Pediatrics (AAP) News* (January, 1992): 21; and Lee, Kellermann et al., "The Epidemiologic Basis for the Prevention of Firearm Injuries," p. 19 to William W. Treanor and Marjolijn Bijlefeld, "Kids and Guns: A Child Safety Scandal," 2d ed. (Educational Fund to End Handgun Violence, 1989). The fund is a nonprofit spin-off of the National Coalition to Ban Handguns.

80. Dolins and Christoffel, "Reducing Violent Injuries," p. 646. See also Weil and Hemenway, "Loaded Guns in the Home."

81. It bears emphasis that Dolins and Christoffel are not unique. Rather their attitude seems general among health advocates. All of the various advocates who consider safety training dismiss it with this or some similar comment. Only one discussion notes the need for study, and the terms in which it does so are significant: "an important research question is whether the safety benefit of [safety] courses is outweighed by their ability to promote an interest in firearms, an interest which

increases the number of firearms in circulation." National Committee, *Injury Prevention*, p. 266. The authors piously add that increasing the number of firearms may cause more accidental injuries with guns. Of course, once again, they nowhere temper this point (or the rest of their discussion) by mentioning the coincidence of a 173 percent increase in handguns with a two-thirds decline in accidental fatalities over a twenty-year period.

82. See, e.g., Stephen Teret, "Public Health and the Law," *American Journal of Public Health* 76 (1986): 1027, 1028; Susan Baker et al., *The Injury Fact Book* (Baltimore: Johns Hopkins, 1984), pp. 90–91; CDC, "Firearms-Related Years of Potential Life Lost Before Age 65 Years—United States, 1980-1991," *Journal of the American Medical Association* 272 (1994): 1246; Stephen Teret and Garen Wintemute, "Handgun Injuries: The Epidemiologic Evidence for Assessing Legal Responsibility," *Hamline Law Review* 6 (1983): 341.

83. Compare CDC, "Firearm-Related Years of Potential Life Lost Before Age 65 Years," p. 1246 (combined homicide/suicide) data to the earlier article by CDC employees Fingerhut and Kleinman, "International and Interstate Comparisons of Homicides Among Young Males," p. 3292.

84. Baker, "Without Guns."

85. John Sloan et al., "Firearms Regulations and Rates of Suicide: A Comparison of Two Metropolitan Areas," *New England Journal of Medicine* 322 (1990): 369.

86. For articles stating or implying this causation see ibid. and the following articles cited above: Calhoun, "From Controversy to Prevention," p. 12; and Fingerhut and Kleinman, "Firearm Mortality Among Children and Youth" and "International and Interstate Comparisons of Homicides Among Young Males"; as well as J. H. Boyd, "The Increasing Rate of Suicide by Firearms," *New England Journal of Medicine* 308 (1983): 872–74; CDC, *Youth Suicide in the United States, 1970-1980* (Atlanta: CDC, 1986); J. H. Boyd and Eve K. Moscicki, "Firearms and Youth Suicide," *American Journal of Public Health* 76 (1985): 587.

87. "Teenage Deaths Increasing Across Europe," *CJ-Europe* (November-December 1991): 4.

88. K. Hawton, "By Their Own Young Hand," *British Medical Journal* 6833 (1992): 1000.

89. CDC, "Firearm-Related Years of Potential Life Lost Before Age 65 Years—United States, 1980-1991," *Journal of the American Medical Association* 272 (1994): 1246.

90. "Sri Lanka [Ceylon] has one of the highest suicide rates in the world (29 per 100,000 population in 1980 [when the U.S. rate was 11.8]. Suicides are especially frequent among young adults, both male and female. Compared to the U.S., the suicide rate for males in Sri Lanka is nearly four times greater; the female rate is

nearly 13 times greater. The most common mode of suicide is ingestion of liquid pesticides." Lawrence R. Berger, "Suicides and Pesticides in Sri Lanka," *American Journal of Public Health* 75 (1985): 587. To the same effect see Ruth H. Haynes, "Suicide in Fiji: A Preliminary Study," *British Journal of Psychiatry* 145 (1984): 433.

91. See Gary Kleck, *Point Blank: Guns and Violence in America* (New York: Aldine, 1991), pp. 238–56.

92. Lois A. Fingerhut et al., "Firearm and Non Firearm Homicide Among Persons 15 Through 19 Years of Age," *Journal of the American Medical Association* 267 (1992): 3048, 3049 table 1. Again, this fact is not discussed, nor is the fact of the far greater firearm availability to rural blacks mentioned. The theme of the cited article is that guns are causing an epidemic of black teenage inner city homicide.

93. Kleck, *Point Blank*, p. 23: "Black households in rural areas are just as likely to have a gun as white households in those areas. . . ." See discussion of black and white homicide and gun possession rates on p. 69.

94. See, e.g., an article by Sam Fields of the National Coalition to Ban Handguns, "Handgun Prohibition and Social Necessity," *St. Louis University Law Journal* 23 (1979): 35, 51. Mr. Fields is, of course, correct that (insofar as it was effective) a handgun ban would almost certainly result in increasing reliance on loaded long guns as defensive weapons. See discussion in *Point Blank*, p. 281.

95. Kleck, *Point Blank*, pp. 280–81. The dangers are particularly great for small children; toddlers cannot operate a handgun, but can easily discharge a long gun if their parents irresponsibly keep it loaded and unsecured in the home.

96. See table 3 on p. 65. N.B.: It may be properly objected that the 14 percent handgun involvement figure is misleading, since in many accidental gun fatalities the kind of firearm was not identified. For that reason table 2 gives a percentage figure assuming the same proportion of handgun involvement in these fatalities as in those in which the kind of firearm can be identified. That figure is 41 percent, which is less than half of the percent of guns kept loaded at any one time.

97. Quoting from Don B. Kates Jr., John K. Lattimer, and Robert J. Cottrol, "The Public Health Literature on Firearms—A Critique of Overt Mendacity" (unpublished paper delivered to the 1993 annual meeting of the American Society of Criminology): "So much deadlier are loaded long guns kept in the home that even today, when handguns are the primary defensive weapon, long guns are involved in almost seven times more accidental fatalities in the home. The trend data indicate the magnitude of the risks involved if a handgun-only ban induced a return to reliance on loaded long guns for home defense: the 'proliferation of handguns' since 1967 has resulted in the handgun largely displacing the long gun as the weapon kept loaded in the home for self-protection. Not coincidentally, since 1967 accidental firearm deaths have *decreased* by almost 60 percent. From the available

data it may be estimated that if the 85.2 percent of loaded handguns in American homes in the year 1980 had been long guns instead, the number of fatal gun accidents would have more than quadrupled, from 1,244 to c. 5,346. Or, to put it another way, an additional 4,100 (or more) lives per year would be lost in accidental shootings in the home if a handgun ban resulted in loaded long guns being kept for home defense in the same numbers in which handguns are now kept." We acknowledged the advice of Professor Kleck for the 1980 home accidental fatality figures and for his assistance and advice in making this estimate.

98. From the NSC volumes *Accident Facts* for the years 1980-1994 respectively. Breakdowns between handgun and other firearm accident fatalities are unavailable for the years before 1979 and after 1991. Breakdowns for 1989-91 appear in *Accident Facts-1994*, p. 11. See also the extended discussion of fatal gun accidents in Kleck's *Targeting Guns*, chap. 9

99. See, e.g., the following previously cited articles: AMA Council on Scientific Affairs, *Public Health Reports*, p. 113; Patterson and Smith, "Firearms in the Home and Child Safety," p. 221; Dowd et al; "Pediatric Firearm Injuries, Kansas City, 1992," and the Webster et al. articles in *Pediatrics*; v. 94, pp. 618ff; and vol. 89, pp. 902, 903, 906–907.

100. Compare the health advocate figures of 365, 500, and 1,000 children killed per year with the actual figure of 273 (averaged over the ten-year period 1980-1989; calculation from figures given in *Point Blank*, table 7.5 and NSC, *Accident Facts-1993*, p. 23). The false health advocate figures are (in ascending order of inaccuracy): the 365 attested to Congress by Dr. Joseph Greensher, representing the American Academy of Pediatrics ("one child under age 15 each day"); 1985-1986 *Hearings on Legislation to Modify the 1968 Gun Control Act*, House Judiciary Committee, Subcommittee on Crime; vol. 1 pp. 164, 170); the "five hundred" per year asserted by Dr. Tanz, who is an AAP advisor (quoted by Joan DeClaire, "Kids and Guns," *View* [September-October 1992]: 30, 33); and the claim that "almost 1,000 children a year" die in gun accidents offered by two of the most prolific health sages. Teret and Wintemute, "Handgun Injuries," p. 346.

There is a substantial time lag on publication of accidental death figures. In 1985, when the latest available figure was 243 (for 1983), Dr. Greensher put the figure at more than 365, roughly a 50 percent exaggeration; in 1992 when the latest available figure was 236 (for 1990), Dr. Tanz put the figure at 500, nearly a 100 percent exaggeration; in 1983 the latest available figure would have been 298 (for 1981), but Teret and Wintemute put the figure at almost 1,000, a 335 percent exaggeration.

101. Compare ten-year average fatal gun accident figure of 273 given in note 99 to NSC *Accident Facts-1992*, p. 65 (giving 1988 bicycle death figures).

102. See, e.g., Bureau of Justice Statistics: *Crime Data Brief*, "Young Black Male

Victims" (Washington: U.S. Department of Justice, December, 1994) showing that black males age twelve to twenty-four are murdered at a rate of 114.9 per 100,000 population, whereas the homicide rate for white males in the same age group is only 11.7. In other words, the black rate is almost ten times greater than of whites of similar age and almost fourteen times greater than the American population as a whole.

103. See, e.g., the Fingerhut articles supra in *Journal of the American Medical Association* vol. 267 at 3048 and 3054 and CDC, *Homicide Surveillance: High-Risk Racial and Ethnic Groups—Blacks and Hispanics 1970 to 1983* (Atlanta: CDC, 1987).

104. Kleck *Point Blank*, p. 23: "Whites are much more likely to own guns or handguns than blacks . . . "

105. Cited in Kates, "Firearms and Violence: Old Premises and Current Evidence," p. 201.

106. See, e.g., Brandon S. Centerwall, "Race, Socioeconomic Status and Domestic Homicide, Atlanta, 1971-72," *American Journal of Public Health* 74 (1984): 813, 815 (reporting results of research and discussing prior studies), Mercy and Rosenberg et al., supra at 16, and Darnell F. Hawkins, "Inequality, Culture, and Interpersonal Violence," *Health Affairs*, 12 (1993): 80.

107. Gary Kleck, "Guns and Violence: A Summary of the Field," *Social Pathology* 1 (1995): 12, 34.

108. Gurr, *Violence in America*, p. 17.

109. O'Carroll, "Correspondence: CDC's Approach to Firearms Injuries," *Journal of the American Medical Association* 262 (1989): 348.

110. Dr. Mark Rosenberg, who directs the CDC's National Center for Injury Prevention and Control, has been quoted avowing his and the CDC's desire to create a public perception of firearms as "dirty, deadly—and banned." Rasberry, *Washington Post*, 19 October 1994, p. A23. In October 1993, the first annual Network Conference of the Handgun Epidemic Lowering Plan (HELP), a group founded and run by Dr. Christoffel, was held in Chicago. Speakers and attendees included Dr. Rosenberg and recipients of various CDC grants. In a September 29, 1993, letter to Dr. Edgar A. Suter, Dr. Christoffel rejected his application to attend the Conference on the ground that participants and attendees were limited to "like-minded individuals who represent organizations [whose goal is to] . . . use a public health model to work toward changing public attitudes so that it becomes socially unacceptable for private citizens to have handguns." See also the approving comments on Dr. Christoffel's group and goals by Dr. Rosenberg (quoted by Somerville, "Gun Control as Immunization").

111. D. P. Rice et al., *Cost of Injury in the United States: A Report to Congress* (Atlanta: CDC, 1989), p. 23. A similar misrepresentation was offered by a premier health advocacy sage, Garen Wintemute, "Firearms as Cause of Death in the

United States," p. 534 ("Since the early 1970s year-to-year changes in new firearm availability and firearms homicide have often occurred in parallel").

112. In that period the accumulated handgun stock increased from 39 million to 65.8 million and the total gun stock from 134.5 million to 198.3 million, an increase from 187.9 to 270.6 in handguns per 1000 Americans and from 627.0 to 815.5 in all guns. Kleck, *Targeting Guns*, table 3.1 In contrast, the homicide rate declined from 9.8 in 1974 to 8.4 in 1988. Bureau of Justice Statistics, *Sourcebook of Criminal Justice Statistics-1989* (Washington, D.C.: U.S. Department of Justice, 1990), p. 365 table 3.118.

For twenty-five-year figures showing a 27.7 percent decline in homicide—despite a 160 percent increase in handgun ownership over the period 1973-97—see Kates and Polsby, "Long Term Non-Relationship of Firearm Availability to Homicide."

113. See Schetky, "Children and Handguns," and her reply to a letter to the editor in "The Pediatric Forum" section of the *Journal*'s January 1986 issue. The Smith and Falk claim is identical except that they only blame handguns for a majority of accidental and criminal gun injuries. G. Smith and H. Falk, "Unintentional Injuries," in Robert W. Amler and H. Bruce Dull, eds., *Closing the Gap: The Burden of Unnecessary Illness* (New York: Oxford, 1987), p. 157.

114. Using multiyear UCR figures antigun health advocate Garen J. Wintemute calculated in 1989 that handguns "are used in 70-75 percent of firearm homicides" (not in 90 percent as Dr. Schetzy asserts). *Injury Prevention Network Newsletter*, p. 20.

115. "Correspondence," *New England Journal of Medicine* 320 (1989): 1216-17 (letter by NRA's Paul H. Blackman and response by Sloan and Kellermann et al.).

116. Sloan and Kellermann et al., "Handgun Regulations, Crime, Assaults," p. 1261.

117. Quoting Wintemute, *Injury Prevention Network Newsletter* p. 21; see also Mercy and Rosenberg, "Public Health Policy for Preventing Violence," p. 19; and Webster, Chaulk, Teret, and Wintemute, "Reducing Firearm Injuries," p. 76.

118. Quoting, respectively: Webster et al., "Reducing Firearm Injuries," 73-9, 73 and Christoffel, "Toward Reducing Pediatric Injuries from Firearms," p. 300. To the same effect see Calhoun, *Injury Prevention Network Newsletter*, p. 15 (most murderers "are neither felons nor crazy," but rather "people involved in family fights and fights over jobs and money, and people who are sad or depressed"; and Pickett and Hanlon, supra, footnote 79 at 496 ("murder is *almost always* an act of blind rage or illogical passion," with victims often guilty of provocative behavior, and "when it happens, the killer as well as the killed is the victim." Emphasis added.).

119. Goldsmith, "Edidemiologists Aim at New Target," p. 675 (quoting, inter alia, the president of the American College of Epidemiology); compare: *American Medical News*, editorial, 20 May 1991 ("uncontrolled ownership and use of firearms" is "one of the main causes of intentional and unintentional injury and death."); See also sources quoted in note 2.

120. Mark Rosenberg, "Violence as a Public Health Problem: A New Role for CDC and a New Alliance with Educators," *Educational Horizons* 62 (summer, 1984): 124-127. Emphasis added.

121. Ibid.

122. Mark Rosenberg et al. "Violence: Homicide, Assault, and Suicide," in Amler and Dull, *Closing the Gap*, p. 166.

123. "Gun Ownership as a Risk Factor for Homicide in the Home," *New England Journal of Medicine*, 329 (October 7, 1993): 1084–91. The authors are Arthur L. Kellermann, Frederick P. Rivara, Norman B. Rushforth, Joyce G. Banton, Donald T. Reay, Jerry T. Francisco, Ana B. Locci, Janice Prodzinski, Bela B. Hackman, and Grant Somes.

124. William G. Cochran and Gertrude M. Cox, *Experimental Designs*, 2d ed. (New York: John Wiley and Sons, Inc., 1992).

125. For discussion of intentional confounding see "Design and Analysis of Experiments" in Klaus Hinkelmann and Oscar Kempthorne, *Introduction to Experimental Design* (New York: John Wiley and Sons, Inc., 1994), p. 361.

126. Quoting from the abstract, p. 1084.

127. Gary Kleck, "Can Owning a Gun Really Triple the Owner's Chances of Being Murdered?" paper presented at the 1999 annual meeting of the American Society of Criminology; available from the author at Florida State University School of Criminology.

128. See Don B. Kates, "The Value of Civilian Arms Possession as Deterrent to Crime or Defense Against Crime," *American Journal of Criminal Law* 18 (1991): 113, 127-29, supplying examples and commenting: "Of course it is tragic when, for instance, an abused woman has to shoot to stop a (current or former) boyfriend or husband from beating her to death. But it is highly misleading to count such incidents as costs of gun ownership by misclassifying them with the very thing they prevent: murder between 'family and friends.' However atavistic or unpatriotic such incidents may be, they are not vigilantism and they are not costs; rather they are palpable benefits of defensive gun ownership from society's and the victims' point of view if not from their attackers."

129. Based on a survey of 2,190 felons in California, Michigan, and Texas prisons of the crimes they had committed in the two years prior to their incarceration, Chaiken and Chaiken determined that a small minority were responsible for most crimes, and particularly the serious ones. The average "violent predator" (their term for these career criminals) reported committing eight assaults, 63 robberies, 172 burglaries, 1,252 drug deals, and 214 miscellaneous other thefts in a one-year period. J. M and M. R. Chaiken, *Varieties of Criminal Behavior* (Santa Monica: Rand, 1982). Compare Marvin E. Wolfgang, *Delinquency in a Birth Cohort* (Chicago: University of Chicago Press, 1972) (between their tenth and eigh-

teenth years, of 9,945 Philadelphia boys born in 1945: 65.1 percent had no offenses; 16.2 percent had one offense; 12.4 percent had a few offenses; and 6.3 percent committed 51.9 percent of the offenses in the cohort—and these were more serious than the generality of offenses committed by the less active); L. W. Shannon, *Assessing the Relationship of Adult Criminal Careers: A Summary* (Washington, D.C.: U.S. Department of Justice, 1982) (5 to 7 percent of a birth cohort in Racine, Wisconsin, were involved in over 50 percent of police contacts and 5 to 14 percent were involved in all felonies in the birth cohort); P. E. Tracy et al., *Delinquency Careers in Two Birth Cohorts* (Chicago: University of Chicago Press, 1990) (between their tenth and eighteenth years, of 13,160 Philadelphia boys born in 1958: 67.2 percent were never arrested; 25.3 percent were arrested four or fewer times; 7.5 percent were arrested five or more times—and accounted for 60.6 percent of the arrests in the total birth cohort).

130. By way of analogy, suppose a study of people who had had a heart attack and then later died of another showed that more of them had taken up strenuous exercise after their first heart attack than had a control group of heart attack victims who had not taken up strenuous exercise after the first attack. That result would suggest that strenuous exercise was a risk factor for people who are at high risk of having a heart attack. But it would not prove anything about the level of risk strenuous exercise imposes on low (or ordinary) risk people who have never had a heart attack.

131. *NEJM-1993*, p. 1089 table 4.

132. Arthur L. Kellermann, personal communication. This research was supported by grants from the Centers for Disease Control and Prevention (CDC) of the National Institutes of Health. The CDC does not require that data resulting from their grants be made available to the public. This is in contrast to the policies of the National Institute of Justice, which requires comparable datasets to be made publicly available.

In 1995 the CDC and Kellermann were subject to severe criticism on this point in Congressional hearings, by witnesses (myself included) and legislators having influence over the CDC budget. Thereafter Kellermann was required by the CDC to archive at least some of his data so that scholars could evaluate it. Perhaps not coincidentally, some of his later publications began revealing data that reflected badly on his earlier conclusions. See, e.g., note number 127 and discussion in the text accompanying it.

133. Daniel D. Polsby, "Firearms Costs, Firearms Benefits and the Limits of Knowledge," *Journal of Criminal Law and Criminology* 86 (fall, 1995): 207, 210.

134. A. Bradford Hill, quoted by J. B. Chassan, *Research Design in Clinical Psychology and Psychiatry*, 2d. ed. (New York: Irvington, 1979).

135. Hinkelmann and Kempthorne, *Introduction to Experimental Design*, p. 22.

136. Patricia L. Brantingham and Paul J. Brantingham, "Notes on the Geom-

etry of Crime," chap. 1 in Paul J. Brantingham and Patricia L. Brantingham, eds., *Environmental Criminology* (Beverly Hills: Sage, 1981); Keith D. Harries, *The Geography of Crime and Justice* (New York: McGraw-Hill, 1974).

137. While the problem of unwillingness to admit gun ownership is not entirely absent as to the homicide case households, it is much less acute. *NEJM-1993*'s authors had police reports as to these households. In cases where the murder weapon was left near the body the police report would presumably so indicate; in cases where it was not, the report would presumably indicate that the home was searched for guns and other occupants (if any) asked about gun ownership and registration records consulted to see if a gun was registered to a person living in the household. The family of the deceased in the case home also had time between the homicide and the interview to go through the effects of the deceased and to discover a gun, if owned. None of this eliminates the possibility that a gun was kept in the homicide household, but that this was concealed from the police and they did not discover it, and the case proxy did not find know of it, or did not admit to it. But that possibility is far better minimized as to the homicide case households than as to the control households. There the accuracy of *NEJM-1993*'s gun ownership finding is entirely dependent on the truthfulness of the interviewees.

138. Kleck, *Point Blank*, appendix 2. We are tempted to remark that the quantitative difference between the bare paragraph they devote to this issue—which is vital to their argument—and the appendix Kleck devotes to it is emblematic of the qualitative difference in scholarship between Kleck and the entire health advocacy literature.

139. *NEJM-1993*, p. 1089. Emphasis Added, this work cites A. L. Kellermann et al., "Validating Survey Responses About Gun Ownership Among Owners of Registered Handguns," *American Journal of Epidemiology* 131 (1990): 1080–84.

140. The state of Tennessee and the city of Cleveland have various handgun registration or transfer regulations. Owners who have not adhered to these regulations have committed an offense which varies in seriousness depending on place of residence. The state of Washington has a permit system for dealer transfer. Additionally, some handgun owners may have heard of the extremely severe limitations on handgun possession in many large cities, e.g., Washington, D.C., New York, and Chicago. All of these would tend to make the owner reluctant to admit to the presence of an unregistered handgun or one which was not subjected to the full observance of transfer regulations. *NEJM-1993* does not mention how many of the guns in either the homicide or the control groups were owned legally.

141. Thomas B. Newman et al., "Designing a New Study, II: Cross-Sectional and Case-Control Studies," in Stephen B. Hulley and Steven R. Cummings, eds., *Designing Clinical Research* (NY: Williams and Wilkins, 1988), pp. 78–86.

142. Ibid.

143. Regarding the *New England Journal of Medicine*'s antigun policies and editorials, see p. 85 in this volume and the following editorials: Jerome P. Kassirer, "Guns in the Household," *New England Journal of Medicine* 329 (1993): 1117; Arnold S. Relman, "More Than Sutures and Transfusions," *New England Journal of Medicine* 297 (1977): 552; Franz J. Ingelfinger, "Therapeutic Action for a National Ill," *New England Journal of Medicine* 278 (1968): 1399. See also generally R. W. Hudgens, "Editorial: Preventing Suicide," *New England Journal of Medicine* 308 (1983): 897–98; J. A. Mercy and V. N. Houk, "Firearm Injuries: A Call for Science," *New England Journal of Medicine* 319 (1988): 1283–84.

"Poisoning the Well" for Gun Control

by Don B. Kates

I have long argued that the cause of moderate gun control has been doomed not by fanatic progun opposition, but by the extremist proposals and vituperative discourse of the antigun movement which impel gun owners to fanatic opposition to measures that, superficially at least, appear moderate and reasonable.[1] In this version of that argument, I focus more on the effects of antigun vituperation because extremist goals (prohibition-confiscation) are detailed in chapter 4.

It is a truism that many gun owners hysterically oppose controls that are indistinguishable from those that they readily accept as applied to automobiles. Yet underlying this irony are crucial differences in the rationale and implications for actual implementation of even apparently identical control mechanisms to firearms rather than cars. Illustrative of the differences is the fact that car regulation is not premised on the basis that cars are evils from which any decent person would recoil in horror—that anyone wanting to possess such an excrescence is atavistic and warped sexually, intellectually, educationally, and ethically. Nor are driver licensing, car registration, and so on, proposed or implemented as ways to radically reduce the availability of cars to ordinary citizens or with the goal of ultimately denying cars to all but the military, police, and those special individuals whom the military or police select to receive permits.[2]

Yet those are the terms many prominent and highly articulate "gun control" (more correctly, gun prohibition) advocates insist on using in promoting any kind of control proposal—regardless of whether it might be defended in more moderate terms.[3] To these advocates just owning a gun is analogous not to owning a car but to driving it while inebriated: "The mere possession of a gun is, in itself, an urge to kill, not only by design, but by accident, by madness, by fright, by bravado."[4]

Gun ownership being a per se illegitimate choice, banning it does not implicate any issue of freedom of choice. And the interests and desires of those who own, or want to own, guns are not entitled to consideration: "the need that some homeowners and shopkeepers believe they have for weapons to defend themselves" is contemptuously dismissed as representing "the worst instincts in the human character."[5] As detailed further below, such assertions that self-defense is atavistic and morally abhorrent run like a leit motif in statements by antigun luminaries and activists, both great and minor.[6]

A pervasive theme of antigun discourse is that gun ownership is a morally illegitimate choice: gun ownership is "simply beastly behavior";[7] the *Atlanta Constitution* editorializes that "the crazy gun lobbyists . . . say guns don't kill people. No, guns are doing something worse—they are killing civilization."[8] "Gun lunatics silence [the] sounds of civilization" a *Miami Herald* columnist declares while another, the distinguished cultural historian Garry Wills, regularly reviles "gun fetishists," "gun nuts" as "anti-citizens," "traitors, enemies of their own *patriae*," arming "against their own neighbors."[9] An even more eminent historian, Richard Hofstadter, applied to gun owners D. H. Lawrence's philippic against " 'the essential American soul' " as " 'hard, isolate and a killer.' "[10] Ramsey Clark, attorney general of LBJ, denounces gun ownership as an insult to the state (for "a state in which a citizen needs a gun to protect himself from crime has failed to perform its first purpose") and a return to barbarism, "anarchy, not order under law—a jungle where each relies on himself for survival."[11]

An alternative ground of denying that the interests of gun owners deserve respect or consideration is that espoused by Arthur Schlessinger Jr., Harriet Van Horne, Rep. Fortney Stark, Dr. Joyce Brothers, Harlan Ellison, and others. They assert that gun ownership involves no real choice;

it is actually only a preconditioned manifestation of sexual inadequacy or perversion.[12] (An amusing sidenote to this assertion is that, though it purports to rely on Freud, it reverses his actual view. Freud saw people who fear or loathe firearms, knives, etc. as sexual hysterics—unconscious victims of a terror that causes them to hysterically confuse long objects or pointed weapons with the penis.[13])

Based on their exhaustive review of gun control literature, Professors Wright, Rossi, and Daly characterize the "antigun" view as holding that gun owners are "demented and blood-thirsty psychopaths whose concept of fun is to rain death on innocent creatures, both human and otherwise."[14] (It is worth noting that this view of gun owners is just a currently respectable bigotry: on average, gun owners are actually more prestigiously employed and better paid than nonowners, are not more sexist or racist, or more likely to suffer from mental illness and do not endorse aggressive violence or express other antisocial attitudes.[15])

As will be demonstrated in chapter 4, these views dominate the antigun movement and fix its ultimate agenda, if not its avowed, short-term agenda. These views, this ultimate agenda, and the vituperative rhetoric that so often accompanies them play into the hand of the gun lobby by convincing gun owners that "gun control" is just a synonym for execration of them.

A Tripartite Debate

To understand the American gun debate requires seeing that it has three sides rather than just the two in which it is normally conceptualized. This is not to deny that the debate is monopolized by the conflict between the antigun view (described above), which dominates the active gun control movement, and the progun view (hysterical opposition to any additional control proposal, however moderate and reasonable). But the debate's monopolization by these opposing high-decibel extremes obscures the relative paucity of their adherents. The fact is that even if those adherents were added together, their combined numbers would not represent more than a minority of the American public.

The vast majority—including a majority of gun owners—espouse the markedly different view I call "procontrol." It differs from the antigun view in recognizing the legitimacy of, and according consideration to, the choice to own guns (especially for self-defense). At the same time, unlike the progun view, the "procontrol" view sees a need to accommodate legitimate gun owner interests to the social imperative for controlling a dangerous instrumentality.[16]

Poisoning the Well for Gun Control

Unfortunately the procontrol consensus has been undermined and frustrated as the American gun debate has been monopolized over the past quarter-century by extreme views that are inimical to compromise and accommodation. Guns are owned by approximately 46 percent of American households.[17] So all the gun lobby needs to do in order to marshal massive opposition against gun control proposals is capitalize on the extremist, vitriolic terms of debate established by antigun advocates. As one analyst notes, exposure to this debate

> convinces America's handgun owners that they are a hated minority whose days are numbered by mortal enemies—enemies who hate *them* more than crime. With the die cast so, gun owners are made to think that *they have everything to lose* if those who loath them have any success at all. [Knowing this, the gun lobby actually] disseminate[s] the nastier [antigun] cartoons and vituperative op-ed pieces in publications read by gun owners to fan the flames of incipient paranoia.[18]

The last point is both remarkable in itself and telling in its implications: in reprinting antigun cartoons the gun lobby is actually paying antigun cartoonists royalties for penning those cartoons! This money is well spent. Essential to mobilizing gun owner opposition is that they be convinced that every gun control proposal is bottomed on hatred for them—that however moderate and reasonable a control may seem, it is actually only a further step toward the hatemongers' ultimate goal of confiscating all guns. Only by thus convincing gun owners can the gun lobby move them to hysterically oppose controls, many of which they themselves deem reasonable and sensible in the abstract. Indispensable to gun lobby success is an antigun discourse which convinces gun owners that "gun control" is not a criminological imperative but a matter of culturally or ethically based hatred of them.

This brings me to a further disclaimer: the subject here is the political dynamic, not courtesy. Gun owner response to antigun vituperation is no less hateful. Among other things, such gun owner response is notoriously counter-productive as political rhetoric. But, in the long run, antigun hatefulness is even more counterproductive. In a nation where more than 100 million potential voters live in households with upwards of 250 million guns, antigun advocates create almost insurmountable opposition to controls by presenting them in terms of hatred and contempt for gun owners. Moreover, what antigun advocates do by heaping contempt on gun owners is alienate those whose compliance is indispensable if gun laws are to work. No doubt antigun crusaders find emotional satisfaction in reviling those who oppose their views as sexually warped "bulletbrains" who engage in "simply beastly behavior," "gun lunatics [who] silence [the] sounds of civilization," "terrorists," and "psychotics,"[19] the "pusher's best friend,"[20] "hunters who drink beer, don't vote and lie to their wives about where they were all weekend"[21]; in characterizing the murder of children as "another slaughter cosponsored by the National Rifle Association,"[22] and in cartooning gun owners as intellectually retarded, educationally backward and morally obtuse thugs, vigilantes, or Klansmen.[23] But the emotional satisfaction of engaging in such vituperation must be weighed against the catastrophic effects it has for the cause of gun control.

In sum, the key to the gun lobby's ability to defeat new controls is the divisive effect of antigun discourse on a consensus that is only procontrol. As discussed below, this is not just a matter of alienating gun owners (though that would probably suffice to stalemate the debate in any event), but of disagreement by most Americans with the moral and social premises underlying the antigun view.

The "Gun Control Paradox"

Sixty-plus years of nationwide polls have documented a virtually universal American consensus for some forms of "gun control."[24] Moreover polls which isolate gun owners as an opinion group find a majority of them also favor controls, many of which are anathema to the gun lobby. The gun lobby's notorious ability over the same period to defeat nearly all legislative proposals embodying this consensus has been called the "gun control paradox."

One may quibble with the "paradox" concept, because some of its proponents give credence to meaningless polls incompetently phrased in terms of public approval of "gun control" (undefined). This is meaningless because it is impossible to divine from an affirmative answer whether respondents are expressing support: (a) for the approximately twenty thousand controls that already exist; (b) for stricter enforcement of these existing laws; (c) for some undefined additional control—much less; or (d) for any specific kind of new control. Amazingly, such incompetent phraseology persists to this day, as do also similarly defective questions seeking to elicit opinion about "stricter" gun laws.[25]

Indicative of the fatuousness of these undefined questions is that where polls do focus on specific new control proposals, one of the most popular is a law *requiring* that judges give severe prison terms to anyone found guilty of a gun crime.[26] Though such a law enjoys apparently uniform support across the spectrum of progun, procontrol, and antigun respondents, it is the "gun control program" of the National Rifle Association. Conversely, anent the measure which antigun advocates deem the primary goal for an acceptable gun control policy, polls consistently show that most Americans reject banning defensive handgun ownership.[27]

Nevertheless, it remains true that large majorities of the American populace support a variety of other control proposals that are anathema to the gun lobby (see note 27). Its ability to defeat these popular proposals has already been explained. The procontrol consensus is constantly undercut by the divisive goals and vituperative rhetoric of a gun "control" movement that is ardently antigun. The first seriously divisive issue is self-defense, which the majority of Americans see as the most compelling reason to have a gun, but the antiadvocate sees as the most compelling reason to forbid them. (This is discussed below under the heading "On the Morality of Personal Self-Defense.")

A broader, but closely related, conceptual dissonance arises over the question of accommodation between the interests involved. Basic to the procontrol concept is that controls must represent a just and reasonable accommodation of the legitimate interests of gun owners to the social imperative of regulating deadly weapons. But in the antigun view, owning a gun is not a legitimate choice, wherefore the interests of those who have made or would make that abhorrent choice deserve no consideration. Guns are simply evil, those who choose to own them being "gun lunatics who silence the sound of civilization," "anticitizens" representing "the worst instincts in the human character," "demented and blood-thirsty psychopaths whose concept of fun is to rain death on innocent creatures, both human and otherwise."

Antigun advocates do not always express themselves in such vituperative terms. But insofar as they acknowledge there might be some legitimate interests in having a gun, those interests (such as target shooting) are clearly only trifling, if not contemptible. As the author of a Ford Foundation study of gun control observes, "gun owners believe (rightly in my view) that the gun controllers would be willing to sacrifice their interests even if the crime control benefits were tiny."[28]

I shall address these matters further in the next section. But first we must consider an alternative explanation of the "gun control paradox." This alternate explanation emphasizes differential levels of commitment between gun control supporters and opponents. Pollster George Gallup has argued that the extreme commitment level of gun owners frightens legislators into seeing gun control as too politically hazardous to embrace: though the great majority of Americans support gun control, few of them are fervent enough to vote against legislators who eschew it; whereas

> citizens who oppose any kind of gun control laws, though constituting a minority of the public, feel so strongly about this issue that they will do anything they can do to defeat such legislation. As a result they have succeeded in keeping strict gun laws from being adopted in most states and by the federal government.[29]

This thesis misanalyzes the tripartite division of views I have limned as if it were only a dichotomy of progun versus antigun. The conceptual error results in empirical falsification. For instance, what does his phrase "strict gun laws" mean? At a very minimum, from the antigun position, "strict gun laws" would include banning defensive handgun ownership. Yet, as discussed above, polls consistently show that only a rather small minority of the American people support such a prohibition. So there is nothing paradoxical about its nonenactment.

Gallup's thesis becomes empirically sustainable only when a third group is recognized—a procontrol majority which is less fanatic than either the pro- or antigun extremists.

Gun Control Plebiscites

More problematic yet is that Gallup's hypothesis is directly contradicted by the outcomes when gun issues have been submitted to plebiscite. Inherent in Gallup's hypothesis is that if "strict gun laws" were put to a plebiscite, the public would enact them. The problem, as Gallup sees it, is that majoritarian sentiment is frustrated because it has to be implemented by legislators who are personally too timorous to translate it into law. Belying this thesis are the overwhelming rejections of sweeping antigun initiatives when put to the voters in Massachusetts, California, and Washington (state) in 1976, 1982, and 1997, respectively. (Also over the past thirty years voters in eleven other states have amended their state constitutions to add guarantees that every responsible, law-abiding adult may possess a gun.[30]) Obviously actual tallies of the electorate provide much better evidence of the views of the voters (in these states at least) than Gallup's polling of only 500 to 1,000 citizens who supposedly represent the views of upwards of 215 million potential voters.

The Massachusetts, California, and Washington initiatives are especially significant because the gun control movement itself chose those states as the ideal places to go on the offensive. These states were chosen because they had exhibited the nation's most "liberal" electoral record and because polls supposedly showed that urban electorates supported outlawing or radically reducing handgun ownership. Of particular significance for my thesis here is the pattern of opinion change in all three states as the campaign progressed. Polls taken at the outset showed both initiatives winning by roughly the same 65 to 71 percent majorities by which they eventually lost. (Not coincidentally, at the outset the sponsors, particularly in California, sought to present the initiative as a handgun registration measure, downplaying its prohibition of new handgun sales.) Subsequent polls showed support steadily eroding as the campaign went on. In other words, the more the proposals were debated—with concomitant exposition of their antigun premises—the more opposition they garnered, until eventually they were defeated by "landslide" margins.[31]

These results dovetail with findings from sophisticated in-depth polls sponsored by both pro- and antigun groups (though using different independent polling organizations). Unlike the short Gallup and Harris polls, which miss nuances because the number of questions asked are severely limited, the sponsored polls involve extensive questioning designed to reveal patterns and attitudes. The results are highly consistent, despite the differing wording and antagonistic sponsors. They show that most Americans support permissive controls on guns similar to those now applied to automobiles and driving: a permit system to disarm felons, juveniles, and the mentally unstable—but without denying ordinary, responsible adults the freedom to choose to own guns for family defense.[32]

My analysis is further confirmed by the gun lobby's defeat in the 1988 Maryland referendum. That referendum's subject was a law passed by the Maryland legislature to prohibit future sales of Saturday-night specials.The law incorporated standards expressly defining the only handguns to be banned as being diminutive and too cheap and poorly made to be useful for self-defense or sport. The law created a commission to apply those standards, its membership including representatives of a gun company, pro- and antigun groups, and law enforcement.

Progun extremists, believing the commission's powers would be abused to outlaw sale of most or all handguns, dragged a reluctant National Rifle Association into mounting a referendum under the state's highly restricted referendum procedure. Far from offering a clear-cut referendum on guns (or just on handguns), the campaign revolved around the fact that the standards embodied in the new law expressly guaranteed every responsible, law-abiding adult freedom to buy any handgun that would be useful for self-defense or sport.

This was confirmed by the denouement (after voters ratified the statute by a 57-43 percent margin). Fifteen months later, two antigun commission members were complaining bitterly that under the standards the commission had been compelled to approve almost 99 percent of handguns submitted to it (10 rejections out of almost 800 models submitted) and that the approved weapons included a 36-shot "assault pistol."[33] Four weeks later, the approved list had grown to 930, including the Mac-10 and 11 "assault pistols." This was particularly ironic since one complaining commissioner, Baltimore Police Chief Cornelius Behan, had just displayed a Mac-11 in a *New York Times* ad (sponsored by Handgun Control, Inc.) calling for a federal ban on such guns. Behan explained that he and the other commissioners had had to approve the Mac-11 because "the Maryland law is designed to take out of circulation [only] highly concealable, poorly manufactured, low-caliber weapons. The Mac-10 and 11 unfortunately don't fit into that category."[34]

It typifies the mutually skewed perspectives of pro- and antigun advocates that both see the 1988 Maryland referendum as a great antigun victory. What the referendum really was is a *procontrol* victory—at the expense of both extremes. Obviously it was a defeat for the gun lobby's fanatic antiregulatory stance. But for the antigun lobby it was a pyrrhic victory attainable only by implicitly conceding the unsalability of its core view to the American people. The fruits of that victory were meager: about 1 percent of handgun models representing perhaps .001 percent of the handguns sold annually in the United States were disapproved for future sale in Maryland (without affecting either handguns currently owned in Maryland or long guns at all). And the victory itself was attained only by the ruinous means of embracing a law that expressly rejects both the antigun purpose of outlawing handguns and the premises underlying that purpose.

On the Morality of Personal Self-Defense

One of those premises is great dubiety about, or even flat rejection of, the legitimacy of self-defense against violence. A half century ago Wechsler could still justify the legal right of deadly force self-defense in terms of the *"universal* judgment that there is no social interest in preserving the lives of the aggressors at the cost of those of their victims."[35] That is not a universal judgment today—which is the reason for the existence of a movement that is ideologically *antigun* rather than interested in rational gun controls. Typical of views that motivate the antigun movement is the reaction of feminist icon Betty Friedan to the trend of women buying firearms for defense against rape and murder. Friedan denounces this trend as "a horrifying, obscene perversion of feminism," asserting "that lethal violence even in self-defense only engenders more violence and that gun control should override any personal need for safety."[36]

Indicative of how widespread such views are in modern America is that in 1985, 13 percent of respondents to a Gallup Poll answered negatively the question "If the situation arose, would you use deadly force against another person in self-defense?" Presumably some respondents were expressing only their personal repugnance at killing rather than any moral imperative. But that is not the whole explanation as is clear from responses to another

Gallup question which was posed at the height of the Bernhard Goetz controversy* in two different samplings taken a month apart. In one survey, 23 percent of the respondents said that self-defense was "never" justified; in the other, 17 percent gave that response.

No less telling is the language in which the Gallup Poll put the question: "Do you feel that *taking the law into one's own hands, often called vigilantism* is justified by circumstances?" [Emphasis added.] The italicized phrase treats the legal right of self-defense as morally, if not legally, wrong. This language is subject to criticism as being highly prejudicial; perhaps even prejudicial enough to impugn the polls' results. But the Gallup organization's considered use of it is itself evidence of a concept which is now quite widespread as is also shown by endemic misuse of the word "vigilantism." That word is constantly misused as if it applied only to private citizens and signified that there is some legal wrong in private citizens using deadly force to defend their own, and their families', lives from violent criminal attack. This is a solecism. Deadly force is clearly legal in such a situation.[37] The misusage does not so much broaden the historical meaning of vigilantism as contradict it.[38]

In contrast to the responses given above, 71 to 80 percent of respondents in the two 1985 Gallup surveys believed there are circumstances in which self-defense is justified. Indeed, 3 to 8 percent of them *volunteered* the assertion that self-defense is *always* justified, despite Gallup's failure to offer that option. Such approval sharply differentiates the beliefs of the majority of Americans from the moral premises embraced by antigun advocates.

In contrast, disapprobation for self-defense—and a desire to make it pragmatically impossible, if not legally so—permeates the antigun movement, surfacing whenever gun issues are debated. However moderate, even innocuous, a new gun control proposal may be, its appearance sparks impassioned verbal attacks to the effect that "the only purpose of a [gun, handgun, etc.] is to kill." The clear implication is that the use of potentially deadly weapon is always wrong—even when necessary to defend against

---

*Bernard Goetz, a New York City resident who had been mugged, began carrying a gun illegally (because carry licenses are unavailable to ordinary people in New York City). Accosted on a subway by several armed African American youths, Goetz shot them, disappeared for a couple of weeks, and then turned himself in. At his subsequent trial, he was found innocent of assault and attempted murder charges but convicted of carrying a gun illegally. An account by a preeminent authority on American criminal law, Columbia Law School professor George P. Fletcher, is *The Trial of Bernard Goetz* (New York: Free Press, 1988), p. 156.

violent felony. To those who dominate the antigun movement the purpose of gun control is to prevent victims from having the means of self-defense.

Illustrative is an article condemning defensive gun ownership that has been repeatedly published by the Board of Church and Society of the United Methodist Church. (As discussed below, the board is the founder and long-term sponsor of the premier antigun group, the National Coalition to Ban Handguns.) The article first appeared in the board's magazine, written by the magazine's editor, Rev. Allen Brockway. Recall that it has always been lawful for victims to use deadly force to repel robbers or rapists or other felons whose acts threaten great bodily harm, maiming, or death;[39] indeed, the maxim "a man's home is his castle" derives from early English cases upholding the use of deadly force against burglars and arsonists.[40] Yet Rev. Brockway solemnly advises women that their Christian duty is to submit to rape rather than do anything that might imperil a rapist's life. Rhetorically posing the question as "Is the Robber My Brother?" Rev. Brockway answers affirmatively, for though the burglary victim or the

> woman accosted in the park by a rapist is [not] likely to consider the violator to be a neighbor whose safety is of immediate concern . . . [c]riminals are members of the larger community no less than are others. As such they are our neighbors or, as Jesus put it, our brothers. . . . [Though violent criminals act wrongfully,] it is equally wrong for the victim to kill, save in those extremely rare circumstances when the unambiguous alternative is one own's death.[41]

Such views are neither unrepresentative of the antigun movement nor uninfluential therein. To reiterate, the National Coalition to Ban Handguns (NCBH), the senior national antigun lobbying group, is the Board of Church and Society's creature. NCBH's national office is in the Methodist Board's Washington building and the board was NCBH's official fiscal agent until 1976 when gun lobby complaints to the Internal Revenue Service threatened the church's tax exemption.[42]

Rev. Brockway's views are not some bizarre expression of male sexist extremism. Rather they just typify the profoundly antiself-defense attitude underlying the antigun movement as the views of Betty Friedan quoted above suggest. (Those interested in an authentically *feminist* approach to firearms issues must look not to antigun luminaries, but to those who argue against banning guns.[43]) Likewise then-New York Gov. Mario Cuomo avowed that Bernhard Goetz was morally wrong in shooting *even if that was clearly necessary* to resist felonious attack: "If this man was defending himself against attack with reasonable force, he would be legally [justified, but] not morally."[44]

Rev. Brockway seems to concede that a woman may shoot a rapist if she knows to a certainty that he will kill her. But another NCBH affiliate, the Presbyterian Church (USA), disagrees. Its official position is that handguns should be banned because a victim may not take an attacker's life under any circumstance, even if she knows he will kill her after the rape. Testifying before a Congressional panel, Rev. Kathy Young, the church's representative, stated: "The General Assembly [of the Presbyterian Church (USA)] has declared in the context of handgun control and in many other contexts, that it *is opposed to 'the killing of anyone, anywhere, for any reason'* (1972)."[45] Rev. Young emphasized that the Presbyterian position is moderate in that it seeks only to ban handguns, not hunting guns. Rifles and shotguns are not condemned because the church sees them as owned "by sports people," unlike handguns, whose purpose is self-defense (see note 45).

Making no distinction between murderers and victims lawfully defending themselves, the Presbyterian Church (USA) proclaims, "There is no other reason to own a handgun (that we have envisioned, at least) than to kill someone with it." Other major religious groups join the Presbyterians in denouncing gun ownership for self-defense as incipient vigilantism and categorically condemning handguns as "weapons of death . . . that are designed only for killing."[46]

The same general sentiments are embraced by HCI's Sarah and James Brady, though in secular form and with concern to preclude defensive possession of long guns as well as handguns. Professor Wills agrees, decrying "individual self protection" as "antisocial behavior" and calling for the confiscation of all handguns (indeed, all firearms kept for self-defense):

> Every civilized society must disarm its citizens against each other. Those who do not trust their own people become predators upon their own people. The sick thing is that haters of fellow Americans often think of themselves as patriots.
>
> Give up your gun the gun nut says, and you give up your freedom. . . . *Trust no one but yourself to vindicate your cause. Not the law. Not your representatives. Not your fellow citizens.* Every handgun owned in America is an implicit declaration of war on one's neighbor. When the chips are down, its owner says, he will not trust any other arbiter but force personally wielded.[47]

While the Bradys assert "the only reason for guns in civilian hands is for sporting purposes,"[48] the *New York Times*, the *Detroit Daily Press*, and many other antigun luminaries go farther yet. They seek to ban and have confiscated all firearms whatever, on the rationale that

> no private citizen has any reason or need at any time to possess a gun. This applies to both honest citizens and criminals. We realize the Constitution guarantees the "right to bear arms" but this should be changed.[49]
>
> One way to discourage the gun culture is to remove the guns from the hands and shoulders of people who are not in the law enforcement business.[50]

To reiterate, despite differences over legislative strategy, those who dominate the gun "control" movement are united in their belief that self-defense is atavistic and morally abhorrent. The natural outgrowth of this point of view is the law which NCBH succeeded in having adopted by the District of Columbia City Council in 1976: householders may not buy handguns and no guns of any type may be kept assembled or loaded for self-defense.[51] While HCI claims to be more moderate than NCBH, it, too, supports this as the ultimate gun control law. (Not only did HCI file a brief supporting the law when it was challenged, in the last several years HCI president Richard Aborn has urged adoption of the same law on cities around the country, as I heard him do on a radio show in San Francisco. For a detailed examination of HCI's prohibitionist views see chapter 4.)[52]

Gun control proposals presented in these terms are patently unacceptable to the kind of people who own guns. Though those peoples' attitudes and psychological profiles are not generally distinguishable from the rest of the population, one respect in which they do differ is in being even more likely than nonowners to approve the use of defensive force against violent felons.[53] This approval seems to transcend political differences: Analysis of another national poll reveals that, while liberals are less likely to own guns than the general populace, those liberals who do own a gun are just as willing as other gun owners to use it if necessary to repel a burglar.[54]

But it cannot be inferred that belief in the legitimacy of self-defense is confined to gun owners. Though such belief is no longer "universal," it was exhibited by the 78 percent of the respondents in the 1985 Gallup Poll who averred that, if the situation arose, they would themselves use deadly force against an attacker. (Of the remaining respondents 9 percent did not know whether they would use deadly force and 13 percent would not.) Even if 50 of those 78 percentage points represent respondents who reside in the roughly 50 percent of households that have guns, that leaves another 28 percentage points (i.e., over half of the nongun owners) who accept the legitimacy of deadly force self-defense. It is little wonder that public enthusiasm for gun control proposals fades as those associated with them express an attitude toward self-defense which is disagreeable to a large majority of the public and vehemently so to upwards of 50 percent of the public.

Conclusion

Why do those I describe as "antigun" insist that advocacy of gun controls include portraying gun owners as "lunatics," "anticitizens," "terrorists," etc.? While this may partially reflect mere cultural antagonism against gun owners, it also involves genuine, ethically based abhorrence of self-defense and consequent abhorrence of the gun owners and the gun as symbols thereof. To reiterate some of the quotations given earlier:

> No private citizen has any reason at any time to possess a gun. . . . [T]he need that some homeowners and shopkeepers believe they have for weapons to defend themselves [represents] the worst instincts in the human character. . . . I see no reason . . . why anyone in a democracy should own a weapon. . . . [W]eapons of death . . . designed only for killing. . . . There is no other reason to own a handgun (that we have envisioned, at least) than to kill someone with it. . . . The mere possession of a gun is an urge to kill.

Antigun insistence on this kind of discourse is indispensable to the gun lobby's success in defeating control proposals that, in principle, enjoy overwhelming support. Instead of dealing with the proposals' individual merits, the gun lobby is enabled to mobilize gun owners' opposition by portraying all "control" as a hate-inspired scheme designed to systematically multiply controls to the ultimate purpose of making gun ownership impossible. It is this discourse which convinces gun owners that "gun control" is not a criminological imperative but an expression of culturally or ethically based hatred of them.

Recognizing this, gun control groups often try to refrain from officially expressing antigun rationales. Unfortunately, that is not enough to counteract the chorus of (more or less) unofficial antigun champions hailing even the most moderate control proposals as steps toward the eventual banning of all guns. In principle, procontrol forces could defuse this by disavowing and vehemently denouncing overtly antigun rationales for moderate controls. But antigun advocates are so numerous and influential in the so-called gun control movement that it is impossible for less extreme forces to repudiate antigun ideology and disassociate their proposals from it. Yet the failure to repudiate antigun extremism makes it impossible to convince skeptical gun owners that a restriction championed by those who revile them does not really do or imply what those enemies claim.

Thus one reason for the defeat of gun controls which seem to have almost universal support is that antigun discourse has made fanatic opponents out of gun owners who would otherwise have been supporters. The second (and related) obstacle to enactment of gun controls is that certain elements that underlie antigun discourse tend to alienate a substantial proportion of even nongun owners who would otherwise support moderate controls. Though polls show that most Americans support "gun control" (undefined), what that means to them (and why they support it) is very different from what (and why) antigun activists support. Close analysis of recent state plebiscites demonstrates this and the baleful effect expression of antigun rationales has upon gun control efforts that otherwise would enjoy overwhelming support. The intense debate in these campaigns exposes how different the public's "procontrol" pragmatism is from the moralism of "antigun" groups.

It is not the innate strength of the gun lobby that defeats gun control proposals. Rather it is antigun zealots whose goals and equally extreme discourse, even when arguing for more moderate controls, alienate a public that would otherwise be open to rational ideas for control.

Notes

1. This chapter is a revision of my paper "Bigotry, Symbolism, and Ideology in the Battle Over Gun Control," presented at the 1990 Annual Meeting of the Law and Society Association and published in a different revision under the same title in the 1992 *Public Interest Law Review*.

2. The antigun strategy of incremental movement toward disarming the general population is documented in chapter 4.

3. See, e.g., Handgun Control, Inc. (HCI) Vice President Jeanne Shield's description, in a May 8, 1978, *Newsweek* interview, of NRA members as macho men who "don't understand the definition of a civilized society." To the same effect, see: Molly Ivins, "If Guns Were Outlawed," *Chicago Sun-Times*, 20 August 1999 and "Ban the Things. Ban Them All," *Washington Post*, 16 March 1993; Garry Wills, "NRA Is Complicit in the Deaths of Two Children," *Detroit Free Press*, 6 September 1994 ("Every civilized society must disarm its citizens against each other"), Charles Krauthammer, "Disarm the Citizenry," *Washington Post*, 5 April 1996 ("ultimately, a civilized society must disarm its citizenry. . . . "). See also discussion and citations given in T. Markus Funk, "Is the True Meaning of the Second Amendment Really Such a Riddle," *Howard Law Journal* 39 (1995): 412 n. 4.

4. Sydney J Harris, *Chicago Daily News*, 11 April 1967. Compare "Taming the Gun Monster: How Far to Go," *Los Angeles Times*, 22 October 1993 and "Taming the Monster: The Guns Among Us," *Los Angeles Times*, 10 December 1993.

5. "Guns and the Civilizing Process," *Washington Post*, 26 September 1972. Compare *New York Times* editorial, 24 September 1975 ("One way to discourage the gun culture is to remove the guns from the hands and shoulders of people who are not in the law enforcement business").

U.S. Senator Dianne Feinstein agrees, confessing that she only refrains from proposing such a law because too few other senators would support her. "If it were up to me I would tell Mr. and Mrs. America to turn them in—turn them *all* in." Quoted by Don Feder, "Gun Control Delusions," *Washington Times*, 30 August 1994.

6. E.g., James Brady, interviewed in *Parade* magazine, "In Step With: James Brady," 26 June 1994, p. 18 (Q: "Aren't any handguns defensible?" A: "For target shooting, that's ok. Get a license and go to the range. [But not f]or defense of the home—that's why we have police departments."). To the same effect see the testimony of Robert Replogle, M.D., University of Chicago professor and cofounder of the Medical Council on Handgun Abuse, before a Congressional Committee: "The only legitimate use of a handgun that I can understand is for target shooting." *Handgun Crime Control Hearings*, 1975-1976 Senate Judiciary Committee [Subcommittee re Juvenile Delinquency Oversight of the 1968 Gun Control Act, vol. 2 p. 1974; and that of Rev. Kathy Young, testifying behalf of the Presbyterian Church, USA that it does not seek to ban rifles and shotguns because they are to be used for sport but only handguns which are illegitimate because their purpose is personal defense—*Hearings on Legislation to Modify the 1968 Gun Control Act*, House Judiciary Committee, Subcommittee on Crime, 1985-86; vol. 1 pp. 127, 128.

7. "Gun Toting: A Fashion Needing Change," *Science News* 93 (1968): 613, 614; see also Harlan Ellison, "Fear Not Your Enemies," *Heavy Metal* (March 1981) and Ralph Luedens, "Wretchedness Is a Warm Gun," *Progressive* 48 (1984): 50.

8. *Atlanta Constitution* (editorial), 20 August 1993, p. A12.

9. References for these and similarly vituperative comments will be found in notes 3 and 7 above, and in chapter 1 note 20.

10. Richard Hofstadter, "America As a Gun Culture," in *American Heritage* (October 1970): 82.

11. Ramsey Clark, *Crime in America* (New York: Pocket, 1970), p. 88.

12. See, e.g., Margo Jefferson, "The Lethal Icon That Is Turning Upon Its Worshippers," *New York Times*, 9 August 1999, p. B2 (describing gun owners as men in need of Viagra "due to their terror of being weak and unmanned"), and Harlan Ellison, "Sex Education Belongs in the Gun Store," *U.S. Catholic* (August 1979). See Emannuel Tanay's views to the same effect quoted in chapter 2.

13. Ellison, "Sex Education Belongs in the Gun Store," *U.S. Catholic* (August 1979).

14. James D. Wright, Peter Rossi, and Kathleen Daly, *Under the Gun: Weapons, Crime and Violence in the United States* (New York: Aldine, 1983), p. 4.

15. See the section titled "The Character of Gun Owners" in chap. 1 above.

16. As discussed below, public opinion polls consistently show most Americans are skeptical that gun controls can do much about crime and particularly dubious about the likelihood of disarming criminals through gun control. The difference between the people I call progun and those I call procontrol may be illustrated by their disparate reactions to the fact that most Americans still support certain gun controls, despite this skepticism. The progun view would condemn this as contradictory and irrational: why support legislation that you see as of little or no use? Those having a procontrol view would see that as the logic of over-simplification: of course it is unrealistic to think that all or most criminals will obey gun laws any more than other laws. But a law is sensible if, while it does not disarm the law abiding, it might cause even one criminal to disarm—or if it might allow his incarceration when he is found illegally in possession of a gun.

17. Gary Kleck, *Targeting Guns* (New York: Aldine, 1997), pp. 98–99.

18. Lance Stell, "Guns, Politics, and Reason," *Journal of American Culture* 9 (1986): 71, 73. Emphasis in original.

19. References for these and similarly vituperative comments will be found in note 9 above.

20. Guest editorial by Senator Edward M. Kennedy, "Pusher's Best Friend, the NRA," *New York Times*, 22 March 1989; See also Pete Hamill, "A Meeting of NRA's Harlem Branch," *New York Post*, 4 April 1989, and the August 7, 1988, *Louisville Courier-Journal*, p. 6 ("The National Rifle Association, its propagandists and it supporters work day and night to make sure that every hood in the country can get his hands on a gun. They couldn't be more guilty if they stood there slip-

ping pistols to the drug dealers and robbers. If justice were done, they would be in prison."). In fact (though it has often obtusely opposed even reasonable controls that affect *law abiding citizens*), the NRA is the principal architect of laws barring gun ownership by anyone who has been convicted of a felony. Don B. Kates, "Handgun Prohibition and the Original Meaning of the Second Amendment," *Michigan Law Review* 82 (1983): 209–10 (citing state laws dating from the early twentieth century and federal laws from the 1930s through the present day).

21. This remark was first made, and then retracted, by then-N.Y. Governor Mario Cuomo. He later apologized to the NRA, writing that "it is unintelligent and unfair" to "disparage any large group." *Time*, May 27, 1985.

22. Editorial cartoon, *Milwaukee Journal*, 22 January 1989, p. 12J.

23. References for these cartoons are supplied in chapter 1, note 20.

24. A magisterial summary will be found in chapter 10 of Gary Kleck, *Targeting Guns: Firearms and Their Control* (New York: Aldine, 1997).

25. Ibid., pp. 328–29.

26. Congressional Research Service, "Attitudes Toward Gun Control," in *Federal Regulation of Firearms: A Report Prepared for the U.S. Senate Judiciary Committee by the Congressional Research Service* (Washington, D.C.: U.S. Government Printing Office, 1982), p. 249 table 7; Kleck, *Targeting Guns*, p. 347.

27. In Kleck's, *Targeting Guns*, table 10.1 shows that support for banning handguns ranged from 31-45 percent in polls taken over the twenty-year period 1975-94. Closer examination shows that support is highly dependent on the way the question is worded. The only question that clearly, unambiguously involved a total ban to civilians garnered only a 23 percent minority (December 1993). Just two weeks later 39 percent supported a law limiting handgun ownership to owners licensed by the police. Other polls have indicated large majorities support a license requirement for owning any kind of gun, but with police having no discretion as to issuance. The license would have to issue to everyone who met certain legally fixed qualifications. Kleck, *Targeting Guns*, pp. 325–26.

28. Mark Moore, "The Bird in Hand: A Feasible Strategy for Gun Control," *Journal of Policy Analysis and Management* 2 (1983): 185, 187-88.

29. George Gallup, *The Sophisticated Poll Watcher's Guide* (Wilmington: Gallup Press, 1972), p. 105.

30. Idaho, Louisiana, New Hampshire, Nevada, West Virginia, Utah, Maine, Virginia, North Dakota, and Nebraska. (In addition, Delaware enacted such a constitutional provision by legislative action.) See discussion in Stephen P. Halbrook, *A Right to Bear Arms* (Westport, Conn.: Greenwood Press, 1989), pp. 118ff., and Robert Dowlut, "Bearing Arms in State Bills of Rights, Judicial Interpretation, and Public Housing," *St. Thomas Law Review* 5 (1992): 203.

31. See generally, L. Brent Bozell and Tim Graham, "An NRA Victory? That's Not Fit to Print," *Wall Street Journal*, 21 November 1997, and David Bordua, "Adversary Polling and the Construction of Social Meaning: Implications in Gun Control Elections in Massachusetts and California," *Law and Policy Quarterly* 5 (1983): 345-66.

32. Bordua, "Adversary Polling and the Construction of Social Meaning: Implications in Gun Control Elections in Massachusetts and California," *Law and Policy Quarterly* 5 (1983): 345-66; James D. Wright, "Public Opinion and Gun Control: A Comparison of Results from Two Recent Surveys," *Annals of the American Academy of Political and Social Sciences* 455 (1981): 24; Kleck, *Targeting Guns*, chap. 10.

33. "Maryland Panel Approves More Guns for Sale," *Washington Post*, 9 January 1990.

34. "No Way Out: Behan Has to Vote for Gun He Hates," *Baltimore Sun*, 9 February 1990.

35. Herbert Wechsler, "A Rationale of the Law of Homicide," *Columbia Law Review* 27 (1937): 701, 736. Emphasis added.

36. Friedan as interviewed by A. Japenga in the March/April 1994 issue of *Health*, p. 54.

37. See, e.g., Don B. Kates and Nancy Engberg, "Deadly Force Self-Defense Against Rape," *U.C.-Davis Law Review* 15 (1982): 873, 877-80.

38. In its accurate and historical context "vigilantism" (a) does not distinguish between private citizens and police, (b) does not necessarily imply deadly force, and (c) would never apply to any *defensive* use of force, even wrongfully excessive force. Rather, vigilantism defines a highly specific kind of wrong: *punishment* of any kind, inflicted by anyone, whether civilian or police officer, on a supposed criminal without due process of law. Vigilantism's limitations may be illustrated by three alternative hypotheticals of the facts in the Goetz case: If Goetz shot in necessary defense against robbers, the shooting was lawful and thus not vigilantism. If Goetz actually but unreasonably feared mere panhandlers were robbers, the shooting was illegal, but not vigilantism. It was vigilantism only if Goetz used deadly force (or any force!) knowing it was unnecessary and for the purpose of arrogating to himself the judicial function of punishing.

In sum, vigilantism is always illegal, whether engaged in by private citizens or police. Conversely, it is oxymoronic to apply the term to lawful conduct either by private citizens or by police.

39. Kates and Engberg, "Deadly Force Self-Defense Against Rape."

40. Ibid. See also Kates, "Handgun Prohibition and the Meaning of the Second Amendment," p. 205 n. 5.

41. Allen Brockway, "But the Bible Doesn't Mention Pistols," *Engage-Social*

Action Forum (May, 1977): 39–40. The entire issue is devoted to antigun articles. It was republished as a separate pamphlet by the Methodist Board of Church and Society under the title *Handguns in the United States.*

42. Alan Gottlieb, *The Gun Grabbers* (Bellevue, Wash.: Merril, 1986), chap. 2. NCBH has now changed its name to Coalition Against Gun Violence to emphasize its current emphasis on banning many rifles and shotguns, as well as handguns. See Don B. Kates et al., "Guns and Public Health: Epidemic of Violence or Pandemic of Propaganda," *Tennessee Law Review* 62 (1995): 515–16.

43. Perhaps because freedom of choice as a value resonates for feminists, there is a substantial feminist literature supporting the right to possess arms for self-defense. See, e.g., Mary Z. Stange and Carol Oyster, *Gun Women: Firearms and Feminism in Contemorary America* (New York: NYU Press, 2000); Nicholas J. Johnson, "Principles and Passions: The Intersection of Abortion and Gun Rights," *Rutgers Law Review* 50 (1997): 97; Mary Z. Stange, *Woman the Hunter* (Boston: Beacon, 1997); Inge Anna Larish, "Why Annie Can't Get Her Gun: A Feminist Perspective on the Second Amendment," *University of Illinois Law Forum* (1996): 467–508; Laura Ingraham, "Why Feminists Should Be Trigger Happy," *Wall Street Journal*, 13 May 1996, p. A18; Mary Z. Stange, "Arms and the Woman: A Feminist Reappraisal," in David B. Kopel, *Guns: Who Should Have Them?* (Amherst, N.Y.: Prometheus Books, 1995); Sayoko Blodgett-Ford, "Do Battered Women Have A Right to Bear Arms," *Yale Law and Policy Review* 11 (1993): 509–560; and Margaret Howard, "Husband-Wife Homicide: An Essay from a Family Law Perspective," *Law and Contemporary Problems* 49 (1986): 63–88.

44. *Newsweek*, 7 January 1985.

45. 1985-1986 *Hearings on Legislation to Modify the 1968 Gun Control Act*, House Judiciary Committee, Subcommittee on Crime, vol. 1, p. 128. Emphasis added.

46. The language quoted in this and the preceding paragraph comes from the Presbyterian statement at the *Hearings on Legislation to Modify the 1968 Gun Control Act*, pp. 127, 128. For similar views from the Union of American Hebrew Congregations and the Board of Church and Society of the Methodist Church (condemning handgun ownership for self-defense as "vigilantism"), see *Hearings on Legislation to Modify the 1968 Gun Control Act*, pp. 121–25, 141. See also the June 19, 1975, Press Statement of the Young Christian Women's Association of the United States.

47. See references cited in chapter 1, note 20.

48. Eckholm, "A Little Control, a Lot of Guns," *New York Times*, 15 August 1993 (quoting Sarah Brady); see note 6 above for James Brady.

49. *Detroit Daily Press* (editorial), 22 January 1968. Statements to the same effect from other antigun luminaries are legion: see, e.g., those of nationally syndicated columnists Molly Ivins and Charles Krauthammer (quoted at note 3 above).

50. *New York Times* (editorial), 24 September 1975.

51. D.C. Code §§ 6-2132(4) and 6-2372.

52. Wright, Rossi, and Daly, *Under the Gun*, chap. 6.

53. Alan J. Lizotte and Jo Dixon, "Gun Ownership and the 'Southern Subculture of Violence,' " *American Journal of Sociology* 93 (1987): 383. This approval of "defensive force" must be distinguished from generally "violent attitudes" (as defined by approval of violence against social deviants or dissenters). Gun owners are no more likely to have generally violent attitudes than are nonowners (Lizotte and Dixon, "Gun Ownership and the 'Southern Subculture of Violence' "). Indeed, the holders of violent attitudes were less likely than the average gun owner to approve of defensive force (perhaps perceiving it would be directed against violent people like themselves).

54. John T. Whitehead and Robert H. Langworthy, "Gun Ownership: Another Look," *Justice Quarterly* 6 (1989): 263.

Absolutist Politics in a Moderate Package

Prohibitionist Intentions of the Gun Control Movement

by Gary Kleck

The Issue: Moderate Overt Agendas vs. Covert Prohibitionist Goals

The debate over gun control has been described as a dialogue of the deaf. The combatants do not listen to one another, or pretend to be unable to understand what their opponents are saying. Gun control advocates, and sympathetic members of the news media, profess to be mystified why anyone would oppose moderate, "reasonable" controls over guns. "How," they ask, "can any serious person reject commonsensical measures like the licensing of gun ownership or the registration of guns? We license drivers and register cars, don't we?"

Gun control opponents, with boring regularity, consistently offer the same explanation: "We fear that moderate gun controls are steps down a slippery slope towards gun prohibition." Advocates then dismiss this response as sheer fantasy on the part of opponents, and even hint, by labeling such beliefs "paranoid," that those who believe such things must be mentally ill. This belief, however, is not confined to a tiny fringe minority. In December 1993, the Gallup organization asked a national sample of adults whether they

129

agreed or disagreed with the following statement: "Gun control measures will eventually lead to stricter laws which will take guns away from all citizens." Among all adults, gun owners and nonowners alike, 50 percent agreed.[1]

Gun prohibition can be defined for present purposes as any gun control measure that would preclude legal ownership or possession of guns, or of handguns, by almost all of the civilian population. This state of affairs can be accomplished by a law labeled as a gun ban, but can also be achieved through restrictive licensing (à la New York City's Sullivan law or English law). Licensing of handguns can be every bit as restrictive as a handgun ban—under the Sullivan Law's licensing system in New York City, less than 1 percent of civilians have a permit allowing them to own a handgun legally.[2]

Likewise, one could gradually ban gun possession by first requiring registration of guns for lawful possession, then passing a law providing that no further guns will be registered. As existing owners died or moved out of the affected jurisdiction, the number of legally owned guns would eventually dwindle to zero. This is how handguns were banned in Washington, D.C., in 1976 and in Chicago in 1982.[3] Or one could ban guns that are "unsafe" by virtue of not having adequate safety devices such as "smart gun technology," gradually increasing the stringency of safety requirements until no guns could meet the standards and still remain affordable for any but the wealthiest gun buyers. Or one could impose a prohibitive tax on guns to achieve the same state of affairs.

There are also partial gun prohibitions that ban gun acquisition or possession among subsets of the population such as convicted felons, alcoholics, young adults, or illicit drug users. Depending on how broadly one defines the prohibited groups, and how widely one expanded the presumption of unfitness to own a gun, combinations of such "partial" prohibition could approach total prohibition. For example, if one banned gun ownership to all persons who had ever been arrested or given a traffic ticket (on the quite reasonable grounds that such persons are relatively more likely to commit violent acts), this measure alone might well deny legal gun ownership to the majority of the population. Lest one think it unlikely that anyone would advocate banning guns among persons with an arrest record but not a conviction, Handgun Control, Incorporated (HCI) Chair Nelson T. (Pete) Shields advocated banning handgun ownership among persons "with a record" of violence "even though such violence did not result in a conviction."[4]

Prohibition, if it were ever attained in the United States, would almost certainly be achieved incrementally. One way to accomplish this would be to advocate bans on individual gun types one at a time until no major types were left unbanned. Thus, in 1979 HCI advocated banning Saturday-night specials (SNSs)—small, cheap handguns—at a time when HCI staff thought that SNSs accounted for as much as two-thirds of handgun sales.[5] HCI then advocated, in 1989, banning "assault weapons," which are an arbitrarily selected subset of semiautomatic guns, which in turn constitute the majority of the handguns (and a large share of long guns as well) sold in the past twenty years.[6]

Many supporters of moderate controls have condemned the National Rifle Association (NRA) for stoking the fears of gun owners that moderate controls will lead to prohibition. For example, Martin Dyckman, associate editor of the *St. Petersburg Times*, asserted in 1993 that "no one is seriously proposing to ban or confiscate all guns. You hear that only from the gun lobby itself, which whistles up this bogeyman whenever some reasonable regulation is proposed."[7] Echoing this claim, Touro College law professor Andrew Herz denounced the gun lobby for "conjuring up visions of powerful gun-grabbing Washington confiscators knocking down the doors of law-abiding citizens" when in fact "virtually no one in the gun control movement calls for confiscation."[8] Or as one strongly procontrol scholar has put it, "NRA leaders have consistently employed a Chicken Little ('the sky is falling') rhetorical style, with constant prophesies of imminent doom."[9] Likewise, in an editorial endorsing national registration and licensing, the editorial writers of the *New York Times* responded to "gun groups that fear [registration] as a first step toward government confiscation of guns" very simply: "Their fear makes no sense."[10]

On the other hand, some observers, and even some gun control advocates, regard it as obvious that many advocates of moderate controls really want prohibition. For example, self-described "proponent of gun control" Andrew McClurg stated that "there is no doubt that the agenda of many Brady bill proponents encompasses much more than the adoption of waiting periods and background checks. Many Brady Bill supporters want to prohibit private possession of handguns altogether." Pulitzer Prize-winning columnist Mike Royko stated it more bluntly: "The ultimate goal of the antigun lobby is to ban the private ownership of all weapons. That is their ultimate goal, although the antigun people won't admit it. It would be foolish strategy."[11]

Among casual observers of the gun debate, there may be some honest confusion regarding the difference between (1) what gun control advocacy groups are currently "proposing" (note Professor Herz' careful phrase "no one . . . *calls for* confiscation" [emphasis added]) and (2) what they would eventually like to bring about, when and if it becomes politically achievable. In this particular dialogue of the deaf, control opponents express their fears of the *ultimate intentions* of control advocates, while gun control supporters act as if the issue was the *current overt agenda* of advocacy groups, i.e., what they overtly "propose" or "call for" at the moment.

It is unlikely that professional advocates do not understand the distinction between ultimate goals or intentions and an organization's current overt agenda, although when responding to opponents' claims, they sometimes act as if they do not. Accused of harboring prohibitionist intentions, they cite their organization's official current legislative agenda. For example, HCI Chairman Pete Shields seemed to deny any intent of his organization to push for stricter controls on long guns in future when he wrote: "Handgun Control, Inc., does not propose further controls on rifles and shotguns."[12] Two features of this phrasing are noteworthy. First, the statement pertained to what HCI "proposes," i.e., its stated policy agenda, rather than what its leadership ultimately wanted. Second, the statement was phrased in the present tense—it said nothing about what HCI might propose in the future. And in fact, within eight years, HCI did push for a ban on various rifles and shotguns.

In light of this confusion, it may be necessary to state more precisely what it is that gun control opponents fear. They argue that many, and possibly most, gun control advocates favor more than just control of guns via moderate regulatory measures, but also want to eventually make it illegal for Americans in general to own guns. They believe that these advocates pursue this goal through a step-by-step or incrementalist strategy, whereby success in getting mild controls passed makes it politically easier to pass stricter controls, eventually culminating, gun control advocates hope, in prohibition.[13]

Gun control opponents also believe (correctly) that most Americans do not support prohibitionist controls, and would be less likely to support moderate controls if they thought they would lead to prohibition, a point with which some control advocates agree.[14] Recognizing this, some gun control advocates, according to opponents, conceal their prohibitionist intentions as a political tactic and do not admit to such ambitions in their public statements of official policy.[15] In any case, the fact that a group's official agenda contains no call for prohibition indicates nothing one way or the other about whether gun control opponents' claims are correct.

Both sides agree that the most prominent gun control advocacy group, HCI, does not openly advocate prohibition and does not include prohibitionist measures in its current policy agenda. Further, most people on both sides would also acknowledge the political truism that American political movements are more likely to achieve their ultimate goals in an incremental fashion than in a single big jump.[16] Thus, if one imagined the strictness of gun control laws to lie along a scale from 0 (no controls) to 10 (prohibition), it is easier to move the law from 0 to 1, then from 1 to 2, and so on, moving gradually up to 10, than it is to jump directly from 0 to 10.

It is common for supporters of a moderate control measure to say something like "This measure may not be much, but it's a good first step," thereby acknowledging their intention to follow an incrementalist strategy. For example, HCI Chair Pete Shields admitted in 1976 that "we're going to have to take one step at a time, and the first step is necessarily—given the political realities—going to be very modest. . . . The final problem is to make possession of *all* handguns and *all* handgun ammunition . . . totally illegal." Likewise, Congressman William Clay (D-St. Louis, Mo.) described the Brady Act as "the minimum step" that Congress should take to control handguns. "We need much stricter gun control, and eventually we should bar the ownership of handguns except in a few cases." Similarly, Congressman Bobby Rush (D-Ill.) was quoted in 1999 as saying that "ultimately, I would like to see the manufacture and possession of handguns banned except for military and police use. But that's the endgame. And in the meantime, there are some specific things that we can do with legislation." Likewise, Barbara Fass, mayor of Stockton, California, supported assault weapons bans, explaining that "I think you have to do it a step at a time and . . . the banning of semi-assault [*sic*] military weapons . . . is the first step."[17]

Commenting on the 1994 federal assault weapons ban, syndicated columnist and prohibition advocate Charles Krauthammer identified a more subtle utility to moderate controls as a part of an incremental strategy: "In fact, the assault weapons ban will have no significant effect either on the crime rate or on personal security. Nonetheless, it is a good idea. . . . Its only real justification is not to reduce crime but to desensitize the public to the regulation of weapons in preparation for their ultimate confiscation."[18]

The current leaders of HCI openly acknowledge following an incrementalist strategy. In a newspaper interview, HCI Chair Sarah Brady's views were summarized as follows: "[Brady] sees the Brady Bill as 'the cornerstone of a serious gun-control policy in America' that will eventually include more restrictions." Brady predicted "that passage of the Brady Bill will soften up Congress for more. 'Once we get this,' she said, 'I think it will become easier and easier to get the laws we need passed.' "[19]

Thus, there is little serious dispute that gun control organizations, including HCI, are pursuing a step-by-step strategy, where attaining moderate controls facilitates gaining stricter controls. The only point on which disputants differ is how far this incrementalist path will be followed. While some of the preceding proponents openly acknowledged advocating an incrementalist strategy that they hoped would end in prohibition, other proponents, such as the leaders of HCI, do not currently admit to any plans to pursue controls that far.[20]

On the other hand, HCI's leaders do not say exactly how far they will pursue further controls, i.e., what their ultimate stopping point will be. A generous interpretation might be that they are merely being practical, recognizing the limits on their ability to foresee the future, and the need to remain flexible. Regardless, their silence on this question effectively holds open prohibition as a future option.

HCI as an organization has never officially stated that it will never support banning possession of all guns or handguns and it certainly has never said that it would actively oppose gun bans. Further, HCI has never in practice opposed a gun ban in its history. Quite the contrary, it has actively supported local and state proposals to ban handguns and has actively defended existing handgun bans passed by local governments. When a ban on handgun possession was passed by the village of Morton Grove, Illinois, and the ordinance was challenged in court, HCI filed an amicus curiae (friend of the court) brief urging the appellate court to uphold the ordinance. In the brief, they described the local handgun ban as "a significant step toward effective state and national handgun regulation."[21] Likewise, in 1978, HCI, under its old name of the National Council to Control Handguns, filed an amicus curiae brief in defense of the Washington, D.C., handgun ban.[22] More recently, in the 1990s, HCI President Richard Aborn has urged other cities to adopt the same law.[23] Thus, HCI at minimum supports local handgun bans.

HCI's support for handgun bans, however, has not been limited to local measures. In the fall of 1976, under its old name of the National Council to Control Handguns, it contributed $16,000 to a state referendum campaign to ban the private possession of handguns in Massachusetts, providing nearly 30 percent of the campaign's financing.[24] Thus, HCI has supported state-level, as well as local, handgun prohibition. It has never publicly repudiated this support.

Some advocacy groups can accurately, though somewhat misleadingly, deny including prohibitionist measures in any formal long-term agenda, for the simple reason that they do not have a formal long-term agenda. Rather, they have only a series of frequently revised short-term agenda, consisting of whatever legislative measures they are lobbying for at the moment. For example, HCI's website merely lists their "legislative priorities" for the current year, but includes nothing resembling a long-term plan.[25] (A document on HCI letterhead purporting to be an outline of HCI's long-term plans, including plans to advocate prohibition, was circulated on the Internet in 1993. It was almost certainly a hoax.)

Indeed, some elements of HCI's agenda often look like ad hoc responses to media coverage of spectacular instances of violence committed with guns or short-lived trends in gun violence, rather than part of any well thought-out, long-term plan. For example, HCI's push for bans on "assault weapons" came not at the time when sales of such guns were reaching their peak in the 1970s or when their criminal use was growing prior to 1988, but only after the news media devoted massive coverage to a handful of mass shootings involving such guns, beginning in 1989 with the Stockton, California, schoolyard shootings.[26]

In general, HCI appears willing to pursue virtually any further restriction on guns that is politically achievable. Following the defeat of the HCI-endorsed Massachusetts referendum to ban the private possession of handguns, HCI chair Shields frankly described HCI's long-term strategy as follows: "We'll take any law we can get. We're prepared to win our battle in bits and pieces and we realize this is going to be a long, slow process."[27] Beyond this, there appears to be little rhyme or reason to changes in their policy agenda. The indiscriminate nature of HCI's support for virtually any increase in gun control restrictiveness, given political attainability, encourages the belief that it would also support prohibition if it, too, became politically achievable.

Certainly there is no consistent relationship between HCI's agenda and emerging research findings, which are selectively cited to support positions apparently adopted on political grounds rather than used to choose among policy options. For example, HCI's 1979 advocacy of bans on Saturday-night specials (SNSs) came in the wake of widely cited research (sponsored by the procontrol Police Foundation) indicating that these guns are *not*, contrary to HCI claims, the preferred weapons of criminals.[28]

Further, HCI has continued its support for banning SNSs despite strong and unrebutted evidence from prison surveys that if gun-using violent criminals were denied SNSs, they would substitute more lethal handgun models or sawed-off long guns, thereby raising the fraction of gunshot victims who would die.[29] Of course, if one hoped to later ban the more lethal handguns and long guns, as well as cheap handguns, substitution would seem less of a problem.

In contrast to HCI, other major gun control advocacy groups openly support prohibition. After HCI, the most prominent national gun control advocacy groups are probably the Coalition to Stop Gun Violence (CSGV), formerly the National Coalition to Ban Handguns, and the Violence Policy Center (VPC). CSGV, organized by the Board of the Church and Society of the Methodist Church in 1975, unambiguously supports prohibitionist controls.[30] Its website states that it advocates "a ban on the sale and possession of handguns and assault weapons."[31] CSGV does not, however, admit to any intentions to ban long guns (aside from the subset they regard as "assault weapons") as well as handguns, so they, too, could harbor covert prohibitionist intentions that go beyond their advocacy of bans on handguns and "assault weapons."

VPC also openly supports handgun prohibition, though a more indirect variant. It supports the Firearms Safety and Consumer Protection Act (H.R. 920), which would grant regulatory authority to the Department of the Treasury that "would subject the gun industry to the same safety standards as virtually all other products sold in America."[32] This does not sound much like a gun ban, until one knows how VPC anticipates this regulatory power being used. In a 1999 *New York Times* op-ed article supporting this bill, VPC's executive director, Josh Sugarmann, wrote that "any rational regulator with that authority would ban handguns."[33] Further, it is hard to imagine regulatory power that would permit banning of handguns that would not also permit the banning of shotguns and rifles, which are both more lethal and more prone to accidental discharge than handguns.[34]

Other organizations do not openly advocate prohibitionist goals as organizations, but are lead by individuals who personally support prohibition. The HELP (Handgun Epidemic Lowering Plan) Network acknowledges only a miscellany of "policy priorities" that do not include any prohibitionist measures, but the organization's chair, Katherine Christoffel, has publicly expressed some of the most extreme and simplistic antigun views ever to appear in print: "Guns are a virus that must be eradicated. . . . They are causing an epidemic of death by gunshot, which should be treated like any epidemic—you get rid of the virus. . . . Get rid of the guns, get rid of the bullets, and you get rid of the deaths."[35]

Still other organizations openly pursue prohibitionist goals without overtly advocating prohibitionist methods. That is, they support the goal of a "gun-free America" or "handgun-free homes" but do not explicitly advocate achieving this by legislation. For example, a recently (1995) formed organization called Ceasefire, Inc. runs newspaper ads and television public service announcements to persuade people that they should not own guns.[36] Thus, organizations of this type have the same goals as prohibitionists without overtly advocating prohibitionist laws.

Finally, there are many organizations that endorse gun prohibition but are not primarily concerned with the gun issue. For example, Common Cause is probably best known for its efforts to reform campaign financing. However, in a 1972 statement presented to a House Judiciary subcommittee, the organization endorsed a "total ban on the sale and manufacture of all handguns" as well as a proposal that "private ownership of handguns also be prohibited." Likewise the U.S. Conference of Mayors, the Unitarian Universalist Association, the American Civil Liberties Union, Americans for Democratic Action, the National Alliance for Safer Cities, the National Board of the Young Women's Christian Association of the U.S.A., and the International Ladies Garment Workers' Union have all at some time endorsed banning the private possession of handguns.[37]

In contrast to CSGV and VPC, HCI does not currently openly advocate gun prohibition. This was not always true, however. Even the leaders of HCI openly admitted their prohibitionist intentions at one time. In repeated public statements early in the organization's history, the long-time chair of

HCI, Pete Shields, explicitly supported handgun prohibition and even acknowledged that HCI was following an incrementalist strategy to attain this long-term goal. In July of 1976, Shields told a reporter for the *New Yorker* that his organization's ultimate goal was "to make the possession of *all* handguns totally illegal" (emphasis in original) and was pursuing an incrementalist strategy in pursuit of the goal. He repeated these points in an interview in September of 1977 with *Parade* magazine.[38]

Further, although HCI no longer mentions the fact in its official materials, it was once a member of the National Coalition to Ban Handguns, only withdrawing after its leaders decided that public opinion was too strongly opposed to a handgun ban for it to be, at that time, a politically achievable goal.[39]

Sometime between September of 1977 and November 15, 1978, HCI changed its policy of open advocacy of handgun prohibition, though without any official public admission that it was doing so and without any public repudiation of its previous positions. This may have been partly a response to a June 1978 Cambridge Reports poll indicating that only about a third of Americans favored banning handgun possession (though this should not have come as a surprise, since a 1975 Gallup poll had already found that only 41 percent favored this measure).[40] In a letter to HCI members dated November 15, 1978, Shields explained that "while many of us might prefer an outright ban of handguns, we are realistic enough to know that such a goal is unattainable in America today."[41] Thus, HCI's change was apparently one of tactics rather than of ultimate goals, a response to political realities rather than a change of heart.

In his 1981 book, Shields acknowledged that polls showed that Americans do not support "an absolute ban on handguns" and he therefore called instead for "a set of strict laws to control the easy access to handguns by the criminal and the violence-prone—as long as those controls don't jeopardize the perceived right of law-abiding citizens to buy and own handguns for self-defense."[42] There are two noteworthy features of this passage. First, Shields's careful phrasing indicated that he did not concede there is any right to own handguns for self-defense—it is merely something "perceived" by people. Second, the reference to public opinion strongly suggested that this limit on HCI's proposals represented a concession to contemporary political realities, and thus was not necessarily the limit of what HCI leaders really wanted to eventually achieve.

Thus, even in 1981, it was unlikely that Shields/HCI opposed handgun prohibition, as distinct from merely recognizing that it was unattainable at the time and should not, for tactical reasons, be openly pursued. Shields stated that HCI supported a ban on the manufacture and sale of SNSs, supposedly especially small and cheap handguns (p. 147), while also asserting that SNSs claimed one-third to two-thirds of handgun sales (p. 148). Thus, in Shield's own mind, HCI was pushing for a ban on a type of gun that may have encompassed the majority of handguns.

Likewise, it is easy to believe that Shields hoped for a future increase in public support for a ban on handguns when one reads his observation that at present (i.e., 1981) "the people do not want an absolute ban on handguns. A total ban is perceived as taking away their right to self-defense, and *until their fear is reduced* they will never agree to such a law" (p. 146, emphasis added).

By 1982, Shields had clarified somewhat the kind of handgun control he wanted: "I'd have restrictive licensing rather than permissive licensing. You would have to prove a need. All we have to prove (now) is that we're not baddies."[43] Shields evidently perceived a significant difference between restrictive licensing and handgun prohibition, given that he denied that his organization was calling for the latter. The most prominent example of restrictive licensing of handgun ownership in operation at the time was that of New York City, where it was extremely hard to get the permit required to own a handgun and, in the 1980s, less than 1 percent of the population had a permit.[44] Thus, in practice the difference between an actual restrictive licensing system and a hypothetical handgun ban is that under the former, 99 percent of the civilian population were forbidden handguns, while under the latter, 100 percent would be prohibited from having them. Further, given the exceptions that typically accompany handgun bans (e.g., security guards, collectible handguns, etc.), licensing regimes may in fact be the more restrictive of the two policies, a point conceded even by prominent gun control advocates.[45]

Nevertheless, HCI has not openly advocated a policy explicitly labeled as handgun prohibition since 1978. Its overt advocacy of prohibition has been limited to SNSs and "assault weapons." HCI, however, has never officially stated that it regards gun prohibition as a bad policy. Instead, it has merely adopted the position that it is not yet achievable.

Why Do Prohibitionist Intentions Matter?

What difference does it make whether or not the more influential gun control advocacy groups harbor prohibitionist intentions, covert or overt? If prohibition would make Americans safer, why should this be a problem?

One problem is that advocacy, covert or overt, of prohibition makes it harder to get more politically feasible and potentially effective measures implemented. Don Kates has argued that the principal political obstacle to passing useful moderate gun controls is the insistence of advocates on extremist antigun principles that would facilitate achieving gun prohibition. This in turn triggers gun owner opposition to moderate controls that become perceived as stepping stones to banning guns.[46]

Two of the more important extremist principles are: (1) there is no significant defensive value to widespread civilian gun ownership, and specifically no significant life-saving or injury-preventing effects, and (2) the Second Amendment does not recognize any individual right to keep or bear guns, but rather recognizes only a right of states to maintain armed militias like the National Guard.[47] The natural implication of these assumptions is that there is no strong reason why we should not ban guns, once political obstacles can be overcome.

By adhering to these assumptions and declining to commit themselves to opposing prohibitionist controls, gun control advocacy groups effectively hold open the option of eventually pushing for prohibitionist controls. In Kates's words, this sort of "extremism poisons the well" for more moderate controls.

In a similar vein, James Wright attributes the "white-hot ferocity of the debate over guns in America" largely to fears of gun owners that gun permits and registration are " 'just the first step' toward outright confiscation of all privately held firearms." Wright notes that criminals rarely obtain guns through the channels that are effectively subject to such regulatory controls, and thus such controls, along with waiting periods, are unlikely to have much impact on criminals. The measures therefore appear to lawful gun owners to be largely aimed at themselves, stimulating speculation on their part as to why the government would want to focus its control efforts on them. "The distinction between ill-considered and evil is quickly lost" and many gun owners end up attributing nefarious motives to advocates of such controls.[48]

Public debate over important issues should be honest concerning what is at stake. Debate over moderate gun controls is dishonest if some advocates harbor unacknowledged desires for prohibition, which they may well pursue in future if the adoption of moderate controls increases the political feasibility of doing so. Such advocates should honestly concede that there is more at stake in conflicts over moderate controls than just the measure being debated at the moment. As even gun control proponent Andrew McClurg has conceded, specifically in connection with the "slippery slope" issue, "the consequences of a proposal are certainly relevant to deciding whether to adopt it," and one of the consequences of passing moderate controls is that their adoption makes it easier (not inevitable) for stricter controls to be passed.[49] Those who favor banning guns, of course, see little problem with covert advocacy of prohibition. From their standpoint, if advocacy groups find it more effective to keep their prohibitionist preferences secret, so much the better.

A credible case for the desirability of prohibition, however, has not been made. Rational support for prohibition implicitly relies on an assumption that is no longer empirically supportable—that gun ownership among noncriminals has no significant violence-reducing effects, and thus banning guns among noncriminals as well as criminals is bound to be beneficial or at least harmless. The best available evidence indicates that defensive gun use is quite common (probably more common than criminal use of guns) and that defensive use is effective, in the sense that victims who use guns in self-defense are less likely to be injured or to lose property than otherwise similar victims who do not use guns.[50]

If gun ownership among noncriminal victims has violence-reducing effects, then disarming noncriminals via prohibition would have violence-increasing effects, which would counterbalance any violence-reducing effects of disarming criminals. And, almost by definition, prohibition laws would be obeyed at a higher rate by noncriminals than by criminals.

Contrary to the bumper sticker slogan, if guns were outlawed, outlaws would not be the *only* people with guns (except in the tautological sense that anyone who violated the law by retaining a gun would, by legal definition, be a criminal), mainly because there would be widespread disobedience by noncriminals as well.[51] Nevertheless, it is almost certainly true that compliance with gun ban laws would be lower among criminals than among noncriminals.

This means that any beneficial effects of gun ownership among noncriminals would be reduced by prohibition proportionally more than would the harmful effects of gun ownership among criminals. Consequently, to the extent that future gun bans actually achieved their proximate goal of reducing overall gun levels, the net effect would probably be harmful.[52]

Banning only handguns, while leaving the more lethal shotguns and rifles available, is even more clearly undesirable. Surveys of criminals indicate that if they were denied handguns, 73 percent of those who commit gun crime frequently would substitute sawed-off shotguns and rifles. Long guns are, on average, far more lethal than handguns. Further, although they are less concealable than handguns, they can easily be made sufficiently concealable for most criminal purposes—most gun crimes do not require a gun as concealable as a handgun.[53]

Even partial substitution of long guns in attacks would outweigh the benefits of denying handguns to some criminals, leading to a net increase in the number of crime victims killed rather than nonfatally wounded. It has been mathematically demonstrated that even if the long guns substituted by persons who otherwise would have attacked with handguns were only twice as lethal as handguns (a conservative assumption), there would be a net increase in homicides following a handgun-only ban even if as few as 44 percent of attackers substituted long guns, a considerably lower rate of substitution than evidence leads us to expect.[54]

Prohibition of guns, like prohibition of alcohol, would also make criminals of millions of otherwise noncriminal Americans, stimulate the expansion of the black market in guns, increase the incentive to steal guns, and create a law enforcement burden of enormous proportions. A survey of Illinois adults in 1978 found that among gun owners (not just criminals), 73 percent said they would disobey a hypothetical federal law requiring them to turn in their guns.[55] If this predicted rate of noncompliance applied to the nation's gun owners today, it would imply that a national gun ban would, at a stroke, make criminals of 45 million Americans who chose to disobey the national gun ban (73 percent of 61.2 million individual gun owners, based on a 30 percent adult gun owning rate among 203.8 million persons age eighteen or over in 2000).[56] There is even a book sold at gun stores and gun shows entirely devoted to advising gun owners how to avoid government confiscation of their guns by hiding or burying their guns.[57]

It might be reassuring to dismiss the 73 percent noncompliance figure as hollow bravado, but actual compliance rates in connection with less stringent, and presumably less disobedience-provoking, measures are similarly poor. In 1989, California required that all "assault weapons" in the state be registered, allowing all of 1990 for gun owners to comply. When few guns had been registered by the December 31, 1990, deadline, the state passed another law allowing a 90-day amnesty period for late registration, and launched a $330,000 publicity campaign to inform gun owners of the requirement. Of the 300,000 to 600,000 "assault weapons" estimated to exist in the state, only 66,303 had been registered by the end of the amnesty period.[58] Thus, even after extraordinary efforts to achieve voluntary compliance with a relatively mild control measure, about 78 to 89 percent of the guns remained unregistered, in defiance of the law.

Evidence of Prohibitionist Intent of the Leaders of the Gun Control Movement

If the official agenda of advocacy groups does not completely convey the full range of long-term goals and policy preferences of the groups' leaders, staff, and activist members, what evidence might help establish their ultimate intentions? Given the impossibility of reading the innermost thoughts of movement leaders, it must be recognized that no evidence on this question can be conclusive. Nevertheless, a mass of circumstantial evidence, falling into the following categories, consistently supports the same conclusion:

1. past political efforts of gun control advocacy groups in the United States;
2. recent precedents of gun prohibition in other Western nations;
3. the manner in which advocates appear to deny prohibitionist intentions;
4. survey data on the general population showing, among those who support moderate controls, the fraction who also support prohibitionist controls;
5. public statements made by leaders and prominent supporters of the gun control movement;
6. the premises and logic of arguments marshaled in favor of moderate controls; and
7. the advocacy of licensing and registration in addition to background checks.

Past Political Efforts of Advocacy Groups

Given the political truism that small changes are easier to bring about than big ones, it is no surprise that the history of the gun control movement has followed an incrementalist path, with each legislative victory leading to a push for further controls. Thus, the passage of the Brady Act (which required a background check to buy a gun from a licensed dealer) in 1994 was immediately followed by lobbying by HCI for the "Brady II" Bill, which requires the registration of guns and the licensing of their owners. Likewise, a ban on the further manufacture and importation of large capacity magazines (LCMs, which hold more than ten cartridges) (part of the 1994 federal assault weapons ban) was followed immediately by HCI advocacy of a ban on the possession of existing LCMs.[59]

In each case, "loopholes" and limitations of earlier measures are identified and remedies proposed. The diagnosis is invariably an inadequate dose of gun control, and the prescription is a bigger dose, i.e., stricter or more extensive controls. Thus, HCI devotes a entire section of its website to discussion of "loopholes" that need to be closed with further legislation.[60] Indeed, each failure of previous control initiatives can be portrayed as further evidence of the need to increase the dosage of gun control. In this sense, nothing succeeds like failure. While each supposed success of a control measure could reasonably be cited as showing the likely value of still more controls, each apparent failure can also be cited as evidence of the need for still stricter controls—heads we win, tails you lose.

HCI has also shown a willingness to expand the scope of the controls it supported with respect to the types of guns covered. At one time the group favored only banning SNSs and regulating other handguns. In his 1981 book, HCI Chair Pete Shields assured his readers that HCI had no intention of pushing for further controls over long guns, i.e., shotguns and rifles: "Handgun Control, Inc. does not propose further controls on rifles and shotguns. Rifles and shotguns are not the problem; they are not concealable."[61] Likewise, the field director of the National Coalition to Ban Handguns (later the Coalition to Stop Gun Violence [CSGV]), Sam Fields, insisted in 1979 that "neither the National Coalition to Ban Handguns, nor any other leading group in the fight for handgun reform, is interested in banning long guns."[62]

Yet, within a decade, as soon as the political opportunity arose to restrict "assault rifles" (which are no more concealable than other long guns), both HCI and CSGV began to lobby for a ban on "assault weapons," an amorphous category largely composed of long guns. The ban was eventually passed in 1994. This reversal of policy might be defended on the grounds that gun crime had changed in the interim, but in fact "assault weapon" use in crime was declining by 1989, the rifle share of gun crime was no higher in 1989 than in 1981, and "assault rifles" were in any case never involved in even as much as 1 percent of gun crimes.[63] This willingness to extend their control efforts to long guns undermines the credibility of HCI and CSGV promises concerning the limits of their future control ambitions.

There are also earlier precedents for moderate gun controls being expanded and made stricter until they reached the status of de facto gun bans. New York's Sullivan Law, passed in 1911, initially allowed almost any adult to get the required permit for possessing a handgun, but legislative amendments and progressively stricter police administration of the law in New York City eventually produced a de facto ban on the private possession of handguns.[64] Likewise, Washington, D.C., initially required only the registration of handguns, but in 1976 it passed a law providing that the District would no longer register handguns, effectively banning any further acquisition of handguns. This handgun "freeze" in the long run will become a handgun ban as registered handgun owners move out of the city or die.[65]

While neither Congress nor any state legislature has passed bans on guns or handguns, this is not because no such legislation has been introduced. Proposals to ban the private possession of handguns have been under consideration by the U.S. Congress since at least 1974. For example, Representative Jonathan Bingham (D-N.Y.) had one version or another of a bill banning private possession of handguns under consideration from at least as early as 1974 to as late as 1981. This bill was supported by HCI, when it was called the National Council to Control Handguns (NCCH). More recently, Senator John Chafee (R-R.I.) introduced a bill in 1992 banning handgun possession, as did Rep. Major Owens (D-N.Y.) in 1993.[66]

At the state level, South Carolina banned possession of all but the largest handguns in 1901.[67] A referendum measure to ban handguns, supported by HCI, was put on the Massachusetts ballot, and defeated, in 1976.[68] And in 1999, the attorney general of Maryland, J. Joseph Curran, proposed banning handguns in that state.[69]

While federal or state bills providing for gun prohibitions have been repeatedly proposed, none have passed in the United States. Nevertheless, several large cities, including Chicago and Washington, D.C., have banned handgun possession. San Francisco also banned handguns in 1982, though the law was later overturned by a state court.[70] And, as noted, New York City has a restrictive licensing law in place that is administered so strictly as to constitute a de facto handgun ban.[71]

Finally, it is worth noting that roughly 40 percent of Americans support banning the private possession of handguns, a figure that has occasionally approached a majority.[72] In this light, it is scarcely reasonable to view the prospect of a national handgun ban as nothing more than a paranoid delusion of extremist gun control opponents. Nor can it be reasonably denied that gun control advocacy groups, including HCI, have followed incrementalist strategies or that milder controls have been regularly followed by calls for stricter controls. The only issue in serious question is exactly how far HCI and similar organizations will pursue the incrementalist strategy.

Recent Precedents of Gun Prohibition in Other Nations

There are ample precedents for moderate gun controls being followed by national gun bans and mass confiscation of guns in the recent history of other nations, in democracies and formerly democratic nations as well as dictatorships. When a military junta took over the formerly democratic government of Greece in 1967 and suspended part of the nation's constitution, it issued an edict that ordered citizens to turn in all guns and ammunition to the authorities. They promised to return "sports guns" to their owners after inspection.[73]

The formerly democratic Philippines had gun registration in place on September 23, 1972, when President Ferdinand Marcos declared martial law and adopted dictatorial powers. He declared that it was his aim to "establish a gunless society," decreed that all firearms and ammunition be turned in, and announced that anyone who retained an unauthorized gun would face ten to fifteen years in prison. Within three months the regime claimed that it had seized 482,248 firearms, though officials guessed that a similar number of guns were still held illegally by the citizenry, and a suspiciously low number of rounds of ammunition had been surrendered.[74]

Bermuda had gun registration in place in 1973 when its governor and an aide were murdered. The government ordered the surrender of all handguns on the island.[75] A year later, in response to rising violence, Jamaica banned the private possession of firearms among all of the nation's two million citizens except the estimated twelve to fifteen thousand (less than 1 percent of the population) holders of private gun licenses.[76]

In 1990, shortly before the breakup of the Soviet Union, Lithuania declared its independence. In response, Soviet President Mikhail Gorbachev used his executive powers to order civilians in Lithuania to surrender private firearms to representatives of the Soviet government within seven days "for temporary keeping" and to authorize the Interior Ministry "to seize such weapons in cases of refusal to turn them in."[77] Registration of firearms was required under Soviet law, so lawful Lithuanian gun owners knew that the Soviet authorities had a list of people who, in effect, "owed them" a gun.[78]

In sum, in recent decades a number of national governments, both democratic and dictatorial, have banned gun possession, required mass turn-ins of guns, and have usually done so with registration laws already in place. The fact that this has happened in other nations does not prove that it is inevitable it will happen in the United States; it only shows that it has happened. Nevertheless, HCI's attitudes toward foreign nations' gun prohibitions may be symptomatic of the organization's view of prohibition in America. None of HCI's publications or website material condemn any of these foreign instances of gun confiscation or prohibition. Indeed, they include nothing but praise for the de facto ban on handguns and rifles in Great Britain, the handgun ban in Australia, and near-ban measures such as restrictive licensing in Germany, partially attributing foreign nations' lower violence rates to these laws.[79]

"Nondenial Denials" of Prohibitionist Intentions

If HCI and similar groups wanted to deny the NRA its most potent emotional tool for stimulating gun owner opposition to moderate controls, they would officially and publicly state that HCI was permanently committed to actively opposing prohibitionist controls, perhaps amending their charter to institutionalize this commitment. They could further strengthen this position by officially endorsing the view that the Second Amendment recognizes an inviolable, though not unlimited, individual right to keep and bear arms, and forbids gun bans that would disarm the mass of American citizens, though it permits a wide variety of rational gun regulations short of prohibition.

Such a position would have the advantage of comporting with the modern scholarly consensus on the Second Amendment. Of forty-eight law review articles published on the Second Amendment in the 1990s, forty-two endorsed the individual rights position, and most of the six minority articles were written by employees of gun control advocacy groups. Such an endorsement would also have the added political benefit of bringing HCI in line with the 78 to 87 percent of Americans who believe that they have a constitutionally guaranteed individual right to keep and bear arms.[80] Further, HCI could concede the now well-established fact that defensive use of guns is commonplace and effective, and that gun ownership among noncriminals therefore has significant violence- and crime-reducing effects.[81]

HCI has never repudiated these two absolutist principles and is not likely to do so in the foreseeable future. Given how potent a political weapon such a move would be, why does HCI not make it? Concerning the Second Amendment and defensive utility issues, HCI leaders would presumably assert that their current positions simply reflect reality, as they see it. They largely ignore the scholarly literature on the Second Amendment—HCI's website as of February 28, 2000, listed just seven articles on the Second Amendment, all but one of them written by their own general counsel, Dennis Henigan—and instead rely largely on ambiguous or even irrelevant federal court decisions as justification for their view that Americans have no individual, Constitutionally guaranteed right to own guns. Likewise, they either ignore evidence on the benefits of defensive ownership of guns or cite feeble one-sided speculations as to why evidence indicating utility is wrong.[82]

On the other hand, another simple explanation of HCI's adherence to these key premises of prohibitionist thought is that HCI leaders in fact either support gun bans, or at least want to hold open bans as an option in the future. Consistent with this interpretation, HCI does not actually deny desiring gun bans in future. Rather, their official policy statements, as found on their website, are silent on the matter and confined to addressing current legislative priorities.[83] When asked about prohibitionist intentions, HCI spokespersons commonly refer to their current agenda, saying HCI is not (present tense) "calling for" prohibition, a "nondenial denial" that obscures the distinction between long-term intentions and current agenda.

Support for Gun Bans Among Moderate Control Supporters in the General Population

It seems a safe assumption that people who belong to advocacy groups devoted to a given issue have, on average, stronger views on that issue than nonmembers and casual supporters in the general population. Thus, NRA members have more strongly anticontrol views than nonmember gun owners or anticontrol members of the general adult population.[84] Correspondingly, HCI members are likely to have more strongly procontrol views than non-members and procontrol members of the general population. Activist members are likely to have still stronger procontrol views than casual members, since it would be their stronger views that would motivate their greater involvement. And leaders and staff, who devote their lives to the issue, probably have the strongest opinions of all.

No surveys have been conducted on HCI members or the HCI leadership or staff (or at least no results have been publicly released), so we can only indirectly infer their views on handgun prohibition from surveys of the general adult population, using the aforementioned assumptions. Recent national surveys indicate that about 67 to 82 percent of the U.S. adult population favors requiring permits to buy guns, 66 to 81 percent favor handgun registration, and 67 percent favor limiting handgun purchases to one a month, all measures favored by HCI.[85] However, surveys conducted in 1999 also indicate that 34 to 50 percent of Americans favor banning the private possession of handguns.[86] Assuming that ban supporters are a subset of those who support less strict controls, these figures imply that most people who favor gun permits, registration, and similarly moderate controls also favor banning the private possession of handguns.

Thus, if one accepts the assumption that HCI members, staff, and leaders are more strongly procontrol than casual gun control supporters in the general population, these survey data imply that most HCI members, staff, and leaders personally support banning handgun possession. Personal opinions do not directly translate into organizational policy, given the restraining effect of political realities, but these data do suggest that the personal views of HCI members would incline them to support banning handguns in the future, should it become politically attainable. And since public support for banning handguns occasionally has approached a majority, it is perfectly possible that achieving a handgun ban could become politically feasible in the near future.

Public Statements Made by Leaders and Prominent Supporters of the Gun Control Lobby

The impression among many gun owners that gun control advocates favor gun bans, and are following a step-by-step strategy to achieve prohibition, is reinforced by numerous public statements made by the leaders of gun control advocacy organizations and by many of their most prominent supporters. A selection of such statements follows.

Of most direct relevance, some leaders of gun control organizations have openly expressed their desires to achieve bans on gun ownership in the long run, as well as their intention to pursue this goal using a step-by-step strategy:

—Nelson T. (Pete) Shields III, Chairman of Handgun Control, Inc.: "Our ultimate goal—total control of handguns in the United States—is going to take time. My estimate is from seven to ten years. The first problem is to slow down the increasing number of handguns being produced and sold in this country. The second problem is to get handguns registered. And the final problem is make the possession of *all* handguns and *all* ammunition—except for the military, policemen, licensed security guards, licensed sporting clubs, and licensed gun collectors—totally illegal."[87]

—J. Elliott Corbett, Secretary and Board Member of the National

Council for a Responsible Firearms Policy, a gun control advocacy group operating prior to the advent of HCI: "I personally believe handguns should be outlawed. . . . Our organization will probably officially take this stand in time but we are not anxious to rouse the opposition before we get the other legislation passed. It would be difficult to outlaw all rifles and shotguns because of the hunting sport. But there should be stiff regulations. . . . We thought the handgun bill [the Gun Control Act of 1968] was a step in the right direction. But, as you can see, our movement will be towards increasingly stiff controls."[88]

—Josh Sugarmann, Executive Director of the Violence Policy Center (describing the use that would be made of regulatory power granted by a bill VPC supported): "Any rational regulator with that authority would ban handguns."[89]

Many important political figures have likewise made clear their preference for gun bans in the long run, though they often revealed their true preferences to the public only after they left office:

—Ramsey Clark, Attorney General of the United States, 1967-1969: "I think we should work for the day when there are no guns at all, at least in urban areas—even for the police on normal duty."[90]

—Pat Brown, former governor of California: "I feel that we should take the general position that handguns should be barred except by police officials and other authorized people, and then try to find out how to seize them in the days ahead."[91]

—Patrick Murphy, former New York City Police Commissioner and President of the Police Foundation: "The time has come for us to disarm the individual citizen."[92]

Many prominent academics have also publicly expressed explicit support for gun prohibition:

—Marvin Wolfgang, arguably the nation's best known criminologist: "My personal choice for legislation is to remove all guns from private possession. I would favor statutory provisions that require all guns to be turned in to public authorities."[93]

—Noted sociologist Morris Janowitz: "I see no reason why anyone in a democratic society should own a weapon."[94]

—Norval Morris, legal scholar and unsuccessful nominee in 1978 to head the federal Law Enforcement Assistance Administration (with coauthor Gordon Hawkins): "Licensing of guns . . . is an excessively cautious, only marginally useful mechanism, other than as a wedge to more rational legislation. We seek a disarmed population."[95]

—Prominent sociologist and Special Advisor to the president in the Carter administration, Amitai Etzioni: "Domestic disarmament . . . would result in a decrease in murder from 40 percent to 45 percent and an estimated decrease in armed robbery of 23 percent to 26 percent."[96]

Etzioni later founded the Communitarian Network, which in 1991 endorsed as part of its platform "domestic disarmament," i.e., the total banning of the private possession of all firearms. Among the signatories to the platform, in addition to Etzioni, were Newton Minnow, Henry Cisneros (former Secretary of Housing and Urban Development in the Clinton administration), Albert Shanker (president of the American Federation of Teachers); pollster Daniel Yankelovich, economist Lester Thurow, and distinguished sociologists Gary Marx, Alice Rossi, Robert Bellah, and Dennis Wrong.[97]

Journalists affiliated with major news outlets also have publicly called for prohibition.

—Juan Williams of the *Washington Post*: "I don't understand why we're piddling around. We should talk about getting rid of guns in this country."[98]

—Michael Gartner, then president of NBC News: "I now think the only way to control handgun use in this country is to prohibit the guns. And the only way to do that is to change the Constitution."[99]

—Jack E. White, National Correspondent of *Time* magazine: "Whatever is being proposed is way too namby-pamby. I mean, for example, we're talking about limiting people to one gun purchase, or handgun purchase a month. Why not just ban the ownership of handguns when nobody needs one? Why not just ban semiautomatic rifles? Nobody needs one."[100]

Other prominent prohibitionists support gun bans covertly, so this support can only be inferred, with some uncertainty, from their public statements. President Bill Clinton is arguably the most prominent of all prohibitionists. One year into his first term, he was asked by a reporter for his opinion on "banning handguns." Given a straightforward opportunity to state whether he personally supported or opposed banning handguns, Clinton instead carefully confined his answer to an assessment of the short-term political achievability of such a measure: "I don't think the American people are there right now. But with more than 200 million guns in circulation, we've got so much more to do on this issue before we even reach that. I don't think that's an option now. But there are certain kinds of guns that can be banned and a lot of other reasonable regulations that can be imposed."[101]

For those who oppose prohibition, the issue of political achievability is irrelevant to their views—if they feel prohibition is a bad idea on the merits, then there is no need to think about whether it is achievable. Consequently, Clinton's focus on achievability would seem to indicate that he supported, or at least did not oppose, the idea of handgun prohibition in principle. In any case, it is indisputable that, given an opportunity to indicate his opposition, if that were his position, Clinton chose not to do so. This in spite of the fact that it would have been in his political interest to do so, given his awareness that "the American people are not there yet," i.e., that opinion polls indicate that most Americans oppose banning handguns.

Further, Clinton managed, in very brief remarks, to twice refer to political conditions "now," thereby stressing that his assessment of political achievability pertained only to the present. The strong implication was that Clinton viewed these conditions as changeable, that the opinions of "the American people" could be "shaped" in future in a more strongly proban direction. Clinton even outlined an incrementalist strategy by which stronger controls could be achieved: ban "certain kinds of guns" (presumably referring to, at minimum, "assault weapons") and impose "a lot of other reasonable regulations."

Among other "reasonable regulations" that Clinton eventually proposed, in addition to banning "assault weapons," was a ban on the possession of handguns by all young adults aged eighteen to twenty. The significance of this proposal is that the ban applies to noncriminals as much as to criminals, i.e., to both the vast majority of young adults who would never commit an act of violence with a handgun, and to the small minority who would. The rationale for this measure is that persons in this age group are more likely to be violent than people in other age groups. This is indeed true (and would also be true if the prohibition covered persons aged eighteen to thirty-nine), but it is also true that only a tiny share of eighteen- to twenty-year-olds will commit an act of gun violence. Thus, we have a prohibitionist argument in its starkest form: everyone must be denied guns to stop the few who would misuse them.

In sum, prohibitionist goals and intentions are frequently endorsed by prominent gun control supporters, and even some leaders of gun control advocacy organizations. This does not prove that all such organizations, including HCI, currently have explicit covert plans to pursue prohibition via an incremental strategy. But it does mean that many prominent people seriously advocate prohibition, that the prospect of gun bans is not merely a phantom menace "whistled up" by the gun lobby, and that it is perfectly reasonable that the leaders and staff of organizations that do not openly advocate prohibition may nevertheless covertly favor it.

The Premises and Logic of Arguments for Moderate Controls

Perhaps the strongest evidence of prohibitionist intentions among gun control advocates, including the leaders and staff of HCI, are the premises and arguments that they use to argue in favor of moderate controls, since the premises and arguments logically lead to prohibitionist conclusions.

HCI now supports bans on both (1) SNSs, which are cheap and small (and thus more easily concealed) yet less lethal than other guns, and on (2) "assault weapons," which are generally more expensive, larger (and thus less easily concealed) and supposedly more lethal than other guns. But if one advocates banning both big guns and little guns, both more lethal and less lethal guns, both expensive and cheap guns, what does that logically leave as guns that are *not* suitable candidates for banning? Can there be any serious arguments, other than ones based solely on changeable political realities, that banning both big guns and little guns is a good idea, but banning middle-sized guns, which are both moderately concealable and moderately lethal, is not a good idea?

HCI has supported and helped organize a campaign of lawsuits by municipal and county governments against gun manufacturers, through their Legal Action Project (LAP). HCI boasts that it has "pioneered innovative theories of gun industry liability" and that, as of August 18, 1999, LAP was co-counsel for fifteen of the twenty-seven cities and counties that had filed suit.[102] Opponents argue that the purpose of the lawsuit campaign is to either drive the gunmakers into bankruptcy from the costs of defending against dozens of frivolous lawsuits, or to increase prices of guns to the point where most people could not afford to buy one, an outcome equivalent to a prohibitive tax. That is, they accuse HCI of trying to ban the further manufacture of guns, using lawsuits to achieve what could not be attained through legislative means.[103] HCI insists that it merely wants to induce the gun companies to "reform" themselves by making safer guns and exerting more control over the distribution and marketing of their guns.[104]

The legal theories used by HCI and the way in which the lawsuits are targeted, however, are inconsistent with HCI's stated justifications. For example, HCI's lawyers have argued that gun companies should be sued for making guns that lack "personalized gun" technology, i.e., locking devices that are an integral part of guns and that permit only authorized users to fire the gun.[105] For most existing gun models, no demonstrably reliable personalized gun technology that would meet HCI's implicit specifications currently exists, making it impossible for gun firms to have installed such devices in these models. For example, among currently manufactured guns, the Magna-Trigger (an existing locking device) can only be installed in large-frame Smith & Wesson revolvers.[106]

Other technologies, such as the Oxford Micro Devices fingerprint lock or the Fulton Arms SSR-6 handgun, might be usable in many types of guns but exist only in the form of unproven prototypes. One such prototype, of the much-touted Colt Z-40, failed to function in one of its first public demonstrations.[107] Still other devices, not true "smart gun" technology, require an affirmative action, such as pushing a lever or putting a wristlet on, to either lock the gun or to make it operable. This makes the devices only marginally better than far cheaper low-tech gun locks. Reliable and affordable personalized gun technology may eventually be developed, but it does not exist yet and may be many years away.[108]

This does not represent an obstacle to HCI lawyers, who assert that gunmakers should also be held liable for harm done due to the firms' failure to develop *new* personalized gun technology in the first place. It is not certain whether it is even possible to develop any sufficiently reliable technology. But even if it could be developed, there is no conceivable technology that gun companies could adopt that would guarantee that HCI would not organize lawsuits against them based on the same basic legal theories. Guns will necessarily always be dangerous as long as they function as guns, i.e., fire a projectile at high velocity. Since there is no known upper limit on human inventiveness and possible future technological developments, someone could always sue gun companies, regardless of the safety technologies they had already developed and installed in their guns, for making guns that are dangerous in a way that hypothetically could have been prevented by some future, theoretically possible, technology. Consequently, no matter how amenable to "reform" some gun manufacturers might be, there is nothing they could do that would guarantee protection from being sued into bankruptcy under HCI-developed theories of manufacturer liability.

In contrast, if HCI were sincerely interested in merely motivating gun companies to become more "responsible," the most effective tactics would be to sue the least responsible firms while "rewarding" the most responsible ones by not suing them. This is not, however, the pattern that HCI-assisted lawsuits have followed. Every major handgun manufacturer in the United States has been sued, regardless of their efforts to improve gun safety, including Colt, Smith and Wesson, and Beretta.[109] Thus, regardless of their efforts to improve gun safety, no handgun maker has been immune, and no firm's efforts were regarded as sufficient.

HCI also helped bring a private lawsuit in California (*Dix* v. *Beretta*) based on the argument that handgun makers should be held liable for harm arising from accidents involving one of their guns, if the firearm did not have a "gun loaded" indicator. Beretta is one of the few companies that make handguns with such a device, yet HCI helped sue Beretta, because, in HCI's view, the gun loaded indicator was inadequate. Likewise, Colt Industries and Smith and Wesson spent millions of dollars developing personalized gun technology of the very type that HCI wants (so far, no reliable prototype has been developed), but HCI nevertheless helped bring suits against these firms as well.[110]

In sum, neither the legal theories HCI has devised nor their choice of targets for lawsuits supports their claims about why they are supporting the lawsuits. On the other hand, HCI's policies are completely consistent with the hypothesis that they are seeking to effectively ban the further manufacture of guns via a wave of lawsuits aimed at bankrupting the gun industry.

One of the bedrock premises of HCI ideology is that guns cannot provide any significant benefit in the form of defensive use. Empirical evidence is overwhelmingly contrary to this premise, but its factual accuracy is irrelevant for present purposes.[111] Rather, the irony of this position is that, given rejection of any constitutionally protected individual right to keep and bear arms, it deprives those who claim to support only limited, nonprohibitionist controls of their only serious rationale for supporting only limited controls and not gun bans. The pleasures associated with recreational uses of guns, such as hunting or target shooting, cannot compare in seriousness with the harms associated with violent uses of guns, such as death and injury linked with crime, suicide, or gun accidents. Therefore, if one accepts the premise that gun availability increases these harms, as gun control advocates obviously do, but also holds to the premise that guns provide no significant capability for reducing death and injury from criminal violence, the only reasonable policy conclusion is that the more we limit gun availability, the less death and injury there will be. Thus, the logical implication is that we should limit gun availability as much as we can, and should pursue gun prohibition as soon as it is attainable.

Indeed, under the assumption that there are no significant violence-reducing effects of gun ownership and use, there is virtually a moral imperative to pursue the strictest controls achievable under prevailing political conditions, right up to and including prohibition. Doing anything less would necessarily mean that there was more death and injury than there would have been with a gun ban. In sum, HCI's premises imply a moral obligation to pursue prohibition.

If the effect of gun availability is overwhelmingly a violence-increasing one, then the fewer guns there are, the better, from a violence-reduction standpoint. If, however, one permits the mass of the population to have guns, by having only the "commonsense" laws that HCI currently advocates, but not a gun ban, this means that a huge supply of guns will remain in civilian hands and thus will continue to be available to criminals, as well as the suicide-prone and accident-prone. Even if all voluntary gun transfers, whether through dealers or private transfers, were somehow eliminated, there would still remain the estimated 750,000 guns stolen each year, mostly in residential burglaries (341,000 household gun theft incidents per year, times 2.2 guns stolen per household theft incident).[112] This is far more than enough to maintain a level of gun ownership among criminals sufficient to sustain the highest known levels of gun violence, since probably no more that a few hundred thousand different guns are used to commit crimes each year.[113]

These facts, when combined with HCI premises, strongly suggest a prohibitionist conclusion: the only realistic way one can effectively deny guns to criminals is to deny guns to everyone, i.e., to ban gun ownership. Once one assumes there are no significant violence-reducing effects of gun ownership, nor any constitutional obstacles to gun bans, there is no significant cost to disarming noncriminals and thus no compelling reason *not* to ban the private possession of guns.

Another variant of this reasoning is evident when gun control supporters discuss the violence-increasing effects of gun ownership, but without addressing who possesses the guns. By omission, gun ownership itself is portrayed as increasing violence, or at best having no effect, independent of the character of those who possess and use the guns, since anyone might do harm with them. The possibility that the power-enhancing impact of weapons might have very different effects on violence depending on whether victims or aggressors possess them is simply not considered, or is superficially dismissed on the basis of one-sided speculation and selective citation of technically inferior or even irrelevant evidence.[114]

Statements made by Clinton administration spokespersons defending its support of gun buyback programs perfectly exemplify this variant of prohibitionist logic. A spokesman for the Department of Housing and Urban Development insisted that even though the programs do not directly disarm criminals, eliminating any gun ultimately reduces the risk of death or injury, explaining that "the first purpose of [gun buybacks] is not trying to stop bad guys from robbing banks or bad guys from shooting each other. The first purpose is to get guns out of homes."[115] Thus, even disarming noncriminals (i.e., persons other than "bad guys") was, according to the Clinton administration, likely to reduce deaths and injuries.

This reasoning is closely related to another premise of HCI/gun control ideology that leads to prohibitionist conclusions. This is the venerable article of faith that the typical killer is a "regular Joe" with little prior record of crime or violence, who therefore is not a "real criminal."[116] This element of the ideology was developed to deal with an obvious objection to gun control as crime control: if only lawbreakers commit crimes with guns, but lawbreakers will not obey gun laws, how can gun laws prevent gun crimes such as gun homicides? The solution to this rhetorical problem was to assert that there were significant numbers of people who, although they did commit a homicide or other crime with a gun, were nevertheless, prior to this isolated violent act, law-abiding enough to obey gun laws. Therefore, gun laws could have prevented their violent acts.[117]

The "regular Joe" imagery of killers implies that a large share of homicides committed with guns are committed by persons who previously showed no significant signs that they were likely to be violent in future. That is, they had no prior criminal convictions, no known record of mental illness accompanied by violent outbursts, no known record of violent reactions to drug use, and so on. The higher the fraction of killers one believes fit this imagery of "normal" killers committing a single isolated act of criminal violence, the more necessary it is to support gun prohibition to reduce homicide, i.e., to deny guns to everyone, not just those with criminal convictions or similar official indicators of high-risk status. If anyone might become violent, everyone must be denied guns.

In its early years, HCI openly advocated handgun prohibition, as CSGV and VPC still do today. None openly advocate banning private possession of all types of guns, presumably because it is currently a political impossibility. Only about 17 percent of U.S. adults support banning all gun ownership.[118] Unfortunately, for reasons noted earlier, banning only handguns, but not long guns, is a fatally flawed policy. Banning only handguns, while leaving over 150 million shotguns and rifles available, would be likely to prove so counterproductive that handgun ban advocates would have to either repudiate their support for any kind of gun prohibition (an unlikely eventuality) or attempt to correct the mistake by pursuing a ban on long guns as well, in hopes of removing the more lethal substitute weapons.[119] Thus, the flaws inherent in handgun-only bans would create strong pressures for an escalation to a complete ban on guns of all types.

The Advocacy of Licensing and Registration in Addition to Background Checks

The principal federal legislative initiative of HCI at the turn of the millennium was the bill informally known as "Brady II," which mandates national registration of guns and licensing of gun owners.[120] It is called Brady II because it is a follow-up to the Brady Act, which required a criminal background check for all persons attempting to acquire a gun from a licensed dealer. Given that a background check already prevents convicted criminals from legally acquiring guns from licensed dealers, what additional violence-reduction benefit could reasonably be expected from licensing owners and registering guns?

For those pursuing prohibitionist goals, the value of licensing and registration is obvious. Licensing and registration make administratively feasible what would otherwise be a utopian effort to disarm the civilian American population. If one eventually got a federal law passed that banned the private possession of guns, or handguns, compliance with the law would obviously be higher if the government possessed a list of all those known to own guns and of the guns that they owned. Under current political conditions, it is unlikely such a list would be used to guide massive, and very expensive, house-to-house searches and confiscations. Rather, the utility of registration records would primarily derive from their value for compelling compliance with gun confiscation, due to gun owners' knowledge that their gun ownership was recorded with the government, and thus that the government knew which citizens "owed" them guns.

Anyone who was on the registration lists who did not turn in all registered guns by a gun ban deadline could be presumed to be in violation of the possession ban, and would be a high-priority candidate for rationally targeted, and thus more constitutionally defensible, law enforcement attention. Since random searches of homes are not likely to be authorized in the United States, registration lists could be used to establish probable cause for issuance of selectively targeted search warrants to find contraband guns.

Registration supporters sometimes even concede the advantages of registration for purposes of selective confiscation of guns from criminals.[121] Pete Shields denied that registration would *lead to* mass confiscation, but never denied that it would be helpful in implementing mass confiscation. Nevertheless, HCI did not propose any government registry of guns in 1981. By 1994, however, after the Brady Act was passed, HCI had expanded its goals to include registration.[122]

The perception that registration could lead to confiscation is by no means a rare one in the United States. In a 1978 national survey, 51 percent of U.S. adults agreed with the statement that "a national gun registration program might well eventually lead to the confiscation of registered firearms by the government."[123] Thus, the belief that registration might have this consequence cannot honestly be portrayed as an idea confined to NRA members or right-wing extremists.

While the value of licensing and registration for enforcing a mass confiscation of guns is self-evident, its violence reduction benefits are completely undocumented. Advocates used to claim that registration would facilitate identifying and convicting criminals who used guns to commit violent crimes, apparently envisioning significant numbers of offenders who registered their guns and then abandoned them at the scene of a crime.[124] The implausibility of this scenario, and the rarity with which police used existing state registration systems to identify suspects, probably contributed to this rationale losing its popularity.[125] Nevertheless, HCI still justifies registration by asserting that it "allows for speedier and more reliable tracing of guns used in crime" and would reduce the number of criminals who "escape conviction because there is no papertrail or evidence linking them to the crime guns they used." HCI does not, however, cite any data from existing state registration systems concerning how often registration records were instrumental in securing criminal convictions.[126]

A second, marginally less dubious rationale is now generally preferred by registration supporters. HCI states that "registration is designed to reduce illegal gun trafficking by providing for more efficient tracing of guns used in crimes" to the dealers involved in illicit gun sales.[127] This rationale is based on the empirically unsupported claim, promoted by the U.S. Bureau of Alcohol, Tobacco, and Firearms (BATF), that a large share of criminals acquire guns as a result of the activities of high-volume gun traffickers, and thus that criminal gun possession could be significantly reduced by identifying and prosecuting these traffickers.[128]

Empirical evidence indicates that such traffickers account for only a tiny share of criminal guns, operate in large numbers only in a handful of places (a few large cities in the Northeast), and that most of the few criminals who get their guns from traffickers could also get guns from other sources if the traffickers did not operate. Instead, theft and private transfers by persons not in the business of dealing guns are the primary means by which criminals acquire guns.[129]

It cannot be accurately argued that registration has never been tried, and thus not given a chance to show its merits. At least a half dozen states have implemented registration (mostly of handguns). Empirical assessments of gun law impact have consistently indicated that state registration laws have no measurable effect on rates of crime or violence.[130]

Licensing of gun owners likewise seems redundant for crime control purposes, once one has background checks on prospective gun buyers, as is already required for purchases from licensed dealers under the Brady Act. These checks could be extended to nondealer transfers by requiring private buyers and sellers to use licensed dealers as brokers, who would then perform the usual checks. This, however, would not require licensing. HCI claims that licensing is needed to permit more thorough background checks, involving fingerprinting and more time-consuming checks of paper records than are possible under the present "instant" background checks. They also argue that licensing would permit better residency verification, thereby disrupting interstate gun running, and would require completion of a gun safety course.[131]

What is most noteworthy for present purposes is that licensing of owners is not needed to accomplish any of these goals. The government could issue certificates of nonfelon status, based on background checks as thorough and prolonged as one could want, without retaining lists of persons receiving the certificates, and then merely require that prospective gun buyers present an up-to-date certificate before a gun could be transferred. Under such a system, there would be no government-controlled list of gun owners generated. Likewise, certificates of completion of a gun safety course, or of residency, could be issued without any government retaining lists of recipients.

Thus, the one goal that HCI's licensing proposal would indisputably achieve that could not be easily achieved by these other means is a federal government list of all legal gun owners. Likewise, the only goal clearly achieved by registration is that it would provide a complete list of guns legally owned by those licensed owners. Thus, the element that HCI appears most intent on achieving is government records of who owns guns and what guns they own. In sum, HCI places highest priority on giving the government a resource that would indisputably facilitate mass confiscation of guns, but that has no documented value for reducing crime or violence.

This does not imply that all supporters of licensing and registration secretly view these as tools for mass confiscation. Some advocates are simply honestly mistaken or unrealistically optimistic about the crime-control value of the measures, while more casual supporters probably have not thought very much about the full set of implications of licensing and registration. On the other hand, the potential that registration records could be used to facilitate mass confiscation cannot have escaped the notice of professional gun control advocates, and is clearly not so dire a prospect that it deters them from supporting registration, on the basis of only the most weakly supported and speculative potential crime-control benefits.

Conclusions

Of the three most prominent gun control advocacy groups, two, CSGV and VPC, openly support handgun prohibition, while the third, HCI, once openly advocated the same thing, but ceased to do so only when it decided that prohibition was, at least for the moment, politically unachievable. The evidence reviewed herein nevertheless supports the proposition that the HCI leadership continues to support handgun prohibition despite apparent disclaimers to the contrary. The premises and logic of HCI's arguments for moderate gun controls lead to prohibitionist conclusions, and its advocacy of federal registration and licensing, when background checks on prospective gun transferees are already in place, suggests a desire to gain the administrative tools for implementing prohibition. HCI currently supports bans on gun types such as SNSs and "assault weapons," has actively supported both state and local handgun bans in the past, has commented favorably on foreign prohibitions, and has neither repudiated its past support of prohibition nor committed itself to opposing prohibition in the future.

Another way to think about this issue is to consider whether there is any evidence that is clearly inconsistent with this conclusion, that affirmatively indicates that the leaders of HCI oppose prohibition, as distinct from merely regarding it as currently unattainable. This chapter was submitted to HCI to give its leaders an opportunity to rebut any of its points prior to publication. HCI did not respond.

The American gun control debate is frequently dishonest. Sometimes the dishonesty is of the banal type common in all political debates—exaggeration, selective attention to evidence and to the possible implications of the evidence, creation of distorted straw man versions of one's opponent's positions, and so on. However, many gun control advocates also distort the gun debate by concealing exactly what it is that they would ultimately like to achieve, and thereby obscuring the full set of consequences of passing the "reasonable" measures that they currently advocate.

Most Americans oppose banning handguns or all guns, and would, as gun ban advocates have conceded, be less likely to support moderate controls if they thought that they would lead to prohibition. Consequently, some gun control proponents choose to be less than forthright about the full set of reasons why they support moderate controls. As a result, the debate over a given moderate control is distorted in that some of the consequences of the control becoming law are not honestly discussed.

In turn, some people who sincerely support only moderate controls and who oppose prohibition are misled as to the full set of possible consequences of their support for measures like registration or licensing. Further, their motives are unfairly impugned by gun control opponents who wrongly lump them in with the many prominent advocates who support moderate controls as stepping stones to prohibition.

As long as gun control advocacy groups like HCI continue to hold open the possibility of the group's future support for prohibition, by declining to formally forswear any such future support, it will be impossible to confine debate to the merits of more moderate controls. Instead the debate over a given control will always be distorted by what ought to be, in an ideal world, irrelevant concerns about the slippery slope implications of passing the measure.

For example, when the Consumer Product Safety Commission (CPSC) was created, Congress denied the agency jurisdiction over firearms and ammunition precisely because of fears that a future administration might use the agency's authority to declare guns and/or ammunition to be dangerous products and to ban their further manufacture. This was unfortunate, since the authority might also have been used, in a less politically toxic environment, to prevent the manufacture of guns with faults that any gun owner would acknowledge to be defects, such as a tendency to discharge if dropped on a hard surface.[132] Now, HCI is pushing to give authority over guns to CPSC, supposedly to get manufacturers to produce guns that are not needlessly dangerous, but concerns over prohibition are again contaminating discussion of the potential merits.[133]

Of course, if people took slippery slope thinking to its logical conclusion with respect to all social problems, it would imply that no solution, no matter how sensible or effective, could be adopted, for fear that it would lead to a harmful overdose of the solution. Conservative advocates of the death penalty would, if they consistently applied slippery slope thinking in all problem areas, have to drop their support, for fear that providing capital punishment for murder would lead to its use to punish shoplifting, then drunk driving, then speeding, littering, and disturbing the peace.[134]

Thus, people are selective about where they choose to apply slippery slope reasoning. Gun control opponents, however, have sound reasons to suspect many advocates of seeking prohibition and for fearing that advocates are trying to create or exploit a slippery slope. Many, probably most, supporters of moderate controls do favor banning the private possession of handguns at minimum, and advocacy groups do believe in premises, and use arguments, that imply prohibitionist conclusions.

Nevertheless, despite decades of effort, gun ban supporters have not managed to increase popular support for prohibition.[135] There is nothing inevitable about a slippery slope leading from moderate gun controls to prohibition. It is perfectly possible to go only so far and then stop. There is, rather, a slippery slope only to the extent that (1) extremist advocates work to create one, by pushing, openly or covertly, for prohibition, and (2) the rest of the citizenry allow them to do so.[136]

The gun control debate is carried out at two levels: (1) the overt debate over whatever moderate regulatory control is currently being considered, and (2) the subterranean or background debate over prohibition measures that are not even under formal consideration. To stop the overt debate from being distorted by the subterranean debate, prominent gun control organizations claiming to support only moderate "commonsense" measures will have to formally, and convincingly, commit themselves to permanent opposition to any future "control" measures that would disarm most of the American population.

Notes

1. Gallup Organization, survey conducted on 17-19 December 1993 for Cable News Network and USA Today. Lexis-Nexis Academic Universe, Public Opinion Online, accession number 0213597.

2. Gary Kleck, *Point Blank: Guns and Violence in America* (New York: Aldine, 1991), p. 355.

3. Chester Britt III, Gary Kleck, and David J. Bordua, "A Reassessment of the D.C. Gun Law: Some Cautionary Notes on the Use of Interrupted Time Series Designs for Policy Impact assessment," *Law & Society Review* 30 (1996): 361-80.

4. Pete Shields, *Guns Don't Die—People Do* (New York: Arbor House, 1981), p. 155.

5. Ibid., p. 148.

6. Gary Kleck, *Targeting Guns: Firearms and Their Control* (New York: Aldine, 1997), pp. 110–12.

7. *St. Petersburg Times*, 12 December 1993, p. 3D.

8. Andrew D. Herz, "Gun Crazy," *Boston University Law Review* 75 (1995): 89.

9. Robert J. Spitzer, *The Politics of Gun Control* (Chatham, N.J.: Chatham House, 1995), p. 125.

10. *New York Times*, 16 May 1992, p. 22.

11. Andrew J. McClurg, "The Rhetoric of Gun Control," *The American University Law Review* 42 (1992): 59.

12. Shields, *Guns Don't Die*, pp. 47–48.

13. Robert J. Kukla, *Gun Control* (Harrisburg, Pa.: Stackpole Books, 1973); Alan Gottlieb, *The Gun Grabbers* (Bellevue, Wash.: Bobbs Merrill, 1994); National Rifle Association (NRA) website at http://www.nra.org, accessed 28 February 2000; see Joseph E. Olson and David B. Kopel, "All the Way Down the Slippery Slope," *Hamline Law Review* 22 (1999): 399-465 for a detailed discussion of how a slippery slope has worked with respect to legal controls over guns in England.

14. Kleck, *Targeting Guns*, pp. 337, 346; Shields, *Guns Don't Die*, p. 146; Edward F. Leddy, *Magnum Force Lobby: The National Rifle Association Fights Gun Control* (Lanham, Md.: University Press of America, 1987), p. 130.

15. Kukla, *Gun Control*; Gottlieb, *The Gun Grabbers*.

16. Gottlieb, *The Gun Grabbers*; Shields, *Guns Don't Die*.

17. Richard Harris, "A Reporter at Large—Hanguns," *The New Yorker*, 26 July 1976, pp. 53, 58; *St. Louis Post Dispatch*, 8 May 1993, p. 1A; *Chicago Tribune*, 5 December 1999, p. C3; "Peter Jennings Reporting: Guns," ABC telecast, 24 January 1990.

18. Charles Krauthammer, "Disarming the Citizenry. But Not Yet," *Wash-*

ington Post, 5 April 1996, p. A19; see also Mike Royko, "Assault on Weapons Missing the Mark," *Chicago Tribune* 6 May 1994, sec. 1, p. 3.

19. *New York Times*, 15 August 1993, sec. 4, p. 4.

20. Shields, *Guns Don't Die*; Handgun Control, Inc. (HCI) website at http://www.handguncontrol.org. Accessed 28 February 2000.

21. Handgun Control, Inc., "Motion of Handgun Control, Inc. for Leave to File a Brief Amicus Curiae." U.S. Court of Appeals for the Seventh Circuit, Quilici et al. vs. Village of Morton Grove, On Appeal from the United States District Court for Northern District of Illinois, Eastern Division, 1982.

22. *McIntosh* v. *Washington*, Atlantic Reporter, 2d series, vol. 395, p. 746.

23. Don B. Kates Jr., "Public Opinion: The Effects of Extremist Discourse on the Gun Debate," in *The Great American Gun Debate*, ed. Don B. Kates Jr. and Gary Kleck (San Francisco: Pacific Research Institute, 1997), p. 110.

24. Judith Vandell Holmberg and Michael Clancy, *People vs. Handguns* (Washington, D.C.: U.S. Conference of Mayors, 1977), p. 70.

25. HCI website, "What's Next: The Complete Handgun Control Legislative Agenda."

26. Kleck, *Point Blank*, pp. 72–73, 95; Kleck, *Targeting Guns*, pp. 117–18, 124–26.

27. Gottlieb, *The Gun Grabbers*, p. 5.

28. Shields, *Guns Don't Die*, pp. 147–48, 157; Steven Brill, *Firearm Abuse: A Research and Policy Report* (Washington, D.C.: Police Foundation, 1977), pp. v, 52, 59–60, 146.

29. James D. Wright and Peter H. Rossi, *Armed and Considered Dangerous: A Survey of Felons and Their Firearms* (New York: Aldine, 1986), pp. 215–23; Gary Kleck, "Handgun-only Gun Control," in *Firearms and Violence: Issues of Public Policy*, ed. Don B. Kates Jr. (Cambridge: Ballinger, 1984); Kleck, *Point Blank*, pp. 83–91.

30. Gregg Lee Carter, *The Gun Control Movement* (New York.: Twayne Publishers, 1997), p. 75.

31. Coalition to Stop Gun Violence (CSGV), CSGV website at http://www.gunfree.org/csgv. Accessed 28 February 2000.

32. Violence Policy Center (VPC) website at http://www.vpc.org. Accessed 21 February 2000.

33. Josh Sugarmann, "Laws That Can't Stop a Bullet," *New York Times*, 4 November 1999, p. A29.

34. Kleck, "Handgun-only Gun Control," pp. 177–85; Kleck, *Targeting Guns*, p. 303.

35. Handgun Epidemic Lowering Plan (HELP) Network website at http://www.childmmc.edu /help/helphome.htm. Accessed 31 March 2000. *American Medical News*, 3 January 1994, 9.

36. Ceasefire, Inc. website at http://www.ceasefire.org. Accessed 31 March 2000.

37. Gottlieb, *The Gun Grabbers*, p. 97; Joseph D. Alviani and William R. Drake, *Handgun Control . . . Issues and Alternatives* (Washington, D.C.: U.S. Conference of Mayors, 1975), pp. 45–46.

38. Harris, "Reporter at Large," p. 58; *Parade*, 18 September 1977, p. 9.

39. HCI website, "About HCI"; Carter, *The Gun Control Movement*, p. 75.

40. Shields, *Guns Don't Die*, pp. 73–74; Kleck, *Targeting Guns*, p. 345.

41. Pete Shields. Letter from Pete Shields to members of the National Council to Control Handguns, 15 November 1978, p. 4.

42. Shields, *Guns Don't Die*, p. 146.

43. Robert Benjamin, "Handgun Opponent: 'Morton Grove Law Could Hurt'," *Chicago Tribune*, 23 January 1982, sec. 1, p. 7.

44. Kleck, *Point Blank*, p. 355.

45. Franklin E. Zimring and Gordon Hawkins, *The Citizen's Guide to Gun Control* (New York: Macmillan, 1987), p. 118.

46. Don B. Kates, Jr., "Public Opinion: The Effects of Extremist Discourse on the Gun Debate," in *The Great American Gun Debate*.

47. HCI website, "Guns in the Home"; "The Myth of the Second Amendment."

48. James D. Wright, "Ten Essential Observations on Guns in America," *Society* 32 (1995): 66.

49. McClurg, "The Rhetoric of Gun Control," p. 85.

50. Gary Kleck, "Crime Control Through the Private Use of Armed Force," *Social Problems* 35 (1988): 1-21; Gary Kleck and Susan Sayles, "Rape and Resistance," *Social Problems* 37 (1990): 149-62; Gary Kleck and Miriam DeLone, "Victim Resistance and Offender Weapon Effects in Robbery," *Journal of Quantitative Criminology* 9 (1993): 55-82; Lawrence Southwick Jr., "Self-Defense with Guns: The Consequences," *Journal of Criminal Justice* 28 (2000): 351–70; Gary Kleck and Marc Gertz, "Armed Resistance to Crime: The Prevalence and Nature of Self-Defense with a Gun," *Journal of Criminal Law and Criminology* 86 (1995): 150-87; see also chapters 6 and 7.

51. Kleck, *Point Blank*, p. 344.

52. Ibid., pp. 344–47.

53. Wright and Rossi, *Armed and Considered Dangerous*, p. 217; Kleck, "Handgun-only Gun Control," pp. 177–85, 188–94.

54. Kleck, "Handgun-only Gun Control," pp. 171–76; Kleck, *Point Blank*, pp. 91–92, 461–65.

55. David J. Bordua, Alan J. Lizotte, and Gary Kleck, with Van Cagle, *Patterns of Firearms Ownership, Regulation and Use in Illinois* (Springfield, Ill.: Illinois Law Enforcement Commission, 1979).

56. Kleck, *Targeting Guns*, p. 99; U.S. Bureau of the Census, *Statistical Abstract of the United States—1999* (Washington, D.C.: U.S. Government Printing Office, 1999), p. 17.

57. Ragnar Benson, *Modern Weapon Caching: A Down-to-Earth Approach to Beating the Government Gun Grab* (Boulder, Colo.: Paladin Press, 1990).

58. *Los Angeles Times*, 20 November 1991, p. A25; 24 April 1992, p. A28.

59. HCI website, "Pending Legislation"; "Federal Legislative Priorities."

60. HCI website, "What's Hot: The Fight to Close Gun Law Loopholes."

61. Shields, *Guns Don't Die*, pp. 47–48; see also pp. 54, 141.

62. Sam Fields, "Handgun Prohibition and Social Necessity," *St. Louis University Law Journal* 23 (1979): 35-36.

63. Compare U.S. Federal Bureau of Investigation, C*rime in the United States, 1989—Uniform Crime Reports* (Washington, D.C.: U.S. Government Printing Office, 1990), p. 11, with U.S. Federal Bureau of Investigation, *Crime in the United States, 1981—Uniform Crime Reports* (Washington, D.C.: U.S. Government Printing Office, 1982), p. 12; Kleck, *Targeting Guns*, pp. 112–17, 141–43.

64. Lee Kennett and James LaVerne Anderson, *The Gun in America* (Westport, Conn.: Greenwood Press, 1975); Kleck, *Point Blank*, pp. 354–57.

65. Britt et al., "A Reassessment," pp. 369–70.

66. National Council to Control Handguns (NCCH), "Statement on the Firearms Issue" (Washington, D.C.: NCCH, 1974); Alviani and Drake, *Handgun Control*; Clarke Rupert, "Handgun Control Legislation: 97th Congress," paper presented at the annual meetings of the American Society of Criminology, 13 November 1981; *Minneapolis Star Tribune*, 15 June 1992, p. 13A; *Congressional Record*, 103d Cong., 2d sess., 1993, 139, pt. 10:9088.

67. Shields, *Guns Don't Die*, pp. 86–87.

68. Holmberg and Clancy, *People vs. Handguns*.

69. *Washington Post*, 20 October 1999, p. A1.

70. *Washington Post*, 26 February 1982, p. A11.

71. Kleck, *Point Blank*, pp. 354–6.

72. Kleck, *Targeting Guns*, p. 345.

73. *New York Times*, 24 February 1967, p. 4.

74. Tillman Durdin, "More Politicians Are Arrested in the Philippines," *New York Times*, 29 September 1972, p. 2; Tillman Durdin, "Publisher Is Held by Manila Regime," *New York Times*, 6 December 1972, p. 8; 3 January 1973, p. 9; Robert Sherrill, *The Saturday Night Special* (New York: Charterhouse, 1973), pp. 272–73.

75. *New York Times* 14 March 1973, p. 8; Sherrill, *The Saturday Night Special*, p. 271.

76. Edward Diener and Rick Crandall, "An Evaluation of the Jamaican Anticrime Program," *Journal of Applied Social Psychology* 9 (1979): pp. 135–36.

77. *New York Times*, 12 March 1990, pp. A1, A16.

78. U.S. Library of Congress, *Gun Control Laws in Foreign Countries* (Washington, D.C.: U.S. Government Printing Office, 1981), p. 177.

79. Shields, *Guns Don't Die*, pp. 60–69; HCI website.

80. See chapter 1 of the present volume; Royce Crocker, "Attitudes Toward Gun Control: A Review," in *Federal Regulation of Firearms*. A report prepared by Congressional Research Service for the U.S. Senate Judiciary Committee (Washington, D.C.: U.S. Government Printing Office, 1982), p. 261.

81. See chapters 6 and 7.

82. Shields, *Guns Don't Die*, pp. 126–27; HCI website, "The Myth of the Second Amendment"; "Guns in the Home"; "Responding to Progun Research."

83. HCI website, "Federal Legislative Priorities."

84. Douglas S. Weil and David Hemenway, "I Am the NRA," *Violence and Victims* 8 (1993): 360-61.

85. Kleck, *Targeting Guns*, pp. 345–47; HCI website, "Federal Legislative Priorities."

86. Kleck, *Targeting Guns*, p. 345; Lexis-Nexis online computer database of public opinion results. Accessed 3 March 2000.

87. Harris, "Reporter at Large," pp. 57-58; *Parade*, 18 September 1977, p. 9.

88. Letter from J. Elliott Corbett, 17 June 1968. Reproduced in *Congressional Record*, 77th Cong., 1st sess., 1968.

89. Sugarmann, "Laws That Can't Stop a Bullet."

90. "Playboy Interview—Ramsey Clark," *Playboy*, August 1969, p. 70.

91. Sherrill, *Saturday Night Special*, p. 272.

92. David Kopel, *The Samurai, the Mountie, and the Cowboy* (Amherst, N.Y.: Prometheus Books, 1992), p. 57.

93. *Time*, 5 July 1968, p. 6; see also Marvin Wolfgang, "A Tribute to a View I Have Opposed," *Journal of Criminal Law and Criminology* 86 (1995): 188.

94. *Time*, 21 June 1968, p. 17.

95. Norval Morris and Gordon Hawkins, *The Honest Politician's Guide to Crime Control* (Chicago: University of Chicago Press, 1970), p. 65.

96. Amatai Etzioni, "Public Policy and Curbing Violence," *International Journal of Group Tensions* 3 (1973): 76.

97. Communitarian Network website at http://www.gwu.edu/~ccps/pop_disarm.html. Accessed 3-10-00.

98. "Fox News Sunday," Fox television, broadcast 23 May 1999.

99. *USA Today*, 16 January 1992, p. 9A.

100. "Inside Washington," broadcast 1 May 1999.

101. *Rolling Stone*, 9 December 1993, p. 45.

102. HCI website, "Gun Industry Lawsuits."

103. National Rifle Association Institute for Legislative Action website, at http://www.narila.org. Accessed 28 February 2000.

104. HCI website, "Gun Industry Lawsuits."

105. Ibid.

106. Website for Tarnhelm Supply company, manufacturer of the Magna-Trigger gun locking device, at http://www.tarnhelm.com. Accessed 29 February 2000.

107. *Discovery*, September 1999, 93.

108. *Washington Post*, 28 February 2000, p. A1.

109. E.g., see the defendants list in the Complaint in San Francisco's suit, HCI website, "Gun Industry Lawsuits."

110. HCI website, "Background Information on 'Personalized Gun' Lawsuit," accessed 20 August 1999; *Discovery*, September 1999, p. 93.

111. See chapters 6 and 7.

112. U.S. Bureau of Justice Statistics, *Guns and Crime*, Crime Data Brief (Washington, D.C.: U.S. Government Printing Office, 1994), p. 2; Philip J. Cook and Jens Ludwig, *Guns in America: Summary Report* (Washington, D.C.: Police Foundation, 1997), p. 30.

113. Kleck, *Targeting Guns*, pp. 90–94.

114. Shields, *Guns Don't Die*, pp. 49–53; HCI website, "Guns in the Home."

115. *Chicago Tribune*, 9 June 2000, p. 1.

116. E.g., Spitzer, *The Politics of Gun Control*, p. 186; Shields, *Guns Don't Die*, p. 124; Alviani and Drake, *Handgun Control*, p. 54.

117. For critiques of this reasoning, see Don B. Kates, Henry E. Schaffer, John K. Lattimer, George B. Murray, and Edwin H. Cassem, "Guns and Public Health: Epidemic of Violence or Pandemic of Propaganda?" *Tennessee Law Review* 62 (1995): 579-84; Kleck, *Targeting Guns*, pp. 235–37.

118. Kleck, *Targeting Guns*, p. 346.

119. Ibid., p. 97.

120. HCI website, "Pending Legislation"; "Federal Legislative Priorities."

121. James Blose and Philip J. Cook, *Regulating Handgun Transfers* (Durham, N.C.: Institute of Policy Sciences and Public Affairs, Duke University, 1980), p. 17.

122. Shields, *Guns Don't Die*, pp. 125–26, 147–52, esp. 150–51; HCI website, "Licensing and Registration."

123. Crocker, "Attitudes Toward Gun Control," p. 262.

124. Blose and Cook, *Regulating Handguns*, pp. 9–10, 16; U.S. Bureau of Alcohol, Tobacco, and Firearms, *1994 Firearms Enforcement Investigative Report* (Washington, D.C.: Department of the Treasury, 1995), pp. 5–6.

125. E.g., compare U.S. Bureau of Alcohol, Tobacco, and Firearms, *The National Tracing Center 1994 Yearend Report* (Washington, D.C.: Department of the Treasury, 1995), pp. 5–6, with U.S. Bureau of Alcohol, Tobacco, and Firearms, *Crime Gun Trace Analysis Report: The Illegal Youth Firearms Market in New York* (Washington, D.C.: Department of the Treasury, 1999), p. 7.

126. HCI website, "Licensing and Registration."

127. Ibid.

128. U.S. Bureau of Alcohol, Tobacco, and Firearms, *Crime Gun Trace Analysis Report.*

129. Wright and Rossi, *Armed and Considered Dangerous*, p. 185.

130. Martin S. Geisel, Richard Roll, and R. Stanton Wettick, "The Effectiveness of State and Local Regulations of Handguns," *Duke University Law Journal* 4 (1969): 676; Douglas R. Murray, "Handguns, Gun Control Laws and Firearm Violence," *Social Problems* 23 (1975): 84-88; Joseph P. Magaddino and Marshall H. Medoff, "An Empirical Analysis of Federal and State Firearm Control Laws," in *Firearms and Violence: Issues of Public Policy*, ed. by Don B. Kates Jr. (Cambridge, Mass.: Ballinger, 1984), 235-38; Gary Kleck and E. Britt Patterson, "The Impact of Gun Control and Gun Ownership Levels on Violence Rates," *Journal of Quantitative Criminology* 9 (1993): 267-71, 274.

131. Kleck, *Targeting Guns*, pp. 388–90; HCI website, "Licensing and Registration."

132. Kleck, *Targeting Guns*, p. 312.

133. HCI website, "Federal Legislative Priorities."

134. Kleck, *Point Blank*, p. 11.

135. Kleck, *Targeting Guns*, p. 345.

136. Kleck, *Point Blank*, pp. 9–12.

Modes of
News Media Distortion
of Gun Issues

by Gary Kleck

A mericans receive most of their information about crime and violence through the mass media rather than from direct personal experience. This information, as it pertains to guns and violence, does not neutrally reflect reality, but is shaped and managed to encourage some conclusions and discourage others. The premise of this chapter is that the nation's most important news sources shape information on gun issues in a way that encourages procontrol conclusions. The purpose of this chapter is to identify and illustrate the forms that this information management takes.

This assertion should not be viewed as part of a broad accusation of liberal bias in the news media generally. While survey evidence does indicate that reporters and editors are somewhat more liberal than the general public, newspapers, magazines, and television and radio stations and networks are owned by wealthy businessmen, and most wealthy businessmen are not liberals.[1] It is unlikely that these wealthy owners would consistently permit their property to be used to promote a liberal ideology they personally oppose.

Instead of procontrol bias being a part of a general liberal bias on the part of news workers, bias on the gun issue is a thing apart, whose persistence may be possible partly because it does not conflict with any strongly

173

held elements of the ideology of the owners of media corporations. Consequently, the gun issue may provide a fairly rare situation where purportedly "liberal" ideas can be repeatedly favored by reporters without provoking intervention from management.

It should also be stressed that it is not being argued that there is a consciously calculated or coordinated campaign to lie about or distort the gun issue. Rather, a variety of information management techniques may be used to produce impressions that news managers honestly believe to be accurate. It is thus not the sincerity of news workers that is in question. The content of news stories is what is at issue in this chapter, not the intentions of the stories' authors. Most news people probably sincerely believe that guns are a major cause of the nation's high rates of violence and that there would be less violence if there was more gun control and fewer guns. Therefore, to be procontrol or antigun is merely to be in accord with the facts, "biased" only in favor of the truth. From this viewpoint, news sources are merely accurately informing the public of a genuinely one-sided issue, rather than slanting the news to create an artificially one-sided picture.

There are occasional outrageous and obvious "smoking gun" examples of antigun/procontrol bias, but these are exceptions to the general rule of more subtle information manipulation. For example, there was the presumably unusual case of a newspaper discontinuing the column of a staff writer for publicly expressing support for positions taken by the National Rifle Association.[2] Sophisticated information management does not rely primarily on lies or crude censorship, but rather on less obviously illegitimate or sloppy techniques.

First and foremost, news stories can shape the audience's views through the omission of accurate, relevant information that would tend to undercut the theme of the story. Biased exclusion of information is both more important and more effective in shaping public opinion than inclusion of inaccurate information. Lies do not further the interests of propagandists in a democracy in the long run, because they are vulnerable to exposure and threaten the future credibility (and possibly the profits) of the news outlet.

Information that contradicts a news story's thesis can be excluded from a story either by a reporter or by an editor or producer. All news stories necessarily must exclude information in the interests of brevity, but exclusions are biased when they are patterned to consistently weed out information contradicting a theme or message favored by the producers of the news. The practice is especially pernicious because, unlike inaccurate or biased statements that are included in a story, excluded facts are generally invisible to the ordinary reader or viewer. Further, there rarely can be any "smoking gun" proving deliberate exclusion because it usually would be impossible to prove that a reporter was aware of the information in the first place.

Second, in deciding which bits of information to include in a story, and, if included, whether to treat the information as factual, different levels of skepticism and different standards for assessing importance can be applied to information supporting the preferred view and to information contradicting it. Information contrary to the preferred view can be subjected to intense and searching scrutiny, or downplayed as unimportant or self-serving, while information supporting the preferred view can be spared any comparable scrutiny and is presented to the audience without comment, or even with comments suggesting the information is credible and of great importance.

Third, differing amounts of "play" can be given to stories with pro- or anticontrol implications. Stories with implications supporting the preferred view can be given coverage that is prominent (front page versus inside page), extended (fifteen column inches versus six), and prolonged (coverage on multiple days rather than just one), while stories with contrary implications can be given little play or ignored altogether.

Fourth, procontrol editorial positions prevail among the nation's major daily press outlets, and such positions can lend credibility and legitimacy to a procontrol stance as the preferred position of responsible and educated persons.[3]

Sins of Omission—Exclusion Bias

Examples of biased exclusion of information are not hard to find in news stories on guns. It should be stressed that in each of the following examples, the omitted information was critical to judging the main theme of the story and could have been included in the story in a single sentence. Therefore, it cannot be argued that the omissions were due to either the information being irrelevant or unimportant, or to space or time limitations making it impossible to include the information.

The major gun-related story of 1989-1991 was the alleged proliferation and criminal use of so-called "assault rifles" (ARs) or, more broadly, assault weapons (AWs), a vague category that encompassed handguns and shotguns as well as rifles. AWs are semiautomatic firearms with a "military-style" appearance. AWs were presented in the press as especially threatening to public safety mainly because they allegedly (1) were more lethal than their ordinary counterparts (especially ARs compared with civilian rifles), (2) had rapid rates of fire, and (3) had large ammunition capacities. The first claim was false, the second either false or true to only a trivial degree, while the third was sometimes true but of negligible significance since incidents of gun violence rarely involve large numbers of rounds fired.

News stories that addressed the rate-of-fire issue commonly hinted or stated that AWs either fired as rapidly as machine guns, or that they might as well do so, since they could easily be converted to fire like machine guns.[4] The convertability claim was inaccurate and was apparently repeated by news sources simply because they did not, as the *New York Times* eventually did, check with the relevant authorities to see if it was true.[5]

The implication that AWs could fire like machine guns was hinted at through descriptions of shootings in which the shooter was described as having "*sprayed*" an area with bullets from his AW. Without making the claim explicit, this wording strongly hinted that ARs were capable of fully automatic fire, i.e., sending out a virtually continuous stream of bullets as long as the trigger was held down and ammunition remained. In fact, AWs can fire only in semiautomatic mode, i.e., one shot is fired for each trigger pull, the same as with ordinary revolvers. (The guns are different from ordinary revolvers in that each shot fired causes the next cartridge to be moved into the firing chamber, and the hammer to be pushed back.)[6] Television network news programs also hinted at the same idea by overlaying reporters speaking about semiautomatic AWs with film of fully automatic weapons being shown on the screen.

Failing to make this distinction explicit could leave the average reader or viewer with the erroneous impression that AWs were machine guns, and that therefore machine guns were being legally sold without significant restrictions. In 1989, *most* news stories about AWs omitted this critical piece of information. A content analysis of a random national sample of 115 newspaper stories on guns and gun control indicated that nearly 80 percent of the sixty-five stories on ARs failed to distinguish fully automatic fire from semiautomatic fire, or to in any way indicate that ARs could not fire like machine guns.[7]

In 1985 and 1986, one of the major gun-related stories concerned armor-piercing ammunition. Numerous examples of biased exclusion of relevant information can be found in stories on these "cop-killer" bullets, projectiles capable of penetrating the body armor worn by police officers. Two facts were consistently omitted from stories on this issue: (1) supporters of restrictions had never documented a single case in which this ammunition actually killed a police officer by penetrating his body armor, and (2) many common types of rifle ammunition had always been capable of penetrating police body armor, and had been widely available for years. Leaving aside whether restrictions on this ammunition were advisable, these facts were obviously relevant to informed public debate about the issue, yet somehow did not make it into print in the nation's leading newspapers.[8] There was at least one exception—the *Los Angeles Times* did mention, in a single article, that no police officer had ever been killed by the bullets. The diligent reader could find it on page 20, in the middle of the twelfth paragraph of a fourteen-paragraph story.[9] Marginalizing the information in this way is only slightly better than omitting it altogether. It could hardly be seriously argued that it is not relevant and important that the "cop-killer" bullet had never killed a cop.

At the very least, the repeated use of an inflammatory and inaccurate term like "cop-killer bullet" was dubious journalistic practice. News sources uncritically accepted a label invented by procontrol activists for propaganda purposes. One presumed justification would be that this term had become the commonly used label for the ammunition in question. This is something of a circular justification, since it became the commonly used term largely because news workers had chosen to accept and disseminate it. While the ammunition certainly is capable of killing a police officer (or civilian for that matter), the term nevertheless is not very descriptive because the same is also true of any other firearms ammunition. The desire for a pithy, hard-hitting label apparently won out over a commitment to accuracy.

One of the difficulties in documenting specific instances of "sins of omission" is that it is usually impossible to be sure that the reporter knew about the information, and therefore one cannot be certain that the information had been deliberately excluded. Usually, one can only be sure that the reporter either did not make enough effort to acquire the information *or* someone excluded it. There are, however, occasional exceptions.

I have given hundreds of interviews about gun issues, sometimes talking for as long as two hours at a time with reporters. Occasionally I have read the stories that print reporters prepared on the basis of interviews with me and others. It was often apparent that reporters had been assigned a story with a preset theme and charged with gathering supportive information. The nature of the theme sometimes became apparent during the course of an interview, and when it was inconsistent with what I knew, I would convey the contrary information to the reporter. Again and again, I have had the experience of providing information that flatly contradicted a procontrol theme of the story as finally published, yet the contradictory information was neither rebutted nor mentioned in the story. Space (or time) limitations can account for omission of information that is marginal or irrelevant to a story, or whose accuracy has been put in doubt, but it cannot account for exclusion of unrebutted information that directly contradicts the principal claims or themes of the story.

On June 14, 1989, I was interviewed by a reporter from *USA Today*. The story concerned child gun accidents and had been stimulated by five gun accidents involving children in Florida, all occurring within a week of each other. I told the reporter that unconnected accidents, and rare events in general, occasionally cluster together in time, that this is bound to happen somewhere, sometime, and that such short-term clusterings were not a sound basis for concluding that there was a significant trend developing. I then told her what the actual national trends had been in recent years—the number of fatal gun accidents involving children (under the age of ten) had dropped sharply, from 227 in 1974 to about 92 in 1987, the latest year for which data were available at the time. (The same was true of accidents in all age groups.) When the story appeared the next day, it was a fairly long article (or as long as they get in *USA Today*—fifty square inches including photo and charts). But it evidently was not long enough to have room for either these facts or any others I provided the reporter.[10] The theme of the article was the supposedly large number of recent child gun accidents, the article's headline being "Spate of shootings spurs Florida to act." The article had room for a statistic provided by a procontrol advocacy group, to the effect that gunshot wounds to children had increased by 300 percent (!) since 1986, in unspecified "large urban areas" (for the nation as a whole, gun violence rates were flat from 1986 to 1988).[11] The article did not, however, have room for the only relevant national data available to the reporters and editors that bore directly on trends in child gun accidents, data that indicated that fatal gun accidents were sharply declining, and had been doing so for many years. Thus, the main theme of the story was flat wrong, and the reporters had good reason to know it was wrong.

One might be tempted to dismiss this sort of selective omission of relevant information as characteristic only of news outlets with a less-than-lofty journalistic reputation. However, CBS News, the organization that Edward R. Murrow built, broadcast a story with the exact same misleading theme, presented even more bluntly. On the *CBS Evening News* for October 11, 1989, anchorman Dan Rather read a story on child gun accidents, describing the problem as "an epidemic that shows every sign of worsening." In fact, the only data reliable for judging national trends in such accidents, mortality statistics, had long indicated precisely the opposite. However, in this case it is impossible to know whether CBS knew about, or made any effort to discover, the relevant figures.[12]

In December of 1989, I gave an interview lasting about an hour to a reporter from the National Public Radio (NPR) affiliate in St. Paul, Minnesota. The interview was done as part of a national effort by NPR affiliates to explore the gun issue, and the resulting reports were distributed to NPR member stations. The bulk of my remarks concerned the considerable evidence indicating the utility of guns for self-defense, as well as evidence indicating that most existing gun laws appear to be ineffective in reducing violence. I also very briefly (for a minute or two) noted the risks of keeping guns for defense in homes with children, and remarked that most crime victimizations occurred in circumstances that do not permit effective defensive use of a gun. When WETA-FM, the NPR affiliate in Washington, D.C., broadcast an excerpt of about thirty seconds from my interview, it was entirely taken from my brief remarks noting the limits and risks of keeping guns for self-defense. None of my extensive (and unrebutted) remarks noting the defensive effectiveness of guns were included. Further, the brief excerpts were placed in a section of the broadcast devoted to arguing a proposition—that keeping a gun for defensive purposes is irrational—that was clearly contradicted by both the bulk of my remarks and by the overwhelming weight of scholarly evidence.[13]

In June of 1989, I gave a series of interviews lasting over two hours to a reporter from *Time* magazine in which I noted, among other things, that gun violence had been decreasing since the early 1980s. While the magazine's story briefly noted, in the text, the decrease in gun deaths in the early and mid-1980s, this was undercut by their twice referring in large type to the "epidemic" of gun violence.[14] If "epidemic" does not mean an increasing or spreading problem, exactly what does it mean?

One section of this article pertained to suicides. Without mentioning any evidence that rebutted the information that I had discussed with the reporter, the article asserted that "most people who attempt to kill themselves do not really wish to die." I had told the reporter that while this claim was true of suicide attempters in general, there was good reason to believe it was *not* true of those who use guns. The article noted that only one in twenty suicide attempts results in death, while, according to one study, 92 percent of gun attempts are fatal. I had told the reporter that the fatality rate in suicide attempts with guns was indeed high, but that the rate was nearly as high in attempts using likely substitutes for shooting, such as hanging, carbon monoxide poisoning, and drowning.

The article described a gun suicide in which the absence of a gun allegedly could have made a difference as to whether the attempter eventually survived. I had told the reporter that one reason that few suicides could be prevented by removing guns was that the people who use guns in suicide typically have a more serious and persistent desire to kill themselves than suicide attempters using other methods. If denied guns, some or all of this group would substitute other methods and kill themselves anyway. The case cited in the resulting article seemed to provide the perfect illustration of my point, since the woman had suffered from "recurring depression" and had made at least three suicide attempts. Yet the article implied that the woman died only because she had found a "swift and certain" method of suicide, and that her depression could have been cured before the next attempt had she not obtained a gun.

In this thirty-one-page article, as finally published, no experts on gun violence were quoted or explicitly cited, with the exception of a single remark by James Wright (p. 61). I have no idea how many other experts were consulted and provided *Time* reporters with information contrary to their preferred views, and can only be sure that they excluded the information that I provided. Professor Wright, however, was interviewed and was quoted in a context that inverted his remarks' original meaning. Wright was quoted as saying that "everyone knows that if you put a loaded .38 in your ear and pull the trigger, you won't survive." His intended meaning was that ambiguously motivated people intending only to make a "cry for help" do not make such attempts with guns. Only people who truly want to die use guns to attempt suicide, and these highly motivated persons would just use other means to kill themselves if guns were not available. Professor Wright has confirmed to me that this was indeed his meaning.[15] However, the remark was quoted in a context that suggested precisely the opposite, that gun victims *would* have survived had guns not been available, because guns are a uniquely lethal method of suicide.

This story illustrates another noteworthy pattern. News stories that give very extended coverage of gun issues (e.g., feature-length newspaper or magazine stories or hour-long broadcast stories) usually make virtually no use of expert commentary. This raises the possibility that reporters did seek out expert information but could not quickly find any acknowledged experts who would confirm the preset themes of the story. By defining the experts' unsupportive remarks as irrelevant, unimportant, or unreliable, reporters would be able to exclude them from the final story on grounds the reporters considered to be legitimate. This must necessarily remain a speculation, however, because news stories do not report which experts were consulted but ignored.

A Speculation About How Exclusion Bias Works

Reporters and editors probably do not decide to exclude certain pieces of information from stories because they know them to be false, but rather because they consider them to be suspect, trivial, or irrelevant to their stories. They are especially likely to arrive at such an assessment, however, when the data do not fit into their general worldview as it pertains to guns and gun control. Such information does not seem to jive with the rest of the information in their possession, leading to the suspicion on the reporter's part that the information may be inaccurate or tainted by the source's personal biases. The information is suspect because it deviates from the accepted orthodoxy, even if the reporter does not know of any solid facts that directly contradict the suspect claims.

Further, since the suspect information would be hard to integrate with the rest of the information in their story, the easiest way for the reporter to handle such anomalous evidence is simply to drop it from the story, a decision that also comports nicely with the general pressure to conserve print space or air time. This sort of decision to exclude can be done in good faith, since it is hard to criticize excluding suspect information.

This process largely works on an individual, ad hoc basis, reporter by reporter, and story by story. However, if reporters for the major news outlets generally share the same worldview on guns and gun control, they will also tend to independently reject the same kinds of troublesome information, without any coordinated conspiracy needed to achieve this result. The result, nevertheless, is essentially the same as it would be if there *were* a calculated conspiracy.

Unfortunately, this phenomenon sets up a vicious circle. Because reporters are themselves consumers of news, they read other reporters' stories on guns, which, of course, excluded the same sorts of suspect information as their own stories did. This reinforces their skewed worldview, which then encourages their later decisions to exclude the suspect information, and so on.

Unbalanced Skepticism Applied to Pro and Con Information

Media bias often results from what might be termed "sloppiness in the service of bias." Because the people who produce and manage the news are operating under deadlines, and under limits on print space, air time, and resources of all kinds, a certain amount of sloppiness and imperfection in news coverage is unavoidable. There are therefore inevitable limits to the thoroughness with which reporters can evaluate debatable claims. However, it is illegitimate bias when reporters selectively direct their reportorial skepticism predominantly toward those advocating ideas with which they disagree, and disproportionately devote their limited resources to debunking such positions, while directing little skepticism at those who espouse more congenial views and devoting little or no time to checking out the factual basis for those views.

Sloppiness in checking out technical claims made about guns is a chronic problem. Consider the case of a newspaper that published a mislabelled photograph to support their claim that a particular "assault rifle" was an unusually powerful and lethal rifle. On January 23, 1989, the *Los Angeles Herald-Examiner* printed a news story that focussed on the "AK-47" (actually a semiautomatic civilian adaptation of the AK-47), the type of gun used in the 1989 Stockton, California, schoolyard killing of five children. The story was accompanied by a photo showing a melon being blown apart by a bullet supposedly fired from the "AK-47." The text made a number of perfectly accurate comments about the high penetrating power of the ammunition used in this gun, but failed to note other attributes of the ammunition that tended to make it *less* lethal than other rifle rounds.[16]

Unfortunately, the shot that had so dramatically blown up the melon had not come from the "assault rifle" in question, or indeed from any kind of rifle. A member of the Los Angeles County sheriff's department had initially been asked by a reporter to fire an "AK-47" round through the melon, which he did, using the fully jacketed, military-style 7.62 x 39 mm ammunition type used in the Stockton shootings. Because the ammunition in question does not in fact create an unusually large wound cavity, it failed to blow up the melon, creating a small hole and merely cracking the melon instead.[17] For comparative purposes, the deputy sheriff was also asked to fire a police handgun round (a 9 mm 115 grain jacketed hollow point) from a Beretta Model 92 pistol, which he did, causing the melon to blow up.[18]

That the rifle ammunition in question does not blow up melons as portrayed was substantiated by tests conducted by *Gun Week*, a weekly firearms newspaper and later in an ABC-TV documentary.[19] Consequently, it was evidently a photograph of the effects of the police handgun round that was published in the newspaper and described in the picture's caption as portraying "the power of an AK-47." Apparently, the photographer or an editor mislabeled the photo of the melon being blown up by the handgun round, identifying it instead as portraying the effects of an AK-47 round. The reporter present at the scene could not be sure whether this was what had happened and the photographer never returned my phone calls.[20] Shortly thereafter, the *Los Angeles Herald-Examiner* went out of business.

After the *Herald-Examiner* published this story, local television stations, including the Los Angeles ABC affiliate, KABC-TV, broadcast filmed demonstrations showing melons being blown up, supposedly by an "AK-47." Finally, one year after the Stockton shooting, the ABC-TV network broadcast an accurate demonstration in which the "AK-47" round merely put a small split in a melon, while ordinary civilian hunting rifle ammunition caused one to explode.[21]

The KABC broadcasts become more understandable in the context of the station's editorial stance. Bill Press, news commentator for KABC-TV, testified to the U.S. Senate that his station's reports on AWs stemmed from a conscious decision on the part of the station to influence the public: "We have involved the public in this issue through our daily commentary. We are working every day with the Los Angeles Police Department. Every time there is an incident using a semiautomatic rifle in the city of Los Angeles, we report it on the news and we ask people to write to the State legislature to ban these weapons."[22]

Numerous other allegations about a variety of guns and ammunition were made in various news stories, could easily have been checked out, but were not. The following claims (stated or implied) all had clear procontrol (or antigun) implications, all were false, and all could have been disconfirmed with a single phone call: (1) AWs are readily convertible to fully automatic fire like a machinegun, (2) ARs are more lethal than ordinary civilian-style hunting rifles, (3) AWs are the preferred weapon of criminals in general, or of drug dealers or youth gangs in particular, (4) large numbers of police officers have been killed with AWs, and (5) large numbers of police officers have been killed with "cop-killer" bullets.[23]

Amount of "Play"— Extent and Prominence of Coverage

Bias can also be evident in the amount of "play" gun stories are given depending on whether their implications are pro- or anticontrol, i.e., the amount of space or air time devoted to a story and the prominence given it— front page versus inside page, lead story in a broadcast, or a later one. Major victories for the anticontrol forces are sometimes downplayed, while procontrol victories are given disproportionately prominent coverage. After advocates manage to persuade a legislature to pass a criminologically insignificant form of gun control, often concerning some rare gun type, the advocates understandably declare a major victory in the war on gun violence. An uncritical press then treats this assessment as objective fact, rather than a political stance taken by an advocacy group. This then contributes to a bandwagon effect, by giving the impression that the procontrol forces are winning.

Trivial procontrol victories such as the banning of nonexistent "plastic" guns, outlawing of "cop killer" bullets, and temporary federal import bans on "assault rifles" have been given front-page treatment, while more far-reaching anticontrol victories like the passage of state preemption bills have been virtually ignored.

A state preemption measure establishes that only the state may regulate guns, wiping out local gun controls and/or preventing local governments from passing new restrictions. The significance of these measures derives partly from the fact that rather than merely eliminating just one form of control, they commonly void entire broad categories of controls, usually virtually all forms of gun control. Further, this does not affect just a single local jurisdiction, but hundreds of local jurisdictions in a given state. Finally, typical preemption measures not only strike down existing controls, but also make local enactment of future controls impossible. All this is of special significance in light of the fact that the nation's strongest gun controls have all been imposed by local governments. The NRA and other anticontrol forces have gained state preemption laws in at least thirty-four states, with at least twenty-three being passed or strengthened in the period from 1982 to 1987.[24] These victories were largely ignored by the national news media, usually being covered only within each affected state.

In sharp contrast, a minor bill allowing a commission to ban certain types of cheap handguns, passed in Maryland in 1988, was given front-page coverage in papers across the nation. (The low frequency of involvement of cheap handguns in crime is documented elsewhere.[25]) To establish the national newsworthiness of what seemed to be, aside from the amount of news coverage itself, a strictly local story in Maryland, news sources falsely claimed that this was "the first state law to outlaw the cheap handguns called Saturday night specials."[26] In fact, at least four other states already had similar statutes on the books: Illinois, Hawaii, Minnesota, and South Carolina. The first three banned both sale and manufacture of the guns, while the last banned only sale. The Hawaii statute was even stronger than the Maryland measure, banning most possession of the guns, as well as sale and manufacture.[27] One major newspaper even made this "first in the nation" claim while directly contradicting itself in another story on the same page, by the same author, noting the existence of these "similar statutes."[28] The only novel element of the Maryland law was the technical details of how authorities would determine which handguns would be prohibited.

Editorial Stances and Other Newspaper Policies

According to historians Lee Kennett and James LaVerne Anderson, "three quarters of the nation's newspapers, and most of the periodical press" support gun control.[29] These authors described the media as "mostly unsympathetic" to the progun forces, stating that, in the 1960s, "large urban dailies with mass circulation—the *New York Times, Washington Post, Los Angeles Times*, and *Christian Science Monitor*—issued continual calls for new and tougher laws. With few exceptions the popular magazines followed suit." They noted that the *Washington Post*, in what may be a record, once published procontrol editorials on the gun issue for seventy-seven consecutive days (pp. 239, 312). Perhaps the *Post* had moderated its views by 1988 when the Maryland handgun referendum was voted on—they published strongly worded proreferendum editorials for only nine consecutive days before the vote.[30]

News organizations regularly insist on the independence of their news coverage and their editorial stances, but media scholar Ben Bagdikian has stated that "studies throughout the years have shown that any bias in the news tends to follow a paper's editorial opinions."[31] This claim received support regarding the gun control issue in Tamryn Etten's study of daily newspaper stories—papers with procontrol editorial policies were more likely to show procontrol bias in their new stories.[32]

The general public apparently is sensitive to a procontrol slant in news stories about gun control. In a 1985 national *Los Angeles Times* poll, people were asked how they thought their daily newspapers felt about stricter gun laws. Among those who thought they knew their paper's stance, 62 percent felt that stance was procontrol. Further, among those who thought they knew their paper's stance, most said they knew this because of the way their paper covered news stories on gun control, rather than from editorials.[33] Apparently, bias in news coverage of gun issues is sufficiently obvious to convey newspapers' gun control preferences even to large numbers of ordinary readers.

Media bias is not exclusively exercised in the newsroom. Advertising industry publications have reported that the advertising departments of national publications, including the *Christian Science Monitor*, *Newsweek*, *Time*, and *Reader's Digest* magazines, as well as the NBC and CBS television networks, have refused to accept paid advertisements from the National Rifle Association.[34] Consequently, gun owner groups are often in the position of not being able to even buy the opportunity to counter the claims of the news media.

Other Forms of Bias

Antigun bias can take even more subtle, even subliminal, forms. In recent years, local television stations have taken to displaying a stylized handgun "insert" or "super" (an image superimposed on the screen) to introduce crime stories, including those not involving handguns. This is done even though less than 1 percent of all crimes, and only 13 percent of violent crimes, involve handguns.[35] Thus, "crime" and "handgun" are repeatedly paired in the minds of viewers, even though handguns are neither a predominant nor even a very common element of crime. A practice that reinforces an association between handguns and violence is not questioned, perhaps because the contribution of handguns to violence, and the high frequency of their use in violent acts, are taken for granted as unquestioned facts, fixed elements of the "consensual paradigm" under which news workers operate.[36]

A Case Study— A CBS Television Documentary

Close examination of a particular case will illustrate some common forms of news media bias as they pertain to gun issues. On March 16, 1989, the CBS television network broadcast an episode of its *48 Hours* news magazine program titled "Armed and Deadly."[37] The program's purported topic was "assault rifles," defined in the documentary as military-style semiautomatic rifles, though the focus often wandered to both fully automatic machine guns and to the broader category of "assault weapons," which includes some types of handguns and shotguns.

While no written analysis can fully convey the emotional and visual impact of a television documentary, the following description covers in some detail all of the major segments of the program, in their original sequence. The subheadings of paragraphs convey what seemed to be the main theme of each segment. I will usually refer to assertions being made by CBS, rather than by particular reporters, to emphasize that the documentary was a collaborative product. All assertions about what is actually true about ARs and AWs are documented elsewhere.[38]

Vivid Images of "Assault Weapon" Violence. The documentary opened with dramatic footage of a trauma center helicopter flying a gunshot victim to a Washington, D.C., hospital. Viewers heard a medical technician speaking to hospital staff over the helicopter's radio, saying that the victim was shot five times with a "high caliber automatic pistol." As it turned out, this was inaccurate; the weapon was evidently an ordinary nine millimeter (9 mm) semiautomatic pistol, i.e., one that is neither automatic in fire nor large in caliber. Thus in a documentary supposedly focusing on "assault rifles," the opening footage did not even pertain to a recent "assault rifle" killing, almost certainly because such events are so rare in any one city, even one as large as Washington, that CBS might have had to wait for months before they could have gotten footage on such a crime.

Perhaps to establish the relevance of footage on a handgun killing, rather than an "assault rifle" killing, a District of Columbia homicide detective was filmed at the hospital claiming that a 9 mm semiautomatic pistol is "just as dangerous as any assault rifle," because it can carry 12 to 17 rounds at a time. CBS did not explicitly vouch for the validity of this ludicrous claim, but simply broadcast the claim without criticism or commentary from gun or medical experts on the lethality of different types of firearms. The statement was incorrect regardless of how one might define dangerousness. The higher lethality of rifles in general (including "assault rifles") compared to handguns (including 9 mm handguns) is one of the few traits that truly do make at least some assault rifles more dangerous than other guns. A 9 mm pistol has neither the muzzle velocity nor maximum magazine capacity that assault rifles commonly have. Thus, CBS conveyed both the message that "assault rifles" are especially dangerous guns and the message that they are no more dangerous than very common semiautomatic handguns, with no evident awareness of the contradiction.

Persuading Viewers the Problem Affects Them, Too. Next, the head of the hospital's trauma unit was interviewed, and he alluded to "this epidemic of violence," implying that criminal gun violence was rapidly increasing. While this was true in the District of Columbia at that moment, it was not true nationally or in most local areas—the number and rate of gun homicides had been fairly stable for years. CBS neither noted this fact nor denied it, but simply presented an unrebutted statement that surely would lead at least some viewers to draw the seemingly obvious, but erroneous, conclusion that the nation, and perhaps their own community, was also undergoing an "epidemic" of gun violence. In fact, the U.S. homicide rate (the most accurately measured violent crime rate) had fluctuated, without any consistent trend, within a narrow range between 7.9 per 100,000 citizens and 8.6 from 1983 through 1988, and had declined sharply from its peak of 10.2 in 1980. Likewise, the share of homicides involving guns fluctuated very slightly between 58 and 61 percent from 1983 through 1988, down from the peak of 68 percent in 1974.[39]

A physician was then interviewed and he argued that the ordinary medical patient might face a shortage of blood or might have important surgery delayed because of the heavy hospital gunshot case load, and implied that trauma centers are closing down and are unavailable to treat automobile accident victims because of the increasing burden of gunshot cases. CBS anchorman Dan Rather asked the doctor whether some trauma centers have "been forced to close" because of "these new pressures," i.e., the alleged increasing numbers of gunshot wounds. The doctor replied, "They have," citing unnamed trauma centers in Chicago, Los Angeles, the District of Columbia, and South Florida that refused to "open their doors to the care of the injured." Note that this response did not actually answer Rather's question, since the doctor did not cite any specific cases of trauma centers *closing* but only some that restricted their services, nor did he explicitly claim that gunshot wounds were the sole or even the principal reason for even these limited restrictions. Rather did not inquire whether the well-known increases in medical malpractice insurance costs, the increasing difficulties of recouping payment from low-income patients, or troubles in finding physicians willing to work in urban emergency rooms might have been more important factors, and moved on to the next segment.

Rather's hinted claim that gunshot wounds were responsible for the closing of urban trauma centers was highly implausible. Washington, D.C., had the highest homicide rate of any large U.S. city at the time, yet even the hospital that treated 30 to 40 percent of the city's adult gunshot patients in the 1980s admitted only about four such patients a week even during the peak violence years of 1983-1990.[40]

This Is a New Crisis, Not the Same Old Thing. Rather stated that only about 4,000 "military-style assault weapons" were imported into the United States in 1986, compared to the first few months of 1989, when over 100,000 importation applications had been submitted. The documentary never claimed that the mechanically identical civilian-appearing semiautomatic rifles are any less dangerous than their military-style counterparts or that imported assault weapons are more dangerous than domestically manufactured ones. (In fact, Rather later asserted that three out of four ARs in the United States were domestically made.) Therefore, it is unclear what the viewer was to learn from trends only in imports of the military-style weapons.

An "assault rifle" is basically a semiautomatic centerfire rifle. It was not mentioned that nonmilitary-style semiautomatic rifles had already been commonplace in the United States for decades, a fact anyone in the firearms industry could have told CBS. No basis was provided for believing that relative increases in the total sales of all semiautomatic centerfire rifles were anywhere as large as was implied by the import figures. In fact, it is not clear that the trend in total sales of these rifles was upward at all. In 1972, well before the popularity of "military-style" ARs began, 360,000 centerfire semiautomatic rifles were produced for civilian sale by domestic U.S. manufacturers, compared to only 149,000 in 1987, well after the increase in AR sales was supposed to have begun. Even taking into account the increase in rifle imports, total sales of semiautomatic centerfire rifles may well have *declined* between 1972 and 1987.[41] While imports of *military-style* semiautomatic rifles did grow in the 1980s, there was little technical difference in these few weapons from the much larger number of ordinary nonmilitary-style semiautomatic rifles that had already been common, and nothing at all of criminological significance in the fact that the weapons were imported.

Citing the import figures appears to have served no other purpose than to impress the viewer with the contrast between the very large 100,000 figure and the very small 4,000 figure. In any case, this supposed trend was the synthetic product of an apples-and-oranges comparison between the number of guns actually imported in the earlier period and the number for which import applications had been filed in the later period. Because it costs an importer no more to apply for the importation of many guns than it does for few guns, the import application figures commonly are much higher than the numbers actually imported.

In the next segment, at a D.C. police firing range, an officer was shown firing first a bolt-action rifle, firing four shots in about nine seconds, and then an AR, firing five rounds in about five seconds, to demonstrate the higher rate of fire of ARs. Because bolt-action rifles are the slowest firing major type of firearm, virtually any other gun type will fire more rapidly than this one. Therefore, this exercise did not demonstrate any unique superiority peculiar to ARs. Then a policewoman was shown firing about 16 or 17 rounds from an AR in about eight seconds. No comparison was made with ordinary revolvers, which are the most common type of gun used by criminals, perhaps because such a comparison would have revealed no perceptible difference in rate of fire.

The police officer erroneously claimed on camera that "when you talk about semiautomatic weapons, you always talk about a large, a lot of, uh, a large capacity hold [sic] ammunition," holding up a magazine that appeared capable of holding about 30 rounds (she later referred to "32 rounds"). In fact, ARs are commonly sold with magazines holding only about five rounds; a 32-round magazine would be the largest magazine commonly sold with an AR, not the typical one.[42] Certainly ARs are not "always" sold or used with large magazines, and CBS cited no evidence they are even typically sold or used with large magazines. Again, CBS did not explicitly endorse the policewoman's claim; they merely presented it to viewers and allowed it to stand unquestioned.

"Assault Rifles" Are Machine Guns Waiting to Be Converted. In the next segment, reporter David Martin related how he found, in two hours, a gunsmith willing and able to convert an AR into a fully automatic weapon. He

did not say how he located him, or whether the ordinary violent criminal would be able to locate such a person. The unnamed "gunsmith" was shown, in a series of seven camera shots lasting a total of fifteen seconds of air time, allegedly converting the gun. The editing of the sequence was rapid and unlike that in the rest of the program, evidently intended to convey the rapidity of the conversion. "Nine minutes later, he had turned it into an automatic rifle," said reporter Martin. While Martin did not say one way or the other whether the man used any unusual, expensive, or specialized machine shop tools, the gunsmith was shown on camera using no tool more exotic than a pair of pliers. In most shots, he was shown using only his hands—he even held the rifle between his legs while working on it, rather than using a vise. Likewise, there was no mention of the need for any additional, hard-to-obtain (or illegal) parts. The viewer was left with the distinct impression that the conversion could be done quickly, without special tools or parts.

According to Ed Owen, chief of the Bureau of Alcohol, Tobacco, and Firearms (BATF) Firearms Technology Branch, it is unlawful to buy or otherwise transfer any guns that are readily convertible to automatic fire, since such guns are defined under federal law as machine guns. Thus, the semi-automatic guns legally on the market at the time of the documentary could not be "readily converted" to fully automatic fire, according to BATF standards. Owens's branch of BATF is charged with, among other things, determining whether guns are convertible to automatic fire. Owen was supplied with a videotape of the CBS "conversion" sequence by an anticontrol group, Gun Owners of America. After viewing the brief tape frame-by-frame, Owen said that while he could not conclusively say that a nine-minute conversion was impossible or whether it had in fact occurred, he "was not aware that a conversion could be done in the manner shown." Thus, one of the nation's leading authorities on conversions had never seen a conversion done in the manner supposedly performed in nine minutes by a gunsmith CBS was able to locate in under two hours.[43]

This becomes more interesting in light of the fact that no one was shown demonstrating the allegedly converted weapon's ability to fire in fully automatic mode. Casual viewers might be forgiven if they thought they *had* seen the weapon fired this way, since the documentary cut directly from the gunsmith segment to footage of Martin firing "an automatic rifle" at a firing range. If viewers were not paying very close attention, they would not have noticed that the gun fired by Martin was different from the rifle supposedly converted. Thus, juxtaposition of the sequences almost certainly left some viewers with the impression that it was the converted weapon's fully automatic capabilities being demonstrated, without CBS actually saying so. The documentary never did say whether anyone checked to see if the "conversion" was successful. It is worth noting that if the conversion did indeed occur, CBS induced the gunsmith to commit a federal crime, assuming he was not licensed to manufacture machine guns.[44]

Assault Rifles Are Especially Dangerous Firearms. In this sequence at the police firing range, reporter Martin fired a fully automatic rifle, noting that he could not fire the gun accurately, and then switched over to semiautomatic fire. He did not note the implication that this difficulty in controlling fire would presumably make the gun less useful for killing people, instead commenting only that "semiautomatic was all the firepower I needed." This remark made it hard to understand the purpose of the conversion sequence. If fully automatic fire does not provide any additional capability for harming people, what purpose was served by attempting to establish how easily ARs could be converted to fully automatic fire?

Martin and a police officer then examined the damage done to a wrecked car at which Martin had fired. The officer pointed to a hole in a side door of the car, saying, "Look at that—straight through the car." Neither he nor Martin noted that the same result could also have been achieved with most medium or large caliber bolt- or lever-action rifles, shotguns loaded with rifled slugs, or even a magnum revolver. The impression left with at least some viewers, but never explicitly stated by anyone, was that ARs have unique or unusually high penetrating or hitting power. In fact, the ammunition most commonly fired from ARs, the .223 round, is smaller than average for a rifle round, and ballistics data indicate that it imparts *less* energy than the average rifle round. Further, one of the principal military advantages of this ammunition is that it usually does not kill, but rather wounds and thereby not only removes the wounded soldier from combat but also diverts enemy resources to evacuate and treat the wounded soldier.

The Procontrol Forces Are Winning. In the next segment, Dan Rather noted that many people had been urging President George Bush to do something about getting ARs "off the streets." At that point, CBS had not actually established that there *were* large numbers of ARs on the streets, but treated it as a given. In fact, even in areas supposedly heavily afflicted by ARs, like Los Angeles, these guns were almost never used by criminals and claimed less than 2 percent of the firearms recovered by police or linked to homicides. Dan Rather then discussed Bush's decision to temporarily ban importation of ARs.

Next, Rather reported the results of a CBS *48 Hours* poll, indicating that 73 percent of the 663 respondents (Rs) supported a "total ban on military-style assault weapons," with 22 percent opposed, and 5 percent missing (no opinion, etc.). The significance of these findings is impossible to gauge in the absence of any evidence indicating that Rs knew what interviewers meant by the term "assault weapons." It is likely that many, perhaps most, of the Rs believed that the guns referred to were capable of fully automatic fire; indeed, true military assault rifles do have this capability. The weapons available to civilians, however, do not. The contrary view was also encouraged by the aforementioned news stories that repeatedly blurred the distinction between automatic and semiautomatic fire and that inaccurately insisted that weapons currently on the market can be readily converted to fire like a machine gun. With this background, it was scarcely surprising that a large majority of Americans favored a ban on private possession of guns that they believed could fire like machine guns, especially since this is already the law of the land.[45] It was not clear whether Rs opposed weapons that have a military appearance, opposed semiautomatic weapons, understood what "semiautomatic" meant, or even knew that the weapons referred to in the question *were* semiautomatic. Given that even news sources were confused about the relevant distinctions, it would be implausible to assume that those who answered the question understood what they were being asked about.

The *48 Hours* documentary itself wandered back and forth between machine guns, "assault weapons," "assault rifles," "military-style assault rifles" and even commonplace semiautomatic pistols. Like CBS, other prominent news sources also have asserted that semiautomatic weapons are little more than fully automatic machine guns waiting to be converted. For example, even though federal law bans guns readily converted to fully automatic fire and no weapons available for sale to the public had this property, the *New York Times* insisted in an editorial that "many semiautomatics can be made fully automatic with a screwdriver, even a paperclip," a claim their own reporters contradicted just eight months later.[46]

Survey researchers know that those contacted in polls are reluctant to admit that they do not know what a surveyor is asking about, and will generally provide a response, however meaningless, to an opinion question. They will even "express an opinion about an issue they could not possibly know anything about, simply because they do not wish to appear empty-headed or uninformed." For instance, they will respond to questions asking about prejudice against imaginary ethnic groups or about nonexistent government officials invented by the surveyors.[47] CBS presented the poll results without commentary, letting viewers draw the seemingly obvious conclusion about the popularity of the restrictions in question.

The Violence Problem Is an Assault Rifle Problem. The next segment was devoted to anecdotal information about the prevalence of ARs "on the streets" and among crime weapons. Two Boston police officers were shown on patrol; they offered the opinion that there were a lot of ARs "out there." Then a police detective was shown in a Fort Lauderdale police property room against a backdrop of dozens or hundreds of confiscated guns. CBS did not report what fraction of these seized guns were ARs. At least forty-seven reports on the prevalence of assault weapons among crime guns recovered by police indicate that less than 1 percent are "assault rifles" and less than 2 percent fall into the more broadly defined assault weapons category.[48]

The detective described how he thought local drug gangs typically killed people—"they'll spray the area, just an indiscriminate shooting. . . . If they hit innocent bystanders along the way, no big deal." CBS did not ask how many times innocent bystanders had been killed in indiscriminate drug-related shootings, did not ask the officer to relate even one such incident, and did not confirm that it had actually happened, even once. Such incidents are in fact extremely rare. (Note again that the word "spray" could suggest, without anyone explicitly saying so, that the guns were capable of fully automatic fire.)

Late in the documentary, in a segment largely devoted to showing machine gun scenes from commercial films, the first and only scholarly expert of any kind to appear or even be cited on the program was interviewed, but on a topic of negligible relevance. Professor David Malamud was questioned about the effect of media violence on real-life violence. None of the research he cited bore specifically on the significance of media portrayals of either weapons generally, or automatic (or semiautomatic) weapons specifically. No gun violence researchers of any kind were interviewed or cited in the program in connection with any of the issues addressed.

A live studio discussion followed, involving two persons: Larry Pratt, spokesman for Gun Owners of America, an organization even more strongly opposed to gun controls than the National Rifle Association, and a man named Joseph McNamara. While Pratt was clearly identified as being a spokesman for an anticontrol group, McNamara was described only as chief of the San Jose police department. Some viewers might assume McNamara had arrived at his views purely on the basis of his experience as a police officer familiar with violent crime. In fact he was a gun control activist, a board member of the Handgun Information Center, a tax-exempt branch of Handgun Control, Inc., has frequently testified in favor of gun control before legislative bodies, and held views arguably as extreme in support of AR restrictions as Pratt's were in opposition.[49]

No police administrator was shown expressing skepticism about the likely efficacy of AR restrictions or the frequency of their involvement in crime. CBS did not overtly describe McNamara as a disinterested or representative spokesman for responsible law enforcement opinion; they merely presented his views without mentioning his affiliation with gun control lobbying groups and without any opposing law enforcement views. Because of his affiliation, Pratt's opinions could be easily dismissed by the viewer as the biased views of a spokesperson for the gun lobby. But a spokesperson clearly affiliated with the "gun lobby" was not "balanced off" by identifying the spokesperson for Handgun Control as such. It is unlikely that spokespersons affiliated with advocacy groups and those not so affiliated would be perceived by viewers as equally credible.

The final sequence concerned the critical event that stimulated the movement to restrict ARs, the January 17, 1989, Stockton, California, schoolyard massacre. Dan Rather stated that the killer, Patrick Purdy, "brought his imported AK-47 to a school playground in Stockton, California. He fired 106 bullets within 120 seconds. Five children were murdered, 29 wounded." The *Los Angeles Times* reported that 110 shots were fired, but over a period of three to four minutes.[50] Their report implied a rate of fire that was only half as rapid as that implied by the CBS figures and that was no faster than that which can be easily sustained by an ordinary revolver, even taking reloading time into account—about one shot every two seconds.

In this and many of the examples previously cited, there is no reason to believe that CBS knew they were misinforming their audience. On the other hand, there is also little reason to doubt that the documentary was intentionally constructed to persuade viewers that ARs represented a major threat to public safety. Its producers probably believed what they were attempting to persuade their audience to believe, even though their message was largely without factual foundation. They did not discover this because they failed to exercise sufficient journalistic skepticism or diligence in seeking out potentially contrary information. They did not bother to check out questionable claims, or seek out expert opinion on dubious propositions, perhaps because they did not seriously entertain the possibility that the assertions were questionable or subject to dispute in the first place.

None of the information management strategies used by CBS are unique to that organization. Other television documentaries about guns have been equally unbalanced, sloppy, and manipulative of viewers. The *48 Hours* program was not an unusual or extreme case. For example, ABC-TV's "America Under the Gun" (broadcast May 9, 1994) or the Discovery Channel's "Vigilantes" (an episode of the *Justice Files* series first aired on February 10, 1998) share the same flaws, while NBC-TV's program *Guns, Guns, Guns* (broadcast in June of 1988) could easily have served as a far more extreme example of shoddy coverage of the issue.

Newsweek and the Invention of a Machine Gun Crisis

Magazines have also manipulated information to create a procontrol impression. The *Newsweek* cover story of October 14, 1985, on machine guns is a prominent example, partly because it appears to be the first place the term "assault weapon" appeared in the press. The cover headline was "MACHINE GUN U.S.A." with a subheadline claiming that "Nearly 500,000 Automatic Weapons Are Now in the Hands of Collectors—and Criminals."[51] In fact, no one had any idea how many automatic weapons were in private hands, least of all *Newsweek*. The 500,000 figure was mentioned only once in the article itself, and then it referred neither to machine guns nor to fully automatic weapons, but rather to semiautomatic military-style assault guns or assault weapons.[52] These weapons fire only one shot per trigger pull, the same as revolvers. But even this number as it pertained to semiautomatic assault weapons was nothing more than a guess supplied by the general counsel of the National Coalition to Ban Handguns. *Newsweek* apparently saw nothing improper about using a guess from a gun control lobbyist as the sole basis for a cover headline. No factual basis was ever provided for the claim of 500,000 machine guns.

The only numbers that did pertain to automatic weapons were the number of federally registered automatic weapons (116,000 at the time, according to BATF) and a guess by the gun control lobbyist that "perhaps 125,000" of the 500,000 assault weapons (a guess derived from a guess) had been converted to full automatic fire. In fact, only 40 percent of the federally registered automatic weapons were even in private hands at the time, implying about 46,000 registered machine guns in private hands—the rest belonged to law enforcement agencies.[53] There was no factual basis whatsoever for the claim that a quarter, or even 1 percent, of assault weapons had been converted to full automatic status. Indeed, even among the guns confiscated by police (presumably more criminally involved than other guns, and thus more likely to have undergone an illegal conversion), semiautomatic assault weapons converted to fully automatic fire are virtually nonexistent.[54]

The article vaguely asserted that these weapons were somehow "raising the risks of criminal violence" yet never cited a single national or even local crime statistic to indicate that the frequency of crimes committed with either machine guns or assault weapons was increasing.[55] Indeed, the authors came up with descriptions of a grand total of two fatal machine gun attacks, occurring in two different years. In lieu of any hard evidence on the prevalence of such incidents, Edward Conroy, a Miami BATF agent, was quoted as claiming that "South Florida is the mecca of illegal automatics, and machine-gun hits are almost commonplace. . . . There are even brazen attacks at stoplights, with grandma and the kiddies getting greased along with the target."[56] In fact, both machine-gun killings and accidental killings of innocent bystanders in drug shootouts (at stoplights or anywhere else) were virtually nonexistent, even in Miami during the peak of its drug-related homicide problem. Perhaps the sort of incident Conroy described did occur once. However, *Newsweek* neither bothered to confirm it nor to question the claim that it was "almost common." Even in Miami less than

1 percent of homicides in 1980 involved machine guns, and none of these involved innocent bystanders being killed.[57]

The *Newsweek* article also contained a long series of half-truths and unsupported assertions similar to those repeated four years later in the CBS *48 Hours* documentary—for instance, that assault rifles are easily converted to fully automatic fire, so the distinction between the these weapons and machine guns is an "increasingly tenuous" one (pp. 48-49); that they pose a major threat to police officers (p. 50); that they are unusually lethal (p. 51); and so on. And, as with the CBS documentary, not a single expert on guns and violence, either favoring or opposing the premises of the story, was quoted or cited. Because few experts in the field could have provided evidence supporting the main propositions of the story, the omission of expert commentary was perhaps understandable.[58]

The Bernhard Goetz Case

Perhaps the most heavily publicized case of a purported defensive use of a gun in recent decades was an incident in which Bernhard Goetz shot four young men in a New York City subway train on December 22, 1984. As the story was handled by the national press, the following were the salient features of the incident. The four individuals who were shot by Goetz had "asked" for money, the stories hinting that they may have merely been panhandling rather than attempting to rob Goetz. The four were "youths" who were merely acting a bit rambunctious, rather than menacing. While the four had prior records of "brushes with the law," the offenses involved were "minor." After shooting two of the four, Goetz shot at least one, possibly two of them, in the back as they were attempting to flee. After turning himself in to police, Goetz confessed to shooting all four, then pausing, seeing one of them already wounded, and firing another shot into the helpless victim. Goetz was described as a "subway vigilante," and writers speculated that the incident would stimulate future criminal use of guns by citizens encouraged to carry guns as Goetz did. Goetz was acquitted of the most serious charges connected with the shootings and was convicted only of unlawful possession of a firearm. The press hinted that Goetz had been treated leniently by the court and reported speculations that the leniency was racially motivated and was due to the fact that Goetz was white and the four victims were black.[59]

The only problem with this account of the case was that nearly all of it was either false, misleading, or unsupported by the available facts. From the very beginning there had been no doubt that the incident began with an attempted robbery. Two of the four victims admitted to police and reporters that they had intended to rob Goetz. (Even twelve years after the incident, the *Los Angeles Times* was uncritically repeating the robbers' claim that "they were only panhandling."[60]) Leaving aside its wisdom or morality, New York State law is clear that victims of robbery may use force, including deadly force, to resist robbery, regardless of whether the robbers are armed or whether the victim could safely retreat.[61]

The victims were not ordinary, rambunctious children—all were eighteen or nineteen years old at the time, and all four had extensive criminal records. At the time of the incident, there were a total of nine convictions, many more arrests, plus twelve cases pending and ten bench warrants for nonappearance in court against the four. While some later news reports conceded this, some also attempted to undercut it by only acknowledging the more minor offenses.[62] In fact, the charges included rape, armed robbery, and assault with a deadly weapon. At the time of the incident Darrell Cabey was awaiting trial on charges of armed robbery with a shotgun, and six months later James Ramseur was arrested for (and later convicted of) the rape and robbery of a pregnant woman, who required forty stitches to close her wounds and had to be hospitalized for four days.

News accounts laid special emphasis on Goetz's videotaped confession in which he stated that, after wounding all four of the robbers, he paused, looked the fourth (Cabey) over, said, "You don't look too bad, here's another," and shot the already-wounded man a second time.[63] Although Goetz did tell police something like this, the confession was contradicted by seven eyewitnesses, who agreed that the shots had all been fired in rapid succession without a pause. No one saw Goetz calmly shoot a helpless man after walking over to him and delivering a speech. Even the prosecutor expressed doubts about whether Goetz spoke, at the scene, the words he later confessed to, though he nonetheless insisted that Goetz had shot one of the men a second time without justification.[64]

The press freely used the term "vigilante" to describe Goetz, but the use was inaccurate. The word derives from "vigilance committee" and traditionally refers to members of groups who seek to punish criminals where the legally constituted authorities are unable or unwilling to do so. Scholars have noted the existence of modern vigilantes, but these are always members of anticrime groups.[65] Strictly speaking, the term "lone vigilante" is an oxymoron since vigilantism is by definition a group activity. More importantly, there was never any clear evidence Goetz set out to punish criminals or sought contact with either the four he shot or any other criminals.[66] Instead, whether morally justified or not, whether excessive or not, Goetz's act was believed by the jury to be an act of self-defense. Further, there is no evidence that this incident encouraged other people to commit illegal acts of self-defense. The only possible effect on criminal behavior documented so far was a pronounced *decrease* in subway robberies in the weeks and months following the incident (drops the New York authorities attributed to added transit police in the subways).[67]

Finally, there is no evidence Goetz was treated leniently by the court, for any reason. There was never any solid legal foundation for doubting that the four young men were attempting to rob Goetz, nor any ambiguity about whether New York state law permits use of force against robbers. Consequently, there was little legal basis for convicting Goetz for shooting the first three men, and only conflicting and inconsistent evidence supporting the charges pertaining to the second wounding of the fourth man.[68] Goetz was convicted of an unlawful weapons possession charge, a Class D felony of which he was undoubtedly guilty. In 1989, of 2,308 people convicted in New York City for illegal gun possession, half received no jail time at all, including the four out of ten who received only probation.[69] Goetz was sentenced to one year in jail (and served over eight months), five years' probation, 280 hours of community service, a $5,000 fine or another year in jail, and was ordered to seek psychiatric help.[70] In short, Goetz was treated more harshly than most less-publicized defendants convicted of the same charge.

One might argue that the acquittal on the shooting-related charges was itself the product of racism. For example, Benjamin Hooks, head of the NAACP, was quoted in the press as asking: "If a white youth had been shot in similar circumstances by a black man, what would have been the outcome?" Oddly enough, a similar incident was in fact handled by the New York courts around the same time, with the races of the participants reversed. According to a newspaper account, a twenty-three-year-old black man named Austin Weeks, while riding a New York City subway train, was accosted by two white teenagers who called him a racist name. Weeks shot and killed one of them with an unlicensed pistol. A Brooklyn grand jury refused to indict Weeks, he never had to face the prolonged trial Goetz faced, and consequently Weeks received no legal punishment of any kind. Thus, in a shooting with a more legally questionable justification (no robbery was involved, but only a verbal provocation) and a fatal outcome, a black man accused of killing a white teenager was treated more leniently than a white man accused of nonfatally shooting four black teenagers. The Weeks case was ignored by the national press.[71]

Is It Bias or Just Random Sloppiness?

It could be argued that these examples merely reflect the inevitable imperfections of work done under a deadline and with limited resources. Reporters are human and make mistakes like everyone else. While this is obviously true, it cannot account for the unbalanced, consistently procontrol character of the flaws. If these flaws were truly just innocent mistakes unrelated to biased views of guns and gun control, they would be randomly distributed and equally likely to be pro- or anticontrol in their implications. They are not.

The prevalence and direction of bias was addressed directly in former reporter Tamryn Etten's content analysis of newspaper stories on gun issues. Etten examined a nationally representative sample of 117 gun stories published in 1989 and selected from *Newsbank*, a database covering virtually all large-circulation, and many small-to-medium circulation, daily newspapers in the United States. Each story was coded for indications of bias in the content of the story, such as unrebutted statements favoring one side or the other, use of words tending to weaken or strengthen the impact of pro- or anticontrol arguments (e.g., advocate Smith "claimed" . . . versus "stated"), use of unattributed facts or opinions, and use of sarcasm directed at advocates or arguments on one side or the other. Using a "net bias" score that measured the excess of procontrol bias over anticontrol bias, Etten's results indicated that 71 percent of the stories contained net bias in one direction or another, and that among stories with some net bias, 81 percent were biased in favor of gun control. Thus, stories biased in favor of the procontrol side outnumbered stories favoring the anticontrol side by a margin of four to one.[72]

Perhaps the most telling evidence of the one-sided character of national news media coverage of the gun debate is the almost total absence of complaints about it from the procontrol side. While the gun press is filled with bitter complaints of antigun bias in the national media, the writings of gun control advocates rarely even mention the issue.[73] Either the latter see little national news coverage to object to, or they are remarkably forbearing in saying anything about it.

Quite the contrary—one especially strong supporter of strict gun controls approvingly described early television news coverage of gun issues as "balanced."[74] And the chairman of Handgun Control, Inc., Pete Shields, all but acknowledged the nation's newspapers as an active ally in the gun control movement: "I would be remiss if I failed to mention the support that the handgun control movement has received from the editorial pages of papers across the nation. Some of these papers have supported the movement for its entire life. As a group, American editorial writers have done a great deal to keep the cause of handgun control before the American public."[75]

This sort of free media support provides more than just the intangible benefits of public good will and organizational legitimacy. Shields recalled the effects of interviews he gave in 1977 to *Parade* magazine and the top-rated *60 Minutes* news magazine program on CBS-TV, crediting them with providing a critical early boost to his organization's growth. "As a result of these two features, we were accorded what you might call 'instant credibility.' The phones [at Handgun Control, Inc.] rang more than ever, and the mail thundered in. The huge number of contributions and letters of support showed us that . . . the American people favored some form of gun control."[76]

Discussion and Conclusions

Etten's content analysis results indicated that strong procontrol/antigun bias is not universal. Some major news sources have covered the gun issue in a competent and balanced fashion, notably PBS television (which produced what may be the best broadcast documentary on the issue, in its

Frontline series), the *Wall Street Journal*, and *U.S. News & World Report*. And there are certainly many local newspapers that also cover gun control issues in a reasonably balanced way, though most of these are small-circulation outlets with strictly local impact. Nevertheless, while antigun bias is not universal among the major national news outlets, it is certainly widespread. Further, it is not balanced by important news sources with a progun bias. No major national news source, broadcast or print, can reasonably be described as biased in a progun or antigun control direction.

Recent research has confirmed the generally antigun tilt of both newspapers and network television coverage of the issue. Research for a 1999 doctoral dissertation addressed how the National Rifle Association (NRA) was treated, examining nearly 1,500 articles appearing in the elite press from 1990 to 1998. The research indicated that coverage of the NRA was far more likely to be negative than coverage of four other major national organizations (87 percent of editorials and op-eds on the NRA were negative), that NRA sources in news stories were more likely to be labeled "lobbyists," and that their views were more likely to be accompanied by negative verbs of attribution such as "claims" or "contends" versus "says." Further, the organization is more likely that other interest groups to be mocked or satirized, and is more than twice as likely to be described as a lobby or "special interest group," while other groups, including Handgun Control, Inc., are likely to be accorded more positive labels such as "citizen group."[77]

The imbalance in coverage is also evident in the broadcast media. An analysis of network news programs broadcast during the period from July 1, 1997, to June 30, 1999, found that gun policy stories favoring gun control outnumbered those opposing it by a ratio of almost ten to one, and that "talking heads" were more than twice as likely to be procontrol than anticontrol.[78]

To be sure, biases in news coverage of gun control are not unique to that issue. The news industry's handling of drug issues may be just as distorted, and coverage of crime issues in general is superficial, sloppy, and uncritical of official views.[79] Nevertheless, the partiality and lack of skepticism towards one side in the dispute seem especially pronounced in connection with gun control.

Why should such bias exist? How can professional journalists, committed to an ethic of objectivity and fairness, nevertheless engage in such unbalanced coverage of an issue and apparently be so unaware of any bias? One possible explanation is that many news professionals do not believe there are two legitimate sides to the gun debate. While there are obviously two parties to the dispute, only one is believed to have a legitimate case to make, one that goes beyond mere narrow self-interest. One possible consequence is that some members of influential news organizations set the gun issue apart, make it an exception, and do not feel bound by customary standards of objectivity and even-handedness where gun control is concerned. It is just an issue involving conflict between the "good guys" and the "bad guys." Consider the following unusually frank excerpt from a form letter sent from the editorial offices of *Time* magazine to a reader who had objected to one of their stories on guns:

> The July 17 (1989) cover story is the most recent in a growing number of attempts on the part of TIME editors to keep the gun-availability issue resolutely in view. Such an editorial closing of ranks represents the exception rather than the rule in the history of the magazine, which has always endeavored to provide a variety of opinions and comment, in addition to straightforward news reporting, as a way of engaging readers in interpreting the significance of issues and events as they arise. *But the time for opinions on the dangers of gun availability is long since gone, replaced by overwhelming evidence that it represents a growing threat to public safety.*[80]

"The time for opinions . . . is long since gone." Were the issue any other one, would any respectable journalist fail to find such a sentiment disturbing? The guns-violence issue was evidently beyond debate in the editorial offices of *Time*. In sharp contrast to the debates among experts on the subject, there were no honestly differing views among the editors on "the dangers of gun availability" or the assertion that it was "a growing threat to public safety." This was not an issue with two sides, which *Time* was obliged to cover fairly, but rather was an issue with only one valid or respectable side. The only remaining issue was how best to convey to the readers of *Time* the indisputable truth that the editors saw so clearly.

The political implications of this imbalance are important. Few would dispute that the mass media influence public opinion and lawmaking in a democracy. Consequently, the one-sided character of much of the news reporting on the gun issue is a serious matter, though clearly not one that has been widely acknowledged among opinion leaders. Media manipulation of information in general has certainly not gone unnoticed.[81] However, the unequal character of the propaganda struggle over guns is not as well known or as frequently addressed by scholars.

Author Roger Caras commented in 1970 on the quality of the debate over guns: "Any careful observer of the battle must be distressed at the ignorance, ill will, and dishonesty apparent on both sides."[82] Caras's assessment was true as far as it went, but its bland evenhandedness obscured the extremely unequal impact of "the ignorance, ill will, and dishonesty" of each side. The purveyors of misinformation are not all equally influential or well-placed to disseminate their views. The indisputably biased publications of the National Rifle Association (NRA) and the rest of the gun press have a combined circulation probably well under ten million (about 5.3 million in 1998, for the four largest circulation gun and outdoor magazines), while *Time* and *Newsweek* alone reach over seven million households every week, and the commercial television networks reach many tens of millions of households every day.[83] The biased views of gun control proponents find a sympathetic outlet in the major print and broadcast media, while the equally biased views of gun control opponents are largely confined to the pages of gun and hunting magazines, where they are read almost exclusively by a comparatively small audience of the already-converted faithful.

Regardless of how successful a political lobbying organization the NRA may or may not be, this power is greatly counterbalanced by the disproportionately procontrol slant of the nation's most influential providers of news.[84] While the NRA has to purchase (when media advertising departments permit it to do so) print and broadcast advertisements in order to reach a substantial share of the general public, procontrol forces are in effect given sympathetic media dissemination of their views free of charge.

When a California referendum to limit private possession of handguns was defeated in 1982 by a 63 percent to 37 percent margin, its supporters attributed its defeat to NRA spending, specifically $5.5 to 7 million spent on print and broadcast advertisements, compared to only $1.5 to 2.6 million spent by proponents.[85] While the ads and air time the NRA bought surely helped its cause, this analysis is misleadingly one-sided because it ignores procontrol messages provided by media outlets free of charge. University of Illinois Professor David Bordua noted that CBS broadcast a fifteen-minute, strongly antihandgun segment on its highest-rated program, *60 Minutes*, just nine days before the referendum vote. Bordua also noted that the referendum was preceded by no fewer than nine procontrol editorials by the *Los Angeles Times*, not to mention similar ones from much of the rest of the state's major newspapers. Proponents of the referendum did not have to buy this mass media help, but it was obviously to their benefit and was certainly intended to persuade voters. Bordua estimated that fifteen minutes of CBS airtime during the *60 Minutes* program would cost about six million dollars if it had been purchased as proreferendum advertising, rather than being granted as a free gift, as it were, by CBS. Depending on a variety of assumptions about the value of various forms of free media exposure, and counting in the value of newspaper editorials and free air time on local TV and radio stations available to proponents under the Fairness Doctrine (still in effect back in 1982), Bordua's analysis indicated that supporters of the referendum may actually have received greater media exposure, paid and unpaid, than opponents.[86]

It is unrealistic to view the gun lobby as the only powerful player in the political struggle over guns. The most important mass media news sources are extremely powerful, and many of the more influential among them have clearly taken sides on the gun issue. For the battle to be portrayed by these media sources as a procontrol David against an anticontrol Goliath is not only inaccurate but also blatantly self-serving. It allows the news media to inaccurately portray themselves as neutral bystanders in a political struggle they merely report, rather than one in which they play an active part. This self-image is especially apparent in news coverage of the procontrol findings of public opinion surveys, which are reported as if public opinion were something that independently existed and evolved on its own, and that the media merely reported, rather than something heavily shaped by the news outlets themselves.

If the media were in fact neutral, and only the NRA and gun control advocacy groups were involved in the conflict, the struggle would indeed be a very unequal one, for the NRA is undoubtedly a better funded lobbying organization than its opposite numbers on the procontrol side. However, the news establishment is not neutral on the gun issue and so the struggle is considerably more equal than one would guess from news stories that narrowly focus on campaign spending and lobbying efforts by the advocacy groups, while ignoring news outlets' crucial, albeit unacknowledged, role as active allies of the gun control movement.[87]

What are the effects of this slanted coverage of the gun issue? First, the public is poorly informed. With limited space and time, bad coverage drives out good coverage, and unbiased sources are drowned out by biased ones. Second, gun owners are made to feel like embattled victims of a disinformation campaign whose distortions can only be fought with further distortions in the opposite direction. Public debate gets deformed by pushing responsible moderates to the extremes, and polarizing the issue. Discussion degenerates into exchanges of increasingly outrageous claims and insults.[88] Finally, the legislative process is warped by inducing lawmakers to focus on highly publicized but substantively trivial sideshow issues like bans on assault weapons, plastic guns, "cop-killer" bullets and Saturday-night specials, rather than addressing more serious, but perhaps less exciting, control measures like gun buyer background checks, or improved enforcement of existing bans on criminal possession and unlawful carrying of guns. Because the news media affect public opinion, politicians can ill afford to ignore the implicit policy agenda set by the news industry when it focuses disproportionate attention on trivial or unproductive policies.

Notes

1. *Los Angeles Times*, 11 August 1985, p. 1.

2. *Brown Deer [Wisconsin] Herald*, 23 March 1989.

3. For general discussions of media influence on public opinion, see Stanley Cohen and Jock Young, *The Manufacture of News: Deviance, Social Problems and the Mass Media* (London: Constable, 1981); Ben H. Bagdikian, *The Media Monopoly*, 2d ed. (Boston: Beacon Press, 1987); Edward S. Herman and Noam Chomsky, *Manufacturing Consent* (New York: Pantheon, 1988).

4. *Newsweek*, 14 October 1985, pp. 48–49.

5. *New York Times*, 3 April 1989, p. A14.

6. Gary Kleck, *Point Blank: Guns and Violence in America* (New York: Aldine, 1991), pp. 66, 70.

7. Tamryn Etten, "Gun Control and the Press: A Content Analysis of Newspaper Bias" (paper presented at the annual meeting of the American Society of Criminology, San Francisco, Calif., November 20–23, 1991).

8. *New York Times*, 20 July 1985, p. 22; *New York Times*, 27 September 1985, p. A30; *New York Times* 7 March 1986, p. A15; *Chicago Tribune*, 7 March 1986, pp. 1–3; *Los Angeles Times*, 19 December 1985, p. II–6; *Los Angeles Times*, 7 March 1986, p. I–15; *Los Angeles Times*, 15 August 1986, p. I–2; *Los Angeles Times*, 29 August 1986, p. I–4.

9. *Los Angeles Times*, 29 August 1986, p. I–4.

10. Carol Memmott and Andrea Stone, "Spate of Shootings Spurs Florida to Act," *USA Today*, 15 June 1989, p. 3A.

11. Kleck, *Point Blank*, pp. 262, 306, 310.

12. *CBS Evening News*, CBS telecast, 11 October 1989.

13. *All Things Considered*, WETA-FM radio broadcast, 17 December 1989; compare with chapters 6 and 7.

14. *Time*, July 17, 1989, compare p. 31 with pp. 3, 30.

15. Letter from Professor James D. Wright, 15 February 1991. For his published views on this point, see James D. Wright, "Guns and Crime," in *Criminology: A Contemporary Handbook* (Belmont, Calif.: Wadsworth, 1991).

16. Emilia Askari, John Crust, and Timothy Carlson, "AK-47: 'Weapon of War' Finds a Home on L.A.'s Mean Streets," *Los Angeles Herald Examiner*, 23 January 1989, pp. A1, A6, A7.

17. Martin Fackler et al., "Wounding Effects of the AK-47 Rifle Used by Patrick Purdy in the Stockton Schoolyard Shooting of 17 January 1989," *American Journal of Forensic Medicine and Pathology* 11 (1989): 185–89.

18. Deputy Sheriff Dwight Van Horn of the Los Angeles County Sheriff's Department, telephone conversation with author, 12 September 1989.

19. *Gun Week*, 5 May 1989, p. 1; "Peter Jennings Reporting: Guns," ABC telecast, 24 January 1990.

20. Emilia Askari, reporter for the *Los Angeles Herald Examiner*, telephone conversaton with author, October 1989.

21. "Peter Jennings Reporting: Guns."

22. U.S. Congressional Research Service, assault weapons: Military-Style Semiautomatic Firearms Facts and Issues, Report 92–434 GOV (1992), pp. 38–39.

23. For documentation of that these claims are inaccurate, see Kleck, *Point Blank*, pp. 70–82.

24. U.S. Bureau of Alcohol, Tobacco, and Firearms, *Firearms State Laws and Published Ordinances—1994*, 20th ed. (1994); *U.S. News and World Report*, 25 April 1988; National Rifle Association, *Legislative Status*, fact sheet on state gun laws (Washington, D.C.: National Rifle Association, 1987).

25. Kleck, *Point Blank*, pp. 84–85.

26. Michael Briggs, "How Maryland Banned Handguns," *Chicago Sun Times*, 29 May 1988, p. 22; *Washington Post*, 12 April 1988, p. A1.

27. Hawaii Revised Statutes, sec. 134–32.

28. Michael Briggs, "Limits on Sales Found Ineffective," *Chicago Sun Times*, 29 May 1988, p. 22.

29. Lee Kennett and James LaVerne Anderson, *The Gun in America* (Westport, Conn.: Greenwood Press, 1975), p. 237.

30. *Washington Post*, 30 October 1988 to 7 November 1988.

31. Bagdikian, *The Media Monopoly*, p. 100.

32. Etten, "Gun Control and the Press."

33. *Los Angeles Times* Poll on the Public and Press, released August, 1985, DIALOG, Public Opinion Online, accessed 10 December 1990.

34. Theresa Fassihi, "NRA Ad from Oklahoma Agency Stirs Controversy," *Adweek*, 26 June 1989, p. 4.

35. U.S. Bureau of Justice Statistics, *Guns and Crime*, Crime Data Brief (Washington, D.C.: U.S. Government Printing Office, 1994).

36. Jock Young, "Beyond the Consensual Paradigm," in *The Manufacture of News: Deviance, Social Problems and the Mass Media* (Beverly Hills: Sage, 1981).

37. *48 Hours*, "Armed and Deadly," CBS telecast, 16 March 1989.

38. Kleck, *Point Blank*, pp. 70–82.

39. U.S. Federal Bureau of Investigation, *Uniform Crime Reports—1989* (and earlier issues, covering 1974–1988) (Washington, D.C.: U.S. Government Printing Office, 1990 [1975–1989]).

40. Daniel W. Webster et al., "Epidemiological Changes in Gunshot Wounds in Washington, D.C., 1983–1990," *Archives of Surgery* 127 (1992): 694–98.

41. Kleck, *Point Blank*, p. 95.

42. Ken Warner, *Gun Digest—1989/43rd Annual Edition* (Northbrook, Ill.: DBI Books, 1988).

43. Ed Owen, Chief of the Firearms Technology Branch of the Bureau of Alcohol, Tobacco, and Firearms, telephone conversation with author, 1989.

44. U.S. Bureau of Alcohol, Tobacco and Firearms, *Federal Firearms Regulation 1988–89* (1988): 14–16.

45. Ibid.

46. *New York Times*, 1 August 1988, p. A14; *New York Times*, 3 April 1989, p. A14.

47. I. A. Lewis and William Schneider, "Is the Public Lying to the Pollsters?" *Public Opinion* 5 (1982): 42–47.

48. Gary Kleck, *Targeting Guns: Firearms and Their Control* (New York: Aldine, 1997), pp. 112–17, 141–43.

49. *New York Times*, 8 June 1986, p. A26.

50. *Los Angles Times*, 18 January 1989, sec. 1, p. 3.

51. Tom Morganthau, "Machine Gun U.S.A.," *Newsweek*, 14 October 1985, pp. 46–51.

52. Ibid., pp. 46, 49.

53. *Los Angeles Times*, 16 November 1986, p. D–4.

54. U.S. Congressional Research Service, "Assault weapons," p. 18—none of 3,527 Washington, D.C., guns recovered by police had been converted to fully automatic fire; Hearings before the Senate Committee on the Judiciary, Subcommittee on the Constitution, on S. 386 and S. 747, 101st Cong., 1st session (1989), p. 379— of over 4,000 Los Angeles guns, six had been converted to fully automatic fire.

55. Morganthau, "Machine Gun U.S.A.," p. 46.

56. Ibid., p. 48.

57. Kleck, *Point Blank*, p. 68.

58. Ibid., pp. 70–82.

59. See, e.g., *Newsweek*, 11 March 1985 or 1 April 1985; *Time*, 21 January 1985.

60. John J. Goldman, "Jury awards millions to victim of shooting by subway gunman," *Los Angeles Times* wire service story appearing in *Tallahassee Democrat*, 24 April 1996, p. 1A. In the civil suit brought by one of the men Goetz wounded, Darrell Cabey, one of only two witnesses called by the defense was reporter Jimmy Breslin. Breslin testified that Cabey himself admitted in an interview that his friends planned to rob Goetz—Larry McShane, "Breslin: Victim Said Goetz 'Looked Like Easy Bait'," *Chicago Sun-Times*, 18 April 1996, p. 20.

61. George P. Fletcher, *A Crime of Self-Defense* (New York: The Free Press, 1988), p. 25.

62. E.g., *Newsweek*, 1 April 1985, p. 23.

63. Ibid.

64. Mark Lesley, *Subway Gunman* (Latham, N.Y.: British American Publishing, 1988), pp. 187–93.

65. Richard Maxwell Brown, "The American Vigilante Tradition," in *Violence in America*, ed. Hugh Davis Graham and Ted Robert Gurr (New York: Signet, 1969).

66. Lesley, *Subway Gunman*, p. 317.

67. *New York Times*, 22 March 1985, p. B4; *New York Times*, 18 April 1985, p. B7.

68. Lesley, *Subway Gunman*.

69. *New York Times*, 29 January 1990.

70. Lesley, *Subway Gunman*, p. 320.

71. Ray Kerrison, "Here's Proof Goetz Verdict Wasn't Racist," *New York Post*, 23 June 1987. A search of the Lexis-Nexis newspaper database found no references to "Austin Weeks" in 1987.

72. Etten, "Gun Control and the Press."

73. Paul Blackman, "Mugged by the Media," *American Rifleman*, June 1987, pp. 34–36, 80–81; Marshall J. Brown, "Wound Ballistics Expert Exposes Media AK Fakery," *Gun Week*, 5 May 1989, p. 1.

74. Carl Bakal, *No Right to Bear Arms* (New York: McGraw-Hill, 1966), p. 127.

75. Pete Shields, *Guns Don't Die—People Do* (New York: Arbor House, 1981), p. 89.

76. Ibid., p. 134.

77. Brian A. Patrick, "Social Movement Pluralism: Negative Media Coverage and National Rifle Association Mobilization" (Ph.D. diss., University of Michigan, 1999), abstract in *Dissertation Abstracts International* 60/7A (2000): 2274.

78. Geoffrey Dickens, "Outgunned: How the Network News Media Are Spinning the Gun Control Debate" (Media Research Center, 2000). Downloaded from Worldwide Web on 12 January 2000 at: http://www.mediaresearch.org/specialreports/newssr20000105b.html.

79. Cohen and Young, *The Manufacture of News*.

80. Form letter from Gloria Hammond, Editorial Offices of *Time*, 1 August 1989. Emphasis added.

81. See, e.g., Cohen and Young, *The Manufacture of News*, concerning media treatment of crime, deviance and social problems; Bagdikian, *The Media Monopoly*, on economic and political issues in general; Herman and Chomsky, *Manufacturing Consent*, on political, especially foreign policy, issues.

82. Roger Caras, *Death as a Way of Life* (Boston: Little, Brown, 1970), p. 122.

83. *The World Almanac and Book of Facts 2000* (Mahwah, N.J.: World Almanac Books, 1999), 182.

84. For evidence casting doubt the NRA's lobbying impact, see Laura I. Langbein and Mark A. Lotwis, "The Political Efficacy of Lobbying and Money: Gun Control in the U.S. House, 1986," *Legislative Studies Quarterly* 15 (August 1990): 414–40.

85. David J. Bordua, "Adversary Polling and the Construction of Social Meaning," *Law & Policy Quarterly* 5 (July 1983): 345–66.

86. Ibid.

87. E.g., *Rolling Stone*, 14 May 1981, pp. 1, 19–25, 70; *New York Times*, 12 April 1986, p. A26; 3 April 1989.

88. See chapter 3.

The Frequency of Defensive Gun Use
Evidence and Disinformation

by Gary Kleck

An ounce of evidence outweighs a ton of speculation

Abbreviations Frequently Used in Chapter Six:

DGU	=	defensive gun use
NCVS	=	National Crime Victimization Survey
NSDS	=	National Self-Defense Survey
NSPOF	=	National Survey of the Private Ownership of Firearms[1]
R	=	respondent (in a survey)

Gun control advocates who argue for laws that would reduce gun availability in various ways often assert that such a measure would be worthwhile even if it could save just one life. Thus, even if nearly all violent people managed to evade a given control mechanism, it might nevertheless be beneficial. The unstated premise of this argument, however, is that there are no countervailing costs attributable to any benefits of gun ownership and use that might be reduced by the control. Suppose, for example, that passing a gun control law indeed saved one life, but also cost two lives by disarming prospective victims who would have used guns defensively to prevent the loss of life. Then the law would actually cost lives, and, other things being equal, would be a bad idea.

To simply assume that gun control measures can only reduce violence, or at worst have no effect, is an irresponsible simplification. Gun control policies should be subject to the same critical standards that apply to other policies, which means that analysts must take seriously—not merely give lip service to—the possibility that the policies could have unintended harmful effects. Whether this is true for gun control depends to a great extent on the frequency and effects of defensive uses of guns. Thus, this chapter, and the next one, address the frequency, nature, and effects of owning, carrying, and using guns for protection.

We begin with the issue of how often Americans use guns for protection. This chapter is as much about the plague of advocacy scholarship, sagecraft, and "junk science" that afflicts the study of guns and violence, and particularly the issue of guns and self-defense, as it is about the methods and results of research in this area.

Early Surveys with Defensive Gun Use Questions

Before any scholarly survey research focused on defensive gun use (DGU), a number of public opinion polls, many focusing on gun ownership, crime, or related issues, asked one or two defensive gun use questions of probability samples of the general adult population. The results and other noteworthy features of these surveys, referred to hereafter as the "gun surveys," are summarized in table 6.1. The surveys differ in many important respects. Some asked about uses of all types of guns, while others were confined to handguns. Some covered a specific time period, asking if the respondent used a gun in, e.g., the past five years, while others asked whether the respondent had ever used a gun defensively at any time in the past. Given the widely varying ages of those questioned, the former method of asking the question is clearly more informative. Some of the survey questions asked about "self-defense," which may narrowly suggest defense of one's own bodily safety, while others asked more broadly about "protection," which could include protection of other people and of property.

Some questions asked only about the respondent's own experiences, while others asked about defensive uses by anyone in the respondent's household. Most surveys asked the defensive use questions of all respondents, but three of them "prescreened" respondents asking the question only of those who reported currently having a handgun or gun in the household. Most surveys specifically excluded uses in the course of military or police duties, but some did not. Some surveys did not distinguish defensive uses against animals from uses against human threats. The better surveys covered a national population, asked about defensive uses during a specific time period, asked the question of all respondents, distinguished civilian use from other uses, and distinguished uses against humans from uses against animals.

Like serious crime victimization, the absolute prevalence of defensive gun use, i.e., the percent of the population that has had this experience, is low. However, when translated into raw numbers of events, as crime figures are commonly reported, the percentages imply large numbers of defensive uses. All of the surveys imply at least 700,000 annual defensive gun uses. The surveys all differed from one another with respect to exactly what set of events was being estimated, but it is possible to adjust estimates from almost all of the surveys to make them somewhat more comparable with each other. Two surveys (Cambridge Reports; *Time*/CNN) cannot yield comparable estimates because the defensive gun use questions were asked only of current gun owners.[3] This is important because a substantial share of defensive gun uses are by persons in households that do not currently own (or at least do not report) guns, because the user employed either a gun belonging to someone else or one that was previously in the household.[4] Surveys that ask the defensive gun use question only of current gun owners will therefore substantially underestimate the frequency of defensive gun uses. The appendix to this chapter explains the computation of adjusted estimates for the thirteen earlier surveys.

The National Self-Defense Survey

The National Self-Defense Survey (NSDS), conducted in the spring of 1993, was the first survey ever devoted to the subject of armed self-defense.[5] It was carefully designed to correct all of the known correctable or avoidable

Table 6.1. Frequency of Defensive Gun Use Based on Thirteen Early Surveys[2]

	Field	Bordua	Cambridge Reports	DMIa	DMIb	Hart	Ohio
Survey:	Field	Bordua	Cambridge Reports	DMIa	DMIb	Hart	Ohio
Area:	California	Illinois	U.S.	U.S.	U.S.	U.S.	Ohio
Year of Interviews:	1976	1977	1978	1978	1978	1981	1982
Population covered:	Noninst. adults	Noninst. adults	Noninst. adults	Registered voters	Registered voters	Registered voters	Residents
Gun Type Covered:	Handguns	All guns	Handguns	All guns	All guns	Handguns	Handguns
Recall Period:	Ever/1,2 yrs.	Ever	Ever	Ever	Ever	5 yrs.	Ever
Excluded Uses Against Animals?	No	No	No	No	Yes	Yes	No
Excluded Military, Police Uses?	Yes	No	No	Yes	Yes	Yes	No
Defensive question asked of:	All Rs	All Rs	Protection hgun owners	All Rs	All Rs	All Rs Households	Rs, Hgun
Defensive question refers to:	Respondent	Respondent	Respondent	Household	Household	Household	Respondents
% Who Used	1.4/3/8.6[a]	5.0	18	15	7	4	6.5
% Who Fired Gun	2.9	n.a.	12	6	n.a.	n.a.	2.6
Implied number of def. gun uses[b] (millions)	3.1	1.4	n.a.	2.1	1.1	1.8	0.8

Table 6.1. (continued) Frequency of Defensive Gun Use Based on Thirteen Early Surveys[2]

Survey:	Time/ CNN	Mauser	Gallup	Gallup	L.A. Times	Tarrance
Area:	U.S.	U.S.	U.S.	U.S.	U.S.	U.S.
Year of Interviews:	1989	1990	1991	1993	1994	1994
Population covered:	"Firearm owners"	Residents	Noninst. Adults	Noninst. Adults	Noninst. Adults	Noninst. Adults
Gun Type Covered:	All guns	All guns	All guns	All guns	All guns	All guns
Recall Period:	Ever	5 years	Ever	Ever	Ever	5 years
Excluded Uses Against Animals?	No	Yes	No	No	No	Yes
Excluded Military, Police Uses?	Yes	Yes	No	Yes	Yes	Yes
Defensive question asked of:	Gun owners	All Rs	Rs in hgun hshlds	Gun owners	All	All
Defensive question refers to:	Respondent	Hsehold	Respondent	Respondent	Respondent	Respondent/ Household
% Who Used	n.a.	3.79	8	11	8[d]	1/2[e]
% Who Fired Gun	9-16[c]	n.a.	n.a.	n.a.	n.a.	n.a.
Implied number of def. gun uses[b] (millions)	n.a.	1.5	0.8	1.6	3.6	0.8

Notes:
a. 1.4 percent in past year, 3 percent in past two years, 8.6 percent ever.
b. Estimated annual number of defensive uses of guns of all types against humans, excluding uses connected with military or police duties, after any necessary adjustments were made, for U.S., 1993. Adjustments are explained in detail in Appendix.
c. 9 percent fired gun for self-protection, 7 percent used gun "to scare someone." An unknown share of the latter could be defensive uses not overlapping with the former.
d. Covered only uses outside the home.
e. 1 percent of respondents, 2 percent of households.

flaws of previous surveys. The authors used the most anonymous possible national survey format, that of the anonymous random digit dialed telephone survey. They did not know the identities of those who were interviewed, and made this fact clear to the respondents. They interviewed a large, nationally representative sample (4,977 completed interviews) covering all adults (age eighteen and over) in the lower forty-eight states who lived in households with telephones, including those with unlisted numbers. They asked defensive gun use questions of all respondents in our sample, asking them separately about both their own defensive gun use experiences and those of other members of their households.

They used both a five-year recall period and a one-year recall period, inquired about uses of both handguns and other types of guns, and excluded occupational uses of guns and uses against animals. Finally, they asked a long series of detailed questions designed to establish exactly what respondents did with their guns, whether they confronted other humans, and with what type of crime each defensive gun use was linked.

A professional telephone polling firm, Research Network of Tallahassee, Florida, carried out the sampling and interviewing. Only the firm's most experienced interviewers were used on the project. Interviews were monitored at random by survey supervisors. All interviews in which an alleged defensive gun use was reported by the respondent were validated by supervisors with call-backs, along with a 20 percent random sample of all other interviews. Of all eligible residential telephone numbers called where a person (rather than an answering machine) answered, 61 percent resulted in a completed interview. Interviewing was carried out from February through April of 1993.

The quality of sampling procedures was likewise well above the level common in national surveys. The sample was not only large and nationally representative, but also stratified by state. That is, forty-eight independent samples of residential telephone numbers were drawn, one from each of the lower forty-eight states, providing forty-eight independent, albeit often small, state samples. Given the nature of randomly generated samples of telephone numbers, there was no clustering of cases or multistage sampling, as there is in the National Crime Victimization Survey (NCVS), and thus no inflation of sampling error due to such procedures.[6] To gain a larger raw number of sample defensive gun use cases, the authors oversampled in the South and West regions, where previous surveys had indicated gun ownership was higher.[7] They also oversampled within contacted households for males, who are both more likely to own guns and to be victims of crimes in which victims might use guns defensively (p. 56). Data were later weighted to adjust for oversampling.

Each interview began with a few general "throat-clearing" questions about problems facing the respondent's community and crime. The interviewers then asked: "Within the past *five years*, have you yourself or another member of your household *used* a gun, even if it was not fired, for self-protection or for the protection of property at home, work, or elsewhere? Please do *not* include military service, police work, or work as a security guard." respondents who answered yes were then asked: "Was this to protect against an animal or a person?" Those who reported a defensive gun use against a person were then asked: "How many incidents involving defensive uses of guns against persons happened to members of your household in the past five years?" and then: "Did this incident [any of these incidents] happen in the *past twelve months?*" At this point, respondents were asked: "Was it *you* who used a gun defensively, or did someone else in your household do this?"

All respondents reporting a defensive gun use were then asked a long, detailed series of questions establishing exactly what happened in the defensive gun use incident. Respondents who reported having experienced more than one defensive gun use in the previous five years were asked about their most recent experience. When the original respondent was the one who had used a gun defensively, as was usually the case, interviewers obtained their firsthand account of the event. When the original R indicated that some other member of their household was the one who had the experience, interviewers made every effort to speak directly to the involved person, either speaking to them immediately, or obtaining times and dates to call them back. Up to three callbacks were made in attempting to directly contact the defensive gun use-involved person.

There were 222 completed interviews with respondents reporting defensive gun uses. Questions about the details of defensive gun use incidents permitted us to establish that a given defensive gun use met all of the following qualifications before it would be defined as a genuine defensive gun use: (1) the incident involved defensive action against a human rather than an animal, but not in connection with police, military, or security guard duties, (2) the incident involved actual contact with a person, rather than merely investigating suspicious circumstances, etc., (3) the defender could state a specific crime that they thought was being committed at the time of the incident, and (4) the gun was actually used in some way—at minimum it had to be used as part of a threat against a person, either by verbally referring to the gun (e.g., "get away—I've got a gun") or by pointing it at an adversary. No effort was made to assess either the lawfulness or morality of the defensive gun uses.

An additional step was taken to minimize the possibility of defensive gun use frequency being overstated. Kleck went through interview sheets on every one of the interviews in which a defensive gun use was reported, looking for any indication that the incident might not be genuine. A case would be coded as questionable if any of four problems appeared to characterize it: (1) it was not clear whether the respondent actually confronted any adversaries, (2) the respondent was a police officer, member of the military, or a security guard, and thus might have been reporting, despite instructions not to do so, an incident that occurred as part of his or her occupational duties; (3) the interviewer did not properly record exactly what the respondent had done with the gun, so it was possible that he or she had not used it in any meaningful way, or (4) the respondent did not state, or the interviewer did not record, a specific crime that the respondent thought was being committed against him or her at the time of the incident. There were a total of twenty-six cases where at least one of these problematic indications was present.

It should be emphasized that the authors did not know that these cases were *not* genuine defensive gun uses; rather, they simply did not have as high a degree of confidence on the matter as with the rest of the cases designated as defensive gun uses, usually because of missing information. Thus, these were *not* cases where there was affirmative information indicating they were not genuine defensive gun uses, but rather cases with less information and thus less basis for confidence about their status. Cases where there was affirmative information indicating that the event did not fit the definition of a defensive gun use were excluded altogether from all estimates. Estimates using all of the apparently genuine defensive gun use cases were labeled A estimates, while the more conservative estimates based only on cases devoid of problematic indications were labeled B estimates.

National Self-Defense Survey Results

Table 6.2 displays a large number of estimates of how often guns are used defensively. These estimates are not inconsistent with each other, but rather measure different things in different ways. Some estimates are based only on incidents that respondents reported as occurring in the twelve months preceding the interview, while others are based on incidents reported for the preceding five years. Both telescoping and recall failure should be lower with a one-year recall period, so estimates derived using it should be superior to those based on the longer recall period. Some estimates are based only on incidents that respondents reported as involving themselves (person-based estimates), while others were based on all incidents which Rs reported as involving anyone in their household (household-based estimates). Because of their more firsthand character, the person-based estimates should be better. Finally, some of the figures pertain only to defensive gun uses involving use of handguns, while others pertain to defensive gun uses involving any type of gun.

The methods used to compute the table 6.2 estimates are simple. Prevalence ("% Used") figures were computed by dividing the weighted sample frequencies (in the top two rows of numbers) by the total weighted sample size of 4,977. The estimated number of persons or households who experienced a defensive gun use (in the third and fourth rows) was then computed by multiplying these prevalence figures by the appropriate U.S. population base—the number of persons age eighteen and over for person-based estimates, and the number of households for household-based estimates. Finally, the estimated number of defensive uses was computed by multiplying the number of defensive gun use-involved persons or households by an estimates of the number of all-guns defensive gun use incidents per defensive gun use-involved person or household. Applying the more generous definitions used with the A estimates, the survey data indicated that each defensive gun use-involved person had been involved in an average of 1.478 defensive gun uses in the previous five years, while each involved household had experienced an average of 1.531 uses. Applying the more conservative definition used with the B estimates, the data indicated that each involved person experienced an average of 1.472 defensive uses in the preceding five years, while each involved household experienced an average at 1.535 uses. The authors did not establish how many defensive gun uses occurred in the past year, and, for past-five-years defensive gun uses, did not separately establish how many of the defensive gun uses involved handguns and how many involved other types of guns. Therefore, for all past-year estimates, and for past-five-years handgun estimates, it was necessary to conservatively assume that there was only one defensive gun use per involved person or household.

The most technically sound estimates presented in table 6.2 are those based on the shorter one-year recall period and which rely on respondents' firsthand accounts of their own experiences (person-based estimates). These estimates, shown in the first two columns, indicate that each year in the United States there are about 2.2 to 2.5 million defensive uses of guns of all types by civilians against humans, with about 1.5 to 1.9 million of the incidents involving use of handguns.

These estimates were larger than those derived from the best previous surveys, indicating that technical improvements in the measurement procedures, contrary to the expectations of Cook, Reiss, and Roth, and McDowall and Wiersema, *increased* rather than decreased estimates of the frequency with which defensive gun uses occur.[8] Defensive gun use is thus just another specific example of a commonplace pattern in criminological survey work (victimization surveys, self-report surveys of delinquency, surveys of illicit drug use, etc.): the better the measurement procedures, the higher the estimates of controversial behaviors.[9]

These estimates may seem remarkable in comparison to expectations based on conventional wisdom, but are quite modest in comparison to various gun-related phenomena. There were probably over 235 million guns in private hands in the United States by the end of 1994, implying that only about 1 percent of them are used for defensive purposes in any one year.[10] In a December 1993 Gallup survey, 49 percent of U.S. households reported a gun, and 31 percent of adults reported personally owning one (p. 99). These figures imply about 47.6 million households with a gun, with perhaps 93 million (49 percent of the adult U.S. population) adults living in households with guns, and about 59.1 million adults personally owning a gun. Again, it hardly seems implausible that 3 percent (2.5 million/93 million) of the people with immediate access to a gun could have used one defensively in a given year. Finally, while the NSDS implied about 670,000 to

Table 6.2 Prevalence and Incidence of Civilian Defensive Gun Use, U.S., 1988-1993[a] (National Self-Defense Survey)

Recall Period:	Past Year				Past Five Years			
Base:	Person		Household		Person		Household	
Gun Types:	All Guns	Handguns	All Guns	Handguns	All Guns	Handguns	All Guns	Handguns
Weighted Sample Cases A:[c]	66	49	79	55	165	132	194	148
B:[c]	56	40	68	46	148	115	172	129
% Used[b] A:	1.326	0.985	1.587	1.105	3.315	2.652	3.898	2.974
B:	1.125	0.804	1.366	0.924	2.974	2.311	3.456	2.592
Persons/ Households A:	2549862	1893079	1540405	1072434	6316811	5053449	3782767	2885822
B:	2163519	1545371	1325918	896945	5665988	4402626	3353794	2515345
Annual Uses A:	2549862	1893079	1540405	1072434	1867249	1493800	1158283	883639
B:	2163519	1545371	1325918	896945	1668067	1296133	1029615	772211

Population Bases: Estimated resident population, age 18 and over, U.S., April, 1993: 192,282,770; estimated households (assuming the 1992-1993 percentage increase was the same as the 1991-1992 increase): 97,045,525 (U.S. Bureau of the Census 1993, pp. 17, 55).

Notes:

a. Defensive uses of guns against humans by civilians (i.e. excluding uses by police officers, security guards or military personnel). All figures are based on weighted data. Some of the estimated DGU counts in the "Past Five Years" section have been revised from those in Kleck and Gertz (1995, p. 184). However, no conclusions, here or elsewhere, are based on these estimates.

b. Percent of persons (households) with at least one defensive gun use during the five years (one year) preceding the interview.

c. A estimates are based on all reported defensive gun uses reported in the survey. B estimates are based on only cases with no indications the case might not be a genuine defensive gun use.

1,570,000 defensive gun uses linked with carrying guns in public places, it also found there were 1.8 to 2.8 billion person-days of carrying guns in public places.[11] Thus, defensive gun uses in public places occurred in less than one in a thousand instances of carrying guns in public places.

Not only do huge numbers of Americans have access to guns, but the overwhelming majority of them are, if one can believe their own statements, willing to use a gun defensively. In a December 1989 national survey, 78 percent of American gun owners stated that they would not only be willing to use a gun defensively in some way, but would be willing to *shoot* a burglar.[12] The percentage willing to use a gun defensively in some way, though not necessarily by shooting someone, would presumably be even higher than this.

Nevertheless, having access to a gun and being willing to use it against criminals is not the same as actually doing so. The latter requires experiencing a crime under circumstances in which the victim has access to a gun. It is unknown how many such opportunities for crime victims to use guns defensively occur each year. It would be useful to know how large a fraction of crimes with direct offender-victim contact result in a defensive gun use. Unfortunately, a large share of the incidents covered by defensive gun use surveys are probably outside the scope of incidents that are likely to be reported to either the National Crime Victimization Survey (NCVS) or police. If the defensive gun use incidents reported in the present survey are not entirely a subset within the pool of cases covered by the NCVS, one cannot meaningfully use NCVS data to estimate the share of crime incidents that result in a defensive gun use. Nevertheless, in a ten-state sample of incarcerated felons interviewed in 1982, 34 percent reported having been "scared off, shot at, wounded or captured by an armed victim."[13] From the criminals' standpoint, this experience was not rare.

This phenomenon, regardless of how widespread it really is, is largely an invisible one as far as governmental statistics are concerned. The defender/victim has little incentive to report this sort of event to the police, and may have strong reasons to not do so, such as the possibility of being arrested for either the violent use of the gun or for a violation of gun laws. Consequently, many of these incidents never come to the attention of the police, while others may be reported, but with victims omitting any mention of their own use of a gun. And even when a defensive gun use is reported, it would rarely be recorded by the police, who ordinarily do not keep statistics on such matters (other than defensive gun uses resulting in a death), since police record-keeping is largely confined to information helpful in apprehending perpetrators and making a legal case for convicting them.

It is also clear that virtually none of the victims who use guns defensively tell interviewers about it in the NCVS. The NSDS estimates imply that less than 5 percent of defensive gun uses among NCVS respondents are reported to interviewers (the 116,000 defensive gun uses estimated from the NCVS, divided by the 2.55 million estimate derived from the NSDS equals .045).[14]

Contrary to unsubstantiated speculations that the NSDS estimates of defensive gun use frequency are too high,[15] there is a considerably firmer basis for believing they are too low, because they do not count any of the following:

1). defensive gun uses people are unwilling to tell strangers about on the phone, often because they involved gun law violations by the respondent (e.g., the gun was carried illegally);

2). defensive gun uses people forgot or wrongly thought were not serious enough to fit into the set of events about which the interviewer was inquiring;

3). defensive gun uses among persons under age eighteen (the NSDS, like other gun surveys, covered only persons eighteen or older, in contrast to the NCVS, which covers persons twelve or older). Persons age twelve to seventeen account for about 24 percent of violent victimizations, and carry guns for protection at about the same rate as adults, so the NSDS may have missed about one quarter of defensive gun uses for this reason alone;[16]

4). additional defensive gun uses in the one-year recall period, beyond the most recent one (NSDS one-year estimates assume a single defensive gun use per defensive gun use-involved person).

Also, the NSDS could not contact persons in households without telephones, who tend to be poorer than the rest of the population. And like most surveys, the NSDS underrepresented African Americans. Since both poor people and minorities are more likely to be crime victims, the effect is that the NSDS underrepresented persons likely to have had a need to use a gun for self-protection.

Later Surveys

At least five more national surveys have been conducted since the NSDS (for a total of nineteen altogether, as of mid-2000), and all yielded DGU estimates supportive of those from the NSDS. The best of these surveys, the Police Foundation's National Survey of the Private Ownership of Firearms (NSPOF), was sponsored by the U.S. Justice Department.[17] The NSPOF was based on a sample only half the size of the NSDS's; was conducted by interviewers and staff with no prior experience with crime surveys, and, unlike the NSDS, apparently did not make callbacks with respondents claiming a defensive gun use. Nevertheless, it was modeled after, and otherwise generally comparable to, the NSDS. Further, it included even more questions about details of alleged defensive gun uses that might disqualify them as genuine defensive gun uses.

The NSPOF strongly confirmed the results of the NSDS, yielding estimates, where comparable, of annual DGU prevalence that were within sampling error of those obtained by Kleck and Professor Marc Gertz. Phillip Cook and Jens Ludwig, however, obscured just how strong the confirmation was by making an erroneous comparison of estimates.[18] Like the NSDS, the NSPOF yielded both A estimates based on all reports that fit the definition of a defensive gun use, and more conservative B estimates that excluded reports based on less complete information. Based on person-based self-reports covering the preceding one year, the NSDS yielded an A estimate of 2.55 million and a B estimate of 2.16 million (table 6.2). Cook and Ludwig claimed that their A estimate, which they said was "directly comparable to the well-known Kleck and Gertz estimate of 2.5 million," was just 1.5 million.[19] While this was within sampling error of the 2.55 million figure, it was nevertheless far lower.

The problem is that Cook and Ludwig reversed their A and B estimates, comparing their more conservative B estimate with the more inclusive Kleck-Gertz A estimate. The estimate from their survey that most closely corresponded to the Kleck-Gertz A estimate of 2.55 million was 2.73 million.[20] Cook and Ludwig's discussion made the difference look like a 70 percent discrepancy, but it was in fact a remarkably small 7 percent difference. Ludwig has since repeated this erroneous comparison.[21]

The journal article version of the Cook-Ludwig report only confused things further, comparing two more estimates derived from the NSPOF that were also not comparable with the Kleck-Gertz A estimate. The first was not comparable because it included defensive gun uses linked with law enforcement, security work or military service, while the second was not comparable because it excluded cases that were included in the Kleck-Gertz A estimates.[22] Ignoring these noncomparable estimates, the Cook-Ludwig results were a remarkably strong confirmation of the Kleck-Gertz NSDS results.

The federal Centers for Disease Control and Prevention (CDCP) fielded a large-scale national survey (n=5,238 completed interviews) in 1994 that asked only about one particular kind of DGU, victims retrieving guns in response to intruders attempting to enter the victim's home.[23] This would roughly correspond to burglary-related defensive gun uses in the NSDS. The NSDS indicated that there were 2.55 million annual DGUs, 33.8 percent of them connected with burglaries (table 6.2), implying 861,853 annual burglary-linked defensive gun uses.[24] The CDCP survey estimated that each year in the United States there are 1,001,127 incidents in which a victim saw an intruder in, or trying to get into, their home and retrieved a gun to deal with the situation. Cases where the person retrieved a gun but never saw the potential intruder are excluded from this estimate. Thus, the CDCP estimate was just 16 percent higher than the NSDS estimate, and well within sampling error. Further, even this modest difference would be still smaller if some of the cases where the respondent did not see the potential intruder were in fact burglaries and the respondent verbally threatened the burglar with the gun. Once again, a large professionally conducted national survey strongly confirmed the NSDS results.

A much smaller-scale survey of 1906 respondents was fielded in 1996. Although its designers did not report any national defensive gun use estimates, it utilized a national probability sample of adults and did ask a defensive gun use question. Deborah Azrael and Professor David Hemenway asked their Rs: "In the past five years, have you used a gun to protect yourself from a person or people?"[25] The phrase "protect yourself" excludes defensive uses on behalf of others. The authors excluded cases involving police, security guard, or military duties (apparently excluding off-duty uses as well as on-duty uses, unlike other researchers). This question had been preceded by the question "In the past five years, has anyone displayed or brought out a gun in a hostile manner, even if this event did not take place as part of commission of a crime?" As the authors acknowledged (p. 290), an unknown share of the positive responses to this somewhat ambiguous question may also reflect defensive gun uses, i.e., experiences in which other people used guns defensively against the respondent. Some defenders who answered yes to the ambiguous first question might have thought it was unnecessary to answer affirmatively to the self-protection question, believing that they had already reported the relevant event.

Nevertheless, it is possible to compute a conservative national defensive gun use prevalence estimate implied by this survey's results for just the "used a gun to protect" question. Of 1,906 respondents, fourteen answered yes to this question, pertaining to the past five years (p. 289). No past-year figures were reported, but both the NSDS and NSPOF found that the ratio of past-year defensive gun uses over past-five-years defensive gun uses was 0.40, so we can estimate this survey would have yielded 5.6 defensive gun uses with a one-year recall period, indicating an annual prevalence of 0.294 percent (95 percent confidence interval: 0.00294 +/- 0.002430, assuming simple random sampling, and an even wider interval without it).[26] Applying these figures to the 1996 U.S. population age eighteen and over of 235,118,000, the estimated annual defensive gun uses would be 690,798 (95 percent confidence interval: 119,885 to 1,262,111). This is a conservative estimate because it excludes the "hostile uses" of guns reported by respondents in this study that could also have been defensive gun uses directed at the respondent. Thus, Hemenway's own survey indicated at least six times as many defensive gun uses as the NCVS estimates that he favors.[27] He and his coauthor did not, however, report this estimate to their readers.

In May of 2000, the Gallup survey organization asked 1,031 U.S. adults: "Not including military combat, have you ever used a gun to defend yourself, either by firing it or threatening to fire it?" and 7 percent responded yes.[28] This survey used a lifetime recall period, failed to exclude uses against animals or uses linked with law enforcement or security work, while arbitrarily excluding defensive gun uses to defend others (" . . . to defend *yourself* . . . "). McDowall et al. found that of 155 respondents who initially reported a defensive gun use without being told to exclude such cases, 30 turned out to involve uses linked with law enforcement or security work.[29] Thus, one can roughly adjust for the failure to exclude such cases by multiplying the estimate by 125/155. Multiplying 7 percent by

125/155, and also applying the adjustments described in the appendix to adjust for use of a lifetime recall period and the inclusion of uses against animals, yields an estimated past-year defensive gun use prevalence of 0.836 percent (95 percent confidence interval: 0.280-1.392 percent, assuming simple random sampling). This is not significantly different from the NSDS estimate of 1.326 percent and implies, based on a projected U.S. population of 203,852,000 residents age eighteen or over, 1,704,449 annual defensive gun uses.

Finally, a *Washington Post* poll fielded in late June 2000 found that 8 percent of U.S. adults had used a gun in self-defense or to protect their property sometime in their lives.[30] Applying the appendix adjustments for the lifetime recall period and the failure to exclude uses against animals yields a one-year prevalence estimate of 1.185 percent, not significantly different from the 1.326 percent estimate from the NSDS. Given about 203,852,000 U.S. adults in 2000, this implies 2,415,448 persons with a defensive gun use in the previous year.

To summarize, there are now at least nineteen professional surveys, seventeen of them national in scope, that indicate huge numbers of defensive gun uses in the United States each year.

Explaining the Deviant National Crime Victimization Survey Results

The only national survey to ever indicate less than about 700,000 annual defensive gun uses is the National Crime Victimization Survey (NCVS), which indicated only about 116,000 defensive gun uses per year from 1993 to 1994.[31] This is less than one twentieth of the 2.55 million estimate yielded by the 1993 National Self-Defense Survey or the 2.73 million estimate from the 1994 National Survey of the Private Ownership of Firearms. How might one account for the extraordinarily deviant estimates produced by the National Crime Victimization Survey?

Some have assumed that the NCVS *must* somehow yield at least approximately reasonable estimates because so much money and technical expertise has gone into developing the survey, and therefore all the other surveys are wrong. For example, Cook accurately, if not very relevantly, noted that "the National Crime Survey [the original name of the NCVS] is a much larger and more sophisticated effort [than the gun surveys], based on questionnaires that have been devised and refined through a program of extensive testing."[32] This is not very relevant because none of this considerable technical refinement was aimed at producing estimates of defensive uses of guns or of other forceful self-protective actions. Further, none of the "extensive testing" has ever addressed whether the NCVS accurately estimates the frequency of these behaviors. External evidence from at least nineteen other surveys strongly indicates that it does not.

The NCVS was designed to produce national estimates of criminal victimizations. Estimates of forceful self-protection actions are merely an incidental byproduct of the considerable effort devoted to achieving this primary goal. The task of estimating forceful defensive actions is, however, so fundamentally different from that of estimating criminal victimizations in general that many of the undoubted virtues of the NCVS for the latter task have no necessary bearing on the former. Ironically, many of the NCVS's features which are advantageous for producing crime estimates, such as being conducted by the federal government, are probably handicaps for estimating DGUs.

Any forceful act of self-protection is a violent act, since by definition it involves either an attack or a threat against another human being. Even when the victim/defender is confident that the act was morally justified, he or she cannot be so certain about how an interviewer would morally assess their actions. A well-recognized problem of survey research is that respondents often do care about what interviewers think and adjust their answers to not raise questionable matters. Further, regardless of whether the act was in fact lawful, few respondents could be certain about its legality. The law of self-defense is extremely complex, and even legal experts are frequently uncertain whether a given forceful act was lawful.[33] Therefore, uncertainty among defensive actors themselves is also likely to be widespread. Finally, leaving aside the legality of the defensive act, a person who defended themselves with a firearm is likely to have carried the gun illegally or otherwise violated gun control laws.

Thus, if an respondent in the NCVS was the victim of a crime in which she/he used defensive force, when the NCVS interviewer asks about self-protective acts, she/he is in effect asking the respondent to confess to an act of violence, an act that may itself be criminal, and that in any case the respondent might think the interviewer would disapprove of. Thus, in connection with forceful self-protection, the NCVS becomes a survey covering controversial and possibly illegal acts committed by the respondent, rather than merely a survey of criminal acts committed against the respondent. The goals of a survey of self-reported deviance are fundamentally different from those of a victimization survey, and are best served by significantly different technical features.

There obviously are some hugely consequential factors responsible for the enormous discrepancy in defensive gun use results between the NCVS and all other surveys. Many features of the NCVS are likely to contribute to an underestimation of defensive gun use frequency. First, interviewers never directly ask respondents about defensive gun use. One could argue that the NCVS cannot even yield a defensive gun use estimate, since one cannot use a survey to estimate the frequency of an experience that is never directly asked about. Instead, after the respondents report that they had been the victim of a crime, the NCVS interviewer merely asks the respondents, "Was there anything you did or tried to do about the incident while it was going on?" and Rs who wish can then volunteer that they used a gun.[34]

Discussing this aspect of the NCVS, Tom Smith, director of the National Opinion Research Center, noted that "indirect questions that rely on a respondent volunteering a specific element as part of a broad and unfocused inquiry *uniformly lead to* undercounts of the particular of interest."[35] In contrast, the gun use surveys directly asked respondents specifically about defensive gun use.

Second, the NCVS is conducted by one branch of the federal government, the U.S. Census Bureau, on behalf of another branch, the U.S. Justice Department. Respondents are told these things at the beginning of the interview, so when respondents are later asked about self-protection actions, those who used guns are aware that they are talking to employees of the federal government.[36] This might not matter much if they were reporting on innocuous topics like how much they spent on home repairs or the number of rooms in their home, but most defensive gun uses involve illegal behavior on the part of the victim, most commonly unlawful carrying of a firearm.[37] Federal government conduct of interviews has a very different significance when respondents are asked to confess to a crime, or gun owners are asked about illegal things they have done with their guns, than when respondents are asked the mostly innocuous questions common in the census. In contrast, most of the gun use surveys were conducted by private survey firms.[38]

Third, respondents in the NCVS are not anonymous. Although respondents are promised confidentiality, interviews begin with interviewers obtaining the respondent's name, address, and telephone number.[39] Thus, questions are answered in the context of the respondent's knowledge that their identities are known to the surveyors. The lack of anonymity might be of little consequence if respondents did not know that they were speaking to employees of the federal government, but gun owners' fears of gun confiscation by the federal government gives a very different significance to nonanonymity in this context.[40] NCVS respondents know that they are speaking to federal employees and that the government knows who they are and where they live. Thus, the combination of government conduct of the survey with nonanonymity could be a powerful deterrent to reporting defensive gun uses. In contrast, in gun use surveys Rs are told the interviews are anonymous.

Fourth, in the NCVS, interviewers ask where the crime occurred before asking questions about self-protection.[41] This means that a respondent who had used a gun for self-protection in a public place knows, by the time the self-protection questions are asked, that he has already revealed where he was when the crime occurred. Almost all of the U.S. population lives in states where it is either completely forbidden for any civilian to possess a gun in a public place, or forbidden to all but the handful who possess a carry permit.[42] The crime of unlawful carrying is generally defined as a felony, frequently results in arrest, and is even subject to mandatory minimum prison sentences of one year or more in at least ten states.[43] Thus, if a victim had used a gun in self-protection in connection with a crime that occurred in a public place, it would usually be impossible for the victim to report the defensive gun use without also confessing to having committed a serious crime.

The NCVS for 1994 indicated that only 14.4 percent of violent crime incidents occurred "at or in respondent's home."[44] The other 85.6 percent occurred in some location where, in order to possess a gun during the incident, the victim would have had to have carried the gun through public spaces. In contrast, gun use surveys ask about details of the incident, including its location, only after asking the defensive gun use questions.

Fifth, for many respondents, gun possession would be unlawful regardless of location. This would apply with special force to the subset of the population most likely to be criminally victimized, criminals. Persons with criminal convictions are prohibited under federal law and most states' laws from possessing guns anywhere, and a common condition of probation or parole is to not possess weapons.[45] In addition, millions of otherwise non-criminal persons possess guns illegally because they lack a permit or license legally required under local or state law. In two Illinois surveys of the general population, Professor David Bordua and his colleagues found that even among respondents willing to report gun ownership, 28 percent did not have the license required of all Illinois gun owners.[46] For all such persons, to admit use of a gun for self-protection or for any other purpose would necessarily entail confessing to unlawful possession of a gun.

Sixth, in the NCVS, no respondents are even asked the self-protection questions unless they are first willing to report a criminal incident and provide some details about it. Thus, any tendency of respondents to underreport personal contact crimes would necessarily also cause an underreporting of defensive gun uses. There is convincing evidence that the NCVS underestimates crime frequency. For example, Cook showed that the NCVS radically underestimates the number of criminal incidents involving gunshot woundings.[47] Based on his best estimate of the number of gunshot woundings reported to police, Cook's data indicated that the NCVS captured only about one-third of the gunshot wound incidents (p. 96). Since all of his proposed explanations for this problem would apply at least as well to other forms of violence, there is reason to expect that victims also radically underreport violent incidents in general. And indeed, based on other comparisons of alternative survey estimates of violent events with NCVS estimates, University of Maryland researchers Colin Loftin and Ellen MacKenzie noted that rapes could be thirty-three times as frequent as NCVS estimates indicate, while spousal violence could easily be twelve times as high.[48] Less serious incidents are underreported still more, since memory failure is greater with less serious offenses.[49]

A specific variant of nonreporting in the NCVS is especially problematic for defensive gun use estimation. The NCVS often fails to elicit positive responses to crime questions where a genuine crime involved no harm to the victim, i.e., the crime was attempted but not completed. Because the vast majority of defensive gun uses involve neither property loss nor injury to the victim, crimes with defensive gun use will often not be reported at all in the NCVS, never mind reported as having involved a defensive gun use.[50] This problem is discussed in greater detail in a later section.

In sum, in order for respondents to report a defensive gun use in the NCVS, they must be willing to confess, to an employee of the federal government, gathering information for the law enforcement branch of that government, to having committed a serious crime, and to do so in the context of a nonanonymous interview, by volunteering the information in response to a general question that does not even directly ask about gun use. It is hard to imagine survey conditions less congenial for gaining meaningful estimates of defensive gun use frequency.

Nevertheless, none of these conspicuous problems prevented University of Maryland criminologist David McDowall from insisting that there is no "solid reason for expecting errors" in NCVS respondents' responses to the self-protection questions.[51] Nor have the problems been regarded as serious enough to prevent the Bureau of Justice Statistics from continuing to disseminate its defensive gun use "estimates" as if they were valid, without a single caveat to potential users.[52] And these seemingly grave flaws did not deter McDowall and Wiersema from stating, based solely on the NCVS, that "armed self-defense is extremely uncommon," or discourage Cook from concluding that he could, with minor qualifications, "accept the NCS-based estimate of 50,000 defensive uses per year against rape, robbery, and assault" and conclude that "the National Crime Survey estimates are a reasonable approximation of reality."[53] Nor were Kellermann and his colleagues prevented from relying solely on the NCVS estimate in drawing the conclusion that "fewer than two crimes in a thousand (are) resisted with a gun."[54] Likewise, writing a report for the National Institute of Justice, Urban Institute researcher Jeffrey Roth showed no qualms about citing only a 70,000 NCVS estimate to support his claim that defensive gun uses are rare, mentioning none of the problems with NCVS, and withholding from his readers any hint that every single other survey had yielded far higher estimates of defensive gun use frequency.[55]

McDowall and others have explored whether the differences between defensive gun use estimates based on the NCVS and those based on other surveys such as the NSDS were due to (1) differing question order (asking about victimization first, then self-protective methods rather than the reverse) or to (2) differing domains of behavior covered by the differing questions in the surveys.[56] To test these ideas, respondents were either asked the NCVS questions first, followed by the gun survey questions, or the reverse.

The most noteworthy of the findings pertained to Hemenway's (1997) speculation that large numbers of respondents fabricate nonexistent defensive gun use experiences. McDowall and his colleagues stated that Hemenway's fabrication hypothesis "requires an interaction between question content and question order," and the authors reported that they "did not find such an interaction."[57] Thus, the results clearly failed to support Hemenway's fabrication hypothesis. The authors, however, declined to draw this conclusion. After having previously stated that they could test this hypothesis with their methods (p. 9), once they obtained results unsupportive of Hemenway's falsification hypothesis, they concluded that their interaction test had "low statistical power" and called for "additional study" (p. 17).

Their results also indicated that using the NCVS questions, and asking them in the NCVS sequence, both yield fewer defensive gun use reports than using the questions and sequence found in the other surveys. In an earlier draft of their paper, the authors had claimed that incidents reported using the gun survey methods but not with the NCVS methods were not really defensive gun uses, but rather were gun uses in connection with "crimes that had not yet occurred."[58] I served as a referee assessing this paper for a journal and suggested, in comments to the authors, a different interpretation. These cases may instead have been defensive gun uses that occurred early in a genuine crime that was in fact already underway. When early defensive gun use averted any harm to the victim, and did so in such a way that it never became certain that the defender's adversary was indeed trying to harm the victim in some way, these ambiguous cases were not likely to be reported in response to NCVS questions. This interpretation was partially incorporated into the published version of the paper, but the authors nevertheless asserted, without any supporting evidence, that gun surveys include in their estimates "defenses against crimes that had not yet occurred."[59]

Early-Intervention Defensive Gun Uses

It would not be legitimate to place early-intervention uses outside the definition of defensive gun use, since it is precisely within this category where one would find the most successful defensive gun uses. A genuine attempted crime that is disrupted in its early stages is still a crime, and defensive use of a gun in connection with such a crime is therefore properly classified as a DGU. In many crime situations, victims can effectively defend themselves only if they do so before the offender attacks or immobilizes them. That is, they can defend themselves either early or not at all. This is especially true where the victim is physically smaller or weaker than the aggressor, as in violence of men against women.[60]

Respondents will often be less certain in early-intervention cases that a criminal attempt was in fact underway, and some reported "defensive gun uses" may have been responses to a "threat" that was perceived but not real. Uncertainty about possible early intervention defensive gun uses would justify placing such cases in a category separate from less uncertain cases, as Kleck and Gertz did with some possible defensive gun uses, but it would not justify simply treating them as cases known to *not* involve defensive gun use.[61] It is inherent in the nature of defensive gun uses or any other preventive measures that, if they are effective, individual cases of harm averted are necessarily ambiguous.

There might be a temptation among those critical of defensive gun use to adopt a heads-we-win, tails-you-lose strategy whereby one assigns a large share of alleged defensive gun uses to either of two categories: (1) those in which no harm is inflicted on the victim, which are classified as fake "defensive gun uses" in response to "crimes that had not yet occurred," and (2) those in which the victim *is* harmed, which are genuine but obviously ineffective defensive gun uses. If one is unwilling to classify an event as a genuine defensive gun use unless one achieves the certainty of criminal intent on the part of the offender that comes from the victim actually being harmed, then by definition there can be no such thing as a genuine and effective defensive gun use.

Some of the difference in results between the NCVS and other surveys may be due to the failure of the NCVS to capture early-intervention defensive gun uses. The McDowall et al. results suggest that a three-to-one difference between the NCVS and other surveys could be due to the NCVS question content and sequence, though it is unknown how much of this reflects NCVS failure to capture genuine DGU events and how much is due to gun surveys capturing "defensive gun use" cases that were not true defensive gun uses because no actual crime was committed.[62]

There is no evidence indicating how large a share of alleged defensive gun use cases involve borderline or ambiguous cases, and thus no sound empirical basis for believing that such cases pose significant problems for defensive gun use estimation. Such cases might be common among all defensive gun uses, but it is unlikely that they would be common among reported defensive gun uses, i.e., those that people are willing to report to interviewers, since respondents are less likely to report ambiguous cases. McDowall and his associates cite a case that seems to fit this scenario, describing a respondent who did not report a crime with a defensive gun use because he "doubted that he could prove he was victimized" (p. 15).

Defensive Gun Use in Crimes with No Harm to the Victim

Another source of the NCVS-gun survey discrepancy is probably more significant. This is the failure of some NCVS respondents to report crimes that they did not regard as sufficiently serious to deserve mention or qualify as relevant to the interviewer's questions. This category of crimes is likely to include both genuinely minor crimes and potentially serious crimes in which the victim nevertheless suffered neither injury nor property loss. Although NCVS interviewers encourage respondents to report less serious crimes (by asking about, and providing examples of, minor crimes) and those in which they did not suffer any harm (asking about threats without injury and attempted thefts), many such events still go unreported in the NCVS.[63]

From the standpoint of estimating harm from crime, the failure of the NCVS to capture no-harm cases is arguably not that serious a problem. On the other hand, from the standpoint of estimating defensive gun use frequency, it is critical because the vast majority of defensive gun uses involve neither property loss nor injury to the victim, and thus are likely to go unreported in response to NCVS questions for this reason alone.[64] In many cases it may be defensive gun use itself that caused a crime to be harmless to the victim, and thus to be perceived by the victim as "minor," which in turn ensured that it was not reported in the NCVS.

Supporting this interpretation, when McDowall and his fellow researchers found respondents who reported a defensive gun use in response to gun survey questions but had not done so in response to pre-vious NCVS questions, and asked these resondents to account for the con-flict, the most common explanation was that the respondent did not think the crime was serious enough to mention when the NCVS victimization questions were asked.[65] Only when the question specifically referring to defensive gun use was asked did it prompt these respondents to report the crime. Some genuine no-harm defensive gun use crime incidents will not be reported in response to NCVS questions because the respondent will wrongly assume them to be too minor to qualify as relevant to the inter-viewer's questions, but would be reported in response to a question specif-ically mentioning defensive gun use because only then is the experience perceived as relevant to the interviewer's questions.

Two kinds of error in answers to defensive gun use questions will dis-tort estimates. A "false positive" occurs when a respondent claims to have had a defensive gun use experience but did not, while a "false negative" occurs when a respondent who had a defensive gun use experience denies it. Respondents who reported a defensive gun use in response to gun survey questions but not to NCVS questions can, for convenience, be called "dis-crepant respondents." McDowall and his colleagues did not cite any dis-crepant respondents who admitted that the defensive gun use reported in response to the gun survey questions was false or distorted. Instead, when discrepant respondents were asked to account for their seemingly inconsis-tent responses, the only specific explanations they offered (excluding "idio-syncratic" responses peculiar to single respondents) were either that they simply misunderstood the questions or that they did not think that the crim-inal offenses involved were serious enough to justify a positive response (pp. 14-15). As far as one can tell from these researchers' evidence, there were (excluding cases that simply did not fit the defensive gun use defini-tion, such as police or military uses) no false positives in their sample.

Nevertheless, the authors interpreted the discrepant reports as false positives, based on the arbitrary decision to view them as reports of inci-dents in which the respondent had overreacted to nonexistent threats and "crimes that had not yet happened," rather than as cases of defensive gun use in the early stages of genuine criminal attempts or cases of defensive gun use against less serious crimes. Thus, there was no logical or empirical foundation for their strongly stated conclusion that "many reports to the other [gun] surveys were false positives (that is, they were not defenses against criminal acts)" (p. 17). The authors did not list any individual cases of false positives or report any counts of the number of cases, among the discrepant reports, that they had confirmed to be false positives, yet they were somehow able to conclude that there were "many" of them.

The authors inserted this non sequitur conclusion into their paper only after the last draft had been reviewed by the referees. Thus, the main conclusion of the paper was not subject to peer review, although the journal that published the paper describes itself as a "refereed publication."[66] When I objected to this evasion of peer review to the editor, he refused to respond to my objections.[67]

When the NCVS was revised in the early 1990s, many of the improvements consisted of increasing the number and variety of specific prompts about crime that might trigger respondents' memories, or more effectively convey to them the full set of crime experiences that the surveyors were interested in. As a result, reports of crime did indeed increase.[68] The lesson for the present debate is that questions specifically referring to defensive gun use apparently serve as better prompts than the NCVS questions for no-harm crimes involving defensive gun use, perhaps because explicit mention of victim gun use more effectively triggers recollection of crimes involving defensive gun use, and more effectively signals to respondents that their crime experience is relevant, based on their gun use, despite the otherwise "minor" character of the no-harm incident.

Telescoping as a Source of Overestimation in the Defensive Gun Use Surveys

"Forward telescoping" occurs when a respondent is asked about the past year but reports incidents that occurred more than a year in the past. Census Bureau research connected with the development of the NCVS, using a one-year recall period, indicated that telescoping could increase reports of crime incidents by no more than a factor of 1.21 (that is, one would get 1.21 times as many reports of crime as actually occurred during the recall period), and thus telescoping in the gun surveys is not likely to have more than a modest effect on defensive gun use estimates.[69]

Hemenway, however, hinted that telescoping inflated crime estimates by 30 to 40 percent, by misciting research on the NCVS reported by researcher David Cantor.[70] Cantor had noted that "bounded" interviews in the NCVS yielded 30 to 40 percent more crime reports than "unbounded" interviews. A bounded interview is one preceded by an earlier interview with the same respondent. Since a previous interview can establish what crime incidents occurred in the previous recall period, researchers can eliminate the effects of telescoping by dropping, from estimates based on the later "bounded" interview, any reports of "out-of-recall-period" events already reported in the previous interview.

For example, suppose that a person interviewed in January 2001 was asked about any crime experiences they had in the preceding six months (July to December 2000) and accurately reported that they had been robbed during that period. Suppose the person was then interviewed again six months later and asked about January to June 2001. If the person erroneously reported that the robbery from the earlier six-month period occurred during the January to June 2001 recall period (i.e., the respondent "telescoped" the incident into the later recall period), the researchers would be able to recognize this as the same incident reported in the previous interview. Thus, because the earlier interview had preceded the later one, the researchers could disqualify the telescoped incident and prevent it from inflating their estimates of the frequency of crime. Further, because interviewers can instuct respondents to report only events that occurred "since the last interview," and the preceding interview provides an easily recalled starting point for the recall period, respondents are less likely to telescope an incident in the first place.

Cantor went to great pains to explain that the 30 to 40 percent difference in crime reports between bounded and unbounded interviews could *not* be viewed as an estimate of the magnitude of telescoping, because the differences in reports of crime were also partly due to respondents failing to report genuine crime experiences in the later interviews, due to "respondent conditioning." That is, once respondents have reported victimizations in previous interviews, they learn that doing so will result in their having to do more work answering questions concerning details of the incidents and endure a longer interview. This causes some of them to falsely deny, in later "bounded" interviews, having being victimized during the most recent recall period. Cantor cautioned that "it is unclear to what degree the drop in reports [of crime] between the first (unbounded) and second (bounded) interviews is due to telescoping or conditioning" (p. 33).

Hemenway, however, cited Cantor's 30 to 40 percent figure without Cantor's caveats, in a sentence immediately following a reference to "a substantial amount of telescoping of criminal victimization" and in the context of a discussion of "false positives" in defensive gun use surveys.[71] Cook and Ludwig also cited the 30 to 40 percent figure in the context of a discussion of telescoping, without mentioning Cantor's caveats.[72] Cook, Ludwig, and Hemenway aggravated the misrepresentation even further by boosting Cantor's 30 to 40 percent to "over 50 percent."[73] Smith even justified his guess of "around 50 percent" telescoping in defensive gun use surveys by citing (in addition to the nonsupportive Cantor report) the degree of telescoping in reports of consumer expenditures on household repairs and of visits to the doctor![74] There is in fact no evidence that forward telescoping causes any more than the upper-limit 21 percent increase in DGU reports that was cited in the original Kleck and Gertz article.[75] In short, telescoping is not likely to cause any significant exaggeration of the frequency of defensive gun use.

Telescoping is not only a fairly minor source of overestimation, but is also counterbalanced by response errors in the opposite direction. Census Bureau evaluations of victim survey methods indicated that for one-year recall periods, the magnitude of overreporting of criminal victimizations due to telescoping is roughly matched by underreporting due to forgetting and other failures to report incidents which actually did occur in the reference period.[76] Thus, false positives are balanced out by false negatives.

The Scholarly Response to Large Defensive Gun Use Estimates

Faced with a huge body of evidence contradicting the rare-defensive gun use theory, its supporters have had little choice but to simply promote the dubious NCVS "estimate" and ignore or discount everything else. Articles in medical and public health journals are typically the most misleading about the volume of contrary evidence, since they usually do not even mention the existence of a large volume of evidence pointing to huge numbers of defensive gun uses. For example, Kellermann and his colleagues mentioned only the NCVS estimate when telling their readers that defensive gun use is rare. While it is possible that these authors did not know of all fifteen of the other surveys that had been conducted by the time their article was written, they certainly should have known of the existence of at least six contradictory surveys, since they were prominently reviewed in a source that they cited.[77]

Further, editors have ensured near-total censorship of contrary information through their publication decisions (see chapter 2). And although these journals commonly provide for letters to the editor, editors of the journals have refused to publish rebuttals or even brief letters challenging the rare-defensive gun use thesis, aside from letters by employees of gun owner organizations, whose views can be easily dismissed by readers as biased. For example, when I wrote a brief letter to the editor to the *American Journal of Public Health* to point out that the journal had published a grossly inaccurate estimate (on the low side) of the frequency of defensive gun uses [McDowall and Wiersema 1994]), the editors refused to publish the letter.[78]

Writers publishing in criminological and social science outlets, where editors and referees tend to be more knowledgeable about violence, must be a bit more sophisticated in obscuring the extent of contrary evidence. Some do so by conceding the existence of contrary evidence but being vague about how much of it there is. For example, sociologists Albert Reiss and Jeffrey Roth obscured the extent of the contradictory evidence by vaguely referring to "a number of surveys" that implied larger estimates and then dropping the matter, with no detailed further discussion of any of the other surveys.[79] Then, later in their essay, they uncritically accepted the dubious NCVS estimate at face value (p. 266), effectively ignoring all the contrary sources. Even at the time they wrote, there were a least eight other surveys yielding defensive gun use estimates, all many times higher than the NCVS estimate. These surveys had been reviewed in sources they cited.[80] Likewise Cook blandly alluded to "a number of surveys," without indicating how many there were, and giving detailed attention to only one of them.[81] University of Maryland criminologists David McDowall and Brian Wiersema gave readers the impression that conclusions in an earlier article were based on results of a single survey, simply by not mentioning any of the other five surveys on which the article's author relied.[82]

On those rare occasions when adherents of the rare-defensive gun use thesis address some of the contrary evidence, they counter empirical evidence with a dense web of one-sided speculations rather than offering better empirical information. Cook set the pattern, speculating that early polls yielding higher defensive gun use estimates did so because respondents were telescoping incidents into the recall period.[83] As previously noted, telescoping has only mild effects that are cancelled out by the effects of respondents forgetting or intentionally failing to report genuine defensive gun uses. Cook offered no evidence that any gun use survey, or indeed any crime-related surveys, are afflicted by more telescoping than recall failure.

Speculation about the flaws in surveys estimating large numbers of defensive gun uses resemble UFO buffs' beliefs that the federal government captured aliens from other worlds at Roswell, New Mexico, in 1947. The reason most people do not share these beliefs is not that they can be proven false—they cannot, since it is impossible to prove a negative. Rather, most people reject them because there is no credible evidence that they *are* true. It is the same with speculations about massive overreporting of defensive gun uses. Since it is impossible to prove a negative, one cannot prove that frequent misreporting of nonexistent defensive gun use incidents does not occur in the gun surveys. There is, however, no affirmative evidence whatsoever that such misreporting occurs often enough to outweigh misreporting in the opposite direction.

In this context, Cook's earlier assessment of the NCVS's adequacy for estimating gunshot wound incidents is worth closer study.[84] When faced with a conflict between low NCVS estimates of the number of criminal gunshot woundings, and far higher estimates implied by data from just four other small samples (all but one of them local in scope), Cook quite reasonably concluded that the NCVS radically underestimated gunshot woundings and that the true figure could be three times larger than the NCVS-based estimate. His reasoning was that the four small-scale bodies of data could not all be radically wrong, so it must be the NCVS estimates that were wrong.

In sharp contrast, when faced with precisely the same conflict between low NCVS estimates of defensive gun uses and no less than thirteen other conflicting bodies of data (nearly all national in scope), Cook concluded that all of the other bodies of evidence were radically wrong, that it was the NCVS that was likely to be more correct, and that it was unlikely that the NCVS could be as seriously inaccurate as the conflicting bodies of data indicated.[85]

Fallacious Reductio ad Absurdum Reasoning

Reporting results from the National Survey of the Private Ownership of Firearms (NSPOF), Cook and Ludwig claimed to have established conflicts between their defensive gun use estimates and crime estimates drawn from other sources, concluding that the defensive gun use results must be erroneous because they implied (1) numbers of defensive gun uses that would claim implausibly large fractions of all crimes in a given category, or (2) implausibly large numbers of defensive woundings of criminals.[86] Their reasoning was fallacious because it relied on the indisputably false premise that we know the total number of crimes in a given category and the total number of gunshot woundings, whether medically treated or not.

The authors cited data on the number of people treated in emergency rooms for nonfatal gunshot wounds and asserted that their own survey's estimates of criminals wounded during defensive gun uses were implausibly high in comparison. In fact, the two sets of numbers are perfectly consistent. Cook and Ludwig effectively ignored the fact that the wounding figures they cited were only estimates of the frequency of gunshot woundings treated in hospital emergency departments, not the *total* number of gunshot woundings.

It is highly unlikely that most criminals wounded by victims would seek medical treatment, since medical personnel are required by law to report gunshot wounds to the police.[87] Because most gunshot woundings are survivable with no more sophisticated medical care than can be administered by the average lay person, most wounded criminals can afford to choose self-treatment over professional treatment at a hospital.[88] And all have extremely strong legal reasons to do so, since seeking professional medical treatment would often be tantamount to surrendering to police for the crime in which they had been wounded. Cook and Ludwig disputed the claim that most such criminals would not receive emergency room treatment, but not by citing contrary evidence or pointing to some logical flaw in the evidence or arguments supporting this assertion. Instead, they simply issued the rather imperious pronouncement that "we find that possibility rather unlikely."[89] They offered no further rationale for this remarkable assessment.

Cook and Ludwig also asserted that the estimated numbers of defensive gun uses connected with particular types of crimes were inconsistent with the total number of crimes of that type, with or without defensive gun uses.[90] For example, they claimed to have shown that the estimated number of defensive gun uses linked with rapes actually exceeded the total number of rapes, as estimated by the NCVS.

Alternate sources of information indicate that only a minority of all crime incidents get reported to the NCVS.[91] Therefore, no matter how large the estimated number of defensive gun uses are in the gun surveys, they could still be a plausibly modest share of *all* crime incidents, including both those effectively covered by the NCVS and those not covered. Consequently, comparing defensive gun use estimates with NCVS estimates of crime or estimates of medically treated gunshot woundings can tell us nothing about whether defensive gun use estimates are plausible.

To give Cook and Ludwig's argument its strongest chance to appear credible, consider rape, the only crime category where the estimated number of crimes with a defensive gun use supposedly exceeded the total number of such crimes as estimated by the NCVS. The NSPOF results, according to Cook and Ludwig, implied 322,000 rapes and attempted rapes in which the victim used a gun defensively, while the NCVS for the same year indicated a total of only 316,000 rapes and attempted rapes, with or without defensive gun use. The defensive gun use figure, however, exceeds the crime total only because Cook and Ludwig made an invalid comparison. The NSPOF defensive gun use estimates actually pertained to defensive gun uses linked with "rape, attempted rape, *other sexual assault*" (emphasis added), while the corresponding number from the NCVS used by Cook and Ludwig, 316,000 covered only "Rape/Attempted rape," even though the NCVS also provided an estimate for the separate category of "Sexual Assault."[92] When the correct figures from properly corresponding categories are used, the NCVS figure is 432,750 rapes, attempted rapes, *and* sexual assaults. The NSPOF estimate of 322,000 defensive gun uses linked with such crimes therefore did not even come close to exceeding the NCVS estimate of the total number of such crimes. Thus, Cook and Ludwig's only instance of a defensive gun use estimate that was supposed to be impossible (as distinct from subjectively "implausible") turns out to be the product of their error.

Nevertheless, even correcting for this mistake, the rape defensive gun use estimate still looks implausibly high at first glance. Cook and Ludwig, however, also reported that their 95 percent confidence interval estimate (which reflects the possible effects of random error in selecting survey respondents) of rape defensive gun uses was 12,000 to 632,000.[93] Unlike estimates of *total* defensive gun uses derived from the NSPOF (and NSDS), which are based on large samples, estimates of defensive gun uses linked with particular subtypes of crime depend on knowing the percent of defensive gun uses linked with a given type of crime, which is based on the far smaller number of defensive gun use cases and is thus highly unstable. Given the lower limit of this extremely imprecise estimate, the NSPOF estimate of rape-linked defensive gun uses was not even mildly implausible compared with the NCVS estimate of all rapes, since the lower limit estimate of 12,000 rapes/sexual assaults with defensive gun use would be less than 3 percent of total rapes and sexual assaults. Therefore, even the appearance of "implausibility" could be the product of nothing more than random sampling error, which in turn was due to the NSPOF's small sample size. There is something vaguely dubious about researchers' arguments being *strengthened* by the inadequacies of their research—the smaller their sample and the more unstable Cook and Ludwig's estimates were, the better their chances of obtaining "implausible" results that would buttress their theory of massive defensive gun use overestimation.

The critics' reductio ad absurdum logic is equivalent to arguing that Gallup presidential election polls cannot accurately estimate the share of the entire electorate voting for the Democratic candidate (something we know they *can* do, usually to within 2 percentage points) because they routinely yield implausible estimates for small subsets of the electorate, such as elderly Hispanic females.[94] One undoubtedly could obtain implausible estimates of voter preference for the Democratic candidate, such as 0 percent or 100 percent, based on a very small number of sample cases, for many subsets of the population. This would imply nothing, however, about the ability of the survey to estimate voter preferences in the entire population. Thus, even if estimates of defensive gun uses linked to a given specific crime type were implausible, which they are not, this would imply nothing about whether estimates of the total number of defensive gun uses, based on the full sample, are accurate.

In any case, the Kleck-Gertz NSDS, which had twice the sample size of the Cook-Ludwig NSPOF and thus considerably less unstable defensive gun use estimates, implied only 209,089 defensive gun uses linked with rapes or sexual assaults.[95] This is less than half the NCVS estimate of "total" crimes in this category. In no crime category were NSDS estimates of defensive gun uses even half the number of NCVS-estimated offenses in the corresponding category.

But, again to give Cook and Ludwig's argument every chance of appearing reasonable, ignore their invalid comparison, ignore sampling error due to an inadequate sample size, and consider just their point estimate of 322,000 rape-linked defensive gun uses. The biggest problem still remains: the NCVS estimate of rape frequency is not complete or exhaustive, and the true total number of rapes is almost certainly far higher. Indeed, rape estimates derived from the present NCVS are two and a half times the size of those derived from earlier versions of the same survey.[96] If the true number of rapes were actually far higher than the NCVS estimate of 316,000, there would be nothing even mildly implausible about there having been 322,000 rapes with DGU.

How much higher could the actual number of rapes be? Reviewing the results of surveys specially designed to study rape, Loftin and MacKenzie (1990) found that the total number of rapes could be as much as thirty-three times as high as NCVS estimates.[97] Thus, instead of there being only 316,000 total rapes per year, there could actually have been anywhere from 316,000 on up to a possible (albeit unlikely) 10.4 million. In sum, there turns out to be no logical foundation whatsoever for the claim that 322,000 rape-linked defensive gun uses is implausible.

Nevertheless, as an indication of just how far Cook and Ludwig were willing to take this reasoning, consider their assertion that "even if the NCVS-based estimates of criminal victimization rates are off by an order of magnitude, the NSPOF-based estimates for DGU are implausible."[98] (The phrase "even if" seems to hint that this degree of underestimation is highly unlikely and that the authors were thus making a generous assumption.) They reported that the NCVS estimates of aggravated assault and robbery in 1994 were 2.48 million and 1.30 million, respectively (p. 123), so if these figures were off by an order of magnitude, Cook and Ludwig were asserting that the defensive gun use estimates would be implausible even if there were in fact 24.8 million aggravated assaults and 13.0 million robberies a year. Yet the NSPOF had implied only 462,000 aggravated assaults and 527,000 robberies with defensive gun use a year. Thus, Cook and

Ludwig were stating that even if defensive gun use data indicated that only 1.9 percent of aggravated assaults or 4.1 percent of robberies involved defensive gun use, they would still regard such defensive gun use estimates as "implausible." It is useful to keep this passage in mind in interpreting what these authors mean when they use the term "implausible."

The Venn diagram in figure 6.1 illustrates hypotheses about the relative frequency of different sets of crime events and the degree of their overlap. The area of circle A represents the true volume of crime that involved a victim-offender confrontation (violent crimes, burglary attempts interrupted by victims, purse-snatchings, etc.), i.e., crimes where a defensive gun use was possible. Circle B represents confrontation crimes that would be captured by the NCVS if everyone in the population were interviewed. Its volume is a third that of circle A, symbolizing the assumption that only a third of confrontation crimes are captured by the NCVS. Circle C represents the set of all defensive gun uses that occurred (all, by definition, in connection with confrontation crimes), whether they could be captured by any survey or not. Its volume is 10 percent that of circle A, reflecting the assumption that a modest 10 percent of confrontation crimes involve a genuine defensive gun use. Finally, oval D represents the set of defensive gun use incidents that would be reported in private surveys like the NSDS or NSPOF if everyone in the population were interviewed.

The volume of oval D implies that private surveys capture only about 50 percent of true defensive gun uses, i.e., there are many false negatives (the area within C but outside D) in the private surveys, while the small share of D that lies outside of C or A implies that there would be few false positives. The minimal overlap between B and C denotes that only a tiny share of true defensive gun uses would be captured by the NCVS. Likewise, the minimal overlap between B and D indicates that almost all of the true defensive gun use incidents that can be captured by the private surveys lie outside the set of incidents that victims are willing to report in the NCVS. Thus, defensive gun uses are for the most part not a subset of crimes that can be captured by the NCVS.

The relative volumes and positioning of these shapes are necessarily hypothetical, given the impossibility of estimating unreported crimes and defensive gun uses, but the diagram is fully consistent with what we do know. The diagram does not prove that any given defensive gun use estimate is correct, but it does prove that the Hemenway-Cook-Ludwig mode of

Figure 6.1 Hypothetical Distribution of Crimes and Defensive Gun Use Incidents

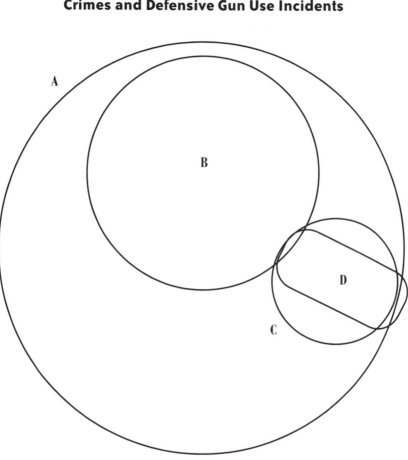

A = The set of all crimes with a victim-offender confrontation

B = The set of confrontation crimes that would be captured by the NCVS (assumed to be 33 percent of A)

C = The set of all confrontation crimes with a true defensive gun use (assumed to be 10 percent of A)

D = The set of confrontation crimes that would be reported in private surveys as involving defensive gun use (5 percent of A, 50 percent of C)

challenging defensive gun use estimates is invalid, since it demonstrates that the defensive gun use estimates based on the private gun surveys are fully compatible with the numbers of crimes reported in the NCVS.

Cook and Ludwig's fallacious claims about implausibly high defensive gun use estimates were later accepted by McDowall and his colleagues, who flatly stated that the defensive gun use outcomes of the gun surveys were "contrary to external evidence," citing Cook and Ludwig.[99] McDowall et al. had apparently read the Kleck and Gertz explanation of why this reasoning was invalid, and neither they nor anyone else has rebutted that explanation.[100]

This dispute cannot reasonably be regarded as just an honest difference of opinion. It is an incontrovertible and obvious logical point that it is impossible to know the total number of rapes, aggravated assaults, robberies, residential burglaries, or gunshot woundings. Indeed, none of the advocates of the rare-defensive gun use theory have disputed this. Therefore, it is impossible to know whether a given estimate of the number of defensive gun uses linked with any one of these types of events would characterize an implausibly large fraction of the (unknowable) total number of events.

McDowall and his coauthors also repeated the same mischaracterization of gunshot wounding estimates that Cook and Ludwig had disseminated, claiming that the number of woundings of criminals implied by the defensive gun use surveys "was larger than independent estimates of *all* serious firearm injuries in the nation."[101] This was plainly inaccurate. The source on which the assertion was based never even claimed to be estimating all gunshot woundings, but rather only firearm injuries "treated in hospital emergency departments."[102] Further, it had been painstakingly explained in multiple sources, which McDowall et al. cited, that the emergency-room estimates to which they alluded were *not* estimates of total woundings and thus could not place an upper limit on the number of defensive gun use-linked woundings.[103] To make it clear that their acceptance of the fallacious reasoning was not inadvertent, McDowall et al. repeated it later in the article: "[Hemenway, Cook, and Ludwig] also show that the Kleck and Gertz study suggests armed defense against implausibly large fractions of other violent crimes."[104]

The Meaning of Internal Inconsistencies in Defensive Gun Use Reports

Cook and Ludwig reported inconsistencies between responses to different questions in seven reported cases of defensive gun use, and concluded that these in-consistencies indicated deliberate falsification of defensive gun use accounts.[105] The main inconsistency, found in all but one of the seven reports, involved respondents reporting a defensive gun use that they asserted (in response to question 72) was linked with a serious violent crime such as a robbery, assault, or rape. But just three questions (and perhaps thirty seconds) later in the interview, these respondents were also recorded as having reported (in response to question 75) that they had not been threatened, attacked or injured.[106]

This is indeed an inconsistency, since every violent crime, by definition, involves an attack or threat to the victim. The question is whether the inconsistency indicates that (1) respondents alleging defensive gun uses were inventing fake events or falsifying parts of their accounts, as Cook and Ludwig preferred to believe, or whether (2) the inconsistencies were the result of survey staff error in recording responses or honest mistakes by respondents with a genuine defensive gun use to report.[107]

Cook and Ludwig arbitrarily rejected the staff error interpretation, based on the fact that 10 percent of interviews were checked by "senior staff" of the survey organization.[108] This was arbitrary because all seven, and most likely six, of the inconsistent defensive gun use cases could have fallen into the unchecked 90 percent. Further, if the "senior staff" were as incapable of recognizing inconsistencies that needed to be resolved as interviewers, supervisor checks would be useless.

The assertion that staff error of some sort occurred in these cases is in one sense indisputably true, since the interviewers and staff both obviously failed to correct conspicuous inconsistencies—the interviewers did not probe for a clarification during the interview, and supervisors did not resolve the inconsistencies afterwards. Even if the inconsistencies *had* been due to respondents falsifying their accounts, the evidence still indicates failures on the part of the survey staff to resolve inconsistencies. Further, data cleaning is supposed to catch and resolve these kinds of flaws, but obviously did not. Thus, these cases indicate, at minimum, poor performance by members of the survey staff.

Even apart from staff error, one would expect a few inconsistencies in honest and otherwise accurate accounts of genuine defensive gun uses. Humans are not error-free robots even when they are being completely honest. In the NSPOF, 50 respondents initially reported a defensive gun use against a human in the past year, and were asked as many as 27 questions concerning details of the incident, potentially providing as many as 1,350 responses that could be crosschecked against one another.[109] After what one suspects was an exhaustive search for inconsistencies, Cook and Ludwig identified all of eight of them (including one incident with two inconsistencies).[110] Some people would be inclined to see this as evidence of remarkably consistent reporting on defensive gun uses, but Cook and Ludwig effectively interpreted anything short of flawless reporting as evidence of falsified defensive gun use accounts.

A less results-oriented approach would be to simply consider which of two alternative interpretations is more plausible: (1) simple staff error and a handful of honest errors by respondents with genuine defensive gun uses to report, or (2) deliberate falsification. To accept the falsification interpretation in this instance requires one to believe that respondents fabricating imaginary events were so inept that they could not keep their stories straight for even thirty seconds at a time, providing blatantly inconsistent responses to questions separated by just two intervening items. Even if respondent falsification were common, falsification this inept seems farfetched. Further, the methodological experiment of McDowall et al. found no significant evidence of falsification of defensive gun use reports.[111]

A less strained interpretation is that even honest respondents will provide a few inconsistent details about genuine experiences, and that careless or poorly trained interviewers occasionally record responses incorrectly, especially on the more complicated questions. For example, some resondents or interviewers may simply have misinterpreted question 75 as an inquiry about any *additional* threat or injury beyond that already established in question 72.

Cook and Ludwig's carefully phrased conclusion was: "At the very least, these apparent contradictions are *consistent with* the idea that a sizable share of DGU reporters are falsifying part of their accounts."[112] Perhaps, but then the fact that some of the respondents were wearing red sweaters when they were interviewed would also be "consistent with" this theory, but hardly supportive of it. The inconsistencies are even more "consistent with" simple staff error or the mistakes that would inevitably be made by respondents with genuine defensive gun uses to report.

Direct Evidence on the Relative Balance of False Positives and False Negatives

Cook and Ludwig were willing to arbitrarily infer respondent falsification from evidence (the seven inconsistent cases) that was of only the most dubious relevance. In contrast, they did not share with readers other information in their possession that bore far more directly on the issue of deliberate falsification of responses. At the end of every NSPOF interview, interviewers were asked to provide their own assessments as to whether respondents either (1) hesitated or otherwise expressed reluctance to answer the initial question about defensive gun use, indicating to the interviewer that the "respondent seemed to be concealing defensive gun use," or (2) gave the impression that the respondent was making up the incident or trying to mislead the interviewer about his/her role in it.[113]

Reanalysis of their dataset provided the results that Cook and Ludwig did not publish.[114] The interviewers reported that respondents seemed to be concealing a defensive gun use in sixty cases, while, within the full pool of reported defensive gun uses in the previous five years, interviewers believed that respondents were either inventing a nonexistent event or misstating their role in it in just thirteen cases. Thus, suspected false negatives outnumbered suspected false positives by a factor of 4.6 to one. If one corrected for both suspected false positives and suspected false negatives, instead of only false positives as Cook and Ludwig did, it would increase the defensive gun use estimate, not decrease it.

To be sure, one could speculate that interviewers, despite the advantages of actually speaking with respondents and hearing their voices and speech patterns, nevertheless could not reliably detect false responses, and to therefore dismiss this inconvenient evidence. It would be harder for Cook and Ludwig to make this argument, however, since they trusted interviewers' judgments enough to exclude claimed defensive gun uses that interviewers suspected to be false positives, solely on the basis of the interviewers' judgments.[115] One could not, however, reasonably argue that these interviewer assessments are completely irrelevant to the issue of misreporting, or less relevant than the handful of ambiguous inconsistencies given so much weight by Cook and Ludwig. Concerns about interviewers' ability to perceive respondent dishonesty might justify reporting their assessments to readers and then attaching caveats to the findings, but it cannot justify withholding from readers the only direct evidence available to Cook and Ludwig on the relative balance of false positives and false negatives.

Circular Reasoning in Numerical Exercises on the Sensitivity of Defensive Gun Use Estimates to False Positives

If only one respondent in a survey had experienced a genuine defensive gun use, then just one more respondent falsely reporting a nonexistent defensive gun use would double the resulting defensive gun use estimate, making such an estimate highly sensitive to the problem of false positives. Note, however, that this sensitivity is a function of the actual defensive gun use frequency. If, in contrast, sixty-six sample respondents had a genuine defensive gun use to report, one or a few false positives would have little effect on estimates, and would have no net effect at all if counterbalanced by false negatives.

Hemenway presented a numerical exercise that, somewhat needlessly, confirmed the self-evident general point that estimates of rare phenomena *could* be highly sensitive to false positives, but also falsely claimed to have demonstrated that in fact the defensive gun use estimates from the NSDS *were* highly sensitive to, and greatly exaggerated by, false positives.[116] He started by pointing out something that is necessarily true of estimates of any relatively uncommon phenomenon. Since there are only a few people with actual defensive gun uses to report, there are only a few people who could provide false negative responses (i.e., falsely deny a true defensive gun use experience), while there are many who potentially could provide false positive responses. Part of the problem seemed to be that Hemenway made no distinction between two very different kinds of claims: (1) There is more hypothetical *potential* for false positives than false negatives, and (2) There are *actually* more false positives than false negatives in defensive gun use surveys. The first statement is a trivial statement of arithmetic fact, while the latter is a non sequitur assertion without the slightest empirical support.

It is worth noting that neither Hemenway nor those who uncritically cite his novel ideas (Cook, Ludwig, McDowall et al.) have ever applied this reasoning to survey estimates of gun crime frequency.[117] Since less than 1 percent of the U.S. population is the victim of a gun crime in any given year, this means that less than 1 percent of the population *could* provide a false negative response, while over 99 percent *could* provide false positives.[118] According to Hemenway's "logic" it is a virtual inevitability that, given such a huge potential for false positives, the NCVS will grossly overstate the frequency of gun crime (and thereby grossly overstate the need for stricter gun control). Either the critics are not interested in a balanced application of such methodological "insights," or they do not really believe in this line of reasoning.

But the core fallacy of Hemenway's argument was that he had to assume his conclusions in order to prove them, an obvious instance of circular reasoning. His assumptions/conclusions were that (1) the true defensive gun use rate is far lower than repeated empirical estimates, such as those of the NSDS, indicate, (2) there is a far higher rate of false positives in reporting defensive gun uses than empirical evidence indicates, and (3) contrary to evidence from other crime-related surveys, the false negative rate is low enough that it produces far fewer false negatives than false positives in a defensive gun use survey.

The argument that Hemenway built on these assumptions, endorsed by Cook and Ludwig and McDowall et al., was as follows:

(1) Despite the unanimous findings to the contrary of nineteen consecutive surveys, defensive gun use is actually extremely rare.
(2) Because defensive gun use is extremely rare, the survey estimates are extremely sensitive to false positives, and therefore not credible.
(3) Because all of the survey estimates are not credible, we can dismiss them.
(4) Since we can dismiss all the survey evidence, no credible evidence remains to indicate that defensive gun use is common, and therefore we can conclude that defensive gun use is extremely rare.[119]

The fallacious character of Hemenway's argument can be illustrated by comparing the implications of two different sets of hypothetical survey results, based on two different sets of starting assumptions: (1) a set that assumes the conclusions that Hemenway was trying to support, and (2) a set that reflects preexisting empirical evidence (correct or not), but does not embody the conclusory assumptions. In table 6.3, panel A repeats one of Hemenway's tables, in which he assumed the aforementioned conclusions.[120] More specifically, he assumed that (1) defensive gun use is virtually nonexistent—it was assumed that only 0.04 percent of respondents had a true defensive gun use in the past year, (2) there were a huge number of false positives in the hypothetical survey—thirty-three times as many as true positives, and (3) there were no false negatives at all.

Panel B shows an alternative version of the table more consistent with empirical evidence. First, it assumes that the true defensive gun use rate is actually somewhat higher than the best surveys indicate (2.04 percent versus 1.33 percent) due to the underreporting common in surveys of other crime-related phenomena.[122] Second, it assumes that false negatives outnumber false positives by a factor of 4.6 to 1, as was indicated by interviewer judgments in the NSPOF.

Comparison of the two tables illustrates that under more realistic assumptions (panel B), the defensive gun use estimate is not very sensitive to false positives, and that the modest effects of these errors are more than counterbalanced by the effects of false negatives. The only reason that Hemenway's table (or either of the other two in his article) supported his claims is because he assumed that defensive gun use is extremely rare, the very issue that was in dispute.[123]

If one does not assume that defensive gun use is virtually nonexistent (panel A), but instead assumes it to be about what the best available surveys indicate (panel B), the number of false positives is not nearly as large relative to true positives. Further, unless one assumes a ratio of false positives over false negatives far higher than is indicated either in defensive gun use surveys or in any other crime-related surveys, the false positives do not cause any net overestimate, never mind the enormous overestimates in which Hemenway believes. One can dispute whether the assumptions underlying panel B are in fact true, but one cannot dispute that Hemenway's conclusions only follow if one accepts them as starting premises of his numerical exercise. His logic is clearly circular and thus fallacious.

Cook and Ludwig later repeated both Hemenway's exercise and his fallacious logic.[124] Like Hemenway, they arbitrarily assumed their conclusions that defensive gun use is virtually nonexistent (assuming it to be 0.1

percent, only 1/13th of the empirically based 1.326 percent) and that nearly all of the people who report defensive gun uses are lying or otherwise wrong. Again, this example would not have supported their conclusions unless it had incorporated the very conclusion they were advocating, that defensive gun use is extremely rare.

One-sided Consideration of Errors in Defensive Gun Use Estimation

Speculation unsupported by evidence is a weak enough foundation for assessing evidence. But it is especially misleading to speculate only in one direction, in this case speculating only about flaws suspected to push defensive gun use estimates up. If one is not willing to seriously consider errors in both directions, one is simply engaging in adversary scholarship or "sagecraft," an enterprise aimed not at discovering the truth, but rather at buttressing predetermined positions.[125] For an overt example of this sort of adversary scholarship, see an article by David Hemenway, along with the response to it by Kleck and Gertz.[126]

The most prevalent, consequential, and crude variety of bias among advocates of the rare-defensive gun use theory is the refusal to consider seriously the possibility of false negatives, and thereby address the relative balance of false positives and false negatives.[127] Without exception, the advocates simply assume that the former outnumber the latter. For example, McDowall et al. (2000, p. 5) noted that there are only a relatively small number of positive responses in defensive gun use surveys, so that "a few false-positive reports could wildly inflate the results," but did not mention the equally obvious implication that equally infrequent false negative reports could wildly *reduce* estimates.[128]

Cook and Ludwig tried to buttress their theory of massive overestimation of defensive gun uses by citing the false positive rate found in a study of drug use that compared self-reports in interviews with urinalysis results, but did not mention to readers the false negatives reported in that same study.[129] For every drug evaluated, the study had indicated that false positives were rare and, more important, that false negatives outnumbered false positives, producing a net underestimate of illicit drug use.[130]

Table 6.3 Circular Reasoning and the False Positive Issue—Hypothetical Distributions of Responses to Survey Questions

Panel A Hemenway's Table 2B[121]—Figures Assume the Conclusions

		Reality		
		DGU	No DGU	Total
Response	Yes	2	64	66
to DGU	No	0	4634	4934
Question	Total	2	4698	5000

Estimated DGU rate: 66/5000=1.33 percent
Actual DGU rate: 2/5000=0.04 percent

Panel B Alternate Figures—Do Not Assume the Conclusions

		Reality		
		DGU	No DGU	Total
Response	Yes	56	10	66
to DGU	No	46	4888	4934
Question	Total	102	4898	5000

Estimated DGU rate: 66/5000=1.33 percent
Actual DGU rate: 102/5000=2.04 percent

Both kinds of response errors almost certainly occur in all defensive gun use surveys, but no matter how many false positives there were, defensive gun use frequency would still not be even slightly overestimated if the number of false negatives were even larger. No one knows how many of each type of error occurs in defensive gun use surveys, but the most direct evidence bearing on this question was information from the NSPOF on interviewer assessments of respondents, which indicated that suspected false negatives outnumbered suspected false positives by a factor of 4.6 (or 4.6 to 1).

There is also a large technical literature on accuracy of responses in crime-related surveys, which advocates of the rare-defensive gun use thesis have declined to confront. This is perhaps understandable, given that this literature indicates that false positive responses are rare in crime-related surveys, and are greatly outnumbered by false negatives.[131] In sum, while no one knows for sure what the relative balance is in defensive gun use surveys, the only direct evidence on the question indicates that false negatives are far more common than false positives, while the indirectly relevant evidence drawn from surveys of other crime-related experiences indicates the same thing.

Cook and Ludwig frankly admitted that they focused their methodological assessment of defensive gun use surveys exclusively on false positives. They justified this one-sidedness by citing their fallacious reductio ad absurdum reasoning and their misinterpretation of the seven inconsistent defensive gun use reports: "Of course it is possible that there are also one or more false negatives in this survey. We focus on the problem of false positives because of the logic of estimating rare events [a reference to their numerical exercise based on circular reasoning], and because we have been persuaded by the evidence offered earlier that the NSPOF estimates overstate the true incidence by a very wide margin [apparently a reference to their fallacious claims that defensive gun use estimates were implausibly high relative to NCVS crime estimates]."[132] That is, they justified the one-sided character of their analysis of errors by citing *previous* one-sided analyses of errors.

Consistent with this bias, Cook and Ludwig's recommendations for "improving" defensive gun use estimates focused exclusively on reducing false positives, an agenda that could only result in revising the defensive gun use estimate downwards.[133] If, however, surveys underestimate defensive gun use frequency, just as they underestimate all other known crime-related experiences, adopting these one-sided suggestions would be worse than useless. By eliminating or adjusting for false positives, while leaving false negatives untouched, they would make estimates that were already too low even worse.

Cook and Ludwig made similarly one-sided use of interviewer judgments about whether respondents were providing false positive or false negative defensive gun use responses. They considered interviewers' judgments to be reliable enough to exclude from defensive gun use estimates those cases in which the interviewer suspected that the respondent was falsely claiming a defensive gun use but did not adjust estimates in any way for the far more numerous cases in which interviewers believed a respondent had falsely denied a defensive gun use in response to the initial defensive gun use question.[134] Indeed, they did not even reveal to readers that cases believed by interviewers to be false negatives even existed, never mind that they were 4.6 times more common than cases the interviewers believed to be false positives. In short, they were willing to use interviewers perceptions about possible errors to adjust defensive gun use estimates downward, but not upward.

Identifying flaws in research can never be, by itself, a justification for dismissing findings or ignoring them altogether. Rather, the identification of known flaws can only justify reducing, in proportion to the seriousness of the known flaws, the weight given to the evidence in drawing conclusions. Evidence based on research that is, on the whole (rather than based on just one or two arbitrarily selected criteria), more technically sound, should be given relatively more weight than evidence generated by less sound research. Speculation about possible, but unsubstantiated, flaws should not be given any weight at all. And still worse than unsubstantiated speculation about flaws is one-sided speculation, since it is both uninformative and systematically distorts readers' understanding of the issues.

Thus, the most pointless and counterproductive mode of assessing evidence is to go down a list of methodology textbook problems and speculate that each one afflicts whatever research one is ideologically uncomfortable with, while declining to do the same with research generating more congenial findings.[135]

Ideologues favor these critical practices because they are powerful and infinitely flexible—they can be used to dismiss even the largest, most consistent, and technically sound body of evidence, and can be used just as easily to discredit good research as bad. The practices can thereby be used to preserve even the most inaccurate beliefs about the world. No preferred proposition about the nature of world need ever be rejected no matter how false, and any proposition, no matter how true, can be made to appear false.

The Rare-Defensive Gun Use Theory: The Creation Science of Criminology

The reasoning used by advocates of the rare-defensive gun use theory is essentially identical to that used by "creation scientists" in challenging modern evolutionary theory. Just as creation scientists propose nonfalsifiable propositions concerning the origins of matter and energy, rare-defensive gun use advocates assert that defensive gun use is rare, and if survey evidence indicates this proposition is false, it only means that nearly all survey estimates of defensive gun use are fraudulent or distorted. Creation scientists speculate about flaws in radiocarbon techniques for dating rocks and fossils to support their view that the earth is too young to have allowed evolution of the species, just as rare-defensive gun use advocates speculate that flaws in survey methods "inevitably" result in overstating the frequency of rare phenomena such as defensive gun uses. Creationists speculate about the meaning of gaps in the fossil record of species, and rare-defensive gun use promoters similarly speculate about why survey Rs might fabricate accounts of nonexistent defensive gun uses, without providing any affirmative evidence of such fabrication actually occurring with any significant frequency.

Creationists bring up evidence that is at least as consistent with evolutionary theory as it is with creation science, such as indications of cataclysmic events like floods, but arbitrarily interpret it as if it were only consistent with their preferred theory. Likewise, when McDowall and his fellow researchers found that questions used in the defensive gun use surveys generate more reports of defensive gun uses than questions used in the NCVS, evidence equally consistent with the view that the NCVS generates many false negatives as with the view that defensive gun use survey questions generate many false positives, the authors arbitrarily interpreted the information as indicating that there were "many false positives" in the defensive gun use surveys. And when Cook and Ludwig found that respondents reporting defensive gun uses occasionally provided a few inconsistent responses about the details of their experiences, instead of interpreting these as the inevitable reflection of imperfect understanding of survey questions and flawed recollections of genuine defensive gun use experiences, they arbitrarily interpreted them as indications of falsified accounts of nonexistent defensive gun uses.

Creationists also knock down false straw-man versions of evolutionary theory that are alleged to be incompatible with evidence of large-scale floods. Similarly, rare-defensive gun use advocates falsely assert that the frequent-defensive gun use proposition is somehow incompatible with NCVS estimates of total crime or estimates of emergency room treatments of gunshot wounds, when in fact there is nothing at all inconsistent about the proposition and the evidence.[136] Speculating your way around evidence that undercuts your beliefs, rather than developing technically better empirical evidence, is no more likely to improve our understanding of defensive gun use than it has proven in explaining the origin of species.

Discouraging the Development
of Better Defensive Gun Use Estimates

Perhaps the most transparently political of all responses to large defensive gun use estimates was that of Jens Ludwig, who frankly admitted that, in his opinion, "far less attention should be devoted to estimating defensive gun use in the future."[137] Ludwig argued that further estimates should be regarded as meaningless as long as anyone could speculate about possible methodological flaws in the surveys, or as long as there was any uncertainty about the moral quality of any of the alleged defensive acts. Ludwig, however, had nothing whatever to say about the uncertainty surrounding the nature of incidents defined as "gun crimes" in the NCVS and did not feel compelled to call for a moratorium on future survey estimates of the frequency of gun crimes.

Faced with overwhelming survey support for the idea that defensive gun uses are common, advocates of the rare-defensive gun use theory have belatedly adopted the view that all the survey evidence must be dismissed because surveys simply cannot yield useful information about how often defensive gun uses occur (unless, it would seem, they indicate, as the NCVS supposedly does, that defensive gun uses are rare). Faced with defeat on the field of survey evidence, they belatedly developed a radical skepticism toward all survey estimates. Cook, for example, insisted that "surveys are a decidedly flawed method for learning about the frequency with which innocent victims of crime use a gun to defend themselves."[138]

Cook and Ludwig, however, were not satisfied with dismissing all previous survey evidence. They also moved to forestall policy use of any future survey evidence by asserting that "even if we could develop a reliable estimate of [defensive gun use] frequency, it would only be of marginal relevance to the ongoing debate over" gun control.[139] Thus, for purposes of public policy, Cook and Ludwig can have no compelling interest in improving defensive gun use estimates, since they would not be willing to give any significant weight to even the most reliable estimates. In light of this attitude, it is hard to understand the motives behind their suggestions for "improving" estimates of DGU prevalence, published just two years later.[140]

Philip Cook and David Hemenway both served with me on the advisory board for the NSPOF, advising on the development of its design. After the

NSPOF results almost exactly confirmed the NSDS results, their response was to assert that surveys inevitably overstate defensive gun use frequency.[141] This appears to be a belated revelation to Cook and Hemenway. In repeated and prolonged meetings of the advisory committee in 1994, during which the members discussed at length the long series of questions asking about DGUs, neither Cook nor Hemenway even once shared with the board their remarkable theory that all that effort was for naught, and that surveys could not generate even approximately accurate estimates of DGU frequency.

Since surveys are the only feasible way we have of measuring the frequency of defensive gun uses, Cook, Ludwig, and Hemenway have transformed their rare-defensive gun use theory into a nonfalsifiable proposition, placing it safely beyond empirical test. Faced with estimates, which he himself helped develop, that radically contradicted the rare-defensive gun use theory, Cook refused to accept the verdict of the evidence. Instead, he and his colleagues have devoted pages of one-sided speculation to explanations of how suspected flaws in their and other surveys might have led to exaggerated defensive gun use estimates.[142]

And, on the off-chance that someone might eventually develop defensive gun use estimates that would be hard to speculate around, Cook, Ludwig, and Hemenway still have a fallback position. They declare that even perfectly accurate defensive gun use estimates would be meaningless and useless, because: (1) we cannot be certain in all cases that reported defensive gun uses were morally correct, (2) it is possible that victims who used guns would have been even better off using other strategies, and (3) it is possible that in some cases there were other means of avoiding trouble altogether, which gun possession and use discourage.[143]

These arguments were based on still more speculation, and ignored certain crucial facts. First, although some reported defensive gun uses indeed are morally ambiguous, in the vast majority of reported cases there is little doubt about who is victim and who is aggressor, and thus little doubt about the moral role of the person wielding the gun. Few reported defensive gun uses occur in connection with "mutual combat" fights in which the combatants are both aggressor and victim. Instead, the vast majority are linked with burglaries, robberies, and sexual assaults, crimes where there is rarely any honest confusion about which party is the criminal and which the victim.[144] Thus, although it is easy enough to imagine many kinds of borderline cases and to cite isolated examples, there is no empirical support for the belief that they are common among the cases reported in defensive gun use surveys. In any case, if one wanted, in a policy analysis, to "count" only the morally clear defensive gun uses as a social benefit, one would be free do so. Completely ignoring unambiguously legitimate cases merely because of the existence of ambiguous cases is irresponsible.

Second, while it is possible that victims using guns defensively *might* have been better off using other self-protective strategies, empirical evidence indicates that, on average, they are not. Among the victim protective strategies on which we have data, defensive gun use is clearly the most effective one, from the standpoint of minimizing either injury or property loss.[145] Leaving aside one-sided speculations about possible deficiencies in the relevant research, we *do* have a fair idea, within the usual limits of multivariate nonexperimental research, what would have happened in defensive gun use cases, considered collectively, had the victims not used guns: a larger share of the victims would have been hurt or lost property. The alternatives that we know about, including nonresistance, are worse than victim use of a gun.

Third, there is no evidence that gun possession or use discourages people from avoiding trouble, or that people treat guns as a substitute for other crime prevention/avoidance strategies, rather than as a supplement. And if "avoiding trouble" includes people restricting their life choices and daily movements so as to make themselves into prisoners in their own homes, one must wonder what cultural values underlie an assumption that avoidance is always the socially preferable alternative. It is hardly self-evident that society is improved by encouraging the law-abiding to abandon valued activities and associations in order to avoid places and times where criminals might be present.

The Relative Frequency of Defensive and Offensive Uses of Guns

McDowall et al. raised the issue of comparing defensive gun use frequency with gun crime frequency, agreeing with Kleck and Gertz that the size of the defensive gun use estimates becomes meaningful only in comparison with another standard, such as the number of criminal uses of guns.[146] The authors then noted that the NCVS estimate of defensive gun uses was much smaller than its estimate of gun offenses, but did not regard it as essential to mention that many of the events they described as "gun offenses" did not, as far as we know, involve a gun being used in an attack or threat by the offender. They were "gun offenses" only in the sense that the offender (according to the victim) possessed a gun at the time of the incident—but did not necessarily use it in any sense. NCVS "gun offenses" are not definitionally comparable with defensive gun uses, since the latter events must involve a gun being *used* in a threat or attack to qualify as a defensive gun use, while for 36.6 to 83.4 percent of NCVS "gun offenses" it is unclear whether there was either an attack or a threat with a gun.[147]

There is also a problem affecting all surveys that contributes to a net undercount of both defensive and criminal gun uses. It has often been recognized that criminals will be among the persons least likely to be interviewed in general population surveys, because of their low income, high mobility, time spent incarcerated, and reluctance to be interviewed even if successfully contacted.[148] Since it is criminals who are in most frequent contact with other criminals, it is they who are potentially most at risk of victimization. Relative to their share of the population, criminals may claim a disproportionate share of both defensive gun uses and gun crime victimizations. Therefore, victimization and gun use surveys share a sampling bias that contributes to underestimating both criminal and defensive uses of guns.

McDowall and his colleagues argued that estimates of defensive and offensive uses of guns should be derived from the same survey, reasoning that this would make them more comparable.[149] However, even under the best circumstances it is unlikely that any one survey can do a good job of estimating both gun crimes and defensive gun uses. The NCVS has distinct advantages for estimating the frequency of gun crime, including the large samples made possible by a large investment of federal dollars, and the high level of cooperation by prospective respondents made possible by the Census Bureau conducting the interviews. On the other hand, federal sponsorship and conduct of the interviews, in the context of nonanonymous interviews, probably create insurmountable obstacles to producing reasonable estimates of defensive gun use frequency. Consequently, the best currently feasible strategy is to compare the defensive gun use results of surveys that optimize conditions for accurate reporting of defensive gun use (such as the gun surveys), with gun crime estimates based on the NCVS.

Regardless of what survey strategies are adopted, it may prove impossible to produce perfectly comparable estimates, whether using a single survey or not, since respondents are not likely to be equally willing to report (1) unlawful things done to them with guns by other people (i.e., gun crime victimizations) and (2) unlawful acts that they themselves had committed (e.g., unlawful possession of a gun, which is involved in most reported defensive gun uses). Thus, defensive gun use experiences are likely to be underreported more than gun crime victimiziond.[150]

Let us nevertheless consider the most recent large-scale national survey that directly asked about both defensive gun use and gun crime victimization. In the 1994 NSPOF, 38 respondents reported a defensive gun use in the past year against a human, not in connection with military, security, or law enforcement work.[151] Respondents were also asked: "During the past twelve months—that is, since last November—has anyone robbed, tried to attack, or attacked you?" and those who replied "yes" were then asked: "Did the perpetrator use a gun in any of these incidents?"[152] Note that there were no further follow-up questions to disqualify any of these cases as gun crimes, so the survey will yield a relatively generous estimate of gun crime. Nevertheless, just nine respondents reported gun crime victimizations in the previous year.[153]

Thus, using the same-survey strategy, defensive gun uses would appear to be about four times more common than gun crimes, supporting (perhaps coincidentally) the conclusion that Kleck and Gertz drew using their methods.[154] It is not being argued that this strategy is in fact the optimum way to go about this task. Rather, the data merely serve to show that one could arrive at substantially the same conclusion about relative frequency of offensive and defensive uses even if one adopted the dubious same-survey strategy, as long as the procedure is confined to surveys that directly ask about both gun crime victimizations and defensive gun uses. The NSPOF results for gun crimes are nowhere to be found in reports by Cook and Ludwig, not even in a chapter titled "Gun Uses and Misuses."[155] Perhaps same-survey comparisons are valid only if they indicate that gun crimes are more common than defensive gun uses, as is the case when one uses the NCVS.

A few other surveys, besides the NCVS or NSPOF, also seem to provide the data for generating estimates of criminal gun use against the respondents, as well as defensive gun use estimates. Unfortunately, the questions supposedly addressing gun crime victimization actually make no distinction between offensive and defensive uses of guns. Instead, they merely ask ambiguous questions like that posed in a December 1993 Gallup poll: "Not including military combat, has a gun ever been used to threaten you in a robbery, mugging or some other situation?"[156] The obvious problem is that a yes answer would be just as accurate for a criminal who had been on the receiving end of a defensive gun use in a robbery or other crime that they had attempted as it would be for a victim of a gun robbery or other gun crime. Thus, these surveys' supposed estimates of "gun crime" actually reflect an inseparable mixture of defensive gun use and gun crime victimization experiences.

Returning to a sounder basis for drawing conclusions, the best estimate of annual defensive gun use frequency, from the NSDS, is 2.55 million in 1993 (table 6.2), while the best, albeit somewhat ambiguous, estimate of gun crime frequency is that of the NCVS, which indicates that in 1992 about 554,000 crimes of all types occurred in which offenders used guns to threaten or attack victims.[157] Thus, defensive uses are about five times more common than criminal uses.

Conclusions

The effect of all the one-sided assessment of methods, suppression of unsupportive evidence, selective reviews of prior research, fallacious logic, and arbitrary interpretation of evidence has been a degradation of scientific standards in the study of guns and violence. Perhaps the most destructive effect of all is the legitimation of one-sided methodological speculation as the equal, and even the superior, of empirical evidence as a basis for drawing conclusions from research. In considering how widespread acceptance of this detrimental practice might be, it should be borne in mind that acceptance, or at least tolerance, of these practices is not confined to a handful of scholars. Every instance of published nonsense requires the collaboration of journal referees who recommend that it be published and of editors who can persuade themselves that the publication of one-sided speculation can somehow make a constructive contribution to scholarly debate. And for every irresponsible scholar who puts one-sided speculations down on paper, there no doubt are others who privately indulge in the same vice. Further, the fact that such material is published sends a message to much larger audiences of scholars that these critical practices are acceptable, thereby legitimating debased intellectual goods and depressing the implied standards of scholarly quality sufficient to gain publication.

The most obviously slanted critique of large defensive gun use estimates published to date was probably that of Hemenway.[158] Perhaps the only thing more shocking than Hemenway's ideological diatribe was the fact that a respectable professional journal, the *Journal of Criminal Law and Criminology*, decided to publish it. Its criminology editor, John Hagan, attributed his decision to publish the paper to the fact that two or three outside reviewers recommended publication. But all that it takes for an editor to get such recommendations is to select reviewers with strong published views consistent with the author's thesis who are willing to overlook its tactics, one-sidedness, speculative character, and lack of supporting evidence.[159]

After Kleck and Gertz supplied Hagan with a long series of documented instances of deceptive claims, logical fallacies, red herrings, inaccuracies, and even potentially libellous insinuations in the Hemenway paper, Hagan did not dispute their claims. Instead, he insisted that publishing Hemenway's paper would somehow "contribute to the debate."[160] To suggest that publishing a long series of falsehoods, red herrings, irrelevancies, libelous insinuations, and personal ideology disguised as scholarly criticism somehow "contributes" to the scholarly debate over gun use is nonsensical. Intellectually debased argumentation only muddies the waters and makes the already difficult task of assessing the evidence even harder.

All of the challenges to large defensive gun use estimates have been thoroughly rebutted. From a crudely political standpoint, however, this is inconsequential. The political functions of a piece like Hemenway's were served the instant an editor decided to publish it. Even if a "critique" is utterly devoid of valid content, and each of its points are thoroughly refuted in the pages of the publishing journal, once the piece appears in print in a journal, propagandists can cite the publication as evidence that large defensive gun use estimates have been "discredited."

And indeed, this is precisely how the Hemenway piece has been cited, even before it was published. In a letter to the *Journal of the American Medical Association*, three public health gun control advocates stated that "the reasons that this survey [the NSDS] is incapable of yielding an accurate estimate of defensive gun use are described at length in the Hemenway article."[161] Apparently a series of unsupported and one-sided speculations was a sound enough basis for these individuals to reject the findings of at least fifteen (at that time) large-scale, professionally conducted surveys.

We can be confident that propagandists will in future cite these one-sided speculations as authoritative proof that large defensive gun use estimates have been "discredited," while procontrol academics who regard themselves as moderates will conclude that while Hemenway and others like him may have overstated a few points, they had nevertheless somehow "cast doubt" on the estimates or "raised serious questions" about them.

The critiques can be cited by gun control advocates, procontrol scholars, and reporters alike in good conscience, as part of a "balanced" presentation of the issue. Hemenway's outrageous and unsupported speculations will be cited in scholarly sources alongside the NSDS estimates, implicitly giving equal weight to careful, empirically based estimates and misleading, evidence-free speculations.[162] The fact that the balance is completely spurious, and that only one side of the debate can present credible supportive empirical evidence, is politically irrelevant. Since it is highly unlikely that either reporters or the rest of the audience for propaganda will bother to read a rebuttal, the complete lack of any intellectual merit to the defensive gun use critiques will not be evident, and thus will not in any way reduce their political utility.

In contrast to advocacy scholarship and political warfare, the effectiveness of science depends on upholding the primacy of empirical evidence over speculation. Scientists are not allowed to ignore or discount evidence merely because they are imaginative enough to conjure up possible flaws in the evidence, for the obvious reason that this can easily be done with even the soundest evidence. Since flawed evidence is the only kind we have, if one rejects flawed evidence, one rejects all evidence. And in the absence of evidence, people tend to fall back on their biases and taken-for-granted preconceptions (euphemistically referred to as "common sense") in drawing conclusions. Once scholars tolerate one-sided speculation, bad ideas are never abandoned because advocates can speculate their way around any evidence.

The hypothesis that many Americans use guns for self-protection each year has been repeatedly subjected to empirical test, using the only feasible method for doing so, surveys of representative samples of the population. The results of nineteen consecutive surveys unanimously indicate that each year huge numbers of Americans (700,000 or more) use guns for self-protection. Further, the more technically sound the surveys, the higher the defensive gun use estimates are (compare the NSDS and NSPOF with earlier surveys). The entire body of evidence cannot be rejected based on the speculation that all surveys share biases that, on net, cause an overestimation of defensive gun use frequency because, ignoring fallacious reasoning, there is no empirical evidence to support this novel theory. At this point, it is fair to say that no intellectually serious challenge has been mounted to the case for defensive gun use being very frequent.

One of the main reasons that elements of the American intelligentsia are reluctant to accept large estimates of defensive gun use frequency, one suspects, is that to do so would put them in agreement with the NRA, an organization so thoroughly demonized within these quarters as to make agreeing with them intolerable. Intellectuals who would normally be perfectly aware of the illegitimacy of using ad hominem standards for judging the validity of an assertion will nonetheless recoil from accepting any conclusion that would put them in agreement with the "evil empire."

Further, if Don Kates is right (chapter 1), some of the resistance to high defensive gun use resistance may be due to a visceral dislike for forceful self-protection actions of all sorts, grounded in a moral repugnance for self-defense. For some, like David McDowall and Colin Loftin, it is self-evident that "collective security requires the disarming and demobilizing of individual capabilities" for self-defense. Some people regard the acceptance of forceful behavior for defensive purposes as moral compromise and a weakening of opposition to violence. In their view, claims of self-defensive use of force are mere rationalizations of what was actually aggressive behavior. For example, referring to defensive gun use surveys, Reiss and Roth insisted that "some of what respondents designate as their own self-defense would be construed as aggression by others," the "others" apparently including Reiss and Roth.[163] Under this view, to see any value in defensive gun use would amount to valuing aggression, since very little of the supposedly "defensive" gun use really was defensive.

Discussion of the merits of DGU estimates in the scholarly community will continue to amount to little more than junk science and advocacy scholarship until a consensus is reached among researchers that speculation, while useful in generating testable hypotheses, should carry no weight at all in assessing evidence and arriving at conclusions. Instead, conclusions, however tentative, should be based solely on the best available empirical evidence. The best survey on defensive gun use frequency indicates 2.55 million defensive gun uses a year in the United States (table 6.2), and this estimate has been repeatedly confirmed by all surveys of comparable technical merit. Until a methodologically better national survey yields a substantially different estimate, honest scholars will have to continue to accept, however tentatively, that millions of Americans use guns for self-protection each year.

Advocates of the rare-defensive gun use theory, however, have shown no interest in developing methodologically better surveys on defensive gun use. Quite the contrary, as soon as it became evident to them that good-quality surveys would continue to yield high defensive gun use estimates, they invented the theory that all surveys are inherently biased to overstate defensive gun use frequency, thus making it impossible, in their minds, to produce valid defensive gun use estimates using surveys.[164] This nihilistic position effectively renders their rare-DGU theory evidence-proof. The only kind of further research on the topic that these critics have called for is transparently one-sided research designed to detect only false positives, and thus to justify revising defensive gun use estimates downward.[165]

Policy Implications of
Large Defensive Gun Use Estimates

It is ironic, in light of all the impassioned scholarly dispute, that large defensive gun use estimates pose no threat whatsoever to the moderate gun controls, such as background checks of prospective gun buyers, that most Americans support. These measures would not deny guns to any significant number of noncriminals, and thus would not prevent defensive gun use among the law-abiding. People who sincerely support only moderate controls, but oppose gun prohibition, should have no political concerns about large defensive gun use estimates.

Such estimates do, on the other hand, constitute a very serious obstacle to promoting gun prohibition, which would deny guns to criminals and non-criminals alike, and thus would reduce whatever benefits defensive gun use may yield. Therefore, in light of the absence of any intellectually serious basis for discounting large defensive gun use estimates, one plausible explanation of why some scholars cling to the rare-defensive gun use theory in the face of overwhelming contrary evidence is that they favor a disarmed populace and accurately perceive high defensive gun use estimates as a significant political obstacle to achieving national gun prohibition.[166]

Appendix—Adjusting Earlier Estimates of Defensive Gun Use

The results of earlier gun use surveys were adjusted to make them more comparable with one another and with the National Self-Defense Survey. The basic idea was to estimate the annual, national estimate of defensive gun uses (DGUs) which each survey would have yielded if it had resembled the NSDS, i.e., if it was a national survey of noninstitutionalized adults (age 18+) that covered uses involving any gun type, excluded uses against animals or uses connected with military, police, or security guard work, had a one-year recall period, and asked the DGU question of all respondents (Rs), not just gun or handgun owners. There was no attempt to adjust for differences in crime or gun ownership levels in different years or locales. For all estimates it was conservatively assumed that there was only one DGU per DGU-involved person or household.

Adjustments

A. Adjustment **A** was applied to surveys inquiring only about uses of handguns, in order to produce an estimate pertaining to all gun types. The NSDS indicated that 79.7 percent of DGUs involved handguns, so the adjustment consists of multiplying a handgun-only estimate by 1.2547 (1/0.797).[167]

B. Adjustment **B** was applied to surveys inquiring about an indefinite period of time ("have you ever . . . "), in order to produce an estimate pertaining to a one-year recall period. The Field poll indicated that the same survey yielded a 1.4 percent prevalence figure for a one-year recall period and an 8.6 percent figure for the unlimited period (see table 6.1, note a), so the adjustment consists of multiplying an "ever used" estimate by 0.16279 (1.4 percent/8.6 percent).

C. Adjustment **C** was applied to surveys inquiring about a five-year recall period, in order to produce an estimate pertaining to a one-year recall period. The NSDS yielded the following ratios of one-year prevalence over five-year prevalence:[168]

C1. All guns, person-based: 1.326/3.315=0.40000

C2. All guns, household-based: 1.587/3.898=0.40713

C3. Handguns, household-based: 1.105/2.974=0.37155

D. Adjustment **D** was applied to surveys that failed to exclude uses of guns against animals, in order to produce an estimate pertaining only to uses against humans. The NSDS indicated that of 244 Rs initially reporting DGUs, 22 had used guns only against animals, so the adjustment consists of multiplying a humans-plus-animals estimate by 0.90984 (222/244).

E. Adjustment **E** was applied to surveys that asked the DGU question only of Rs who reported personally owning a gun or handgun, in order to produce an estimate pertaining to the entire population and thus reflecting uses among those who do not report current ownership of a gun. The NSDS indicated that only 59.5 percent of Rs reporting DGUs reported current personal ownership of a gun (p. 187), so the adjustment consists of multiplying a gun-owners-only estimate by 1.68067 (1/0.595).

F. Adjustment **F** was applied to surveys that asked the DGU question only of Rs who lived in households reporting a gun, in order to produce an estimate pertaining the entire population and thus reflecting uses among those who do not live in a household reporting current ownership of a gun. The NSDS indicated that only 79.0 percent of Rs reporting DGUs reported current household ownership of a gun (p. 187), so the adjustment consists of multiplying a gun-owners-only estimate by 1.26582 (1/0.790).

G. Adjustment **G** was applied to surveys that inquired only about DGUs that occurred outside the R's home, in order to produce an estimate pertaining to all DGUs, regardless of location. The NSDS indicated that

62.7 percent of DGUs occurred outside the R's home (p. 185), so the adjustment consists of multiplying an outside-the-home-only estimate by 1.59490 (1/0.627).

Population Bases Used

Estimated resident population, age 18 or older, as of March, 1993: 190,673,523. Estimated U.S. households as of March, 1993: 96,391,000.[169]

Adjustments Applied

Survey	Population Based Used	Adjustments Applied	Other Information Used
Field	Persons	A,D	Used the 1.4% past-year figure
Bordua	Persons	B,D	
DMIa	Households	B,D	
DMIb	Households	B	
Hart	Households	A,C3	
Ohio	Persons	A,B,D	26.4% of U.S. households had handguns in 1993 (average of 5) national surveys
Mauser	Households	C2	46% of households
Gallup 91	Persons	A,B,D	reported a gun; 47% of these reported a handgun
Gallup 93	Persons	B,D,E	31% of Rs personally owned gun
L.A. Times	Persons	B,D,G	Used "1% of Rs" figure
Tarrance	Persons	C1	

Computational Procedures

Typically, the prevalence figure reported for the survey (e.g., the proportion of adults who had used a gun for protection) was multiplied times the appropriate population base (e.g., number of U.S. resident adults) and then times each of the necessary adjustment factors. In cases where the prevalence figure applied only to gun owners (or some subset thereof) the number of gun owners had to be computed first, using the gun owner prevalence figures generated in the same survey, or, in one case, figures generated in other national surveys conducted in the same year.

Illustrative Example

The 1993 Gallup poll estimate required considerable adjusting, so it serves as a useful example. In that survey, among persons reporting that they personally owned a gun (who constituted 31 percent of the entire sample), 11 percent reported that they had ever used a gun for protection. The survey did not exclude uses against animals. The estimate was therefore computed as follows:

$$190{,}673{,}523 \times 0.31 \times 0.11 \times 0.16278 \times 0.90984 \times 1.68067 = 1{,}618{,}428$$

			B	D	E	
Population (# Adults)	% of pop. that owns guns	% of owners w. DGU	1 year vs. "ever"	Humans only	Entire pop. vs. only gun owners	Est. DGUs

Notes

1. Gary Kleck and Marc Gertz, "Armed Resistance to Crime: The Prevalence and Nature of Self-Defense with a Gun," *Journal of Criminal Law & Criminology* 86 (1995): 150–87; Philip J. Cook and Jens Ludwig, *Guns in America* (Washington, D.C.: The Police Foundation, 1997); Philip J. Cook and Jens Ludwig, "Defensive Gun Uses: New Evidence from a National Survey," *Journal of Quantitative Criminology* 14 (1998): 111–31.

2. Field Institute, "Tabulations of the Findings of a Survey of Handgun Ownership and Access Among a Cross Section of the California Adult Public" (San Francisco: Field Institute, 1976); Bordua et al., *Patterns of Firearms Ownership;* Cambridge Reports, *An Analysis of Public Attitudes;* DMI (Decision-Making-Information), *Attitudes of the American Electorate Toward Gun Control* (Santa Ana: DMI, 1979); Ohio, *Ohio Citizen Attitudes Concerning Crime and Criminal Justice*, the Ohio Statistical Analysis Center, Division of Criminal Justice Services (Columbus,

Ohio: Ohio Department of Development, 1982); Peter D. Hart Research Associates, Inc., "Violence in America," questionnaire, with marginal frequencies, used in October 1981 survey (Washington, D.C.: Peter D. Hart Research Associates, 1981); Quinley, "*Time*/CNN Poll;" Gary A. Mauser, "Armed Self-Defense: The Canadian Case," *Journal of Criminal Justice* 24 (1996): 400; Graham Huebner, "Handguns in America," *The Gallup Poll Monthly* 308 (1991): 43; Gallup/CNN/*USA Today* Poll of December 1993 (Dialog, Roper Center for Public Opinion, accession number 00213628); *Los Angeles Times* poll of April 1994 (Dialog, Roper Center for Public Opinion, accession number 00214862); *U.S. News and World Report* Poll of May 1994 (Dialog, Roper Center for Public Opinion, accession number 00220137).

3. Cambridge Reports, *An Analysis of Public Attitudes Towards Handgun Control* (Cambridge, Mass.: Cambridge Reports, Inc., 1978); Hal Quinley, memorandum reporting results from 1989 *Time*/CNN Poll of Gun Owners, dated 6 February 1990 (New York: Yankelovich Clancy Shulman survey organization, 1990).

4. Kleck and Gertz, "Armed Resistance," pp. 177, 187.

5. Ibid.

6. U.S. Bureau of Justice Statistics, *Criminal Victimization in the United States, 1993* (Washington, D.C.: U.S. Government Printing Office, 1996), pp. 139–40.

7. Gary Kleck, *Point Blank: Guns and Violence in America* (Hawthorne, N.Y.: Aldine, 1991), pp. 56, 57.

8. Philip J. Cook, "The Technology of Personal Violence," *Crime and Justice* 14 (1991): 54-56; Albert J. Reiss and Jeffrey A. Roth, "Firearms and Violence," in *Understanding and Preventing Violence*, ed. Albert J. Reiss and Jeffrey A. Roth (Washington, D.C.: National Academy Press), pp. 265–66; David McDowall and Brian Wiersema, "The Incidence of Defensive Firearm Use by US Crime Victims, 1987 Through 1990," *American Journal of Public Health* 84 (1994): 1982-84.

9. Michael J. Hindelang, Travis Hirschi, and Joseph G. Weis, *Measuring Delinquency* (Beverly Hills: Sage, 1981); U.S. Bureau of Justice Statistics, *Criminal Victimization 1993*, pp. 149–51.

10. Gary Kleck, *Targeting Guns: Firearms and Their Control* (New York: Aldine, 1997), pp. 97, 99.

11. Kleck and Gertz, "Armed Resistance," pp. 174, 184–85; Gary Kleck and Marc Gertz, "Carrying Guns for Protection: Results from the National Self-Defense Survey," *Journal of Research in Crime and Delinquency* 35 (1998): 208.

12. Quinley, "*Time*/CNN poll."

13. James D. Wright and Peter H. Rossi, *Armed and Considered Dangerous* (New York: Aldine, 1986), p. 155.

14. David McDowall, Colin Loftin, and Stanley Presser, "Measuring Civilian Defensive Firearm Use: A Methodological Experiment," *Journal of Quantitative Criminology* 16 (2000): 4.

15. David Hemenway, "Survey Research and Self-defense Gun Use: An Explanation of Extreme Overestimates," *Journal of Criminal Law and Criminology* 87 (1997): 1443-44; Cook and Ludwig, "Defensive Gun Uses," p. 128.

16. U.S. Bureau of Justice Statistics, *Criminal Victimization in the United States, 1994* (Washington, D.C.: U.S. Government Printing Office, 1997), 6, 8; Kleck and Gertz, "Carrying Guns," pp. 200–201.

17. Cook and Ludwig, *Guns in America*.

18. Ibid., p. 62.

19. Kleck and Gertz, "Armed Resistance," p. 184; Cook and Ludwig, *Guns in America*, p. 62.

20. Cook and Ludwig, *Guns in America*, p. 62.

21. Jens Ludwig, "Gun Self-Defense and Deterrence," *Crime and Justice*, forthcoming.

22. Cook and Ludwig, "Defensive Gun Uses," p. 121.

23. Robin M. Ikeda, Linda L. Dahlberg, Jeffrey J. Sacks, James A. Mercy, and Kenneth E. Powell, "Estimating Intruder-Related Firearm Retrievals in U.S. Households, 1994," *Violence and Victims* 12 (1997): 363-72.

24. Kleck and Gertz, "Armed Resistance."

25. Deborah Azrael and David Hemenway, "'In the Safety of Your Own Home': Results from a National Survey on Gun Use at Home," *Social Science & Medicine* 50 (2000): 287, 290.

26. Kleck and Gertz, "Armed Resistance," p. 184; Cook and Ludwig, *Guns in America*, p. 63.

27. Hemenway, "Survey Research," p. 1432.

28. Gallup Organization, "WOMEN.COM Million Mom March Gun Survey" (Lexis-Nexis Academic Universe, Roper Center for Public Opinion Research, accession number 0358375).

29. McDowall et al., "Measuring Civilian Defensive Firearm Use," p. 10.

30. *Washington Post*, 9 July 2000, p. B5.

31. McDowall et al., "Measuring Civilian Defensive Firearm Use," p. 4.

32. Cook, "The Technology of Personal Violence," p. 55.

33. Cynthia Gillespie, *Justifiable Homicide* (Columbus: Ohio State University Press, 1989).

34. U.S. Bureau of Justice Statistics, *Criminal Victimization 1993*, p. 133.

35. Tom W. Smith, "A Call for a Truce in the DGU War," *Journal of Criminal Law and Criminology* 87 (1997): 1462–63. Emphasis added.

36. U.S. Bureau of the Census, *National Crime Survey: Interviewer's Manual*, NCVS-550 Part D—How to Enumerate NCS (Washington, D.C.: U.S. Government Printing Office, 1986).

37. Kleck and Gertz, "Armed Resistance," pp. 155–56.

38. See sources to table 6.1 in note 2.

39. U.S. Bureau of the Census, *Interviewer's Manual*, D2-5a, D4-5, D4-18.

40. See chapter 4.

41. U.S. Bureau of Justice Statistics, *Criminal Victimization 1994*, pp. 120, 123.

42. Kleck, *Targeting Guns*, p. 193.

43. Kent M. Ronhovde and Gloria P. Sugars, "Survey of Select State Firearm Control Laws," in *Federal Regulation of Firearms*, report prepared by Congressional Research Service for the U.S. Senate Judiciary Committee (Washington, D.C.: U.S. Government Printing Office, 1982), pp. 204–5.

44. U.S. Bureau of Justice Statistics, *Criminal Victimization 1994*, p. 59.

45. Ronhovde and Sugars, "State Firearm Control Laws," pp. 204-5.

46. David J. Bordua, Alan J. Lizotte, and Gary Kleck, with Van Cagle, *Patterns of Firearms Ownership, Regulation and Use in Illinois* (Springfield, Ill.: Illinois Law Enforcement Commission, 1979).

47. Philip J. Cook, "The Case of the Missing Victims: Gunshot Woundings in the National Crime Survey," *Journal of Quantitative Criminology* 1 (1985): 91-102.

48. Colin Loftin and Ellen J. MacKenzie, "Building National Estimates of Violent Victimization" (paper presented at the National Research Council Symposium on the Understanding and Control of Violent Behavior, Destin, Fla., 1-6 April 1990), pp. 22–23.

49. U.S. Bureau of Justice Statistics, *Reporting Crime to the Police*, BJS Special Report (Washington, D.C.: U.S. Government Printing Office, 1985).

50. See chapter 7.

51. David McDowall, "Firearms and Self-Defense," *Annals* 539 (1995): 137.

52. U.S. Bureau of Justice Statistics, *Guns and Crime*, Crime Data Brief (Washington, D.C.: U.S. Government Printing Office, 1994), p. 2.

53. McDowall and Wiersema, "Incidence of Defensive Firearm Use," 1984; Cook, "The Technology of Personal Violence," pp. 56, 62.

54. Arthur L. Kellermann, Lori Westphal, Laurie Fischer, and Beverly Harvard, "Weapon Involvement in Home Invasion Crimes," *Journal of American Medical Association* 273 (1995): 1761.

55. Jeffrey A. Roth, "Firearms and Violence," National Institute of Justice Research in Brief (Washington, D.C.: U.S. Government Printing Office, 1994), p. 4.

56. McDowall et al., "Measuring Civilian Defensive Firearm Use."

57. Hemenway, "Survey Research"; McDowall et al., "Measuring Civilian Defensive Firearm Use," pp. 9, 17.

58. David McDowall, Colin Loftin, and Stanley Presser, "Measuring Civilian Defensive Firearm Use: A Methodological Experiment," paper submitted to the *Journal of Quantitative Criminology*, 1999.

59. McDowall et al., "Measuring Civilian Defensive Firearm Use," p. 15.

60. Gillespie, *Justifiable Homicide*, pp. 67–77.

61. Kleck and Gertz, "Armed Resistance," p. 163.

62. McDowall et al., "Measuring Civilian Defensive Firearm Use," pp. 12, 15.

63. U.S. Bureau of Justice Statistics, *Criminal Victimization 1994*, pp. 114–16; Linda R. Murphy and Richard W. Dodge, "The Baltimore Recall Study," in *The National Crime Surveys: Working Papers, Volume I: Current and Historical Perspectives*, ed. Robert G. Lehnen and Wesley G. Skogan (Washington, D.C.: U.S. Goverment Printing Office, 1981), p. 19.

64. Kleck and Gertz, "Armed Resistance," p. 185; see studies reviewed in chapter 7.

65. McDowall et al., "Measuring Civilian Defensive Firearm Use," pp. 14–15, 17.

66. *Journal of Quantitative Criminology* 16 (2000): inside cover.

67. Michael Maltz, editor of the *Journal of Quantitative Criminology*, e-mail to author, 7 August 2000.

68. U.S. Bureau of Justice Statistics, *Criminal Victimization 1993*, pp. 2–3, 170.

69. Richard Dodge, "The Washington, D.C., Recall Study," in *The National Crime Surveys*, vol. 1, p. 14; Kleck and Gertz, "Armed Resistance," p. 171.

70. Hemenway, "Survey Research," p. 1439; David Cantor, "Substantive Implications of Longitudinal Design Features: The National Crime Survey as a Case Study," in *Panel Surveys*, ed. Daniel Kasprzyk, Greg Duncan, Graham Kalton, and M. P. Singh (New York.: Wiley, 1989), p. 73.

71. Hemenway, "Survey Research," p. 1439.

72. Cook and Ludwig, *Guns in America*, p. 73; Ludwig, "Gun Self-Defense."

73. Philip J. Cook, Jens Ludwig, and David Hemenway, "The Gun Debate's New Mythical Number: *How* Many Defensive Uses per Year?" *Journal of Policy Analysis and Management* 16 (1997): 466.

74. Smith, "Truce in the DGU War," p. 1468.

75. Kleck and Gertz, "Armed Resistance," p. 171.

76. Dodge, "Washington, D.C., Recall Study;" Murphy and Dodge, "Baltimore Recall Study"; Anthony G. Turner, "The San Jose Recall Study," in *The National Crime Surveys*, vol. 1.; Henry Woltman, John Bushery, and Larry Carstensen, "Recall Bias and Telescoping in the National Crime Survey," in *The National Crime Surveys*, vol. 1.

77. See chapter 2; Kellermann et al., "Weapon Involvement," note 24, citing Gary Kleck, "Crime Control Through the Private Use of Armed Force," *Social Problems* 35 (1988): 1–21.

78. McDowall and Wiersema, "Incidence of Defensive Firearm Use."

79. Reiss and Roth, "Firearms and Violence," pp. 265, 266.

80. Kleck, "Crime Control"; Kleck, *Point Blank*, pp. 265–66.

81. Cook, "The Technology of Personal Violence."

82. McDowall and Wiersema, "Incidence of Defensive Firearm Use"; Kleck, "Crime Control," p. 3.

83. Cook, "The Technology of Personal Violence," pp. 54–55.

84. Cook, "The Case of the Missing Victims."

85. Cook, "The Technology of Personal Violence," pp. 54–56.

86. Cook and Ludwig, *Guns in America*, pp. 68–71; Cook and Ludwig, "Defensive Gun Uses," pp. 122–24.

87. Roberta K. Lee, Richard J. Waxweiler, James G. Dobbins, and Terri Taschetag, "Incidence Rates of Firearm Injuries in Galveston, Texas, 1979-1981," *American Journal of Epidemiology* 134 (1991): 519.

88. See medical studies reviewed in Kleck, *Targeting Guns*, pp. 3–5.

89. Cook and Ludwig, *Guns in America*, p. 70.

90. Hemenway, "Survey Research," pp. 1441-43.

91. Loftin and MacKenzie, "Building National Estimates."

92. Questionaire for the National Survey of the Private Ownership of Firearms (NSPOF), appendix to codebook for The Police Foundation, note 113; Cook and Ludwig, *Guns in America*, p. 70; Cook and Ludwig, "Defensive Gun Uses," p. 123; U.S. Bureau of Justice Statistics, *Criminal Victimization 1994*, p. 6.

93. Cook and Ludwig, "Defensive Gun Uses," p. 123.

94. Gallup Organization, *The Gallup Poll Monthly* 33 (1992): 326.

95. Kleck and Gertz, "Armed Resistance," pp. 184–85.

96. U.S. Bureau of Justice Statistics, *Criminal Victimization 1993*, p. 152.

97. Loftin and MacKenzie, "Building National Estimates."

98. Cook and Ludwig, "Defensive Gun Uses," p. 123.

99. McDowall et al., "Measuring Civilian Defensive Firearm Use," p. 5, citing Cook and Ludwig, "Defensive Gun Uses."

100. Ibid., citing Gary Kleck and Marc Gertz, "The Illegitimacy of One-Sided Speculation: Getting the Defensive Gun Use Estimate Down," *Journal of Criminal Law and Criminology* 87 (1997): 1446–61.

101. McDowall et al., "Measuring Civilian Defensive Firearm Use," p. 5. Emphasis added.

102. Joseph L. Annest, James A. Mercy, Delinda R. Gibson, and George W. Ryan, "National Esimates of Nonfatal Firearm-Related Injuries," *Journal of the American Medical Association* 273 (1995): 1749, 1753.

103. Kleck, *Targeting Guns*, pp. 3–5; Kleck and Gertz, "The Illegitimacy of

One-Sided Speculation," pp. 1452–54, cited in McDowall et al., "Measuring Civilian Defensive Firearm Use," p. 19.

104. McDowall et al., "Measuring Civilian Defensive Firearm Use," p. 15.

105. Cook and Ludwig, *Guns in America*, pp. 125–26.

106. "NSPOF Questionaire."

107. Cook and Ludwig, "Defensive Gun Uses," p. 126.

108. Ibid., p. 125.

109. Ibid., p. 129; "NSPOF Questionaire," questions 59–85.

110. Cook and Ludwig, "Defensive Gun Uses," p. 125.

111. McDowall et al., "Measuring Civilian Defensive Firearm Use," p. 17.

112. Cook and Ludwig, "Defensive Gun Uses," p. 126. Emphasis added.

113. "NSPOF Questionaire," questions 116, 117.

114. The Police Foundation, *National Study of Private Ownership of Firearm in the United States, 1994* [Computer file]. ICPSR version, Radnor, Pa: Chilton Research Services [producer] (Ann Arbor, Mich.: Inter-University Consortium for Political and Social Research [distributor], 1998).

115. Cook and Ludwig, *Guns in America*, p. 61; Cook and Ludwig, "Defensive Gun Uses," pp. 121, 129.

116. Hemenway, "Survey Research," pp. 1435–37.

117. Cook and Ludwig, "Defensive Gun Uses"; McDowall et al., "Measuring Civilian Defensive Firearm Use."

118. U.S. Bureau of Justice Statistics, *Criminal Victimization 1994*, pp. 6, 64.

119. Hemenway, "Survey Research," pp. 1435–37; Cook and Ludwig, "Defensive Gun Uses," pp. 123–24; McDowall et al., "Measuring Civilian Defensive Firearm Use," pp. 5, 15.

120. Hemenway, "Survey Research," p. 1445.

121. Ibid.

122. Kleck and Gertz, "The Illegitimacy of One-Sided Speculation," pp. 1457–59.

123. Hemenway, "Survey Research," pp. 1444–45.

124. Cook and Ludwig, "Defensive Gun Uses," pp. 115–16.

125. William R. Tonso, "Social Problems and Sagecraft: Gun Control as a Case in Point," in *Firearms and Violence: Issues of Public Policy*, ed. Don B. Kates Jr. (Cambridge: Ballinger, 1984).

126. Hemenway, "Survey Research"; Kleck and Gertz, "The Illegitimacy of One-Sided Speculation."

127. Kleck and Gertz, "The Illegitimacy of One-Sided Speculation."

128. McDowall et al., "Measuring Civilian Defensive Firearm Use," p. 5.

129. Cook and Ludwig, "Defensive Gun Uses," p. 115.

130. Lana D. Harrison, "The Validity of Self-Reported Data on Drug Use," *The Journal of Drug Issues* 25 (1995): 94.

131. Kleck and Gertz, "The Illegitimacy of One-Sided Speculation," pp. 1457–59.

132. Cook and Ludwig, *Guns in America*, p. 75; Philip J. Cook and Jens Ludwig, "You Got Me: How Many Defensive Gun Uses per Year?" Paper presented at the annual meetings of the Homicide Research Working Group, Santa Monica, California, on 17 May 1996.

133. Cook and Ludwig, "Defensive Gun Uses," pp. 127–28; Smith, "Truce in the DGU War," p. 1469.

134. Cook and Ludwig, *Guns in America*, p. 61; Cook and Ludwig, "Defensive Gun Uses," pp. 121, 129.

135. E.g., Hemenway, "Survey Research"; Cook et al., "New Mythical Number"; Ludwig, "Gun Self-Defense."

136. E.g., compare Walter T. Brown, *In the Beginning: Compelling Evidence for Creation and the Flood* (Phoenix, Az.: Center for Scientific Creation, 1996), with Christopher McGowan, *In the Beginning: A Scientist Shows Why the Creationists Are Wrong* (Amherst, N.Y.: Prometheus Books, 1984).

137. Ludwig, "Gun Self-Defense."

138. Cook and Ludwig, "You Got Me."

139. Ibid.

140. Ludwig, "Gun Self-Defense"; Cook and Ludwig, "Defensive Gun Uses," pp. 127–28.

141. Cook and Ludwig, "You Got Me"; Hemenway, "Survey Research."

142. Cook and Ludwig, *Guns in America*, pp. 68–76; Cook and Ludwig, "Defensive Gun Uses," pp. 122–27; Cook et al., "New Mythical Number."

143. Cook and Ludwig, "You Got Me"; Cook and Ludwig, *Guns in America*, pp. 75–76; Cook and Ludwig, "Defensive Gun Uses," p. 128.

144. Kleck and Gertz, "Armed Resistance," pp. 174, 185.

145. See chapter 7.

146. McDowall et al., "Measuring Civilian Defensive Firearm Use," 116; Kleck and Gertz, "Armed Resistance," p. 169.

147. Kleck and Gertz, "Armed Resistance," pp. 169–70.

148. E.g., Cook, "The Case of the Missing Victims."

149 McDowall et al., "Measuring Civilian Defensive Firearm Use," p. 18.

150. Kleck and Gertz, "Armed Resistance," p. 171.

151. Cook and Ludwig, *Guns in America*, p. 62.

152. NSPOF Questionaire, questions 51, 52.

153. Author's analysis of data in The Police Foundation, "National Study."

154. Kleck and Gertz, "Armed Resistance," p. 170.

155. Cook and Ludwig, "Defensive Gun Uses"; Cook and Ludwig, *Guns in America*, pp. 45–56.

156. Gallup Organization, "Gallup Short Subjects," *Gallup Poll Monthly* 339 (1993): 48–58; for similarly ambiguous questions, see Azrael and Hemenway, "In the Safety."

157. Kleck and Gertz, "Armed Resistance," pp. 169–70.

158. Hemenway, "Survey Research"; see rebuttal in Kleck and Gertz, "The Illegitimacy of One-Sided Speculation."

159. *Journal of Criminal Law and Criminology* 87 (1997): vii.

160. John Hagan, criminology editor of the *Journal of Criminal Law and Criminology*, personal conversation with author, Tallahassee, Florida, 26 March 1997.

161. Vernick, Teret, and Webster, 1997, p. 703.

162. E.g., Cook and Ludwig, *Guns in America*; Cook and Ludwig, "Defensive Gun Uses"; McDowall et al., "Measuring Civilian Defensive Firearm Use."

163. David McDowall and Colin Loftin, "Collective Security and the Demand for Legal Handguns," *American Journal of Sociology* 88 (1983): 1148; Albert Reiss and Jeffrey Roth, *Understanding and Preventing Violence* (Washington, D.C.: National Academy Press, 1993), p. 266.

164. Cook and Ludwig, "You Got Me;" Cook and Ludwig, *Guns in America*; Cook and Ludwig, "Defensive Gun Uses"; Hemenway, "Survey Research."

165. Cook and Ludwig, "Defensive Gun Uses," pp. 127–28.

166. See chapter 4.

167. Kleck and Gertz, "Armed Resistance," p. 185.

168. Ibid., p. 184

169. U.S. Bureau of the Census, *Current Population Reports, Series P-25* (Washington, D.C.: U.S. Government Printing Office); U.S. Bureau of the Census, *Statistical Abstract of the United States* (Washington, D.C.: GPO), p. 58.

The Nature and Effectiveness of Owning, Carrying, and Using Guns for Self-Protection

by Gary Kleck

A huge volume of empirical evidence now supports the idea that defensive gun use is common in the U.S., occurring about 2.5 million times a year. The best estimates of defensive gun use frequency exceed even the highest estimates of the number of crimes committed with guns. But regardless of how common defensive gun use may be, is it effective? That is, are crime victims who use guns to protect themselves less likely to be hurt or to lose property than those who do not resist or adopt other self-protection measures? Under what circumstances does defensive gun use occur? How is it related to the carrying of firearms in public places, and how often do people carry guns? Does the ownership and defensive use of guns deter criminals from attempting crimes in the first place? This chapter addresses these and related questions.

Issues of Armed Resistance to Criminals

The belief that guns provide effective self-protection for at least some people some of the time is nearly universal. Even proponents of stringent gun control who assert that guns are not effective defensive devices for civilians nearly always make exceptions for police officers and the like. The rationale for police having guns is based at least partly on the idea that police need and can effectively use guns to defend themselves and others. Doubts about the defensive utility of guns, then, appear to rest on any of three beliefs: (1) civilians do not need any self-protective devices, because they will never confront criminals, or at least will never do so while they have access to a gun; (2) they can rely on the police for protection, or (3) they are not able to use guns effectively, regardless of need.

There is certainly some merit to the first belief. Most Americans rarely face a threat of serious physical assault, and some will never do so. Nevertheless, NCVS estimates indicate that 83 percent of Americans will, sometime over the span of their lives, be victims of violent crime, an event that, by definition, involves direct confrontation with a criminal.[1] Further, the most common location for such a confrontation is in or near the victim's home, i.e., the place where victims would be most likely to have access to a gun if they owned one.[2] While it cannot be stated what share of these incidents will transpire in a way that would allow the victim to actually use a gun, it is clear that a large share of the population will experience such an incident.

The second idea, that citizens can depend on police for effective protection, is plainly false. It implies that police can serve the same function as a gun in disrupting a crime in progress, before the victim is hurt or loses property. Police cannot do this, and indeed do not themselves even claim to be able to do so. Instead, police primarily respond reactively to crimes *after* they have occurred, questioning the victim and other witnesses in the hope that they can apprehend the criminals, make them available for prosecution and punishment, and thereby deter other criminals from attempting crimes. Police officers rarely disrupt violent crimes or burglaries in progress; even the most professional and efficient urban police forces rarely reach the scene of a crime soon enough to catch the criminal "in the act."[3] More generally, the idea that the modern police are so effective in controlling crime that they have rendered citizen self-protection obsolete is wildly at variance with a large body of evidence that police activities have, at best, only very modest effects on crime.[4] In any case, the fact that huge numbers of crimes still occur is obvious proof that the existence of modern police forces has not made other ways of dealing with crime, whether or not involving victim self-defense, unnecessary.

The third idea, that civilians are not generally able to use guns effectively, requires more extended consideration. Gun control proponents sometimes argue that only police have the special training, skills, and emotional control needed to wield guns effectively in self-defense. They hint that would-be gun users are ineffectual, panic-prone hysterics, as likely to accidentally shoot a family member as a burglar.[5] Incidents in which householders shoot family members mistaken for burglars and other criminals do indeed occur, but they are extremely rare. Studies reviewed elsewhere indicate that fewer than 2 percent of fatal gun accidents involve a person accidentally shooting someone mistaken for an intruder.[6] With about 900 fatal gun accidents in 1998, this implies that there were fewer than eighteen incidents of this sort that year.[7] Compared with 2.55 million annual defensive uses of guns, this translates into about a 1-in-142,000 chance of a defensive gun use resulting in this kind of accident.

Evidence pertaining to police use of firearms also indicates that civilians who use guns for self-protection are actually less likely to shoot innocent parties than police officers. To be fair, though, crime victims usually have the advantage of knowing who the offender in the crime is, while police officers often enter crime situations where they cannot distinguish offenders from victims or bystanders (chapter 1).

It is important to distinguish at this point two discrete issues addressed in this chapter: (1) the effectiveness of individual instances of civilian gun use against criminals in preventing injury and the completion of the crimes involved, and (2) whether such actions, and gun ownership in general, can deter criminal attempts from being made in the first place. Actual defensive use of guns by victims in specific criminal attempts could disrupt the attempt, preventing the criminal from injuring the victim or obtaining property (disruptive effects). On the other hand, the general fact of widespread civilian gun ownership, or ownership by specific individuals or identifiable groups, could deter some criminals from making the criminal attempts in the first place (deterrent effects). We turn first to the disruptive effects of actual defensive gun use on the outcomes of crime incidents.

The Effectiveness and Risks of Victim Resistance with Guns

Violent crimes and burglaries are inherently dangerous events, and no victim strategy, including nonresistance, is completely safe. Victim actions may improve the victim's situation, make it worse, or may simply be ineffectual. In the 1994 National Crime Victimization Survey (NCVS), 64.5 percent of victims thought that their self-protection actions helped their situation, while only 8.8 percent thought that it hurt their situation (the rest thought there was no effect or mixed effects).[8] But these were merely subjective impressions, and victims may be biased toward viewing their actions as effective, because to do otherwise would be to perceive their choices as foolish or ineffectual. Thus, it is preferable to use more objective information, based on the actual outcomes of crimes in which victims adopted various self-protection strategies.

The NCVS provides the largest, most nationally representative samples of crime incidents available. Further, it provides detailed data on the self-protection actions of victims and the outcomes of crime incidents. Thus, it provides the most authoritative basis we have for judging the effectiveness and risks of victims' defensive actions. The most current data from the NCVS cover the period from 1992 to 1998.

The rates of injury, property loss, and other measures of crime outcomes are shown for each self-protection measure, by crime type, in table 7.1. For the most part, crime incidents have been divided according to the NCVS "Type of Crime" classification, whereby each incident is classified according to the most serious crime elements that were involved. "Robbery" includes incidents where the offender used or threatened force in an attempt, successful or not, to obtain property. "Assault" covers crimes where a threat or attack occurred, but there were no elements of robbery or rape. Finally, "confrontational burglaries" is not a "Type of Crime" class, but rather encompasses all crimes occurring in the respondent's home that involved an offender who was not authorized to be in the home; who was getting into, or trying to get into, the home; and that occurred while the respondent was home. Thus, these are cases of illegal entry where a confrontation was possible and some direct self-protection measure could have been taken by the victim during the incident. These are mostly cases that

Table 7.1 Effectiveness and Risks of
Victim Self-Protection Measures (percentages)[9]

(Data weighted by Incident Weight)

Crime Type:[a]	Confrontational Robbery			Assault		Burglary[b]		
		Post-SP			Post-SP		Post-SP	
SP Measure	Injury	Injury	Loss	Injury	Injury	Injury	Injury	Loss
Attacked O with gun	8.5	0.0	8.5	48.9	5.9	26.5	0.0	4.2
Threatened O with gun	13.5	9.0	16.3	24.9	3.0	10.0	2.6	16.6
Any SP with gun	12.8	7.7	15.2	27.9	3.6	9.5	2.2	15.0
Attacked O with other weapon	41.9	1.6	34.4	60.7	7.8	30.4	7.3	6.3
Attacked O without weapon	52.1	7.7	46.9	82.7	8.6	64.3	5.4	13.5
Threatened O with other weapon	15.9	0.0	23.3	30.6	2.8	15.8	0.0	0.0
Threatened O without weapon	30.0	5.8	29.3	57.1	13.6	28.5	7.1	20.8
Defended self, property[c]	51.4	9.8	52.1	83.3	10.0	61.9	12.8	12.0
Chased, tried to catch O	34.4	9.6	60.3	58.2	9.0	10.2	0.0	26.7
Yelled at O, turned on lights	40.2	10.6	49.8	63.3	10.8	17.0	4.4	9.7
Cooperated with O, pretended to	12.6	6.5	81.5	37.6	14.7	38.1	15.5	37.9
Argued, reasoned with O	31.0	14.1	52.8	56.9	15.2	39.3	11.7	11.8
Ran/drove away, tried to	32.3	4.9	41.5	38.4	5.4	36.2	29.3	14.9
Called police, guard	23.6	3.4	56.0	48.5	4.6	12.9	2.8	14.3
Tried to attract attention	45.6	14.0	41.1	70.4	6.7	39.5	21.2	16.1
Screamed from pain, fear	69.3	22.0	68.6	94.1	12.6	73.6	21.6	19.4
Other self-protection measures	25.2	8.4	58.8	42.4	6.8	8.2	2.3	10.5
All SP measures	34.0	7.2	52.8	58.1	7.8	20.4	4.1	12.5
No SP measures at all	23.6	—	83.6	55.2	—	6.6	—	52.8
All incidents	30.2	4.5	69.9	57.4	5.9	14.2	2.2	30.5

Notes:

a. Crime type of each incident was defined according to Bureau of Justice Statistics Type of Crime classification, which is based on the most serious crime element in the incident.

b. Unauthorized person entered or tried to enter R's home while R was in the home.

c. Struggled, ducked, blocked blows, held onto property.

started out as residential burglaries, and thus crimes of stealth, but a few may be home invasion robberies where offenders intended to confront victims, or crimes with elements of sexual assault or other kinds of assaults.

Several outcome measures can be distinguished. "Injury" measures whether the victim suffered any kind of physical injury. "Loss" refers to whether the victim lost any property during the crime. Finally, a significant recent improvement in the NCVS allows analysts to separately identify injuries inflicted after the victim engaged in some form of self-protection ("post-SP injury"). This is important, because these are injuries that could have been provoked by the SP measure and thus could be regarded as a cost of self-protection, whereas injuries inflicted before the victim used the self-protection measure could not be so regarded. Of course, it should be stressed that even among post-self-protection injuries, some might have been inflicted even in the absence of self-protection, so the rate of post-self-protection injury should be regarded as an upper limit estimate of the rate of injury that was provoked by victim self-protection.

Consistent with the chapter 6 discussion, no victims of rape or sexual assault reported using a gun to either attack or threaten an offender, so it is impossible to directly assess defensive gun use for these crimes. The self-protection measures most similar to defensive gun use were attack or threat with other (nongun) weapons, but there were also few cases of these self-protection measures in connection with rape. The limited data indicate that these were the most effective methods of avoiding completion of the rape and of avoiding additional injury. Thus, if guns are more intimidating than knives to criminals, by extension one would expect defensive gun use to be the most effective measure for avoiding rape completion and additional injury (see p. 294–95 for a more detailed discussion of rape).

In general, self-protection measures of all types are effective, in the sense of reducing the risk of property loss in robberies and confrontational burglaries, compared to doing nothing or cooperating with the offender. The most effective form of self-protection is use of a gun. For robbery the self-protection measures with the lowest loss rates were among victims attacking the offender with a gun, and victims threatening the offender with a gun. For confrontational burglary, attacking with a gun had the second lowest loss rate of sixteen self-protection measures, bested only by another mode of armed self-protection, threatening the offender with a nongun weapon.

Regarding injury, although many victims are hurt in personal contact crimes, few are injured after using self-protection measures, and thus there is little injury that could have been provoked by victim resistance. Almost all the injury comes before, or simultaneous with, defensive actions. For example, only 11.8 percent of rape victims who used some self-protection measure were injured after doing so, while the figures are 10.8 percent for sexual assault victims (results not shown in table 7.1), 7.2 percent for robbery victims, 7.8 percent for assault victims, and 4.1 percent for victims of confrontational burglaries. Further, nonresistance does not guarantee safety, since 23.6 percent of robbery victims who did not resist were injured, while the rate was 55.2 percent for nonresisting assault victims, and even 6.6 percent in confrontational burglaries. Likewise 26.8 percent of rape victims who did not resist nevertheless suffered some additional injury, as did 27.4 percent of nonresisting sexual assault victims.

Victims who used guns were less likely to be injured than crime victims who did not resist, but their post-self-protection injury rates were not significantly different from those of victims using many other self-protection measures. Robbery victims who used guns were about as likely as other resisting victims to suffer a post-self-protection injury, while gun-wielding assault victims were somewhat less likely to suffer such an injury, as were burglary victims who used guns. Victim resistance rarely provokes offenders into attacking the victim, regardless of the form the resistance takes. Consequently, while defensive gun use is generally safe, it does not appear to be as uniquely safe among self-protection methods as data from earlier NCVS data suggested.[10] Nevertheless, there does not appear to be any increase in injury risk due to defensive gun use that counterbalances its greater effectiveness in avoiding property loss.

It has been conjectured that these low rates of injury and property loss are not really due to victim defensive gun use, but rather are attributable to the victim having some opportunity for advanced preparation to deal with the crime. The argument is that crimes with defensive gun uses are unusual in that the criminal failed to surprise the victim, allowing the victim to retrieve a gun, and that this lack of surprise would also make the criminal more vulnerable to any form of self-defense.[11] This is a clever speculation that cannot be tested with the NCVS or any other existing body of evidence. The NCVS does, however, provide some data relevant to the general underlying idea that defensive gun users face more favorable crime circumstances.

These data indicate that victims who use guns for self-protection actually face *less* favorable circumstances than other victims, and that the post-self-protection injury rates for defensive gun use, low though they are, may still be misleadingly high compared to other self-protection measures because victims who used guns faced tougher crime circumstances. More dangerous situations apparently prompt victims to adopt more dangerous self-protection measures. Two pieces of information available in the NCVS support this view. First, victims who used guns were substantially more likely than victims in general or victims using other self-protection measures to face offenders armed with guns—32.7 percent of victims who attacked the offender with a gun, and 21.8 percent of those who threatened the offender with a gun, faced offenders with guns, compared to only 6.8 percent of all victims who used self-protection measures, and 2.2 percent of all victims.[12] Second, victims who used guns were more likely to face multiple offenders—33.2 percent of victims who attacked offenders with a gun and 34.5 percent of those who threatened with a gun confronted multiple adversaries, compared to 20.6 percent of all those who used self-protection measures, and 6.2 percent of all victims. These findings are consistent with the view that crime circumstances likely to appear more dangerous to victims are more likely to push victims into using guns. They are contrary to the speculation that crime outcomes are better for gun-wielding victims merely because other circumstances of the crime made successful outcomes more likely.

Based on the 1992-1998 NCVS data, 20.8 percent of robberies, assaults, and confrontational burglaries in which a victim used a gun for self-protection resulted in some kind of injury to the victims. But most of this injury occurred prior to the victim's use of any self-protection measures. Only 3.6 percent of all gun-using victims in these crimes were injured after use of self-protection. Even if one made the extreme assumption that all of this post-self-protection injury was provoked by the victim gun use (i.e., none of it would have occurred anyway, in the absence of victim gun use), it is fair to say that victim gun use almost never provokes a criminal into attacking the victim.[13]

How serious are the injuries suffered by those who use guns to resist criminals? The NCVS ask victims about whether they received medical care for their injuries, and if so, what kind of care. This can be regarded as a rough measure of the seriousness of injuries, though it necessarily reflects availability of medical care as well. Of all gun-using victims, 1.3 percent were injured and received some sort of medical care, including self-treatment. Most of this was not, however, professional medical care. Only 0.6 percent of all gun-using victims received medical care at a doctor's office, clinic, emergency room, and/or hospital. Finally, none of the gun-using crime victims in the NCVS dataset were injured and received treatment requiring an overnight stay in a hospital. Professional medical treatment was apparently limited to that which could be delivered prior to the patient being released the same day. In sum, defensive gun use rarely provokes criminals to attack victims, and on the rare occasions that gun-using victims are injured after using their guns, the injuries are almost always minor.

Multivariate Analysis of Robbery and Armed Resistance

The simple rates of injury and property loss associated with each method of SP reflect the influence of other crime circumstances as well as that of the SP measure itself. To better isolate the effect of the self-protection measures alone, it is important to statistically control for other crime circumstances that might influence injury or crime completion. Thus, an analyst can compare crimes where the victim used a given self-protection measure with crimes without such self-protection used, using multivariate statistical procedures to control for other factors. The results of such a multivariate analysis provide a response to those who assert that one cannot know how an incident would have turned out had the victim not used the self-protection measure that they in fact used. When one compares, for example, crimes in which the victim engaged in defensive gun use with otherwise similar crimes in which the victim did not engage in defensive gun use, the latter cases in effect show how the former cases would have turned had the victim not engaged in defensive gun use.

Multivariate analysis is especially important in judging the relative effectiveness and safety of different self-protection tactics because, as noted, crime victims who use guns seem to face tougher crime circumstances than those who adopt other tactics—more numerous adversaries who are more likely to be themselves armed with guns. Thus, simple analyses of self-protection and the crime outcome alone can be misleading because they confound the effects of victim self-protection actions with the effects of associated crime circumstances.

The simple percentage table results concerning robbery completion and injury rates are, however, supported by more sophisticated multivariate analysis of NCVS robbery incidents. In a logistic regression analysis, Kleck and Miriam DeLone found that robbery victims who used guns in self-protection were significantly less likely to either be injured or lose their property than victims who used any other form of self-protection or who did nothing to resist.[14] This was true even when controlling for other characteristics of the robbery situation that could influence the effectiveness of defensive actions, such as the number of robbers, the number of victims, whether the robbery occurred in a private place, whether it occurred when it was dark, whether the robbers were armed, the age and gender of victims, and so on. Thus, there is no support for the speculation that gun defenders do well merely because of other advantageous crime circumstances associated with defensive gun use.

Multivariate Analysis of Rape and Armed Resistance

The NCVS data did not permit anything meaningful to be said about gun resistance in rape because there were no relevant sample cases to analyze. However, we may gain some strong hints about the results of gun resistance from an analysis of all forms of armed resistance by rape victims. Grouping together instances of resistance with guns, knives, or other weapons, Kleck and doctoral student Susan Sayles found, in a multivariate analysis of national victim survey data from 1979 to 1985, that rape victims using armed resistance were less likely to have the rape attempt completed against them than victims using any other mode of resistance.[15] These results confirmed those of criminologist Alan Lizotte using city victim surveys.[16] Further, there was no significant effect of armed resistance causing the rapist to inflict additional injury beyond the rape itself. Again, these multivariate results indicate that there is no empirical evidence to support the speculation that successful outcomes of armed resistance to rapists are due to the crime circumstances associated with such resistance.

In light of the robbery and assault findings indicating that gun resistance is at least as effective as armed resistance using other weapons, it is a reasonable inference that the same would be true for rape. Indeed, this would seem especially likely with rapes, given that rape victims are nearly all women, and guns are the weapon type whose effectiveness is least dependent on the physical strength of its user.

A recent multivariate study of assaults against women lumped all forms of self-protection together, but distinquished post-self-protection injury from pre-self-protection injury. Controlling for twelve other possible determinates (only three of which had a significant association), the authors found that women who used self-protection were less likely to suffer injury. The most interesting finding of the research was that the apparent effect of resistance on injury was actually reversed when the analysts distinguished post-self-protection injury from other injury. This indicated that previous research without this refinement that had suggested detrimental effects of resistance was misleading.[17]

The Police Chief's Fallacy

Joseph McNamara, former chief of the San Jose, California, police department, testified before a Congressional committee considering gun legislation: "We urge citizens not to resist armed robbery, but in these sad cases I described, the victims ended up dead because they produced their own handguns and escalated the violence. Very rarely have I seen cases where the handgun was used to ward off a criminal." Likewise, Quinn Tamm, former executive director of the International Chiefs of Police, once asserted that most persons possessing firearms "are a menace to themselves and their families."[18] In light of the foregoing evidence, why do some police say such things? While some, like Chief McNamara and Mr. Tamm, strong gun control advocates, may be motivated by political considerations, it is doubtful that this is true for all officers. Instead, police advice may well logically follow from the resistance experiences of victims with whom officers have had contact. The problem with relying on this sample of resistance cases is that it is substantially unrepresentative of the experiences of crime victims in general—the cases McNamara and other police officers have seen are not like the far more numerous cases they have not seen.

Most crimes are not reported to the police, and the crimes most likely to go unreported are the ones that involve neither injury nor property loss, i.e., those that had successful outcomes from the victim's viewpoint. For example, among robberies reported to the NCVS, only 24 percent of those with no injury or property loss were reported to police, while 72 percent of those with both were reported. Likewise, assaults without injury are less likely to be reported than those with injury.[19] By definition, all successful defensive gun uses fall within the no-injury/no-property-loss category, and thus are largely invisible to the police. Consequently, police never hear about the bulk of successful defensive gun uses, instead hearing mostly about an unrepresentative minority of them dominated by failures. To conclude that armed resistance is ineffective or dangerous, based on the experiences of this sort of unrepresentative sample of victims, can be called, in honor of former Chief McNamara, "the police chief's fallacy." At present, advising victims to not use guns to resist criminal attempts seems imprudent at best, reckless at worst. As criminologists Edward Ziegenhagen and Dolores Brosnan concluded: "victims can and do play an active part in the control of crime outcomes regardless of well-intentioned but ill-conceived efforts to encourage victims to limit the range of responses open to them. Victims can, and do, exercise a range of optional responses to robbery far beyond those conceived of by criminal justice professionals."[20]

The Myth of Criminals Taking Guns from Gun-wielding Victims

It has often been claimed that many people who attempt to use guns for self-protection have the gun taken from them by the criminal and used against them.[21] This type of incident is in fact virtually nonexistent. In the 1992-1998 NCVS sample, it was possible to identify crime incidents in which the victim used a gun for self-protection and lost a gun to the offender(s). Only 0.2 percent of incidents involving defensive gun use also involved the victim losing a gun to an offender—there was only a single sample case of such a thing happening in the NCVS dataset. Even this single case did not necessarily involve the offender seizing a gun from a victim using it for self-defense. Instead, a burglar might, for example, have been leaving a home with one of the household's guns when a resident attempted to stop him, using a different household gun. Thus, the 0.2 percent figure represents an upper limit estimate of the relative frequency of these events.

Researchers Albert Reiss and Jeffrey Roth tried to support this argument by citing misleading data on the frequency with which police officers are killed with their own guns. They reported that sixty-four police officers, 19 percent of those killed with guns in 1984-1988, were killed "when their service weapons were turned against them."[22] The purpose of citing the 19 percent figure was not made explicit, but in context the number clearly hinted that defensive gun use, even by experienced gun users like police, frequently leads to tragedy. This hinted inference was illogical, and the data do not in any way support the idea that defensive gun use frequently leads to a gun being taken away from the user by the criminal.

A meaningful measure of risk would have compared the number of police officers killed with their own gun with a measure of exposure to this risk, such as the number of police officers, or the number of times that they carried or used their guns defensively. There are about 600,000 police officers in the United States.[23] Virtually all of them carry guns for defensive purposes, essentially every working day, 250 or more days per year. Even if each averaged just one actual defensive use of a gun (e.g., it was drawn and at least pointed at someone) per year, this would imply 600,000 annual defensive gun uses by police, with thirteen or fewer per year resulting in an officer losing his gun and being killed with it, or 0.002 percent.

Even taking the Reiss-Roth figure at face value, it is misleading—the authors misadded killings (there were sixty-three deaths of this type, not sixty-four), and the 19 percent (actually 18 percent) figure was drawn from an unrepresentative time period. For the entire 1974-1990 period, the share of killings involving the officer's gun was 13.5 percent, a third less than 19 percent. And for the most recent year available to Reiss and Roth, 1990, there were only three officers killed with their own guns in the entire United States, 5.4 percent of the total killed.[24]

Finally, even on those rare occasions when police officers are killed with their own guns, the event almost never involves a gun being taken from an officer trying to use it defensively. A study of eleven such cases indicated that only one involved the gun being taken from the officer's hand. Instead, the gun is usually snatched from the officer's holster.[25] That is, officers have their guns taken from them when they are *not* using them for self-protection. Contrary to Reiss and Roth, gun owners of any kind, police or civilian, almost never, while using guns for protection, have their weapons taken from them and used against them.

Self-Defense Killings and Woundings of Criminals

Most uses of guns for either criminal or defensive purposes are much less dramatic or consequential than one might think. Only a tiny fraction of criminal gun assaults involve anyone actually being wounded, even nonfatally, and the same is true of defensive gun uses. Neither victim nor offender is hurt in the vast majority of cases. Indeed, it is partly because defensive gun use is as effective it is in preventing further harm that most defensive gun use incidents turn out to be as undramatic and inconsequential as they do.

In the typical defensive gun use, the victim merely points the gun at the offender, or displays or verbally refers to the weapon in a threatening way ("Stop right there—I've got a gun"), and this is sufficient to accomplish the ends of the victim. Nevertheless, most gun owners questioned in surveys assert that they would be willing to shoot criminals under some circumstances. A 1989 *Time*/CNN survey found that 80 percent of gun owners thought that they would get their guns if they believed someone was breaking into their home, and 78 percent said they would shoot a burglar if they felt threatened.[26]

Despite this stated willingness of gun owners to shoot under certain circumstances, few defensive gun uses in fact involve shooting anyone. The rarest but most serious form of self-defense with a gun is a defensive killing. These events are too rare to show up in surveys, even those with huge samples. The only national data bearing on their frequency is a partial count of civilian justifiable homicides compiled by the FBI based on police reports. This count, however, excludes (1) homicides ultimately ruled noncriminal by prosecutors, judges, or juries but reported to the FBI as criminal homicides because that is how initial police investigations routinely classify such events; (2) cases that local police label as civilian justifiable homicides but that are not reported as such to the FBI; and (3) defensive homicides recorded as "excusable" rather than justifiable homicides. These apparently are mostly cases of self-defense against assault but with no other felony (such as a robbery or rape attempt) involved. Detailed local homicide data suggest that the total number of civilian lawful defensive homicides could be four times higher than the FBI civilian justifiable homicide count.[27]

In 1998, there were 167 firearms civilian justifiable homicides reported to the FBI, compared to 379 in 1980 and 316 as recently as 1994.[28] These counts imply perhaps 668 lawful defensive killings with guns in 1998, while the number was 1264 in 1994, and 1516 in 1980. These estimates are all very rough, but regardless of which are used, defensive killings occur in less than a 10th of 1 percent of the estimated 2.5 million annual defensive gun uses.

Nonfatal gun woundings are far more frequent than fatal shootings. Cook reviewed data that indicated that only about 15 percent of gunshot wounds known to the police are fatal, implying a ratio of about 5.67 (85 percent nonfatal/15 percent) fatal nonfatal gun woundings known to the police to each fatal one.[29] However, police are unlikely to learn of many defensive woundings because the victims were criminals, some of whom were shot in the course of attempting crimes. Medical personnel are required by law to report treatment of gunshot wounds. Therefore, criminal victims of defensive gun use woundings who want to avoid a police interrogation about how they were wounded are unlikely to seek professional medical care for any but the most life-threatening wounds.[30] Consistent with this view, even among the presumably mostly noncriminal victims who reported suffering gunshot wounds in crime incidents in the NCVS in 1992 through 1998, 25.8 percent did not receive any professional medical care.[31]

The 1994 National Self-Defense Survey (NSDS) found that 8.3 percent of victims reporting a defensive gun use claimed that they had wounded the criminal, but interviews did not establish how the respondent knew that the criminal was wounded.[32] The marksmanship implied by this many woundings, compared to the number of incidents in which victims tried to shoot criminals, was implausibly high, the "hit rate" exceeding that of police officers. Therefore, it is likely that in many of these cases, victims who had fired their guns were merely guessing that they had shot the criminal. Reanalysis of data from the 1994 Police Foundation survey indicates that of eight reported woundings of criminals, the victim actually saw blood in only four cases.[33] If half of the supposed defensive woundings reported in the NSDS were actual woundings, this indicates that about 4.15 percent of the 2.55 million defensive gun uses involved a wounding, implying about 106,000 defensive woundings in 1993. But since this estimate relies on a wounding rate based on only a handful of sample cases, this estimate is subject to huge sampling error, and so should be taken with a large grain of salt.

It is unknown how many of the criminal victims of these woundings would have received professional medical care, but the share is likely to be small given that most gunshot wounds require no more medical care than a lay person can deliver. This implies that most criminals shot in the course of attempting a crime could afford to rely exclusively on self-treatment, and thereby avoid contact with police and the attendant risks of incarceration for the crime that provoked the wounding. And, of course, few of those criminals who were treated in emergency rooms or hospitals would be recorded in hospital records as victims of DGU, since medical personnel would ordinarily have no basis for knowing this, unless the patient foolishly confessed it to them. More likely, the criminals would simply be recorded as victims of "gun assaults," otherwise unspecified. Consequently, estimates of emergency room/hospital-treated wounds are of little use in estimating the frequency of defensive woundings.[34]

Keeping Loaded Guns in the Home

That defensive gun uses are common is not surprising in light of how many Americans own guns for defensive reasons and keep them ready for defensive use. A 1994 national survey found that 46 percent of gun owners have a gun *mainly* for protection, while in a 1989 survey, 62 percent said that protection from crime was at least *one* of the reasons they owned guns. A December 1993 Gallup poll indicated that 49 percent of U.S. households contained a gun, and 31 percent of U.S. adults personally owned a gun.[35] With 97,107,000 households and 192,323,000 persons age eighteen or over in 1994, these figures translate into about 47.6 million households with guns, 59.6 million adults who personally owned a gun, 27.4 million adults who owned guns mainly for protection, and about 37.0 million who owned them at least partly for protection. Thus, the 2.55 million people using guns defensively each year are only 4 percent of all who personally own guns and less than 7 percent of those who have guns for defensive reasons.

Further, many gun owners, and almost certainly a majority of those who own guns primarily for protection, keep a household gun loaded. The 1994 Police Foundation survey found that 16.4 percent of all guns, and 34.0 percent of handguns, were kept loaded and unlocked, i.e., ready for immediate use (referred to hereafter as "the ready status"). Applied to the national gun stock at the end of 1994 of 84.7 million handguns, 150.0 million long guns, and 235.7 million total guns, these figures imply 28.8 million handguns, 9.9 million long guns, and 38.7 million total guns kept loaded and unlocked at any one time. Thus, three quarters of the guns kept in this status are handguns, which are most commonly kept in the bedroom, where they are ready for nighttime use.[36]

Reanalysis of these data indicates that of handguns kept loaded and unlocked, 83.3 percent were owned by persons who said their most important reason for owning a handgun was "self-defense or protection." Very likely most, and probably nearly all, of the remaining 16.7 percent also owned handguns for self-defense, as a secondary reason (secondary motives were not addressed in this survey).[37] It is a common failing of studies of gun storage practices that they do not separately identify gun owners for whom protection is a secondary reason for owning a gun, or fail to determine reasons for ownership at all.[38] This flaw conceals or obscures the fact that virtually everyone who keeps a gun in the ready status owns the gun at least partly for defensive reasons, thereby blurring the extent to which gun owners have what they would regard as a rational reason for storing guns this way.

Some scholars have claimed that, by storing guns loaded and unlocked, many gun owners keep guns in violation of safety rules promulgated by gun owner organizations such as the National Rifle Association (NRA). They then profess to be puzzled by their finding that this "unsafe" storage pattern is as common, or more common, among those who have received formal firearms safety training.[39] This is misleading because the NRA in fact supports keeping guns unloaded and locked, *except* when the gun is kept for defensive reasons, stating that "a gun stored primarily for personal protection must be ready for immediate use. It may be kept loaded, as long as local laws permit and every precaution is taken to prevent careless or unauthorized individuals from gaining access."[40] Some writers misrepresent the NRA's position by not mentioning the exception for defensive guns.[41] Since nearly all of the guns kept in this ready status are owned for defensive reasons, this means that in fact very few gun owners violate the safety rules concerning gun storage that are promulgated by the NRA.

The most common argument against keeping guns in the ready status for self-defense is that it could lead to accidents or other violence involving guns because unauthorized persons, especially small children, could gain access to the gun. This argument is of limited relevance for several reasons. First, it is common for adolescents, especially in small towns and rural areas, to personally own guns with their parents' knowledge and approval. A member of this group would not be an "unauthorized person," but rather would be the gun's owner and thus would often be the person with the key or combination to any lock on the gun. And among adolescents who possess their own gun without a parent's knowledge (e.g., an urban gang member), access to these guns obviously could not be affected by their parents' locking and storage practices. The failure of gun owners in other households to secure their guns against theft is more likely to play a role in such an adolescent obtaining a gun.

Excluding accidents among preadolescent children (under age thirteen), there is no evidence that any significant number of misuses of guns are committed by persons gaining unauthorized access to guns. More than 99 percent of all suicides and homicides are committed by persons age thirteen or over, that is by persons old enough to own their own guns.[42] As far as we know, virtually everyone who commits an assaultive act of violence or attempts suicide with a gun, and virtually every adult or adolescent who accidentally shoots someone, had "authorized" access to the gun that was used, most commonly because it was the shooter's own gun.

Second, gun accidents among preadolescent children, which *are* likely to involve unauthorized users, are extremely rare. In the entire United States in 1996, there were only 78 FGAs involving victims under age thirteen (compared to 855 accidental deaths in this age group due to drowning, 724 due to fire, and 2,415 due to motor vehicle accidents). Analysis of 1979-1994 Mortality Detail File data indicates that 36.35 percent of FGAs involving victims under age thirteen involved a handgun (among cases with a known gun type).[43] Thus, for 1996, an estimated twenty-eight FGAs with preadolescent victims involved handguns, the type of gun that accounts for at least three quarters of guns kept in the ready status.

Third, most gun-owning households have neither children nor adolescents (and probably rarely or never have visits from youngsters). More specifically, the practice of keeping guns in the ready status is largely confined to households without children or adolescents. Data from a large-scale 1994 national survey indicated that 79 percent of U.S. households that kept at least one gun unlocked and either loaded or stored with ammunition had no children under the age of eighteen (and data from another 1994 national survey put this figure at 76 percent). Data from the 1994 Police Foundation survey indicate that only 5.4 percent of households with children under age eighteen owned guns and kept at least one gun loaded and unlocked.[44]

Further, data indicated that households with preadolescent children are only about half as likely to keep guns in the ready status as those with only adolescents.[45] Thus, perhaps 4 percent of households with preadolescent children, and perhaps 8 percent of households with only adolescents (which would roughly average out to the aforementioned 5.4 percent for households with children of any age), have guns kept loaded and unlocked. In the Police Foundation survey, among households with a gun in the ready status, 16.6 percent had children under eighteen, so a reasonable rough estimate would be that perhaps 10-14 percent had preadolescent children.[46] Thus, the risk of a resident preadolescent child obtaining access to a gun is irrelevant for 86 to 90 percent of households with guns in the ready status.

Finally, the argument is one-sided in not taking account of deaths and injuries that are prevented because a crime victim had quick access to a gun and was able to use it effectively for self-protection. We do not know how many of the 2.55 million annual defensive gun uses, or the nearly one million defensive gun uses in the home, were only possible because the victim had quick access to a gun.[47] The number is not, however, likely to be zero, in light of the fact that criminals rarely give their victims advance warning of their criminal plans, and thus time to make preparations.

To describe storing a gun in the ready status as "unsafe" implies a one-sided focus on danger to household members from the household gun, and effectively prejudges the question of whether the harm of shootings committed with the household gun by unauthorized users outweighs the benefit of quick access to guns for self-protective purposes.[48] This is unreasonable, given that it would require only a tiny fraction of the one million home defensive gun uses to involve a life saved due to quick access to a gun to counterbalance the subset of twenty-eight deaths of preadolescent children in handgun accidents that might have been caused by the gun being stored in the ready status.

In any case, there are compromise modes of storage that permit guns to be safely kept loaded, yet secured in some way—storage modes that provide both security against unauthorized access and quick access by authorized users for defensive purposes. For those who can afford to spend $150 or more, a handgun can be safely stored, in a loaded condition, inside a lockbox that can be quickly opened, but only by persons with the correct combination or key. With the better variants of these products, the user can gain access to the gun in under ten seconds, yet unauthorized users cannot gain access at all. I know of no documented case where a person was killed in an act of gun violence as a result of a lockbox being defeated. Further, the lockbox, if securely fixed to a relatively immovable object, can strongly discourage gun theft.[49]

For those who cannot afford a lockbox, locks that are placed on the gun, such as trigger locks, cable locks, and various other gun locks offer cheap, next-best alternatives. These cost as little as $10 and are also effective in preventing unauthorized use of the gun. They also have various shortcomings that could theoretically allow, or cause, accidents when used on loaded guns.[50] In the absence of evidence on whether these risks have actually resulted in real-world injuries or deaths, about all that can be said is that there is a potential risk to storing a gun loaded using the less expensive security alternatives. Nevertheless, they are clearly better than not securing the gun at all, and for many gun owners may be the only security measure that they can afford. Further, locks that go on a gun, even if they in fact render the gun unusable for unauthorized persons, may nevertheless fail to deter some gun thieves, and some gun locks do nothing to make theft physically difficult or impossible.

Given that most gun criminals acquire their guns directly or indirectly as a result of theft, probably the strongest rationale for keeping guns stored in a secure manner of some sort is to reduce gun theft and thereby reduce acquisition of guns by criminals.[51] It is far more common for violence to be committed by criminals using stolen guns than for it to be committed by persons gaining unauthorized access to guns in their own home. Therefore, arguments for keeping guns stored more securely are more sensibly grounded in efforts to reduce gun theft than in dubious efforts to persuade people of the dangers of guns kept in their own homes.

Perhaps the most prominent example of such dubious efforts is the case-control homicide study of physician Arthur Kellermann and his colleagues, who claimed that because homicide victimization was 2.8 times more likely among persons who kept guns in their homes than among persons in gunless homes, this meant that home gun ownership caused a higher risk of being murdered.[52] The more empirically supported interpretation of their findings is that the same factors that put people at greater risk of violent victimization (e.g., engaging in dangerous activities, frequenting dangerous places, or associating with dangerous people) also motivate people to acquire guns for self-protection.

The credibility of Kellermann's interpretation collapsed when it was found that his own data indicated that no more than 1.67 percent of the homicides committed in the three urban counties he studied were committed with a gun kept in the victim's home. Guns in the victim's household almost never had anything to do with his or her murder, and could not have caused a tripling of the risk of being murdered. People may well be endangered by guns possessed by dangerous people outside their own homes, but their risk of being victimized is not significantly increased by the guns kept in their own homes.[53]

Carrying Guns for Protection

Carrying firearms for protection in public places is one of the most active forms of gun use for both defensive and criminal purposes. Unlawful carrying of guns probably accounts for the majority of arrests for weapons violations, and virtually all gun crime committed in public places necessarily involves carrying of firearms by criminals. On the other hand, about 0.7 to 1.6 million defensive gun uses occur each year in public places and thus entail gun carrying.[54]

Persons who wish to have guns available for defensive purposes in public spaces must necessarily carry guns, legally or illegally, to do so. This carrying is done either on the carrier's person (e.g., in a holster, purse, etc.) or in a vehicle. The latter is more common than the former, possibly because legal controls are less strict over carrying in a vehicle than on the person.[55] The gun is usually carried concealed, a practice facilitated by the fact that 93 percent of the guns carried for self-protection are handguns.[56] While there are no sound data on the question, almost certainly the vast majority of these guns are carried loaded. Thus, protective gun carrying is typically concealed carrying of a loaded handgun.

The NSDS indicated that 3.8 percent of American adults carry a gun on their person for protection, 6.6 percent carry in their vehicles, 2.1 percent do both, and a total of 8.8 percent do either kind of gun carrying for self-defense. The mean number of days carried each year per carrier was 138 days of carrying on the person and 146 days of carrying in a vehicle (figures that could overlap due to days on which people did both kinds of carrying). For the entire adult population, there were nearly a billion person-days of carrying on the person and 1.8 billion person-days of carrying in a vehicle in 1992. One implication of these figures is that the NSDS estimate of one million annual defensive gun uses in public places represents less than one in a thousand of the number of instances of carrying guns.[57]

Because criminals are especially likely to become crime victims themselves, they have especially strong reasons to carry guns for self-protection, as well as for criminal purposes. Further, most gun carrying by Americans is clearly unlawful. Although national surveys indicate that 5 to 11 percent of U.S. adults carry guns outside their home for protection, only about 1 percent of U.S adults have a permit to carry firearms.

Nevertheless, most people who carry guns for protection are not criminals other than in the sense that they are violating gun laws, and nearly all instances of gun carrying are done without any intent to commit a crime, apart from the unlawful carrying itself. This can be inferred from the facts that even the highest estimates of gun crime indicate that there are less than a million violent crimes committed with guns each year, many of which did not involve carrying in public, while the NSDS indicated that there are over a billion person-days of gun carrying for protection each year. Thus, less than one in a thousand instances of gun carrying results in a gun crime. Unless criminals almost never follow criminal intentions with criminal actions, only a tiny fraction of instances of gun carrying are done with the intention of committing a violent crime.

This has important implications for the enforcement of laws forbidding gun carrying. If the vast majority of instances of gun carrying are for exclusively defensive purposes, and less than one in one thousand will result in a gun crime, this implies that practically none of the gun carriers that police officers might randomly stop and frisk in public places would be criminals on their way to or from a crime. Only to the extent that police are able to somehow distinguish, presumably based on visible cues, gun carriers with criminal intentions from gun carriers with purely noncriminal intentions, will a nonnegligible share of street searches be of criminals on their way to or from a gun crime. Thus, few crimes are directly disrupted or prevented by the arrest of the prospective offender for unlawful carrying.

Instead, the value of enforcement of carry laws is more likely to lie in its deterrent effect on carrying of guns by criminals. Even with a low "batting average" in identifying criminal gun carriers, with enough searches police can generate significant numbers of carry detections and arrests in high crime areas. While most carrying, even among criminals, is for defensive reasons, it is also true that most gun crimes, because they do not occur in the offender's home, necessarily involve carrying a gun through public spaces. Thus, reducing gun carrying by criminals, however achieved, could have significant crime control value.

The problem is that enforcement of carry laws will deter carrying among noncriminals and criminals alike. Indeed, even when police try to avoid arresting "otherwise innocent persons" found in unlawful possession of a firearm in a public place, many of those arrested have no prior criminal record.[58]

Thus, to indiscriminantly deter all gun carrying, regardless of whose carrying is deterred, implies deterring the gun carrying that makes possible effective defensive uses of guns, as well as deterring the carrying that facilitates crime. And if criminals are less likely to be deterred from carrying than noncriminals, enforcement of carry laws would reduce defensive uses of guns in public places more than criminal uses. Since the number of defensive gun uses in public places (approximately one million) is at least as large as the number of gun crimes that involve carrying guns, this cannot be dismissed as a trivial consideration.[59]

Kleck and Gertz suggest that one way out of this dilemma is to make a sharper distinction among criminal and noncriminal gun carriers, by making it easier for noncriminal adults to get legal permits to carry guns.[60] Then, when police arrested people for unlawful, i.e., unlicensed, carrying, a larger share of the arrestees would be criminals in some significant sense, beyond their status as gun law violators. Likewise, purely defensive carrying would not be deterred as much since a larger share of it would be lawful and thus not subject to arrest.

Implementation of this policy is effectively already underway in over thirty states, inasmuch as that many states now have nondiscretionary "shall issue" laws that require authorities to grant carry permits to resident adult applicants without criminal records. Some critics feared that expanding access to carry permits would increase gun violence in public places, but evaluations of these laws generally indicate either no impact on crime rates or beneficial effects.[61]

Further, permit revocation data indicate that there is virtually no violent gun crime among permit holders that could be attributable to licensed carrying. There is little foundation for the fear that these laws would result in many carry permit holders committing violent crimes in public with their guns. In the first thirteen years after Florida passed its carry law, of 697,553 licenses issued (including renewals), only 123 had been revoked as a result of conviction for a violent crime involving a gun (about 9.6 per year), representing about one-twentieth of one percent of the 248,049 permits valid as of June 30, 2000. Further, no permit holder has committed a criminal homicide resulting from gun carrying authorized by the permit.[62]

While the carry law evaluations generally show no impact on crime rates, none directly assessed the impact of the laws on rates of defensive carrying or use of guns. It is possible that they increase the number of defensive gun uses in public, and thereby increase the share of crimes that victims successfully disrupt, and thus the number of crimes in which they are able to avoid injury or property loss. A lower fraction of crimes resulting in injury or property loss would not show up in ordinary crime rate statistics.

Psychological Effects of Keeping Guns for Protection

If some people get guns in response to crime or the prospect of being victimized in the future, does gun ownership have any reassuring effects? Once a gun is acquired, does it make its owner feel safer? Reducing fear would be an intangible benefit distinct from the objective utility that a gun has when it is actually used for defensive purposes.

A 1989 national survey of U.S. gun owners asked them: "Does having a gun in your house make you feel more safe from crime, less safe, or doesn't it make any difference?" While 42 percent of the gun owners felt more safe, only 2 percent felt less safe, and the rest said it made no difference.[63] Since only 27 percent of the owners had a gun mainly for protection from crime, and only 62 percent had a gun even partially for protection from crime, it is not surprising that some owners felt having a gun made no difference in their feelings of safety. It presumably was not supposed to make any difference, since their guns were owned for recreational reasons. Assuming that those who felt safer fell largely among those 62 percent (or 27 percent) of owners who had guns for protection, one can infer that most defensive gun owners feel safer from crime as a result of their gun ownership.

A 1990 national survey directly confirmed this. Among persons whose primary reason for owning a gun was self-defense, 89 percent replied yes to the question "Do you feel safer because you have a gun at home?" Among gun owners who did not feel safer, 96 percent were persons whose primary reason for owning was something other than defense.[64] When asked: "Overall, do you feel comfortable with a gun in your house or are you sometimes afraid of it?" 92 percent of gun owners in the *Time*/CNN poll said that they were comfortable, 6 percent were sometimes afraid, and 2 percent were not sure.[65]

Gun owners also believe that gun ownership actually makes them safer. For example, in a national survey conducted in January 1981, respondents were asked: "How do you feel about having a gun in your house? Do you think it makes things safer or do you think it makes things more dangerous?" This question wording differed from that of the CNN/*Time* and Mauser polls in that it focused on the respondent's beliefs concerning the actual effect of guns on their safety, rather than how gun ownership made them feel. Among respondents in gun owning households giving valid responses, 58 percent felt having a gun in their house "makes things safer," 30 percent felt things were about the same, and 11 percent felt it made things more dangerous.[66] In sum, most gun owners, including many who do not even have a gun for defensive reasons, feel comfortable with guns, feel safer from crime because of them, and believe their guns actually make them safer.

Finally, even among those who do not personally own guns but live in a household with guns, few feel less safe because of the guns. In the 1994 Police Foundation survey, only 4.8 percent of gunless residents of gun households felt "not at all safe" or "not very safe" "knowing that someone in your household has a gun."[67]

It has been claimed that higher rates of gun ownership reduce community feelings of safety, based on a single survey's finding that most people responded "less safe" to the question "Thinking specifically about guns, if more people in your community were to acquire guns, would that make you feel more safe, less safe, or the same?"[68] The problem with this question is that it does not distinguish between more guns among criminals and more guns among noncriminals. As far as one can tell from these ambiguous results, everyone who responded "less safe" was exclusively concerned with increases among criminals or other high-risk subsets of the population.

In any case, this conclusion depended on respondents' assessments of a hypothetical (as well as ill-defined) future situation. In contrast, another study directly assessed the impact of actual gun ownership rates on fear of crime among a nationally representative sample of urban residents, estimating the association between survey measures of fear and gun levels in the city in which each respondent lived. The findings indicated that community gun ownership rates, as distinct from the individual's own gun ownership, reduce the fear of walking in one's own neighborhood at night, and have no effect on feelings of safety in one's home. These patterns prevailed among both gun owners and nonowners.[69] This combination of findings makes sense, since people might benefit from other people's possession and defensive use of guns when outside their homes, but are unlikely to benefit from other people's gun ownership when in their own homes.

These results support the view that the Hemenway findings were a reflection of a narrow fear of criminals having guns, and not of fear generated by higher gun ownership levels in the community as a whole. In sum, research indicates that gun ownership not only makes gun owners feel safer, but also may indirectly reduce some kinds of fear of crime among nonowners.

The Nonsense Ratio

When gun control advocates and public health scholar/advocates discuss ownership of guns for defensive purposes, they often bring up one of the oddest statistics in the gun control debate. In 1975 four physicians published an article based on data derived from medical examiner files in Cuyahoga County (Cleveland). They noted that during the period of 1958 to 1973, there were 148 fatal gun accidents (78 percent of them in the home) and 23 "burglars, robbers or intruders who were not relatives or acquaintances" killed by people using guns to defend their homes. They stated that there were six times as many home fatal gun accidents as burglars killed. (This appears to have been a miscomputation—the authors counted all 148 accidental deaths in the numerator, instead of just the 115 occurring in the home.) On the basis of these facts, the authors concluded that "guns in the home are more dangerous than useful to the homeowner and his family who keep them to protect their persons and property" and that "the possession of firearms by civilians appears to be a dangerous and ineffective means of self-protection."[70]

These conclusions were a complete non sequitur. The authors presented no evidence of any kind bearing on the issue of whether guns are "ineffective" means of self-protection, no counts of defensive uses, and no estimates of the fraction of defensive uses that prevented completion of crimes or resulted in injury. Even concerning the accidental gun deaths, the authors did not establish that any of the accidents occurred in connection with defensive uses or even that the guns involved were owned for defensive reasons. The connection between the accidents and defensive gun ownership was simply assumed rather than demonstrated.

The authors clearly treated the six-to-one ratio as if it were somehow a cost-benefit ratio, a comparison that could say something about the relative benefits and risks of defensive gun ownership. The ratio cannot serve such a purpose. The numerator is not a meaningful measure of risk for the average gun-owning household, and the denominator has no bearing at all on the defensive benefits of keeping a gun. Gun accidents are largely concentrated in a very small, high-risk subset of the population.[71] For everyone else, the risks of a fatal gun accident are negligible, so the population-wide accident rate is an exaggeration of the risk borne by the typical gun-owning household.

More importantly, the number of burglars killed does not in any way serve as a measure of the defensive benefit of keeping a gun. As scholar Barry Bruce-Briggs wryly noted, "The measure of the effectiveness of self-defense is not in the number of bodies piled up on doorsteps."[72] Thus, the one protection-related event the authors did count is not even itself a benefit. Defensive gun owners do not have guns for the purpose of getting a chance to "bag a burglar." Being forced to kill another human being, burglar or not, causes psychic trauma that may endure for years. To assess defensive benefits would entail estimating the number of burglars captured, frightened off, deterred from attempting burglaries, or displaced to unoccupied premises where they could not injure any victims. The authors measured none of these things. As previously noted, well under 0.1 percent of defensive gun uses involve a criminal being killed, so a count of justifiable homicides covers a minuscule share of defensive gun uses beneficial to crime victims.

This study was unwittingly replicated eleven years later by two other physicians who apparently were unaware of the Cleveland et al. study (or at least did not cite it) or of the criticism to which it had been subjected. This later analysis had all the same problems as its predecessor, measured no beneficial uses of guns, used the same specious reasoning, and arrived at the same non sequitur conclusion: "The advisability of keeping firearms in the home for protection must be questioned."[73]

Bruce-Briggs described this sort of study as "ingeniously specious" and briefly dismissed it.[74] Most serious gun scholars ignore these studies (e.g., the massive review by Wright et al. [1983] did not mention the Rushforth et al. study at all), and even the strongly procontrol Philip Cook conceded that the nonsense ratios entail a "strange comparison," but they are favorites of procontrol propagandists and scholars who publish in medical journals. Those who have uncritically cited the Kellermann and physician Donald Reay evidence as if it were relevant to an assessment of the relative risks and benefits of keeping guns for self-defense also include criminologists David McDowall and Brian Wiersema, as well as Reiss and Roth.[75]

The benefit of defensive gun ownership that would be parallel to lives lost to guns would be lives saved by defensive use of guns. However, it is impossible to directly count lives saved, so it may never be possible to form a meaningful ratio of genuinely comparable quantities. Nevertheless, it is worth considering what a more meaningful comparison of lives lost and saved due to guns might look like. In 1993, there were 39,595 deaths involving guns, including homicides, suicides, fatal gun accidents, deaths by legal intervention, and deaths where it was undetermined whether the injury was accidentally or purposely inflicted—the highest gun death total in U.S. history.[76] Results from the NSDS indicated that in 1992 there were about 340,000 to 400,000 defensive uses of guns where the user would state, if asked, that the use almost certainly saved a life.[77] Even if as little as a tenth of these subjective assessments reflected objective reality, the number of life-saving defensive uses of guns would equal the number of gun-related deaths.

Further, a meaningful comparison would take account of the fact that many deaths involving guns would have occurred even in the absence of the guns, so the gun death count is not a count of deaths that are attributable to guns, i.e., that would have been avoided had guns not been available. That number would necessarily be smaller than the number of deaths in which a gun was used. For example, 57 percent of gun deaths in 1998 were suicides, and most gun suicides would probably occur even if a gun were not available.[78] Conversely, no one can be sure a death would have occurred had a victim not used a gun defensively, so we cannot obtain a conclusive count of lives saved by defensive uses of guns either. The preceding discussion serves only to indicate what a more meaningful comparison of comparable quantities would require, and to show that one cannot dismiss out of hand the possibility that gun use saves as many, or more, lives as it takes. In contrast, the nonsense ratios computed by Kellermann and Reay and their predecessors have no bearing whatsoever on the relative merits of keeping a gun in the home for self-defense.

The Nature of Defensive Gun Use

The National Self-Defense Survey provides details on exactly who is involved in defensive gun uses and what they do in those incidents.[79] The data support a number of broad generalizations. First, much like the typical gun crime, many of these cases were relatively undramatic and minor compared to fictional portrayals of gun use. Only 24 percent of the gun defenders reported firing the gun, and only 8 percent reported wounding an adversary. This parallels the fact that criminals shot at victims in only 17 percent of the gun crimes reported in the NCVS and inflicted gunshot wounds on victims in only 3 percent of the incidents.[80] Further, low as it is, even an 8 percent wounding rate is probably too high, for reasons previously discussed—in only about 4 percent of defensive gun uses did the victim claim to have wounded the criminal and to have seen the offender's blood, allowing the victim to be confident that the criminal was wounded.

About 37 percent of these incidents occurred in the defender's home, with another 36 percent near the defender's home. This implies that the remaining 27 percent occurred in locations where the defender must have carried a gun through public spaces. Adding in the 36 percent that occurred near the defender's home and that may or may not have entailed public carrying, 27 to 63 percent of the defensive gun uses entailed gun carrying.

Guns were most commonly used for defense against burglary, assault, and robbery. Cases of "mutual combat," where it would be hard to tell who is the aggressor, or where both parties are aggressors, would be some subset of the 30 percent of cases where assault was the crime involved. However, only 19 percent of all defensive gun use cases involved *only* assault and no other crime where victim and offender are more easily distinguished. Further, only 11 percent of all defensive gun use cases involved only assault and a male defender (there was no information on sex of offenders); some subset of these could have been male-on-male fights. Thus, very few of the reported defensive gun uses fit the "mutual combat" model of a fight between two males, where both parties are at once victim and aggressor. This is not to say that such crimes where a gun-using combatant might claim that his use was defensive are rare, but rather that few of them are in this sample. Instead, cases where it is hard to say who is victim and who is aggressor apparently constitute an additional set of questionable defensive gun uses lying largely outside of the universe of more one-sided events that survey respondents are willing to report.

The kinds of incidents that respondents are willing to report as defensive gun uses to interviewers tend to be particularly clear-cut crimes, i.e., the kinds of events in which it is clear that some sort of crime was being committed and in which it is clear which combatant was the victim and which was the offender. Ambiguous or borderline cases, no matter how frequently they may in fact occur, contributed almost nothing to the NSDS estimate of defensive gun use frequency.

One reason crime victims are willing to take the risks of forcefully resisting the offender is that most offenders faced by victims choosing such an action are unarmed, or armed only with less lethal weapons. Relatively few victims try to use a gun against adversaries who are themselves armed with guns—offenders were armed with some kind of weapon in 48 percent of defensive gun use incidents, but had guns in only 18 percent of them. On the other hand, the NCVS data indicated that crime victims who use guns are more likely to face gun-armed offenders than victims adopting other strategies.

The distribution of guns used in defensive gun uses is similar to that of guns used by criminals. NCVS and police-based data indicate that about 90 percent of guns used in crime are handguns, and the NSDS indicated that 80 percent of the guns used by victims were handguns.[81]

Incidents where victims use a gun defensively are almost never gunfights where both parties shoot at one another. Defenders fired their guns in only 24 percent of the crimes and shot at their adversaries in only 16 percent of the incidents. Likewise, the offender shot at the defender in only 4.5 percent of the cases. Consequently, it is not surprising that only 3 percent of all of the incidents involved both parties shooting at each other. More typically, crime incidents are asymmetric—only one party has a gun, and that party dominates the incident and determines its outcome.

The offenders were strangers to the defender in nearly three quarters of the incidents. This may partly reflect the effects of sample censoring. Just as the NCVS appears to detect less than a tenth of domestic violence incidents, the NSDS probably missed some cases of defensive gun use against family members and other intimates.[82]

While victims face multiple offenders in only about 23 percent of *all* violent crimes, the victims in the NSDS sample who used guns faced multiple offenders in 53 percent of the incidents.[83] This mirrors the observation that criminals who use guns are also more likely than unarmed criminals to face multiple victims.[84] Having a gun allows either criminals or victims to successfully confront a larger number of adversaries. Many victims facing multiple offenders probably would not resist at all if they were without a gun or some other weapon. Another possible interpretation is that some victims will resort to a defensive measure as potentially consequential as wielding a gun only if they face the most desperate of circumstances.

Another way of assessing how serious these incidents appeared to the victims is to ask them how potentially fatal the encounter was. Respondents were asked: "If you had *not* used a gun for protection in this incident, how likely do you think it is that you or someone else would have been *killed?* Would you say almost certainly not, probably not, might have, probably would have, or almost certainly would have been killed?" About 15.7 percent of the respondents stated that they or someone else "almost certainly would have" been killed, with another 14.2 percent responding "probably would have" and 16.2 percent responding "might have." Thus, nearly half claimed that they perceived some significant chance of someone being killed in the incident had they not used a gun defensively.

It should be emphasized that these are just stated perceptions of participants, not objective assessments of actual probabilities. Further, the assessments were offered only because interviewers asked for them, not because respondents volunteered them. Crime victims obviously do not have the ability to know how crimes would have turned out had they behaved differently, and respondents in the NSDS did not claim to have such abilities. Rather, they were merely responding helpfully to a necessarily hypothetical question posed to them by the interviewers. Some defenders also might have been bolstering the justification for their actions by exaggerating the seriousness of the threat they faced.

Who Is Involved in Defensive Gun Use?

What do the NSDS data tell us about the kinds of people who use guns for self-protection and how they might differ from other people? Nearly 40 percent of the people reporting a defensive gun use claimed they did not personally own a gun at the time of the interview. Some might have used someone else's gun, while others may have gotten rid of a gun since the defensive gun use incident. About a quarter of the defenders reported that they did not even have a gun in their household at the time of the interview, irrespective of who it belonged to. Some gun owners were probably falsely denying their ownership of a gun.

Gun defenders are more likely to carry a gun for self-protection, consistent with the large share of defensive gun uses that occurred away from the defender's home. They were also obviously more likely to have been a victim of a burglary or robbery in the past year, a finding which is a tautology for those respondents whose defensive gun use was in connection with a robbery or burglary committed against them in the preceding year. Gun defenders were also more likely to have been a victim of an assault since becoming an adult.

Spending time away from home at night places people at greater risk of victimization, but defenders spend no more of their time like this than other gun owners, and these two groups spend only slightly more time like this than those who do not own guns.

Defenders are more likely to believe that a person must "be prepared to defend their homes against crime and violence" rather than letting "the police take care of that," compared to either gun owners without a defensive gun use or nonowners. Whether this attitude is cause or consequence of defenders' defensive actions is impossible to determine with these data.

It might be suspected that some supposedly defensive uses of guns were actually the aggressive acts of vengeful vigilantes intent on punishing criminals. If this were true of gun defenders as a group, one would expect them to be more supportive of punitive measures like the death penalty. In fact, those who reported a defensive gun use in the NSDS were no more likely to support the death penalty than those without such an experience, and were somewhat *less* likely to do so compared with gun owners as a group. Similarly, gun defenders were no more likely than others to endorse the view that the courts in their area do not deal harshly enough with criminals.

Perhaps the most surprising finding of the NSDS was the large share of reported defensive gun uses that involved women. Both because of their lower victimization rates and lower gun ownership rates, one would expect women to account for far less than half of defensive gun uses. Nevertheless, 46 percent of the reported defensive gun uses involved women. This finding could be an artifact of males reporting a lower fraction of their defensive gun uses than women. If a larger share of men's allegedly defensive uses of guns were actually partly aggressive actions, this would imply that a larger share would be at the "illegitimate" end of the scale and thus less likely to be reported to interviewers. Further, men may be less likely than women to report their defensive gun uses because the former believe they are more likely to be prosecuted for their actions. Consequently, although women may well use guns defensively as often as this survey indicates, males may account for a still larger number, and larger share, of defensive gun uses than the NSDS data indicate.

A disproportionately large share of defenders are black or Hispanic, compared to the general population, and especially in comparison to gun owners. Likewise, defenders are disproportionately likely to reside in big cities compared to other people, and especially so when compared to gun owners, who are disproportionately from rural areas and small towns. Finally, defenders are disproportionately likely to be single. These patterns are all probably at least partly due to the higher rates of crime victimization among minorities, big city dwellers, and single persons.[85] On the other hand, defenders are not especially likely to be poor. The effect of higher victimization among poor people may be cancelled out by the lower gun ownership levels among the poor.[86]

Deterrence of Crime Due to Fear of Gun-Armed Victims

To deter a crime means to cause a criminal to refrain from even attempting the crime, due to fear of some negative consequence. If there is a deterrent effect of defensive gun ownership and use, it should be facilitated by a criminal being able to realistically anticipate a potential victim using a gun to disrupt the crime, and possibly injure or even kill the criminal. The types of crimes most likely to be influenced by this possibility are crimes occurring in homes—where victims are most likely to have access to a gun—and in the kinds of business establishments where proprietors keep guns. In line with the preceding information about where defensive uses commonly occur, crimes such as assault in the home, residential burglary, and retail store robbery would seem to be the most likely candidates to be deterred. About one in eight residential burglaries occurs while a household member is present, and, by definition, all robberies, rapes, assaults, and homicides involve direct contact between a victim and an offender.[87] To be sure, in many of these incidents the offender has the initiative, often taking the victim by surprise, and the situations often develop too quickly for victims to get to their guns. On the other hand, the most common single location for violent crimes, especially homicides and assaults between intimates, is in or near the home of the victim or the home of both victim and offender, where access to a gun would be easier.[88]

In 1993 there were twice as many defensive gun uses against violent offenders and burglars as arrests for violent crime and burglary—arrests numbered about 1,160,000 in the United States in 1993. Being threatened or shot at by a gun-wielding victim is thus a more likely consequence of such criminal activity than arrest, and far more likely than conviction or incarceration. This is not surprising since there are only about 600,000 police officers in the United States, fewer than a quarter of whom are on duty at any one time.[89] There are, on the other hand, tens of millions of civilians who have immediate access to firearms and are well motivated to disrupt crimes directed at themselves, their families, or their property.

There is direct, albeit not conclusive, evidence on the deterrent effects of victim gun use from surveys of imprisoned criminals. Wright and Rossi interviewed 1,874 felons in prisons in ten states and asked about their encounters with armed victims and their attitudes toward the risks of such encounters. Among felons who reported ever committing a violent crime or a burglary, 42 percent said they had run into a victim who was armed with a gun, 38 percent reported they had been scared off, shot at, wounded, or captured by an armed victim (these were combined in the original survey question), and 43 percent said they had at some time in their lives decided not to commit a crime because they knew or believed the victim was carrying a gun.[90] Note that the 38 percent of felons who were scared off, etc., by an armed victim are necessarily a subset of the 42 percent who encountered an armed victim. This implies that 90 percent (38/42=.90) of the prisoners who had encountered an armed victim had been scared off, shot, wounded or captured at least once by such a victim.

Concerning the felons' attitudes toward armed victims, 56 percent agreed with the statement that "most criminals are more worried about meeting an armed victim than they are about running into the police," 58 percent agreed that "a store owner who is known to keep a gun on the premises is not going to get robbed very often," and 52 percent agreed that "a criminal is not going to mess around with a victim he knows is armed with a gun." Only 27 percent agreed that committing a "crime against an armed victim is an exciting challenge."[91] Further, 45 percent of those who had encountered an armed victim reported that they thought regularly or often about the possibility of getting shot by their victims. Even among those without such an encounter the figure was 28 percent. These results agree with findings from informal surveys of prisoners.[92]

Clearly, prisoners are biased samples of criminals and prospective criminals, since their presence in prison itself indicates that deterrence was not completely effective with them. In light of this bias, prison survey results supporting a deterrence hypothesis are all the more impressive, given that the most deterrable criminals and those deterred from crime altogether will not be included in prison samples. Further, being "scared off by a victim" is not the sort of thing a violent criminal is likely to want to admit, especially in prison, where maintaining a fearless image can be critical to survival. Thus, incidents of this nature may well have been underreported. These results, therefore, may reflect a minimal baseline picture of the deterrent potential of victim gun use.

There is no serious multivariate research directly bearing on the deterrent effects of civilian gun ownership or defensive use. There is research indirectly addressing the issue by assessing the impact of laws permitting more citizens to carry concealed guns in public, but this work does not directly measure gun ownership, defensive use, or even actual rates of gun carrying (as distinct from the minority of gun carrying authorized by a permit). Economists John Lott and David Mustard found that crime rates declined in states with right-to-carry laws after the laws went into effect, to a greater extent than in states without the laws, and attributed these decreases in a greater perception of risk from victims among prospective offenders. Deterrence was necessarily very indirectly inferred, and crime decreases that might have been attributable to other factors were attributed to unmeasured changes in criminal perceptions of risk.[93] Nevertheless, it remains plausible that, given the considerable publicity surrounding these legal changes, criminal perceptions of risk were altered and that this reduced crime rates.

In addition, there is mostly anecdotal evidence concerning crime trends before and after incidents in which civilian gun training programs were implemented or guns were used for self-defense, followed by substantial news media coverage. Highly publicized incidents of this sort arguably can be expected to produce sharp changes among prospective criminals in awareness of the risks of encountering an armed victim, just as might highly publicized changes in law that allow more prospective crime victims to carry guns in public.

For example, highly publicized programs to train citizens in gun use amount to "gun awareness" programs that could conceivably produce sharp changes in prospective criminals' awareness of gun ownership among potential victims. If citizen gun ownership does exert any deterrent effect, then this effect should be intensified during these episodes of victim gun-related publicity. Thus, an ongoing, pervasive deterrent effect which would ordinarily be invisible becomes potentially detectable through examination of trends in deterrable crimes. Further, unlike gradual increases in mass gun ownership, the impact of these programs can be examined because they have specific times of onset and specific spans of operation which make it easier to say when they might be most likely to affect crime. Nevertheless, the limited work in this area has precisely the same shortcomings as work on permissive concealed carry laws, as well as being based on far more circumscribed bodies of data.

From October 1966 to March 1967 the Orlando (Florida) police department trained more than 2,500 women to use guns.[94] Organized in response to demands from citizens worried about a sharp increase in rape, this was an unusually large and highly publicized program. It received several front page stories in the local daily newspaper, the *Orlando Sentinel*, a cosponsor of the program. An analysis of Orlando crime trends showed that the rape rate decreased by 88 percent in 1967, compared to 1966, a decrease far larger than in any previous one-year period. The rape rate remained constant in the rest of Florida and in the United States. Interestingly, the only other crime to show a substantial drop was burglary. Thus, the crime targeted decreased, and the offense most likely to occur where victims have access to guns, burglary, also decreased.[95]

Criminologist Gary Green interpreted the results of the Orlando study as indicating a partial "spillover" or displacement of rape from the city to nearby areas, i.e., a mixture of absolute deterrence of some rapes and a shift in location of others. Green also suggested that the apparent rape decrease might have been due to allegedly irregular crime recording practices of the Orlando city police department, but did not present any evidence of changes in police reporting practices over this period, beyond the sharp changes in the rape rates themselves.[96]

Criminologists David McDowall, Alan Lizotte, and Brian Wiersema applied Box-Tiao ARIMA methods to the annual Orlando rape data. Despite their claims to the contrary, fourteen time points are not sufficient for purposes of diagnosis and model identification, and it is generally considered inappropriate to apply ARIMA methods to such short series.[97] Further, such a small sample makes it unlikely that any but the most extreme causal effects could pass a significance test. As the authors blandly put it: "small numbers of observations imply . . . low power against a maintained hypothesis."[98] In this case, a more informative observation would have been that even the largest possible causal effect, i.e., the total elimination of rape in Orlando, would not have been statistically significant. Since Orlando averaged fourteen rapes per year before the training program, the authors' impact parameter of -11.3846 implied an *81* percent drop (-11.3846/14=-0.81), virtually identical to the simple before-and-after percentage drop of 88 percent), yet this huge decrease was statistically insignificant, largely due to the authors' very small sample. A parameter of -14, implying a 100 percent drop, would also have been insignificant.

Given this, the purpose of applying significance tests in this analysis was hard to discern. The authors stated that the observed crime changes "could easily be attributed to chance" (p. 504), by which they apparently meant that there was at least a 5 percent chance of this. Since the series was not selected by a random chance selection process, it is unclear exactly what chance process the authors thought produced the huge drops in rape. If the significance test result is set aside as inappropriate or unimportant, then the main finding of McDowall et al. was that the Orlando program was indeed associated with a huge (81 percent) drop in rape, the ARIMA results confirming the conclusions of the earlier study.[99] Interestingly, in a previous study, when a statistically insignificant finding supported a hypothesis they favored, McDowall and Loftin favorably cited and accepted the finding as relevant and supportive, with no emphasis on the significance of the test results.[100]

A much smaller firearms training program for business operators was conducted with 138 people from September through November of 1967 by the Kansas City (Missouri) police, in response to retail businessmen's concerns about store robberies.[101] The city had a population of 507,000, so the per capita participation rate was less than 1/90th of that achieved in Orlando.[102] Nevertheless, results from the Kansas City program support the hypothesis that the program caused crime rates to be lower than they otherwise would have been. While the frequency of robbery increased sharply from 1967 to 1968 by 35 percent in the rest of Missouri, 20 percent in the region, and 30 percent in the United States, it essentially leveled off in Kansas City and declined by 13 percent in surrounding areas, even though robberies had been increasing in the five years prior to the training program and continued to increase again in 1968. Thus, the upward trend showed a distinct interruption in the year immediately following the program.

This cannot be attributed to some general improvement in conditions generating robbery rates elsewhere in the nation, region, or state, since robbery rates were increasing elsewhere. Nor can it be attributed to improvements in conditions producing violent crime in general in Kansas City, since robbery was the only violent crime to level off. Something occurred in the Kansas City area in the 1967-1968 period that caused an upward trend in robberies to level off, something that was not occurring in other places and that was specifically related to robbery. Interestingly, Kansas City also experienced a leveling off in its sharply upward trend in burglary, suggesting a possible "byproduct" deterrent effect like that suggested by the Orlando data.[103]

The finding of no change in robberies in Kansas City, while robberies were increasing in control areas, suggests that the training program had a "dampening" effect, preventing the city from experiencing the increases occurring elsewhere. McDowall et al. (1991) confirmed these findings with ARIMA methods (pp. 548-9), yet concluded that they indicated "no effect."[104] Interestingly, two of the authors (McDowall and Wiersema), when faced with an essentially identical combination of findings in another study (no significant change in the target crime, combined with significant increases in control series), concluded that the intervention had a "dampening effect."[105] The most obvious difference is that the intervention they felt had a dampening effect was a gun control law. Applying a more consistent set of interpretive standards, the McDowall et al. Kansas City results confirmed those of the earlier study.

The two gun training episodes are not unique. They resemble instances of crime drops following gun training programs elsewhere, including decreases in grocery robberies in Detroit after a grocer's organization began gun clinics, and decreases in retail store robberies in Highland Park, Michigan, attributed to "gun-toting merchants."[106]

Awareness of the risks of confronting an armed victim may also be increased by highly publicized individual instances of defensive gun use. After Bernhard Goetz used a handgun to wound four robbers on a New York City subway train on December 22, 1984, subway robberies decreased by 43 percent in the next week, compared to the two weeks prior to the incident, and decreased in the following two months by 19 percent, compared to the same period in the previous year, even though nonrobbery subway crime increased and subway robberies had been increasing prior to the shootings. However, because New York City transit police also increased the number of officers on the subway trains immediately after the shootings, any impact uniquely attributable to the Goetz gun use was confounded with potential effects of the increase in numbers of officers.[107]

The hypothesis of deterrent effects of civilian gun ownership is also supported by the experience of Kennesaw, Georgia, a suburb of Atlanta with a 1980 population of 5,095.[108] To demonstrate their disapproval of a ban on handgun ownership passed in Morton Grove, Illinois, the Kennesaw city council passed a city ordinance requiring heads of household to keep at least one firearm in their homes. The step was consciously symbolic, as only a token fine of $50 was provided as a penalty, citizens could exempt themselves simply by stating that they conscientiously objected to gun possession, and there was no active attempt to enforce the law by inspecting homes. It is doubtful that the law substantially increased household gun ownership; the mayor of Kennesaw guessed that "about 85 percent of Kennesaw households already possessed firearms before the ordinance was passed."[109] Instead, the significance of the ordinance and the associated publicity is that they presumably increased the awareness among criminals of the prevalence of guns in Kennesaw homes.

In the seven months immediately following passage of the ordinance (March 15, 1982, to October 31, 1982), there were only five residential burglaries reported to police, compared to forty-five in the same period in the previous year, an 89 percent decrease.[110] This drop was far in excess of the modest 10.4 percent decrease in the burglary rate experienced by Georgia as a whole from 1981 to 1982, the 6.8 percent decrease for south Atlantic states, the 9.6 percent decrease for the nation, and the 7.1 percent decrease for cities under 10,000 population.[111]

This decrease, however, is not conclusive evidence of a deterrent effect, since small towns have small numbers of crimes and it is not clear that any deterrent effect, no matter how large, would be detectable in an area with monthly crime trends as erratic as those found in small towns. For example, an ARIMA analysis of monthly burglary data found no evidence of a statistically significant drop in burglary in Kennesaw.[112] This study, however, was both flawed and largely irrelevant to the deterrence hypothesis. The Kennesaw ordinance pertained solely to home gun ownership, and thus its deterrent effects, if any, would be evident with *residential* burglaries. This study blurred any such effects by using a data source that lumped residential and nonresidential burglaries together. The difference between the two numbers apparently can be very large—the authors report thirty-two total burglaries for 1985, while a *New York Times* article (which the authors cited) reported only eleven "house burglaries" for that year.[113] The authors also used raw numbers of burglaries rather than rates. Kennesaw experienced a 70 percent increase in population from 1980 to 1987. Burglary increases due to sheer population growth would obscure any crime-reducing effects of the ordinance. The effects of these two errors can be very large, as indicated below:[114]

Raw Numbers or Rate?	Total Burglaries or Just Residential?	Percent Change 1981-82	Percent Change 1981-86
Raw	Total	-35	-41
Rate[a]	Total	-40	-56
Raw	Residential[b]	-53	-80
Rate[a]	Residential[b]	-57	-85

a. Based on linear interpolation of 1980 and 1987 population figures

b. Based on "house burglaries" reported in the aforementioned *New York Times* article.

Thus the authors' methods apparently obscured much of the decrease in the residential burglary rate—an 85 percent reduction in the residential burglary rate was buried inside a far more modest 35 percent reduction in the raw number of total burglaries.

Also, the use of total burglary data ignores the implications of an extended discussion (immediately following Kleck's Kennesaw discussion, cited by McDowall et al.), in which it was argued that a major effect of residential gun ownership may be to displace burglars from occupied homes to less dangerous targets (see also next section).[115] Since nonresidential targets, especially stores and other businesses left unoccupied at night, would fit into the latter category, one would expect a displacement from residential burglaries to nonresidential burglaries, as well as a shift from occupied residences to unoccupied ones. Thus, the hypothesized deterrent effect on occupied residential burglary could occur with no impact at all on total burglaries. Consequently, the exercise by McDowall and his colleagues has no clear relevance to the gun deterrence hypothesis.

McDowall et al. tried to test the gun deterrence hypothesis with data pertaining to the impact of handgun bans passed in two Chicago suburbs. Evanston and Morton Grove, Illinois, passed local bans on handgun possession in the 1980s. Both ordinances applied only to handguns, allowing homeowners to remain armed with the more lethal shotguns and rifles. Therefore, the only households that hypothetically could have become gunless as a result of the ordinances would have been those that (1) owned only handguns, (2) obeyed the law and got rid of all handguns, and (3) did not replace the handguns by acquiring long guns. Although half of U.S. households own guns, only 7 percent own only handguns. Thus, only some very law-abiding subset of this 7 percent would be disarmed by a handgun ban.

Citizens would have to have been very law-abiding indeed to be disarmed by these bans, since authorities depended almost entirely on voluntary compliance. The ordinances were not seriously enforced; the Evanston deputy police chief publicly announced that the police would not actively search out handguns. Only 74 charges were brought for violations over the first three years after the Evanston ordinance was passed, and only 116 handguns were handed in or confiscated, in a city with over 5,000 admitted handgun owners.[116]

Applying ARIMA methods to monthly burglary counts, McDowall et al. detected burglary declines in both cities (significant in Morton Grove and not significant in Evanston). The authors believed that passage of the ordinances should have led burglars to believe that fewer homes were armed with guns, leading to a reduced deterrent effect of guns and an increase in burglary, if a gun deterrence effect had previously been operating. The lack of significant increases in burglaries, they argued, was evidence that no such deterrent effect had been operating.[117]

McDowall et al. were puzzled by the burglary declines, stating that "there is no convincing mechanism to explain how a handgun ban could generate such a reduction" (pp. 553-54). There is, however, such a mechanism, though perhaps not one that would be convincing to these authors. There is little reason to believe that there was any actual reduction in gun-armed households in either Evanston or Morton Grove, and certainly no evidence that prospective burglars believed that there was a reduction. Indeed, to the extent that burglars perceived any change at all, some might have reasonably supposed that at least a few gun owners upgraded their weapons by exchanging their less-lethal handguns for more lethal long guns.

Both of the Evanston and Morton Grove measures, however, were preceded by extended and highly publicized debate, with advocates stressing the "handgun scourge" in their communities and emphasizing the need to reduce the excessive prevalence of handguns. Thus, in the absence of any significant amount of actual disarming, the dominant effect of these episodes could have been an increased awareness, among prospective criminals, of continuing victim gun possession, engendered by the public debate over the measures. Thus, the problem with these episodes as tests of the gun deterrence hypothesis is that one could reasonably expect either increases or decreases in crime following the bans, even if the hypothesis were correct.

It needs to be stressed that the results of these "natural experiments" are not cited for the narrow purpose of demonstrating the short-term deterrent effects of gun training programs or victim gun use. There is no reason to believe that citizens used the gun training in any significant number of real-life defensive situations, nor any solid evidence that gun ownership or defensive uses increased in the affected areas. Rather, the results are cited as evidence on the question of whether routine gun ownership and defensive use by civilians have a pervasive, ongoing impact on crime, with or without such programs or incidents. This ongoing impact is merely intensified and made more detectable at times when criminals' awareness of potential victims' gun possession is dramatically increased, thereby offering an opportunity to detect an effect that is ordinarily invisible. A few diverse examples of how this awareness might come to be increased have been described. Other examples would be general stories in the news media about gun ownership, increases in gun sales, and so on.

All of these cases, although consistent with the gun deterrence hypothesis, can provide only weak anecdotal evidence. There is no technically sound nonexperimental methodology that allows researchers to conclusively separate the effects of an intervention, whether a gun training program or a new gun control law, from the effects of thousands of contemporaneous changes in variables which affect crime trends. Consequently, at present it seems unlikely we will ever have strong evidence bearing on the gun deterrence hypothesis, or at least none based on local case studies like those discussed here. In particular, the univariate interrupted time series design of the type relied on by McDowall and his colleagues, with or without ARIMA analysis, cannot be considered adequate for this purpose.[118]

Guns and the Displacement of Burglars from Occupied Homes

Residential burglars devote considerable thought, time and effort to locating homes that are unoccupied. In interviews with burglars in a Pennsylvania prison, criminologists George Rengert and John Wasilchick (1985) found that nearly all of the two hours spent on the average burglary was devoted to locating an appropriate target, casing the house and making sure no one was home. There are at least two reasons why burglars make this considerable investment of time and effort: to avoid arrest and to avoid getting shot. Several burglars in this study reported that they avoided late-night burglaries because it was too difficult to tell if anyone was home, explaining, "That's the way to get shot."[119] Burglars also stated that they avoided neighborhoods occupied largely by persons of a different race because "you'll get shot if you're caught there" (p. 62). Giving weight to these opinions, one of the thirty-one burglars admitted to having been shot on the job (p. 98). In the Wright-Rossi survey, 73 percent of felons who had committed a burglary or violent crime agreed that "one reason burglars avoid houses when people are at home is that they fear being shot."[120]

The nonconfrontational nature of most burglaries in the United States is a major reason why associated deaths and injuries are so rare—an absent victim cannot be injured. Don Kates has argued that victim gun ownership is a major reason for the nonconfrontational nature of burglary and is therefore to be credited with reducing deaths and injuries by its deterrent effects.[121] This possible benefit would be enjoyed by all potential burglary victims, not just those who own guns, because burglars seeking to avoid confrontations usually cannot know which homes have guns, and must try to avoid any that are occupied.

If burglary victims did not have guns, the worst a burglar would ordinarily have to fear would be breaking off a burglary attempt if faced with an unarmed occupant who called the police. A typical strong, young burglar would usually have little reason to fear attack or apprehension by unarmed victims, especially if the victim confronted was a woman or an older person. Further, there are obvious advantages to burglarizing occupied premises— the burglar has a much better chance to get the cash in victims' purses or wallets, and cash is the most attractive of all theft targets.

To be sure, even under no-guns conditions, many burglars would continue to avoid occupied residences simply because contact with a victim would increase their chances of apprehension by the police. Others may have chosen to do burglaries rather than robberies because they were emotionally unable or unwilling to confront their victims and thus would avoid occupied premises for this reason. However, this does not seem to be true of most incarcerated burglars. Prison surveys indicate that few criminals specialize in one crime type, and most imprisoned burglars report having also committed robberies. In the Wright and Rossi survey, of those who reported ever committing a burglary, 62 percent also reported committing robberies.[122] Thus, most of these burglars were temperamentally capable of confronting victims, even though they presumably preferred to avoid them when committing a burglary.

Results from victim surveys in three foreign nations indicate that in countries with lower rates of gun ownership than the United States, residential burglars are much more willing to enter occupied homes. A 1977 survey in the Netherlands found that residents were home in 48 percent of burglaries, compared to just 9 percent in the United States the previous year. In the British Crime Surveys of 1982, 1984, 1988, and 1992, researchers found that 43 percent of burglaries were committed with someone at home. And criminologists Irvin Waller and Norman Okihiro reported that 44 percent of burglarized Toronto residences were occupied during the burglaries, with 21 percent of the burglaries resulting in confrontations between victim and offender.[123] The huge differences between the United States and Great Britain and Canada cannot be explained by more serious legal punishment in this country, since the probability of arrest and imprisonment and the severity of sentences served for common crimes were, at the time, no higher in the United States than in these other nations.[124]

If widespread civilian gun ownership helps deter burglars from entering occupied premises, what might this imply regarding the level of burglary-linked violence? NCVS data indicate that when a residential burglary is committed with a household member present, it results in a threat or attack on the victim 30.2 percent of the time.[125] While only 12.7 percent of U.S. residential burglaries are against occupied homes, the occupancy rate in the aforementioned three low gun-ownership nations averaged about 45 percent. What would have happened if U.S. burglars had been just as willing to enter occupied premises? In 1985 the NCVS counted 5,594,420 household burglaries, about 214,568 of which resulted in assaults on a victim (5,594,420 × .127 × .302). Assume that 30.2 percent of the occupied premise burglaries resulted in assaults on a victim (the same as now), but also assume that the occupancy rate had increased to 45 percent, as in the low gun-ownership nations. This would imply about 760,282 assaults on burglary victims (5,594,420 × .45 × .302 = 760,282), 545,713 more than actually occurred. This change alone would have represented a 9.4 percent increase in all NCVS-estimated violent crime in 1985. If high home gun ownership rates in the United States really do account for the difference in burglary occupancy rates between the United States and other nations, these figures indicate that burglary displacement effects of widespread gun ownership may have a significant downward impact on violence rates.

Conclusions

Gun use by private citizens against violent criminals and burglars is a more common negative consequence for violent criminals than legal actions like arrests, a more prompt negative consequence of crime than legal punishment, and is more severe, at its most serious, than legal system punishments. On the other hand, only a small percentage of criminal victimizations transpire in a way that results in defensive gun use; guns certainly are not usable in all crime situations.

Serious predatory criminals perceive a risk from victim gun use that is roughly comparable to that of criminal justice system actions, and this perception may deter criminal behavior. Nevertheless, a deterrent effect of widespread gun ownership and defensive use has not been conclusively established, any more than it has been for activities of the legal system. Given the nature of deterrence, it may never be conclusively established.

Nevertheless, the most parsimonious way of linking these facts is to conclude tentatively that civilian ownership and defensive use of guns deters violent crime and reduces burglar-linked injuries.

Victim gun use is associated with lower rates of property loss in robberies and confrontational burglaries, and is not significantly different from other self-protective measures with respect to victim injury. Less than 6 percent of gun-using victims are injured following their gun use, and nearly all of the injuries suffered are minor. Thus, defensive gun use is effective.

Economic inequality, a history of racism, and other factors have created dangerous conditions in many places in America. Police cannot provide personal protection for every American. While gun ownership is no more an all-situations source of protection than the police, it can be a useful supplementary source of safety in addition to police protection, burglar alarms, guard dogs and all the other resources people exploit to improve their security. These sources are not substitutes for one another. Rather, they are complements, each useful in different situations. Possession of a gun gives its owner an additional option for dealing with immediate danger. If other sources of security are adequate, the gun does not have to be used, but where other sources fail, it can preserve bodily safety and property in some situations.

One can dream of a day when governments can eliminate violence and provide total protection to all citizens. In reality, the American legal system has never even approximated this state of affairs, and is unlikely to do so in the foreseeable future. Given the oppressive governmental practices that might be necessary to provide complete protection, it is not even clear that this would be a desirable goal. If predatory crime can be reduced, the private resort to violence for social control should decline. Indeed, as noted earlier, the drop in violent crime in the United States in the 1990s was accompanied by a sharp drop in civilian justifiable homicides and probably a corresponding drop in total defensive gun use.

Nevertheless, the widespread defensive use of guns against criminals will persist as long as Americans believe crime is a serious threat and that they cannot rely completely on the police as effective guardians. Until then, scholars interested in gun control, crime deterrence, victimology, the routine activities approach to crime, and in social control in general need to consider more carefully the significance of millions of potential crime victims armed with deadly weapons.

Implications for Crime Control Policy

Undesirable though such a state of affairs may be, much of social order in America may depend on the fact that millions of people are armed and dangerous to criminals. The availability of deadly weapons to the violence-prone contributes to violence by increasing the probability of a fatal outcome of combat. However, this very fact may raise the stakes in disputes to the point where only the most incensed or intoxicated disputants resort to physical conflict, with the risks of armed retaliation deterring attack and coercing minimal courtesy among otherwise hostile parties. Likewise, rates of commercial robbery, residential burglary injury, and rape might be still higher than their already high levels were it not for the dangerousness of the prospective victim population.

Thus, gun ownership among prospective victims may well have as large a crime-reducing effect as the crime-increasing effects of gun possession among prospective criminals. This would account for the failure of researchers to find a significant net effect on rates of crime like homicide and robbery of measures of gun ownership that do not distinguish between gun availability among criminals and availability in the largely noncriminal general public. The two effects may roughly cancel each other out.[126]

Guns are potentially lethal weapons whether wielded by criminals or by victims. They are frightening and intimidating to those they are pointed at, whether these be criminals or victims. Guns thereby empower both those who would use them to victimize and those who would use them to prevent their victimization. Thus, they are a source of both social order and disorder, depending on who uses them, just as is true of the use of force in general.

The failure to fully acknowledge this reality can lead to grave errors in devising public policy to minimize violence through gun control. While some gun laws are intended to reduce gun possession only among relatively limited "high-risk" groups such as convicted felons, through measures such as background checks, others are aimed at reducing gun possession in all segments of the civilian population, both criminal and noncriminal. Examples would include the Morton Grove and Evanston handgun possession bans, near approximations of such bans in New York City, Chicago, and Washington, D.C., "assault weapon" bans, prohibitions of handgun sales, and laws banning the carrying of concealed weapons in public places.

By definition, laws are most likely to be obeyed by the law-abiding, and gun laws are no different. Therefore, measures that theoretically apply equally to criminals and noncriminals are almost certain to reduce gun possession more among the latter than the former. Because very little serious violent crime is committed by persons without previous histories of serious violence, there are at best only slight direct crime-control benefits to be gained by reductions in gun possession among noncriminals, even though reductions in gun possession among criminals could have more substantial crime-reducing effects.[127]

Consequently, one has to take seriously the possibility that "across-the-board" gun control measures could decrease the crime-control effects of noncriminal gun ownership more than they would decrease the crime-causing effects of criminal gun ownership. For this reason, more narrowly targeted gun control measures like bans on felon gun possession and background checks are preferable.

Skeptics sometimes argue that while a world in which there were no guns would be desirable, it is also unachievable. The evidence presented here raises a more radical possibility—that a world in which no one had guns would actually be *less* safe than one in which nonaggressors had guns and aggressors somehow did not. As a practical matter, the latter world is no more achievable than the former, but the point is worth raising as a way of clarifying what the goals of rational gun control policy should be. If gun possession among prospective victims tends to reduce violence, then reducing such gun possession is not, in and of itself, a social good. Instead, the best policy goal to pursue may be to shift the distribution of gun possession as far as practical in the direction of likely aggressors being disarmed and currently armed nonaggressors being left armed. To disarm noncriminals in the hope that this might somehow indirectly help reduce access to guns among criminals, e.g., by reducing gun theft, is not a risk-free policy.

These categories are, of course, simplifications. Some serious aggressors are also victims of serious aggression, and most people are at least occasionally aggressors in some very minor way. However, while it is clear these two groups overlap to some extent, it is equally clear that they can be, and routinely are, distinguished in law, e.g., in statutes that forbid gun possession among persons with a criminal conviction and allow it among those without one. Further, while a great deal of violence is committed by persons without criminal convictions, it is also true that convicted felons are far more likely to be violent aggressors in the future than nonfelons. The idea that a significant share of serious violence is accounted for by previously nonviolent "average Joes," as in a "crime-of-passion" homicide, is a myth.[128]

Consequently, a rational goal of gun control policy could be to tip the balance of power in prospective victims' favor, by reducing aggressor gun possession while doing nothing to reduce nonaggressor gun possession. This would contrast sharply with across-the-board restrictions that would affect nonaggressors as much as, or more than, aggressors.

Notes

1. U.S. Bureau of Justice Statistics, *Lifetime Likelihood of Victimization*, BJS Technical Report (Washington, D.C.: U.S. Government Printing Office, 1987), p. 3.

2. Lynn A. Curtis, *Criminal Violence: National Patterns and Behavior* (Lexington, Mass.: Lexington, 1974), p. 176.

3. Samuel Walker, *Sense and Nonsense About Crime* (Pacific Grove. Calif.: Brooks/Cole, 1989), pp. 134–35.

4. Ibid., pp. 116–43.

5. Joseph D. Alviani and William R. Drake, *Handgun Control . . . Issues and Alternatives* (Washington, D.C.: U.S. Conference of Mayors, 1975); Matthew G. Yeager, Joseph D. Alviani, and Nancy Loving, *How Well Does the Handgun Protect You and Your Family?* Handgun Control Staff Technical Report 2 (Washington, D.C.: United States Conference of Mayors, 1976).

6. Gary Kleck, *Point Blank: Guns and Violence in America* (New York: Aldine de Gruyter, 1991), p. 289.

7. National Safety Council, *Accident Facts—1999 Edition* (Chicago: National Safety Council, 1999), p. 9.

8. U.S. Bureau of Justice Statistics, *Criminal Victimization in the United States 1994* (Washington, D.C.: U.S. Government Printing Office, 1997), p. 68.

9. U.S. Bureau of Justice Statistics, *Incident Files*.

10. Gary Kleck, "Crime Control Through the Private Use of Armed Force," *Social Problems* 35 (1988): 1–21; Gary Kleck and Miriam DeLone, "Victim Resistance and Offender Weapon Effects in Robbery," *Journal of Quantitative Criminology* 9 (1993): 55–82.

11. Albert J. Reiss and Jeffrey A. Roth, "Firearms and Violence," in *Under-*

standing and Preventing Violence, ed. Albert J. Reiss and Jeffrey A. Roth (Washington, D.C.: National Academy Press, 1993), p. 266; for a similar speculation, see also Thompson et al., "Epidemiology of Injuries," p. 243.

12. See also Kleck and DeLone, "Victim Resistance in Robbery."

13. Ibid.

14. Ibid.

15. Gary Kleck and Susan Sayles, "Rape and Resistance," *Social Problems* 37 (1990): 149–62.

16. Alan J. Lizotte, "Determinants of Completing Rape and Assault," *Journal of Quantitative Criminology* 2 (1986): 203–17.

17. Martie P. Thompson, Thomas R. Simon, Linda E. Saltzman, and James A. Mercy, "Epidemiology of Injuries Among Women after Physical Assaults: The Role of Self-Protective Behaviors," *American Journal of Epidemiology* 150 (1999): 242.

18. Joseph D. McNamara, "Statement of Joseph D. McNamara, Chief of Police, San Jose, Ca," Hearing Before the Committee on the Judiciary, House of Representatives, 99th Congress, 1st and 2nd Sessions on Legislation to Modify the 1968 Gun Control Act, Part 2, 19 February 1986, p. 989; Alviani and Drake, *Handgun Control*, p. 52.

19. U.S. Bureau of Justice Statistics, *Reporting Crimes to the Police*, BJS Special Report (Washington, D.C.: U.S. Government Printing Office, 1985), p. 3.

20. Eduard Ziegenhagen and Dolores Brosnan, "Victim Responses to Robbery and Crime Control Policy," *Criminology* 23 (1985): 693.

21. Pete Shields, *Guns Don't Die—People Do* (New York: Arbor House, 1981), pp. 49, 53; McNamara, "Statement," p. 989.

22. Reiss and Roth, "Firearms and Violence," p. 266.

23. U.S. Federal Bureau of Investigation, *Crime in the United States 1993—Uniform Crime Reports* (Washington, D.C.: U.S. Government Printing Office, 1994), 288.

24. U.S. Federal Bureau of Investigation, *Law Enforcement Officers Killed and Assaulted*, issues for 1974–1990 (Washington, D.C.: U.S. Government Printing Office, 1975–1991).

25. U.S. Federal Bureau of Investigation, *Killed in the Line of Duty* (Washington, D.C.: U.S. Government Printing, 1992), p. 40.

26. Hal Quinley, memorandum reporting results from *Time*/CNN Poll of Gun Owners, dated 6 February 1990 (New York: Yankelovich Clancy Shulman survey organization, 1990), p. 9.

27. Kleck, *Point Blank*, pp. 111–16.

28. U.S. Federal Bureau of Investigation, *Crime in the United States 1997—Uniform Crime Reports* (Washington, D.C.: U.S. Government Printing Office, 1998), p. 22; Kleck, *Point Blank*, p. 148.

29. Philip J. Cook, "The Case of the Missing Victims: Gunshot Woundings in the National Crime Survey," *Journal of Quantitative Criminology* 1 (1985): 91–102.

30. Gary Kleck, *Targeting Guns: Firearms and Their Control* (New York: Aldine, 1997), p. 3–5.

31. U.S. Bureau of Justice Statistics, *National Crime Victimization Surveys, 1992–1998—Concatenated Incident Files* [computer file], ICPSR ed. (Ann Arbor, Mich.: Inter-university Consortium for Political and Social [distributor], 2000).

32. Gary Kleck and Marc Gertz, "Armed Resistance to Crime: The Prevalence and Nature of Self–defense with a Gun," *Journal of Criminal Law and Criminology* 86 (1995): 185.

33. Police Foundation, *National Study of Private Ownership of Firearms in the United States, 1994* [computer file], ICPSR version, Radnor, Penn.: Chilton Research Services [producer], 1994 (Ann Arbor, Mich.: Inter-university Consortium for Political and Social Research, 1998).

34. Kleck, *Targeting Guns*, pp. 3–5; Joseph L. Annest, James A. Mercy, Delinda R. Gibson, and George W. Ryan, "National Estimates of Nonfatal Firearm-Related Injuries," *Journal of the American Medical Association* 273 (1995): 1749–54.

35. Philip Cook and Jens Ludwig, *Guns in America* (Washington, D.C.: Police Foundation, 1997), p. 38; Quinley, *Time/CNN Poll;* Kleck, *Targeting Guns,* p. 99.

36. Cook and Ludwig, *Guns in America,* pp. 20–21; Kleck, *Targeting Guns,* p. 97.

37. Police Foundation, *National Study.*

38. Douglas Weil and David Hemenway, "Loaded Guns in the Home," *Journal of the American Medical Association* 267 (1992): 3033–37; David Hemenway, Sarah J. Solnick, and Deborah R. Azrael, "Firearms and Community Feelings of Safety," *Journal of Criminal Law and Criminology* 86 (1995): 121–32; Yvonne D. Senturia, Katherine Kaufer Christoffel, and Mark Donovan, "Gun Storage Patterns in US Homes with Children," *Archives of Pediatric and Adolescent Medicine* 150 (1996): 265–69; Mark A. Schuster, Todd M. Franke, Amy M. Bastian, Sinaroth Sor, and Neal Halfon, "Firearm Storage Patterns in US Homes with Children," *American Journal of Public Health* 90 (2000): 588–94.

39. Weil and Hemenway, "Loaded Guns;" Philip Cook and Mark C. Moore, "Gun Control," in *Crime*, ed. James Q. Wilson and Joan Petersilia. San Francisco: Institute for Contemporary Studies; Cook and Ludwig, *Guns in America*, p. 22.

40. National Rifle Association, *Home Firearm Safety: Guidelines for Handling and Storing Guns in the Home* (Washington, D.C.: National Rifle Association, 1990), p. 37.

41. Schuster et al., "Firearm Storage," p. 588; Cook and Ludwig, *Guns in America*, p. 20.

42. U.S. National Center for Health Statistics, *Deaths: Final Data for 1998* (Washington, D.C.: U.S. Government Printing Office), p. 67; U.S. Federal Bureau of Investigation, *Crime in the United States 1998—Uniform Crime Reports* (Washington, D.C.: U.S. Government Printing Office, 1999), p. 220.

43. National Safety Council, *Accident Facts 1999*, 32; U.S. National Center for Health Statistics, *Mortality Detail Files, 1968–1994* [Computer file], ICPSR ed. (Ann Arbor, Mich.: Inter-university Consortium for Political and Social Research [distributor], 1997).

44. Computed from data in table 3, Schuster et al., "Firearm Storage," p. 592; Gail Stennies, Robin Ikeda, Steven Leadbetter, Barbara Houston, and Jeffrey Sacks, "Firearm Storage Practices and Children in the Home, United States, 1994," *Archives of Pediatric and Adolescent Medicine* 153 (1999): 588; Police Foundation, *National Study*.

45. Schuster et al., "Firearm Storage," p. 591.

46. Police Foundation, *National Study*.

47. Kleck and Gertz, "Armed Resistance," pp. 184–85.

48. E.g., Weil and Hemenway, "Loaded Guns."

49. Lyn Bates, "The Inside Story on Lockboxes," *Women & Guns* (July/August 2000): 18–22, 48–50.

50. Lyn Bates, "Another Look at Gun Locks," *Women & Guns* (May/June 2000): 16–23.

51. James D. Wright and Peter H. Rossi, *Armed and Considered Dangerous: A Survey of Felons and Their Firearms* (New York: Aldine, 1986), p. 196.

51. Arthur L. Kellermann, Frederick P. Rivara, Norman B. Rushforth, Joyce G. Banton, Donald T. Reay, Jerry T. Francisco, Ana B. Locci, Janice Prodzinski, Bela B. Hackman, and Grant Somes, "Gun Ownership as a Risk Factor for Homicide in the Home," *New England Journal of Medicine* 329 (1993): 1084–91.

53. Gary Kleck, "Can Owning a Gun Really Triple the Owner's Chances of Being Murdered?" *Homicide Studies* 5 (2001): 64–77; Gary Kleck and Michael Hogan, "National Case-Control Study of Homicide Offending and Gun Ownership," *Social Problems* 48 (1999): 275–93.

54. David J. Bordua, Alan J. Lizotte, and Gary Kleck, with Van Cagle, *Patterns of Firearms Ownership, Regulation and Use in Illinois* (Springfield, Ill.: Illinois Law Enforcement Commission, 1985); Kleck and Gertz, "Armed Resistance," p. 210.

55. James D. Wright, Peter H. Rossi, and Kathleen Daly, *Under the Gun: Weapons, Crime and Violence in America* (New York: Aldine, 1983), pp. 252–55.

56. Police Foundation, *National Study*.

57. Gary Kleck and Marc Gertz, "Carrying Guns for Protection: Results from the National Self-Defense Survey," *Journal of Research in Crime and Delinquency* 35 (1998): 208.

58. Kenneth Carlson, *Mandatory Sentencing: The Experience of Two States* (Washington, D.C.: National Institute of Justice, 1982), p. 6.

59. Kleck and Gertz, "Carrying Guns," pp. 200, 208, 210.

60. Ibid., p. 220.

61. Tomislav V. Kovandzic and Thomas B. Marvell, "The Impact of Florida's Right-to-Carry Concealed Firearm Law on Crime Rates" (paper presented at the annual meetings of the American Society of Criminology, Toronto, 20 November 1999); John Lott and David B. M. Mustard, "Crime, Deterrence, and Right to Carry Concealed Handguns," *Journal of Legal Studies* 26 (1997): 1–68.

62. Florida Department of State—Division of Licensing, website at http://licgweb.dos.state.fl.us/stats/cw_monthly.html, Accessed 15 August, 2000; Don B. Kates and Daniel D. Polsby, "Long-Term Nonrelationship of Widespread and Increasing Firearm Availability to Homicide in the United States," *Homicide Studies* 4 (2000): 196.

63. Quinley, *Time*/CNN Poll.

64. Gary A. Mauser, unpublished tabulations from a 1990 national survey, produced at the author's request.

65. Quinley, *Time*/CNN Poll, p. 10.

66. Los Angeles Poll Number 39 [machine-readable dataset], Los Angeles, Calif.

67. Cook and Ludwig, *Guns in America*, p. 43.

68. Hemenway et al., "Feelings of Safety," pp. 122–23.

69. Gary Kleck, "Do Higher Gun Ownership Levels Reduce Community Feelings of Safety?" (Tallahassee, Fla.: School of Criminology and Criminal Justice, Florida State University, 2000).

70. Norman B. Rushforth, Amasa B. Ford, Charles S. Hirsch, Nancy M. Rushforth, and Lester Adelson, "Violent Death in a Metropolitan County: Changing Patterns in Homicide (1958–74)," *New England Journal of Medicine* 297 (1977): 504–5; for an earlier version of this argument, see also George D. Newton and Franklin Zimring, *Firearms and Violence in American Life*, A Staff Report to the National Commission on the Causes and Prevention of Violence (Washington, D.C.: U.S. Government Printing Office, 1969), p. 64.

71. Kleck, *Targeting Guns*, pp. 304–13.

72. B. Bruce-Briggs, "The Great American Gun War," *The Public Interest* 45 (1976): 39.

73. Arthur L. Kellermann and Donald T. Reay, "Protection or Peril? An Analysis of Firearm-related Deaths in the Home," *New England Journal of Medicine* 314 (1986): 1557–60.

74. Bruce-Briggs, "Gun War," p. 39.

75. Philip J. Cook, "The Technology of Personal Violence," in *Crime and*

Justice: A Review of Research, vol. 14, ed. Michael Tonry (Chicago: University of Chicago Press, 1991), p. 62; Wright et al., "Under the Gun"; Yeager et al., *Does the Handgun Protect?* p. 4; Alviani and Drake, *Handgun Control*, p. 8; Senturia et al., "Gun Storage Patterns"; David McDowall and Brian Wiersema, "The Incidence of Defensive Firearm Use by US Crime Victims, 1987 Through 1990," *American Journal of Public Health* 84 (1994): 1982–84; Reiss and Roth, "Firearms and Violence," p. 267.

76. U.S. National Center for Health Statistics, *Deaths*, p. 71.

77. Kleck and Gertz, "Armed Resistance," pp. 176–77.

78. U.S. National Center for Health Statistics, *Deaths*, 67; Kleck, *Targeting Guns*, pp. 269–75, 284–86.

79. Kleck and Gertz, "Armed Resistance."

80. U.S. Bureau of Justice Statistics, *Guns and Crime*, Crime Data Brief (Washington, D.C.: U.S. Government Printing Office, 1994), p. 2.

81. U.S. Bureau of Justice Statistics, *Criminal Victimization 1994*, p. 64; U.S. Federal Bureau of Investigation, *Crime in the United States 1994—Uniform Crime Reports* (Washington, D.C.: U.S. Government Printing Office, 1995), p. 18.

82. Colin Loftin and Ellen J. MacKenzie, "Building National Estimates of Violent Victimization" (paper presented at the National Research Council Symposium on the Understanding and Control of Violent Behavior, Destin, Fl., 1–6 April 1990), pp. 22–23.

83. U.S. Bureau of Justice Statistics, *Criminal Victimization 1994*, p. 38.

84. Cook, "Technology of Violence," p. 32.

85. U.S. Bureau of Justice Statistics, *Criminal Victimization 1994*, pp. 12, 16, 49.

86. Kleck, *Point Blank*, p. 56.

87. U.S. Bureau of Justice Statistics, *Household Burglary*, BJS Bulletin (Washington, D.C.: U.S. Government Printing Office, 1985), p. 4.

88. U.S. Bureau of Justice Statistics, *Intimate Victims: A Study of Violence Among Friends and Relatives* (Washington, D.C.: U.S. Government Printing Office, 1980), p. 22; Curtis, *Criminal Violence*, p. 176.

89. U.S. Federal Bureau of Investigation, *Crime in the United States 1993—Uniform Crime Reports* (Washington, D.C.: U.S. Government Printing Office, 1994), pp. 217, 288.

90. Wright and Rossi, *Armed and Considered Dangerous*; James Wright and Peter Rossi, *Armed Criminals in America: A Survey of Incarcerated Felons, 1983* [Computer file], ICPSR version. James Wright and Peter Rossi [producers], 1983. Inter-university Consortium for Political and Social Research [distributor], Ann Arbor, Mich., 1986.

91. James Wright and Peter Rossi, *Armed Criminals in America: A Survey of*

Incarcerated Felons, 1983 [Computer file], ICPSR version. James Wright and Peter Rossi [producers], 1983. Inter-university Consortium for Political and Social Research [distributor], Ann Arbor, Mich., 1986.

92. Wright and Rossi, *Armed and Considered Dangerous*; Gordon R. Firman, "In Prison Gun Survey the Pros Are the Cons," *The American Rifleman* (November 1975): 13; Mitchell Link, "No Handguns in Morton Grove—Big Deal!" *Menard Times* (prison newspaper of Menard, Illinois, Federal Penitentiary) 33 (1982): 1.

93. Lott and Mustard, "Right to Carry"; Kleck, *Targeting Guns*, pp. 371–72.

94. Alan S. Krug, "The Relationship Between Firearms Ownership and Crime Rates: A Statistical Analysis," *The Congressional Record*, 90th Cong., 2d sess. (30 January 1968): H570–2.

95. Gary Kleck and David J. Bordua, "The Factual Foundations for Certain Key Assumptions of Gun Control," *Law & Policy Quarterly* 5 (1983): 282–88.

96. Gary S. Green, "Citizen Gun Ownership and Criminal Deterrence," *Criminology* 25 (1987): 75.

97. David McDowall, Alan Lizotte, and Brian Wiersema, "General Deterrence Through Civilian Gun Ownership," *Criminology* 29 (1991): 546; Richard McCleary and Richard A. Hay Jr., with Errol E. Meidinger and David McDowall, *Applied Time Series Analysis for the Social Sciences* (Beverly Hills: Sage, 1980), p. 20.

98. McDowall et al., "General Deterrence," p. 546.

99. Kleck and Bordua, "Factual Foundations," pp. 284–88.

100. David McDowall and Colin Loftin, "Collective Security and the Demand for Legal Handguns," *American Journal of Sociology* 88 (1983): 1150; Gary Kleck, "Capital Punishment, Gun Ownership, and Homicide," *American Journal of Sociology* 84 (1979): 882–910.

101. U.S. Small Business Administration, *Crime Against Small Business*, Senate Document No. 91–14 (Washington, D.C.: U.S. Government Printing Office, 1969), pp. 253–56.

102. U.S. Bureau of the Census, *1980 Census of the Population. Volume I: Characteristics of the Population*, Chapter B—General Population Characteristics, United States Summary, table 46 (Washington, D.C.: U.S. Government Printing Office, 1983).

103. Kleck, *Point Blank*, pp. 134–35, 151.

104. McDowall et al., "General Deterrence," pp. 548–49.

105. Patrick W. O'Carroll, Colin Loftin, John B. Waller, David McDowall, Allen Bukoff, Richard O. Scott, James A. Mercy, and Brian Wiersema, "Preventing Homicide: An Evaluation of the Efficacy of a Detroit Gun Ordinance," *American Journal of Public Health* 81 (1991): 578.

106. Krug, "Firearms Ownership," H571.

107. *Tallahassee Democrat* 25 January 1985, p. 1A; *New York Times* 22 March 1985, p B4; 18 April 1985, p. 87.

108. U.S. Bureau of the Census, *1980 Census*, p. 832.

109. Dave Schneidman, "Gun-totin' Town Gets an Apology," *Chicago Tribune*, 8 April 1982, p. 15.

110. Mark K. Benenson, Memorandum recording telephone conversation with Kennesaw, Georgia, Police Chief Ruble, 4 November 1982.

111. U.S. Federal Bureau of Investigation, *Crime in the United States 1982—Uniform Crime Reports* (Washington, D.C.: U.S. Government Printing Office, 1983), pp. 45–47, 143.

112. David McDowall, Brian Wiersema, and Colin Loftin, "Did Mandatory Firearm Ownership in Kennesaw Really Prevent Burglaries?" *Sociology and Social Research* 74 (1989): 48–51; McDowall et al., "General Deterrence."

113. William E. Schmidt, "Town to Celebrate Mandatory Arms," *New York Times*, 11 April 1987, pp. 6–7.

114. Population based on linear interpolation of 1980 and 1987 population figures. "Residential burglary" counts are "house burglaries" reported in Schmidt, "Mandatory Arms."

115. Kleck, "Crime Control," pp. 15–16.

116. Kleck, *Point Blank*, p. 55.

117. McDowall et al., "General Deterrence," pp. 553–54.

118. Gary Kleck, Chester Britt, and David J. Bordua, "The Emperor Has No Clothes: Using Interrupted Time Series Designs to Evaluate Social Policy Impact," *Journal on Firearms and Public Policy* 12 (2000): 197–247.

119. George Rengert and John Wasilchick, *Suburban Burglary: A Time and Place for Everything* (Springfield, Ill.: Charles Thomas, 1985), pp. 30, 62, 98.

120. Wright and Rossi, *Armed Criminals*.

121. Don B. Kates Jr., *Guns, Murders, and the Constitution*, Policy Briefing, Pacific Research Institute for Public Policy (San Francisco: Pacific Research Institute, 1991).

122. Wright and Rossi, *Armed Criminals*.

123. Richard Block, "The Impact of Victimization, Rates, and Patterns: A Comparison of the Netherlands and the United States," in *Victimization and Fear of Crime: World Perspectives*, ed. Richard Block (Washington, D.C.: U.S. Government Printing Office, 1984), p. 26; Pat Mayhew, Natalie Aye Maung, and Catriona Mirrlees-Black, *The 1992 British Crime Survey* (London: Her Majesty's Stationary Office, 1993), table A4.6; Irvin Waller and Norman Okihiro, *Burglary: The Victim and the Public* (Toronto: University of Toronto Press, 1978), p. 31.

124. James Q. Wilson, "Crime and Punishment in England," *The Public*

Interest 43 (1976): 18–19; U.S. Bureau of Justice Statistics, *Imprisonment in Four Countries*, BJS Special Report (Washington, D.C.: U.S. Government Printing Office, 1987).

125. U.S. Bureau of Justice Statistics, *Household Burglary*, p. 4.

126. E.g., Philip J. Cook, "The Effect of Gun Availability on Robbery and Robbery Murder," in *Policy Studies Review Annual*, ed. Robert Haveman and B. Bruce Zellner (Beverly Hills: Sage, 1979); Gary Kleck, "The Relationship Between Gun Ownership Levels and Rates of Violence in the United States," in *Firearms and Violence: Issues of Public Policy*, ed. Don B. Kates Jr. (Cambridge, Mass.: Ballinger, 1984); see also David J. Bordua, "Firearms Ownership and Violent Crime: A Comparison of Illinois Counties," in *The Social Ecology of Crime*, ed. James M. Byrne and Robert J. Sampson (New York: Springer-Verlag, 1986).

127. Chapter 1; Kleck and Bordua, "Factual Foundations."

128. Ibid.

The Second Amendment

A Right to Personal Self-Protection*

by Don B. Kates

From the enactment of the Bill of Rights through most of the twentieth century, the Second Amendment was understood to guarantee to every law-abiding responsible adult the right to possess arms. Until the mid-twentieth century courts and commentaries deemed that the amendment confirmed the people in their right to keep and bear their private arms, albeit nineteenth-century Supreme Court decisions held it subject to the nonincorporation doctrine under which none of the Bill of Rights were deemed applicable against the states. In a 1939 case which is its only full treatment, the Supreme Court accepted that private persons may invoke the Second Amendment but held that it guarantees them only freedom of choice of militia-type weapons, i.e., high quality handguns and rifles, but not "gang-

---

*This chapter is adapted from portions of two articles, Don B. Kates, "The Second Amendment and the Ideology of Self-Protection," *Constitutional Commentary* 9 (1992): 87, and Randy E. Barnett and Don B. Kates, "Under Fire: The New Consensus on the Second Amendment," *Emory Law Journal* 45 (1996): 1139. References for the first two paragraphs have been deleted; readers should instead refer to two articles by Professor David B. Kopel: "The Second Amendment in the Nineteenth Century," *Brigham Young Law Review* (1998): 1359; and "The Supreme Court's Thirty-Four *Other* Gun Cases: What the Supreme Court Has Said About the Second Amendment," *Saint Louis University Public Law Review* 18 (1999): 99.

ster weapons" like sawed-off shotguns, switchblade knives and (arguably) "Saturday Night Specials."[1]

In the 1960s this individual right view was challenged by scholars arguing that the Second Amendment guarantee extends only to the states' right to arm formal military units. The states' right view attained predominance, being endorsed by the American Bar Association, the American Civil Liberties Union and such texts as Lawrence Tribe's *American Constitutional Law*. During the 1980s, however, a large literature on the Amendment appeared, most of it rejecting the states' right view as inconsistent with the text ("right of the people," not "right of the states") and with new research findings on the immediate legislative history, the attitudes of the authors, the meaning of the right to arms in antecedent American and English legal thought and the role that an armed citizenry played in classical liberal political philosophy from Aristotle through Machiavelli and Harrington to Sidney, Locke, Rousseau and their various disciples.

So overwhelming has this literature proven that it has even produced a recantation from Professor Tribe.[2] Indicative of the current Supreme Court's probable view is a 1990 decision which, though focusing on the Fourth Amendment, cites the First and Second as well in concluding that the phrase "right of the people" is a term of art used throughout the Bill of Rights to designate rights pertaining to individual citizens (in contrast to the states).[3]

The issue on which my discussion here will focus is the notion—widespread among proponents of the individual right view—that the purpose of the right to arms is so "the people" may rise up altogether against a tyrant who has seized control of the nation. While that is not wholly wrong, it is a misleading way to think about a right whose central purpose is personal self-defense.

The underpinnings of the classical liberal belief in an armed people are obscure to us because we are not accustomed to seeing political issues in criminological terms. But the classical liberal worldview was criminological, for lack of a better word. It held that, for the benefit of society as well as themselves, citizens must be prepared to defend against crime—a concept that included not just apolitical outlaws but tyrannical ministers and pillaging foreign or domestic soldiers (soldiers being, in fact, largely criminals inducted from jails[4]).

To natural law philosophers' defense of self was "the primary law of nature," the primary reason for man entering society.[5] Indeed, it was not just a right but a positive duty: God gives man both life and the means to defend it; the refusal to do so reviles God's gift; in effect it is a Judeo-Christian form of hubris. Indicative of the intellectual gulf between that era and our own is that Montesquieu—who was, with Sir William Blackstone, the writer most cited by late-eighteenth-century Americans—could rhetorically ask what today might be seriously disputed, "Who does not see that self-protection is a duty superior to every precept?"[6]

Radiating out from this view of self-defense as the most basic of rights came the multiple chains of reasoning by which contemporary thinkers sought to resolve diverse questions. For instance, seventeenth- and eighteenth-century treatises on international law were addicted to long disquisitions on individual self-protection from which they attempted to deduce a law of nations.[7]

More important for present purposes, John Locke adduced from the right of self-defense his justification of the right(s) of individuals to resist tyrannical officials and, if necessary, to band together with other good citizens in overthrowing tyranny: God gives man life, liberty, and property. Slavers, robbers, and other outlaws who would deprive him of these rights may be resisted even unto death because such usurpation places them in a "state of war" against the honest man; likewise, when government seeks to divest the subject of life, liberty, or property it dissolves the compact by which he has agreed to governance and enters into a state of war with him— wherefore it may be resisted the same as any other criminal usurper.[8] Likewise Algernon Sidney declared: "Swords were given to men, that none might be slaves, but such as know not how to use them"; a tyrannical minister is "a public enemy"; every man may rightfully use his arms rather than submit to "the violence of a wicked Magistrate, who having armed a crew of lewd villains," subjects him to murder and pillage. "Nay, all Laws must fall, human societies that subsist by them be dissolved, and all innocent persons be exposed to the violence of the most wicked, if men might not justly defend themselves against injustice. . . . "[9]

Thomas Paine would "gladly" urge "all the world to lay aside the use of arms, and settle matters by negotiation, but unless the whole will, the matter ends, and I take up my musket and thank heaven He has put it in my power." Because "the invader and the plunderer" will not give up their arms, "others *dare not* lay them aside. . . . Horrid mischief would ensue were" the law-abiding "deprived of the use of them; . . . the weak will become a prey to the strong."[10] Similarly did Cesare Beccaria assail arms bans as a paradigm of simplistic legislation reflecting "false ideas of utility." His discussion deserves quotation in full, because Thomas Jefferson laboriously translated it and copied it in longhand into his personal compilation of great quotations:

> False is the idea of utility that sacrifices a thousand real advantages for one imaginary or trifling inconvenience; that would take fire from men because it burns, and water because one may drown in it; that has no remedy for evils, except destruction. The laws that forbid the carrying of arms are laws of such a nature. They disarm those only who are neither inclined nor determined to commit crimes. Can it be supposed that those who have the courage to violate the most sacred laws of humanity, the most important of the code, will respect the less important and arbitrary ones, which can be violated with ease and impunity, and which, if strictly obeyed, would put an end to personal liberty—so dear to men, so dear to the enlightened legislator—and subject innocent persons to all the vexations that the quality alone ought to suffer? Such laws make things worse for the assaulted and better for the assailants; they serve rather to encourage than to prevent homicides, for an unarmed man may be attacked with greater confidence than an armed man. They ought to be designated as laws not preventive but fearful of crimes, produced by the tumultuous impression of a few isolated facts, and not by thoughtful consideration of the inconveniences and advantages of a universal decree.[11]

Self-Protection as Benefit to the Whole Community

The ideas underlying the Second Amendment are also obscured to us by the distinction we tend to draw between self-protection as a purely private matter and defense of the community which we tend to think of in terms of the police. Today, incidents in which police thwart a violent criminal are often seen is as very different from incidents in which civilians defend themselves or others. When police defend citizens it is deemed (and lauded as) defense of the community. Yet civilians defending self and family tend to be seen as exercising what is, at best, a purely personal privilege serving only the particular interests of those defended, not those of the community at large. Such influential and progressive voices in American life as Garry Wills, Ramsey Clark, and the *Washington Post* go further yet, declaring those who own firearms for family defense "anticitizens," "traitors, enemies of their own *patriae*," arming "against their own neighbors"[12] and denouncing "the need that some homeowners and shopkeepers believe they have for weapons to defend themselves" as representing "the worst instincts in the human character,"[13] a return to barbarism, "anarchy, not order under law—a jungle where each relies on himself for survival."[14]

The notion that the truly civilized person eschews self-defense, relying on the police instead, or that self-defense disserves the public interest, could not have occurred to the Founding Fathers, there being no police in eighteenth-century America or England. In the tradition from which the Second Amendment derives it was not only the unquestioned right, but a crucial element in the *moral* character of every free man to be armed and willing to defend family and community against crime both individually and by joining with his fellows in hunting criminals down when the hue and cry went up, and in more formal posse, and militia patrol duties, under the control of justices of the peace or sheriffs.[15] In this milieu, individuals who thwarted a crime against themselves or their families were seen as serving the community as well.

This failure to distinguish the value of self-protection to individuals as opposed to the community helps account for the vast difference between today's thought and seventeenth- to nineteenth-century liberal discourse on crime, self-protection and community interest. Without apparent consciousness of any difference, liberal discourse addressed issues of community defense as if it were only individual self-protection writ large. Thus, Montesquieu confidently asserted that "the life of governments is like that of man. As the former has a right to kill in case of natural defense, the latter have a right to wage war for their own preservation."[16] Likewise, Thomas Paine cited the indubitable right and need for "the good man" to be armed against "the vile and abandoned" as irrefutable evidence of the right and need of nations to arm for defense against "the invader and plunderer."[17] Algernon Sidney and John Locke adduced from the right of individual self-defense their justification of the right(s) of individuals to resist tyrannical officials and, if necessary, to band together with other good citizens to overthrow tyranny. (See notes 8 and 9.)

Thus a crucial point for understanding the Second Amendment is that it emerged from a tradition that viewed general possession of arms as a positive social good, as well as an indispensable adjunct to the premier individual right of self-defense. Moreover, arms were deemed to protect against every species of criminal usurpation, including "political crime," a phrase which the Founding Fathers would have understood in its most literal sense. Whether murder, rape, and theft be committed by gangs of assassins, tyrannous officials and judges, or pillaging soldiers, rather than outlaw bands, was a mere detail; the criminality of the "invader and plunderer" lay in his violation of natural law and rights, regardless of the guise in which he violated them. The right to resist and to possess arms therefore—and the community benefit from such individual and/or concerted self-protection—remained the same.

Political Functions of the Right to Arms

The views of Locke and Sidney—so controversial in their own time that they were the basis of the prosecution's case in the trial that resulted in Sidney's execution—had became settled orthodoxy by the mideighteenth century. Thus we find Edward Gibbon, a Tory member of Parliament. in the circle of George III casually remarking, in the course of defining "monarchy":

> [U]nless public liberty is protected by intrepid and vigilant guardians, the authority of so formidable a magistrate will soon degenerate into despotism. . . . A martial nobility and stubborn commons, possessed of arms, tenacious of property, and collected into constitutional assemblies, form the only balance capable of preserving a free constitution against enterprises of an aspiring prince.[18]

Similarly, Sir William Blackstone's description of the right to arms combined the individual self-protection rationale and the criminological premises so foreign to the terms of the modern debate over the Second Amendment. Blackstone placed the right among the "absolute rights of individuals at common law"—those rights he saw as preserving to England its free government and to Englishmen their liberties. Yet what Blackstone was referring to was individuals' rights to have and use personal arms for self-protection. He describes the right as being "for self-preservation and defense," self-defense being "the primary law of nature which [cannot be] taken away by the law of society"—the "natural right of resistance and self-preservation, when the sanctions of society and laws are found insufficient to restrain the violence of oppression." Yet Blackstone saw this right to personal arms for personal self-defense as a political right of fundamental importance. For his discussion of the "absolute rights of individuals" ends with the following:

> In these several rights consist the rights, or, as they are frequently termed, the liberties of Englishmen. . . . So long as these remain inviolate, the subject is perfectly free; for every species of compulsive tyranny and oppression must act in opposition to one or [an]other of these rights, having no other object upon which it can possibly be employed. . . . And, lastly, to vindicate these rights, when actually violated or attacked, the subjects of England are entitled, in the first place, to the regular and free course of justice in the courts of law; next, to the right of petitioning the King and parliament for redress of grievances; and, *lastly, to the right of having and using arms for self-preservation and defense.*[19]

Why did Blackstone regard the right to possess arms for self-protection as a political matter? How could he have grouped (what we at least conceive as no more than) a privilege to have the means of repelling a robber, rapist, or cutthroat with such political rights as access to the courts and to petition for redress of grievances?

The Armed Freeholder Ideal of Virtuous Citizenship

[An omitted section of this article describes several historical situations in which the possession (or prohibition) of arms for personal self-protection had concrete political effects.] But no less important in the classical liberal worldview was the moral and symbolic significance of the right to arms.

Arms possession for protection of self, family, and polity was both the hallmark of the individual's freedom and one of the two primary factors in his developing the independent, self-reliant, responsible character which classical liberal political philosophers deemed necessary to the citizenry of a free state. The symbolic significance of arms as epitomizing the status of the free citizen represented ancient law. From Anglo-Saxon times "the ceremony of freeing a slave included the placing in his hands of" arms "as a symbol of his new rank." Likewise in Norman times, "the *Laws of Henry I* stipulate[d] that a serf should be liberated by" a public ceremony involving "placing in his hands the arms suitable to a freeman." Anglo-Saxon law forbade anyone to disarm a free man, and Henry I's laws applied this even to the man's own lord.[20] Such precedents were particularly important to theorists like Blackstone and Jefferson to whom the concept of "natural rights" had a strongly juridical tinge relating to the English legal heritage.

The Anglo-American legal distinction between free man/armed and unfree/disarmed flowed naturally into the classical liberal view that the survival of free and popular government required citizens of a special character—and that the possession of arms was one of two keys in the development of that character. From Nicoli Machiavelli and James Harrington classical liberal philosophy derived the idea that arms possession and property ownership were the keys to civic *virtu*. In the Greek and Roman republics from whose example they took so many lessons, every free man had been armed so as to be prepared both to defend his family against outlaws and to man the city walls in immediate response to the tocsin warning of approaching enemies. Thus did each citizen commit himself to the fulfillment of both his private and his public responsibilities.

The very survival of republican institutions depended upon this moral (as well as physical) commitment—upon the moral and physical strength of the armed freeholder: sturdy, independent, scrupulous, and upright, the self-reliant defender of his life, liberty, family, and polity from outlaws, oppressive officials, despotic government, and foreign invasion alike. That the freeholder might never have to use his arms in such protection mattered naught. (Indeed, one basic tenet classical political theory took from its criminological premises was that of deterrence: if armed and ready the free man would be least likely ever to actually have to defend. Simply to be armed, and therefore able to protect one's own, was enough; this moral commitment both developed and exemplified the character of the virtuous republican citizen.)

Commitment, duty, and responsibility were also viewed as a positive right (at least when challenged) because, to the virtuous citizen carrying out his responsibilities to family and duties to country was a right. And this right/obligation to be armed inevitably will be challenged, for it is the nature of absolutism to want to disarm the people. Nor is this simply for the physical security despotism gains in monopolizing armed power in the hands of the state, thereby rendering the people helpless. Disarmament also operates on the moral plane. The tyrant disarms his citizens in order to degrade them; he knows that being unarmed

> palsies the hand and brutalizes the mind: an habitual disuse of physical force totally destroys the moral; and men lose at once the power of protecting themselves, and of discerning the cause of their oppression.[21]

Thus, when Machiavelli said that "to be disarmed is to be contemptible," he meant not simply to be held in contempt, but to deserve it; by disarming men tyrants render them at once brutish and pusillanimous.

It was in this tradition of civic virtue through armament that Thomas Jefferson (who believed that every boy of ten should be given a gun as he had been) advised his fifteen-year-old nephew:

> A strong body makes the mind strong. As to the species of exercises, I advise the gun. While this gives a moderate exercise to the body, it gives boldness, enterprise and independence to the mind. Games played with the ball, and others of that nature, are too violent for the body and stamp no character on the mind. Let your gun therefore be the companion of your walks.[22]

The Efficacy of Arms and Self-Defense

Of course the reasons for the Founding Fathers' belief in arms possession were not limited to purely moral premises. Indeed, the Founders and their intellectual progenitors had an almost boundless faith in the pragmatic, as well as the moral, efficacy of widespread arms possession. They would be not at all surprised that no twentieth-century military has managed to suppress an armed popular national insurgency, a fact which accounts for the modern histories of Afghanistan, Algeria, Angola, Cuba, Ireland, Israel, Madagascar, Nicaragua, Vietnam, and Zimbabwe, to name only the most prominent examples. Classical liberal thought espoused an almost boundless faith in the efficacy of civilian arms possession as deterrent and defense against outlaws, tyrants, and foreign invaders alike. James Madison confidently assured his fellow countrymen that a free people need not fear government "because of the advantage of being armed, which the Americans possess over the people of almost every other nation."[23] Arming the people is, according to Locke's followers John Trenchard and Walter Moyle,

> the surest way to preserve [their liberties] both at home and abroad, the people being secured thereby as well against the domestic affronts of any of their own [fellow] citizens, as against the foreign invasions of ambitious and unruly Neighbors.[24]

This faith in the efficacy of arms buoyed up Locke and his English and American followers against their opponents' charge that their advocacy of a right to resistance and even revolution would lead to sanguinary and internecine disorders. To the contrary, they replied, that is what will come from disarming the people. Unchecked by the salubrious fear of its armed populace, government will follow its natural tendency to despotism. Tyrannous ministers will push their usurpations to the point that even an unarmed people will arise *en masse* to take their rights back into their bloody hands regardless of casualties.[25] But where the people are armed it would rarely, if ever, come to this, for, as Thomas Paine asserted, "arms like laws discourage and keep the invader and plunderer in awe and preserve order in the world as well as property."[26] To avoid domestic tyranny, wrote Trenchard and Moyle, the people must be armed to

> stand upon [their] own defense; which if [they] are able to do, [they] shall never be put upon it, but [their] swords will grow rusty in [their] hands; for that nation is surest to live in peace, that is most capable of making war; and a man that hath a sword by his side, shall have least occasion to make use of it.[27]

CONCLUSION

The self-defense origins of the Second Amendment were many and complex. The Founders believed: (1) Personal self-defense is the cardinal natural right—*and* includes the right to possess arms for defense of self, home, and family. (2) The right of self-defense exists against murder, rape, robbery, and other crime, whether perpetrated by apolitical criminals or by a tyrant or his agents for political purposes (as Sidney put it: "a wicked magistrate" and his "crew of lewd villains"). (3) Derivative of the individual right of self-defense is the right of individuals to join together for collective defense—and in the ultimate extreme—to the right to overthrow tyrants and return government to its proper course.[28] (4) The existence of an armed populace will generally avert the necessity of actual resistance, much less revolution, by deterring government and rulers from their inherent tendency to tyrannize and oppress. Finally, the Founders believed (5) "that the perpetuation of a republican spirit and character in [a free] society depended upon the freeman's possession of arms as well as his ability and willingness to defend both himself and his society."[29]

No less important in shaping the amendment was the Anglo-American legal tradition in which there were no police and the very idea of empowering government to place an armed force in constant watch over the populace was vehemently rejected as a paradigm of abhorrent French despotism.[30] Notwithstanding the evident need for municipal police, it would be another forty to fifty years before police were commissioned in either English or American cities. Even then they were specifically forbidden arms, under the view that if these were needed they could call armed citizens to their aid. (Ironically, the only gun control in nineteenth-century England was the policy forbidding police to have arms while on duty.[31])

In the absence of a police, the American legal tradition was for responsible, law-abiding citizens to be armed and see to their own defense and for most military-age males to chase down criminals in response to public hue and cry and to perform the more formal police duties associated with their membership in the *posse comitatus* and the militia. It was the possession of arms in these contexts which the Second Amendment constitutionalized. "The right" to arms refers to that which preexisted in American common and statutory law, i.e., the legal right to possess arms, which was enjoyed by all responsible, law-abiding individuals, including both militiamen and those exempt from militia service (e.g., the clergy, women, conscientious objectors, and men over the age of militia service).

Nor should it be thought that the Founding Fathers would have repudiated their belief in the right of self-defense—and of individuals to be armed for self-defense—if they had anticipated the replacement of the militia and *posse comitatus* by modern police agencies. [The omitted portion of this article details the attempts by Louis XIV and the Stuart kings of England to penalize political and religious dissent by disarming their opponents in an era of rampant crime and violence.] It would have seemed imprudent to rely on government to protect an unarmed citizenry, given the oppressive use of soldiers in Stuart England and Bourbon France and in search and other enforcement of unpopular laws on the colonists prior to the Revolution. Rather, those examples confirmed the worldview of classical liberal philosophy founded in the dictum the Founders drew from Aristotle that just and popular governments rest upon widespread popular possession of arms, whereas basic to tyrants is "mistrust of the people; hence they deprive them of arms."[32]

Notes

1. *United States* v *Miller*, 307 U.S. 174 (1939).

2. See *American Constitutional Law* (2000).

3. *United States* v. *Verdugo-Uriquez* 494 U.S. 259, 265 (1990).

4. R. Weighley, *History of the United States Army* (New York: Macmillan, 1967), p. 19. An omitted portion of this article discussed the seventeenth-century French and English kings' practice of billeting criminous troops on their enemies as a punishment and means of surveillance. Throughout the eighteenth century, criminal offenses by English soldiers and sailors in the colonies were a constant occurrence, and a subject of constant antagonism between Americans and the English military which refused either to punish their men or to turn them over to local justice. See generally Pauline Maier, *From Resistance to Revolution: Colonial Radicals and the Development of American Opposition to Britain, 1765-76* (New York: Knopf, 1976).

5. Quoting 3 W. Blackstone, *Commentaries* *4; see generally, T. Hobbes, *Leviathan*, chap. XIII (1651; reprint London: George Routledge & Sons, 1894) and Robert Shalhope, "The Ideological Origins of the Second Amendment," *Journal of American History* 69 (1982): 599 and Stephen P. Halbrook, *"That Every Man Be Armed": The Evolution of a Constitutional Right* (Albuquerque: University of New Mexico, 1984). For the philisophical views of the Founding Fathers particularly, see *"That Every Man Be Armed,"* chaps. 3 and 4 and Clayton E. Cramer, *For the Defense of Themselves and the State* (Westport: Praeger, 1994).

6. C. Montesquieu, *Spirit of the Laws*, vol. 38 of *Great Books of the Western World*, trans. Thomas Nugent (Chicago: Encyclopedia Britannica, 1990), p. 217. As to the frequency of citation of Montesquieu and Blackstone see Donald Lutz, "The Relative Influence of European Writers on Late Eighteenth Century American Political Thought," *The American Political Science Review* 78 (1984): 194, table 3.

7. See, e.g., J. J. Burlamqui, *The Principles of Natural and Politic Law*, trans. T. Nugent (Cambridge: Cambridge University Press 1807), pp. 112–13, 119, 121. Emme de Vattel, *The Law of Nations: Principles of the Law of Nature*, trans J. Chitty (London: T. & J.W. Johnson, 1854), p. 22.

8. J. Locke, *An Essay Concerning the True Original, Extent, and End of Civil Government (Second Treatise of Government)* (1694) in Thomas Cook, ed., *Two Treatises of Civil Government* (New York: Haffner, 1947), pp. 119, 129–30.

9. A. Sidney, *Discourses Concerning Civil Government* (London, 1698), pp. 175, 180–81, 266–67, 270.

10. I have here combined quotations from two different essays by Paine, one an editorial in his *Pennsylvania Magazine* (quoted in A. J. Ayer, *Thomas Paine* (Chicago: University of Chicago Press, 1988), p. 8, the other in M. Conway, ed., *Writings of Thomas Paine* 1 (New York: Putnam, 1894): 56. Emphasis in original.

11. C. Beccaria, *An Essay on Crimes and Punishments* (1764), trans. Henry Paolucci (Chicago: Bobbs-Merrill 1963), pp. 87–88.

12. See the following columns by Garry Wills: "Or Worldwide Gun Control," *Philadelphia Inquirer*, 17 May 1981; "Handguns That Kill," *Washington Star*, 18 January 1981; and "John Lennon's War," *Chicago Sun-Times*, 12 December 1980.

13. *Washington Post* editorial, "Guns and the Civilizing Process," 26 September 1972.

14. R. Clark, *Crime in America* (New York: Pocket, 1971), p. 88.

15. Robert Shalhope, "The Armed Citizen in the Early Republic," *Law & Contemporary Problems* 49 (1986): 125, 126–33; Don B. Kates, "Handgun Prohibition and the Original Meaning of the Second Amendment," *Michigan Law Review* 82 (November 1983): 204, 224, 241–51; Joyce Lee Malcolm, "The Right of the People to Keep and Bear Arms: The Common Law Perspective," *Hastings Constitutional Law Quarterly* 10 (1983): 285, 290-92.

16. Montesquieu, *Spirit of the Laws*, pp. 224–25.

17. *Writings of Thomas Paine*, p. 56. See generally, Halbrook, supra, *That Every Man*, and the articles cited in note 15.

18. 1 *Decline and Fall of the Roman Empire* 53 (New York: Modern Library edition 1957), p. 53.

19. 1 *Commentaries* *121, *143-44; see also 3 *Commentaries* *4. Emphasis added.

20. A. V. B. Norman, *The Medieval Soldier* (London: Crowell 1971), p. 73; D. Whitelock, ed., *English Historical Documents c. 500–1042* (London: Eyre & Spottiswoode, 1955), p. 427, *The Assize of Arms* (1181), reprinted in Douglas and C. Greenaway, eds., *English Historical Documents*, vol. 2 (London: Eyre & Spottiswoode, 1953), p. 416.

21. Joel Barlow (1792) quoted in Shalhope, "The Armed Citizen in the Early Republic," p. 132.

22. J. Foley, ed., *The Jefferson Cyclopedia* (New York: Russell & Russell, 1967), p. 318. Compare J. G. A. Pocock, *The Political Works of James Harrington* (Cambridge, Cambridge U. Press, 1977), pp. 54, 145: "It was Harrington who first stated in English terms, the theses that only the armed freeholder was capable of independence and virtue"; the republican political philosophers espoused "the rapturous oratory of . . . King People [based] not merely on rotatory balloting but on the union of 'arms and counsel', bullets and ballots, in a setting in which the citizens appeared in arms to manifest their citizenship, casting their votes even as they advanced and retired in the evolutions of military exercise."

23. Federalist 46 (Madison) in *The Federalist Papers* (New York: Arlington, 1966), pp. 294, 299.

24. J. Trenchard and W. Moyle (1697) quoted in Shalhope, "The Armed Citizen in the Early Republic," p. 128.

25. Don B. Kates, "Minimalist Interpretation of the Second Amendment," in E. Hickok, ed., *The Bill of Rights: Original Meaning and Current Understanding* (Charlottesville: University of Virginia Press, 1991), p. 132.

26. *Writings of Thomas Paine*, p. 56.

27. Trenchard and Moyle (1697), quoted in Shalhope, "The Armed Citizen in the Early Republic," p. 12.

28. For the philisophical tradition of the Founders see Hobbes, Locke, Sidney, Blackstone, and Montesquieu cited above. A typical statement of the Founders' views is Sam Adams's inclusion in the "Natural Rights of the Colonists as Men" of the rights to "life, liberty and property"—"together with the right to support and defend these in the best manner they can." Quoted by Joyce Lee Malcolm, *To Keep and Bear Arms: The Origins of an Anglo-American Right* (Cambridge: Harvard, 1994), p. 149. Comparable statements from Story, Kent, Eden, Paine, Madison, Dwight, and Barlow are cited in Randy E. Barnett and Don B. Kates, "Under Fire: The New Consensus on the Second Amendment," *Emory Law Journal* 45 (fall, 1996): 1177–79 notes 182–89.

29. Shalhope, "The Armed Citizen in the Early Republic," p. 138.

30. Frank Morn, "Firearms Use and the Police: An Historic Evolution of American Values," in Don B. Kates, ed., *Firearms and Violence: Issues of Public Policy* (Cambridge: Ballinger, 1984).

31. The British tradition of unarmed policing persists to this day because crime, particularly violent crime, fell rapidly throughout nineteenth-century England; in contrast, as American violence increased police seized the right to be armed by refusing to patrol unarmed. Morn, "Firearms Use and the Police"; Colin Greenwood, *Firearms Control: A Study of Armed Crime and Firearms Control in England and Wales* (London: Routledge & Kegan Paul, 1971), chap. 1.

32. Quoting Aristotle, *Politics*, trans. J. Sinclair (New York: Penguin, 1962), p. 218.

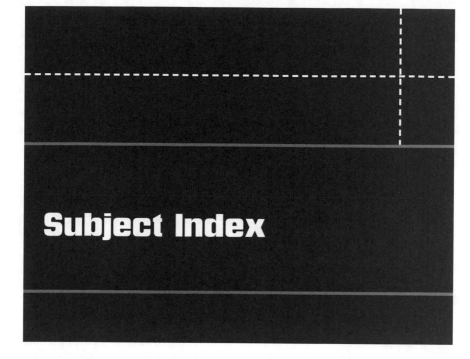

Subject Index

American Bar Association, 344
American Civil Liberties Union, 46, 137, 344
American Constitutional Law, 344
American Journal of Epidemiology, 50
American Journal of Public Health, 242
American Medical Association (AMA), 48
American Society of Criminology, 45, 52
Amnesty International, 46
antigun health advocacy literature, 32, 33, 34, 35, 36–38, 39–40, 42, 45 46, 47, 49, 51, 52 56, 57, 59, 62, 64, 66, 68, 70, 72, 73, 74, 84
armor-piercing ammunition ("cop-killer" bullets) 177, 184, 185, 208
assault, 36, 200, 245, 246, 247, 250, 253, 266, 286, 288, 289, 290, 291, 292, 294–95, 296, 300, 314, 317, 318, 319, 330

assault weapons/rifles, 131, 133, 135, 136, 139, 143, 145, 153, 154, 163, 176–77, 183, 184, 185, 188, 189, 190, 191, 193, 194, 195, 196, 197, 198, 199, 208, 333
Atlanta Constitution, 108

Brady Act/Brady Bill, 46, 131, 133, 134, 144, 160, 161, 162
Bureau of Alcohol, Tobacco and Fire-arms (BATF), 161, 192, 198
burglar, burglary, 36, 42, 120, 158, 224, 227, 248, 250, 266, 286, 287, 288, 289, 290, 291, 292, 296, 298, 311, 312, 314, 317, 318, 319, 321, 324, 325–26, 327, 328–30, 331, 332

Name Index